Social Research Methods by Example

Social Research Methods by Example shows students how researchers carry out work on the cutting edge of social science. The authors illustrate every point through engaging, thought-provoking examples from real research. The language is jargon-free, making research methods less intimidating and more relatable. The text is divided into three major sections, the first of which introduces students to the principles of research through examples from various fields. The second section walks students through the major types of social science research, with each chapter focusing on a different technique. The third section shows students how to carry out basic quantitative data analysis in SPSS. The final chapter shows how technological advances have changed the way researchers are working, and looks at the direction of social science research in the future.

Social Research Methods by Example not only introduces students to the principles of social science research, but gives them a toolbox to carry out their own. By the time they are finished with the book, students will be conversant with many of the most important studies in the history of social science. They will understand not only how to conduct research, but also how the field has evolved over time.

Yasemin Besen-Cassino is an Associate Professor of Sociology at Montclair State University, in New Jersey. She is the author of *Consuming Work: Youth Labor in America* (Temple University Press 2014). Her work focuses on gender, work, and youth. Her work has appeared in many academic journals as well as popular outlets such as BBC4. She is currently serving as the Book Review Editor of *Gender & Society*.

Dan Cassino is an Associate Professor of Political Science at Fairleigh Dickinson University, in Madison, New Jersey. He is the author of *Fox News and American Politics*, and the coauthor, with Yasemin Besen-Cassino, of *Consuming Politics: Jon Stewart, Branding and the Youth Vote in America*. His work has appeared in academic journals, popular outlets including *Newsweek* and *The Harvard Business Review*, as well as in frequent television and radio appearances. He received his PhD from Stony Brook University in 2005, and did post-doctoral work at Princeton before coming to Fairleigh Dickinson.

Besen-Cassino and Cassino have found a way to introduce us to the attraction and exhilaration of social research in the most direct and authentic way—by walking us through real studies of real social situations. Their accounts of how the most imaginative and successful social scientists have engaged with complex and intriguing situations make this work a page-turner, drawing the reader willingly into the challenges of social inquiry.

James B. Rule, *Center for the Study of Law and Society, University of California, Berkeley*

This is the research methods book I was waiting for! What differentiates this book is how it uses concrete, easy-to-follow examples to illustrate every aspect of research methods from hypothesis development to dissemination.

Selcuk R. Sirin, *J. K. Javits Professor, New York University*

Social Research Methods by Example

Applications in the Modern World

Yasemin Besen–Cassino & Dan Cassino

Routledge
Taylor & Francis Group

NEW YORK AND LONDON

First published 2018
by Routledge
711 Third Avenue, New York, NY 10017

and by Routledge
2 Park Square, Milton Park, Abingdon, Oxon, OX14 4RN

Routledge is an imprint of the Taylor & Francis Group, an informa business

Library of Congress Cataloging-in-Publication Data
Names: Besen-Cassino, Yasemin, author. | Cassino, Dan, 1980- author.
Title: Social research methods by example : applications in the modern world / Yasemin Besen-Cassino & Dan Cassino.
Description: New York, NY : Routledge, 2017. | Includes bibliographical references and index.
Identifiers: LCCN 2016043212| ISBN 9780415790901 (hardcover : alk. paper) | ISBN 9780415790918 (pbk. : alk. paper) | ISBN 9781315212791 (ebook)
Subjects: LCSH: Social sciences--Methodology. | Social sciences--Research.
Classification: LCC H61 .B47335 2017 | DDC 300.72/1--dc23
LC record available at https://lccn.loc.gov/2016043212

ISBN: 978-0-415-79090-1 (hbk)
ISBN: 978-0-415-79091-8 (pbk)
ISBN: 978-1-315-21279-1 (ebk)

Typeset in Bembo by
Servis Filmsetting Ltd, Stockport, Cheshire

Printed and bound in the United States of America by Sheridan

Brief Contents

Detailed Contents

Preface

The text you're holding is different from any other social science research methods book on the market. Unlike research methods that tell students about research, this text shows students how real researchers carry out work on the cutting edge of social science, showing how social science works, rather than just telling. Each chapter consists of a number of case studies, which describe the methods and findings of new, classic, or interesting work in the social sciences, and the text then uses these examples to illustrate the concepts that students need to master in order to analyze studies, and carry out their own research. For the instructor, these chapters can function as lecture notes, introducing the students to the craft of research through interesting and thought-provoking examples. The examples come from a wide range of disciplines including sociology, political science, women and gender studies, psychology, and criminology. It is, therefore, an interdisciplinary textbook that will appeal to a wide range of students.

For the students, rather than dry theoretical instruction, this textbook will illustrate every point through engaging, colorful, and thought-provoking examples. Rather than abstract ideas, each concept, technique, or idea is demonstrated through real life, not made up for class research. While other texts resort to examples from biology and other physical sciences, everything in this text is drawn from the social sciences, and nearly all of it is research that students could conceivably carry out themselves. The language is jargon-free and accessible, making research methods less intimidating and more relatable.

The text is divided into three major sections. In the first, comprised of the first five chapters, students are introduced to the general principles of social science research through examples from various fields, and encompassing the range of social science techniques, from ethnography, survey analysis, experiments, and interviews. The second section, running from chapters six through eleven, shows students how to carry out the major types of social science research, with each chapter focusing on a different technique. The third section, in chapters twelve and thirteen, go in-depth to show students how to carry out basic quantitative data analysis in SPSS. The final chapter shows how advances in technology have changed the way in which researchers are working, the types of questions that they can answer, and gives some idea of the direction of social science research going forward.

The first chapter introduces the students to the concept behind social research. In this chapter, we focus on the central components of social research. This chapter shows how to think like a social scientist and how to approach the scientific process. Students are shown why it's necessary to carry out rigorous social scientific research in order to understand human behavior and society, and how social science allows researchers to do so. Key ideas include the scientific process, dependent and independent variables, and levels of measurement.

Chapter 2 shows how social scientists move from abstract ideas and social problems to variables that can be measured in the real world. Unlike biologists or chemists, social scientists deal with abstract concepts, like racism or body image, requiring that they find ingenious ways to turn theoretical constructs into things that can actually be observed. In this chapter, we also introduce the concept of validity, in its many forms, as a way of talking about the potential problems that can arise from flawed measurements of a concept.

Chapter 3 introduces the idea of ethical research practices. Before we delve into how social science researchers actually collect data, we review the rules and guidelines of ethical research practices, in part by tracing the decisions made by researchers who have violated those rules. Because, as social scientists, we make use of human participants, it's vital that we treat them with respect, and acknowledge their role as partners in the research process. As with the other chapters, there's a focus on the logistics of the process, as we show how researchers do everything from designing a consent form, to determining the proper amount of monetary incentives for a study, to navigating the ethics board application process.

Chapter 4 reviews the essential role of theories in social sciences. Theories are never right or wrong but are simply different ways of looking at the social world: different lenses to study social phenomena. The choice of the lens leads the researcher to highlight different aspects of the social world. In addition, the cross-sectional nature of much of the research carried out in the social sciences means that theory becomes one of the major ways in which researchers establish causality. In addition to showing students how theory plays into the research process, we also review the major theoretical perspectives used in modern social science, and show how the use of those theoretical perspectives shapes the decisions made by the researcher.

The fifth chapter turns to the last step of the research process before the start of data collection: the literature review process. In this chapter we explore the most effective ways to utilize library and electronic sources to find the academic journal articles and books necessary to ground research in the existing findings. The chapters also show students how to write and organize existing research using different organizational techniques, and reviews different methods of citations. Again, the focus is on how to actually carry out the process: the chapter includes guides on how to use popular platforms like J-Stor and Google Scholar to find the articles needed to build up the literature review.

Chapter 6 begins the second part of the book, in which we turn to specific research methods, starting with qualitative techniques. In this chapter, we start with one of the most important qualitative techniques: ethnographies. We show students how researchers can give up their own lives to immerse themselves in the field and walk in someone else's shoes to capture their lived experience and understand from their perspective. We also show how nonparticipant ethnographers can go into the field to systematically observe how others live, from how workers at a coffee shop spend their time, to the experiences of college freshmen, to whether parents buckle their children into grocery store shopping carts. We review relative advantages and disadvantages of participant and non-participant observations, focus on different techniques of taking fieldnotes, as well as techniques to allow the researcher to be accepted by the people they meet in the field.

Chapter 7 continues the discussion of qualitative methods and focuses on conducting in-depth, qualitative interviews, and focus groups. In this chapter, we focus on writing effective questions for semi-structured, in-depth interviews, and show how the responses to these questions can reveal things that no other social techniques can show. In addition to formulating the questions, we also discuss techniques to conduct face-to-face interviews and discuss interview techniques.

Chapter 8 begins the transition from qualitative to quantitative research, by showing students how to carry out rigorous content analysis research. Examples of research show students how books, television shows, advertisements, movies, and music can be used as data sources to tell researchers about everything from informal norms of criminals to how students structure "friends with benefits" relationships. In this chapter, we show how students can systematically analyze such secondary sources and provide evidence.

In Chapter 9, we show students how to design and run experiments. The examples used here show the students how to design an experimental study, from the basics to more advanced designs, like the gold standard Solomon 4 group. This chapter also includes a special focus on the ethical and logistical challenges facing researchers who make use of experimental designs, and the benefits, such as an increased ability to show cause and effect, that result from their proper use.

Chapter 10 begins our discussion of survey research. In this chapter, we focus on writing survey items, and explore how items can be phrased in order to get at the real attitudes held by the people answering them. We also show the different types of survey questions that can be utilized to offer both visual interest and capture the most honest and complete answers. Finally, this chapter explores the relative advantages and disadvantages of using various survey techniques and different levels of measurement for each question.

Of course, it's not enough to write survey items: they also have to be administered. Chapter 11 focuses on the various ways in which researchers get the items that they write to respondents, from mail surveys to telephone surveys to online studies. The chapter also explores the costs and benefits of each of the main techniques for administering surveys, and the potential pitfalls that come from them. We also discuss sampling techniques, and show students how researchers recruit participants to ensure the representative samples.

The third section of the book begins in Chapter 12, which looks at basic univariate data analysis, showing both the principles of how to carry it out, and the logistics of actually doing the analyses using SPSS. Students learn not only why researchers do these analyses, but how to input a survey into SPSS, how to understand an imported dataset, and how to calculate measures of central tendency, dispersion, frequencies as well as graphs.

While Chapter 12 focuses on descriptive statistics, Chapter 13 moves into more advanced statistical methods, including calculation of margins of error and regression analysis. Once students have collected data using the techniques discussed in previous chapters, they need to analyze it, and this chapter gives them the tools that they need to explore the relationships between two or more variables. We explore statistical techniques such as correlations, bivariate and multivariate regression, and show how to do them in SPSS.

The last chapter, Chapter 14, aims to give a flavor of the future of research methods. Just as society is changing constantly, so is social science research. In this chapter, we review some of the newest and most cutting-edge research we see in social sciences today. As we discuss these emerging new studies, we also focus on some of the future directions for research methods and important methodological and ethical questions that rise from these new directions.

Overall, the goal is to introduce students not just to the principles of social science research, but to give them a toolbox to actually carry the research out. By the time that they are done with the book, students will have learned not only how to do research, but seen the evolution of the field over time, and be conversant with many of the most important studies in the history of social science. Writing this text has been both enjoyable and a learning experience for us, as we explore sides of social science that we otherwise would never see, and it's our hope that it will be just as enjoyable for you.

Yasemin Besen-Cassino
Dan Cassino
August, 2016

Acknowledgments

We would like to thank our methods professors over the years: Ferhunde Ozbay, Timothy Moran, Stanley Feldman, Matthew Lebo, and Kris Kanthak. We would like to thank Edip and Zeynep Besen for all their support during the writing of the book. We would like thank the anonymous reviewers for their valuable feedback throughout the project. Montclair State University's Distinguished Scholar Program provided a one-semester leave for the completion of this project—to them we are grateful. Finally we would like to thank the editorial team at Routledge and our editor Samantha Barbaro for her vision and her support of this project.

CHAPTER 1
Introduction to Research Methods

Learning Objectives

- Be able to explain the interaction between the individual and the environment
- Be able to identify variables
- Be able to identify components of the wheel of science and describe the processes of the scientific method
- Be able to describe the concept of causality
- Be able to identify different levels of measurement

EFFECTS OF SOCIETY: WHY OUR ENVIRONMENT MATTERS!

Jonah Berger, Marc Meredith, and S. Christian Wheeler— Polling Places and Vote Choice (2008)

A common criticism of social science research is that it's not really necessary. We don't need scientists to figure out why people do what they do—if we want to know, we can just ask people. Everyone believes that they have reasons for their behavior, and that they know what those reasons are, but social science allows researchers to show that while people may have reasons for their actions and beliefs, they don't always know what those reasons are. The phenomena that social scientists study don't exist in a vacuum; they're embedded in a social structure, in a physical place, and among other people, and this context has enormous effects on people's behavior. The fact that these effects are often invisible to the individuals they're affecting doesn't make them any less real.

Berger, Meredith, and Wheeler (2008) examined how people voted in a 2000 Arizona ballot initiative. The initiative—called Proposition 301—asked voters to increase the state sales tax from 5 percent to 5.6 percent, in order to fund an increase in education spending. Now, there are many factors that might lead voters to support or oppose this measure: whether they're Republicans or Democrats, their attitudes toward education, their income, their gender, whether or not they have school-age children. Researchers often ask voters coming out of polling places why they voted the way they did, and voters typically say things like, "I care about education," or "I don't want higher taxes." Almost none of these voters, however, will say that they were influenced by *where* they voted. While individual votes are secret, the researchers were able to look at how people voted on Proposition 301 in each of 2,027 polling places and see how the results differed based on the actual polling place.

Some of the polling places were government buildings or community centers; others were churches or schools. Berger, Meredith, and Wheeler (2008) found that the location of the polling place had a significant effect on how people voted on the proposition: when people voted in a school, they were about 2 points more likely to support raising taxes to fund education (55 percent versus 53 percent). The results show that there are a significant number of voters who apparently cast their ballot the way that they did because they were voting in a school—but it's unlikely that many of these voters realized this. They thought that they were voting a certain way for their own reasons, but carefully constructed social science research can tell us what was really happening.

This book explores the ways in which social scientists explore the effects of the social environment on individual and group behaviors. It is a handbook for social scientists, not just outlining how social scientists study phenomena, but also describing some of the most important studies in the last 100 years of social science research. When done right, social science can understand people better than they understand themselves, and the job of this book is to teach readers how to do it right.

THINKING THROUGH VARIABLES:
HOW RESEARCHERS WORK

Brian Wansink—Mindless Eating (2006)

Overeating has moved from an individual problem to a major social problem, with increasing numbers of Americans being classified as overweight or obese, and government healthcare programs being stretched by the added expense. To understand how to get people to eat less, it's necessary to understand why people eat more—and this is why Brian Wansink, a professor of consumer behavior and nutrition science, founded Cornell's Food and Brand Lab. There are all sorts of potential explanations for why people overeat—the taste of the food, the smell, hunger—and the job of social science research is to isolate these potential causes and determine which ones really matter.

Wansink (2006) argues that the cause of most overeating is the availability of food: People eat more simply because there's more around. To test this, he designed a series of studies in which he looked at all of the potential causes for why people eat too much. In one of these studies, people in Chicago were given tickets to see the afternoon matinee of a new action movie. When they showed up, the people who were part of the study—a group social scientists refer to as **participants**, a term which has replaced the older **subjects**—were given a surprise: a free bucket of popcorn. The movie was scheduled to start at 1:05 in the afternoon, right after lunch, so many of the participants who arrived at the movie theater had just eaten. The goal here was to try and make sure that the participants weren't eating the popcorn just because they were hungry.

Once they came in, the participants were randomly given either a medium-sized bag of popcorn or an extra-large bucket, which Wansink describes as being "bigger than their heads." The researchers believed that the participants who were given the extra-large bucket would eat more, just because there's more available, but there's a problem. What if the participants eat more just because the popcorn tastes good? In addition to controlling for the hunger of the participants, the researchers also have to control for the taste of the popcorn.

All of these factors—how hungry the participants are, the size of the popcorn they're given, how good the popcorn tastes—are all variables. The key aspect of **variables** is that they vary within the study, taking on different values, as opposed to constants, which remain the same. Within society, age is a variable—some people are older or younger than others—so researchers can examine the effect of age. If something is not a variable in the study, it's a constant, and researchers aren't able to look at any effects it may have. For instance, if all of the participants in a study are men or college students, then there's no way for researchers to determine how being a man or being a college student affects whatever the study is looking at.

The variable that a social scientist is interested in explaining is referred to as a **dependent variable**. The dependent variable is the outcome; the researcher believes that it is caused by the other variables in the model. These variables, the ones that cause the dependent variable, are the **independent variables**. One of the first steps in any social science study is to think through these variables, and a big part of being a social scientist is seeing the world in terms of independent and dependent variables, cause and effect.

In this case, the dependent variable is how much the participants eat, measured by the amount of popcorn eating and the number of calories consumed. While there is only one dependent variable, there can be multiple independent variables. In this case, the independent variables include the amount of popcorn that's available and how hungry the participants are.

Problem of Spuriousness

Before Wansink 2010 can be sure that availability leads his participants to overeat, he has to control for other variables, like the taste of the popcorn. What if the reason why people overeat is not simply because the popcorn is there, but rather because they enjoy the taste? Good popcorn might be so warm and buttery that the participants just can't resist it. Participants who get the larger buckets will eat more because it's so good. This would be a problem of **spuriousness**. *Spuriousness* refers to the unwanted effects of lurking variables (also called *confounds*, especially in experimental studies), independent variables that aren't accounted for but have an impact on the dependent variable regardless. If there's spuriousness, it might look like an independent variable is causing the dependent variable when, in fact, an unmeasured third variable is driving the relationship.

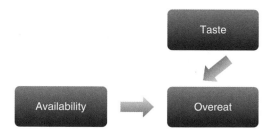

To eliminate this potential problem, Wansink (2006) and his team made sure that no one was eating the popcorn because they liked the taste. Rather than give the participants warm, buttery popcorn, the researchers gave them cold popcorn that had been popped five days beforehand and stored in sterile containers until it squeaked like plastic and was described as being like "eating Styrofoam packing peanuts" by one of the participants. At the end of the movie, the participants were given a survey asking them about how much they had consumed. When asked, "Do you think you consumed more because you had the larger size?"

they generally said no. The responses were things like "That wouldn't happen to me," "Things like that don't trick me," or "I'm pretty good at knowing when I'm full."

In reality, though, participants who were given the larger buckets of squeaky popcorn ate more. After weighing the buckets, researchers concluded that the participants who were randomly assigned to get the larger buckets consumed 173 more calories, approximately equal to 21 more dips into the bucket. This is 53 percent more than those given the medium-size buckets. Based on these findings, it seems likely that the participants were eating more popcorn not because they were hungry, or because it tasted good, but simply because it was there. Again, the participants don't say that they're eating more just because there's more there—Wansink would argue that they're not thinking about why they eat at all—but a carefully designed study can allow researchers to know more about why people do things than the people themselves know.

Still, this is just one study, and one of the hallmarks of social science is what's called *triangulation*, or measuring the same theory in different ways in order to be more certain about the findings. In addition to availability, Wansink (2006) argues that people rely on social cues in order to decide how much to eat. One of Wansink's labs also doubles as a fine dining restaurant twice a month, offering an all-inclusive, prix-fixe dinner for less than $25. In all respects, it looks like a high-end fine dining restaurant, with the big difference being that the diners are actually participants in experiments. In 2004, diners on one night got a special treat: a free Cabernet Sauvignon. It was not a special wine, though: it was a $2 bottle of Charles Shaw from Trader Joes (known as Two Buck Chuck). However, the labels of the bottles were changed. Diners on the left side of the restaurant were offered the same wine with a label for Noah's Winery, located in California. The diners on the right side got an identical label for Noah's Winery, except the location was listed as North Dakota.

Even though they were given the same wine, diners who were given wine with North Dakota labels had lower expectations and rated the wine as tasting bad and their food as inferior in taste and quality. Diners who were given wine with the California label ate 11 percent more of their food and lingered 10 minutes more at their tables after dinner. Even though the wine and the food provided were identical, the label on the bottle made the diners on the left think of the meal as a special occasion. They ate more without any idea about what was causing them to do so.

Social scientists also have to be careful about the trap of **monocausation**. While natural scientists often deal with phenomena that have one cause (increased pressure leads to increased heat, for instance), the phenomena that social scientists are most interested in have multiple and overlapping causes. Sorting out all of these causes is made even more difficult by the fact that people are embedded in a social context, and it's necessary to understand not just how individual-level causes are affecting the individual, but also how the other people around that individual are influencing his or her behavior.

It may seem that Wasink has overeating all figured out, but there are almost always more causes—more independent variables—that could be important.

For instance, psychology professor John DeCastro (1990) shows that even the presence of others makes us eat more: Diners eat 35 percent more if they eat with one other person than they would if they dined alone. If people eat with a group of seven or more, they consume 96 percent more food than they would consume alone! Of course, all of these factors may matter more, or less, depending on the availability of food and the social context of the meal, both of which increase the amount that people eat. While there's one main dependent variable in these studies—the amount that people eat—there are generally many independent variables, enough that the search for more causes is never really over.

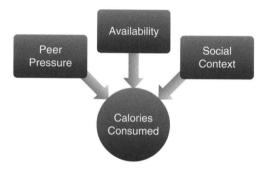

In all of the above examples, the **unit of analysis** was the individual: why one person, rather than another, chooses to overeat. However, social scientists are limited to the individual unit of analysis. One of the main motivations for studying overeating is the increasing proportion of Americans who are overweight or obese, so it might make sense to compare the United States with other countries. In this case, the unit of analysis would be the country, and the researcher would look at how differences in the types and quantities of food consumed at the national level have an impact on the overall rates of obesity. In the past, researchers have used such analyses to look at the effect of soy consumption, olive oil consumption, and the availability of fast food on obesity rates. When researchers have a smaller focus and study individuals and small groups, this is called **micro perspective**. When the unit of analysis is larger, such as countries and institutions, this is called a **macro perspective**. The perspective adopted by the researcher will determine the types of questions the researcher asks as well as the methods used to answer these questions.

There's no correct unit of analysis for approaching a certain problem, and one unit of analysis often provides explanations that simply couldn't be uncovered in another. For instance, the individual unit of analysis shows the importance of social context on overeating, a result that wouldn't be possible just by looking at the national unit of analysis. Similarly, the national level of analysis shows the importance of corn products in determining the obesity rates, a result which wouldn't be obvious from the individual-level analysis.

It's often helpful to approach the same problem from both a micro and a macro level, making use of multiple units of analysis as a part of triangulation. However, when researchers deal with aggregates, they can often fall prey to

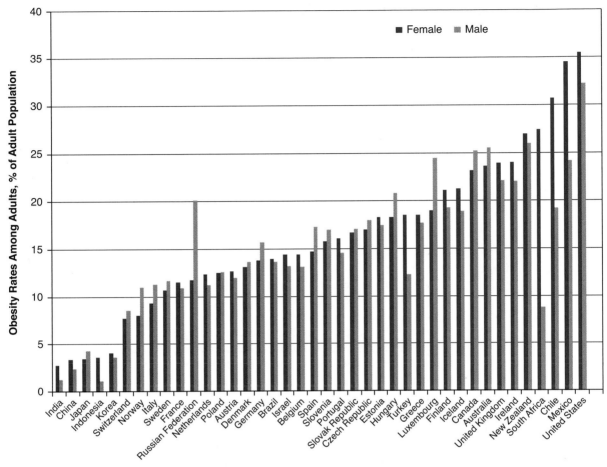

Based on OECD Health Data, 2011 The full OECD report on obesity is online at
http://www.oecd.org

the **ecological fallacy.** The ecological fallacy refers to coming to erroneous
conclusions and assumptions about individuals based on research on groups.
Based on the national-level data, researchers might come to the conclusion
that the greater availability of fast food in the United States is one of the causes
of the high obesity rate. It might be tempting, then, to assume that individual
Americans' obesity can be attributed to the availability of fast food, but that's not
necessarily the case. Conclusions based on one unit of analysis may or may not be
applicable to another unit of analysis. Some Americans may be more likely to be
obese because of the presence of fast food, but obesity might be more related to a
sedentary lifestyle, or high levels of stress, in others. Assuming that aggregate-level
findings apply to individuals is the heart of the ecological fallacy, and researchers
must be careful to avoid it.

THE SCIENTIFIC METHOD

Donald Dutton and Arthur Aron—High Bridges and Arousal (1974)

Good studies in the social sciences are often able to explain human behavior better than individuals can explain it themselves. In Berger, Meredith, and Wheeler's (2008) study of voting in Arizona, for instance, they were able to show a significant influence of polling place on vote choice, but that doesn't mean that they can extend their results to individual voters, who may or may not have been influenced by the polling place. Doing so would be an example of the ecological fallacy, and it would also violate one of the main hallmarks of social science research. Berger, Meredith, and Wheeler's results (people who voted in a school or church were more likely to support the tax increase) apply in the aggregate but not necessarily to any individual. If an individual voter wasn't influenced by the polling place, it doesn't mean that the finding isn't valid. If a finding doesn't seem to apply to you or your friend or your uncle, it doesn't mean that it isn't otherwise true.

A good example of this comes from Donald Dutton and Arthur Aron's (1974) research on physiological arousal and attraction. If researchers were to ask people what led them to be attracted to a potential romantic partner, there's a myriad of qualities that people might list: looks, sense of humor, money, common interests. However, when social scientists test these traits, they typically find that there's only a minimal relationship between what people say they're looking for in a romantic partner and who they actually pick. It may seem that attraction is deeply personal, but that doesn't mean that social science can't tell us about why people are attracted to one another.

When Dutton and Aron (1974) looked at attraction, they treated it like a physiological state. People who are attracted to someone else tend to blush, sweat, feel butterflies in their stomach, and dilate their pupils. Their body temperature elevates, their blood pressure goes up, and adrenaline is released. Dutton and Aron argue that any process that replicates these symptoms will lead people to experience attraction. To test this, the researchers set up in two different bridges over the Capilano River in North Vancouver, British Columbia. The first bridge, the Capilano Canyon Suspension Bridge, is a 5-foot wide, 450-foot long bridge that is made out of wooden board connected by wire cables. It is described by Dutton and Aron as having "a tendency to tilt, sway and wobble, creating the impression that one is about to fall over the side." The second bridge that connects the two sides of the canyon is a wider and firmer bridge, only 10 feet above shallow water and surrounded by high handrails.

Participants in the study were approached by an interviewer of the opposite gender and asked to take part in a psychology experiment on the effects of scenic exposures on creative expression. First, they were asked to fill out a survey on their age, education, and previous visits to the bridge. Then, they were shown a picture of a woman covering her face with one hand and reaching with the other hand and were asked to write a short story or narrative about the picture. They did this while on the bridge to which they had been assigned.

After the participants had finished writing their narrative, the interviewer wrote his or her phone number on the corner of the survey and told the participants that they could call if they had any questions about the study. The researchers were looking at two dependent variables. First, they looked at the sexual content of the stories or narratives that the participants produced. Even though there was no obvious sexual or romantic content in the picture, many participants mentioned sexual intercourse, a kiss, or a lover in their story—and participants who wrote their story on the wobbly, narrow, dangerous-seeming bridge were much more likely to include these features in their story.

The second dependent variable the researchers were interested in dealt with the phone number the participants were given. A large proportion of the male participants called the interviewer, ostensibly to ask about the study, but really to ask her out on a date. Participants who had met the interviewer on the dangerous-seeming bridge were much more likely to call, indicating that they were more attracted to the interviewer.

Now, these participants might have good reasons that they were attracted to the interviewer, but Dutton and Aron (1974) argue that one of those causes is certainly misattribution of arousal. They were more attracted to the interviewer than they otherwise would be because they were in a fear- or anxiety-producing situation. They experienced elevated blood pressure, dilated pupils, butterflies in their stomach, and so forth because they were near a high bridge. However, they were unable to tell the difference between arousal caused by anxiety and arousal caused by attraction, so they were much more likely to call the interviewer for a date. These results suggest why people may like going to scary movies or eating spicy food on dates—they may make it more likely that their date will be attracted to them.

Now, none of this means that any particular individual is attracted to someone else purely because of some misattribution of arousal in the past. It just means that this is a tendency that exists among people in general. Dutton and Aron's (1974) findings, like all findings in social science, are applicable only in the aggregate. Whether they apply to one person in particular is beside the point.

What their findings do show, however, is the power of a well-designed study in the social sciences. Individuals may think that they know why they do what they do, but social science research can often point to factors that they were simply unaware of. It's hard to imagine that any of Dutton and Aron's (1974) participants thought they were attracted to the interviewer because of the view from the bridge. These individual experiences—what are sometimes called *anecdotal evidence*—don't tell us much, and the key to social science is to move away from individual anecdotes, personal experiences, and habits and toward a systematic study. Social science is a systematic practice where researchers study patterns of behavior among large groups of individuals and establish aggregate patterns of behavior. Just like researchers would never try to apply findings from a national-level study to individual-level explanations, they should never apply aggregate findings to particular individuals. People who were on to the high bridge were more likely to call the interviewer for a date, but that doesn't mean that researchers can explain why any one participant did what he did. Establishing these sort of patterns is only possible when the research is carried out in a systematic way: All of the participants in Dutton and Aron's study were treated in the exact same way, except for the bridge that they were on. If there were other differences, it's possible that they would be responsible for any difference between the groups.

In addition to being systematic and focusing on aggregates, good social science research is also **generalizable**. While the results of a study are based on findings from a relatively small group—anywhere from dozens to hundreds of participants or survey respondents—the conclusions of the research should be applicable to a much larger group.

Finally, scientific research should be **replicable**. The details of the research procedures and methodology must be provided in detail so that other researchers can replicate the study. It's always possible that there was some factor that the researchers overlooked, or that there was some random factor that led to nongeneralizable findings. Triangulation can help resolve this issue, but it's also important that other researchers can do the study again, to test if the findings are the same at a different time, with different participants, or in a different setting. In the case of Dutton and Aron's (1974) study, other researchers might use the same questionnaire while participants watch a roller coaster or stand near the window of a tall building to see if the results hold up.

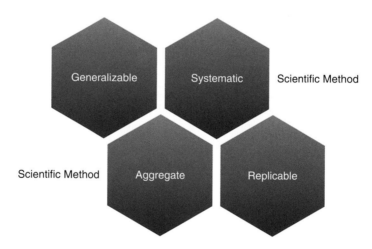

Social scientists always begin their research with a **theory**. Theories are systematic ways of looking at the world and examining phenomena; they guide social scientists in terms of telling them which independent variables should be important, which units of measurement are appropriate, and which research technique is best to study a particular phenomenon. In everyday life, when people say, "I have a theory!" they don't really mean theory. Theories are never right or wrong but are simply established ways of thinking and looking. These theories will also guide researchers as to their **hypotheses** about what the likely result of a study will be. These hypotheses are statements, based in theory, about the relationship between variables. In Dutton and Aron's (1974) research, for instance, they drew on existing research and theories about the misattribution of arousal in order to inform their hypotheses that participants near the seemingly dangerous bridge would use more sexual imagery in their stories and be more likely to call the interviewer.

Once researchers have formed these hypotheses, they make use of systematic social science research techniques to test the hypotheses and, based on the results, come to empirical generalizations about wider groups. These generalizations, in turn, tell researchers about the applicability of theories to real-world phenomena and become the basis for new theories or modifications of existing theories. These new theories are subject to hypotheses and testing themselves; this cyclical nature of scientific inquiry is referred to as the *wheel of science*. Dutton and Aron's work on arousal has led other researchers to examine the circumstances under which arousal is or is not misattributed. Their hypotheses and methods draw from Dutton and Aron (1974), and later researchers in turn draw on them.

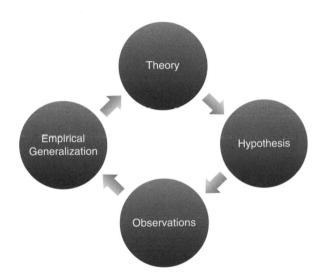

CAUSALITY AND SPURIOUSNESS

Edward E. Jones—What Flattery Gets You (1965)

The job of any social scientist is to think through the relationships between variables, but these relationships aren't always simple. For example, researchers have spent a great deal of effort trying to understand why people become friends. Do people like others who praise them? Who agree with what they do? Who have similar interests? People often don't know why they're friends—and rarely think about what caused the friendship in the first place. Popular explanations point to agreement and praise as essential characteristics in a friendship. Dale Carnegie's classic self-help book, *How to Make Friends and Influence People* (1964), has influenced millions of readers to try and get others to like them by agreeing with them and praising them—if someone praises others, he writes, they'll be liked in return. Such common-sense explanations sound great; after all, people don't seem to like it when someone says nasty things about them. But social science research is necessary because such common-sense explanations are often wrong.

Psychologist Edward Jones (1965), for example, shows that praise and flattery will not get you everywhere. In an experiment, participants came into his lab and were interviewed by a graduate student. After the interview was over, the graduate student went into another room, but the participant was able to hear some of the comments that the graduate student was making about the participant. Participants were randomly assigned to hear positive comments, negative comments, or neutral comments. Some participants also heard the graduate student say that he or she had an ulterior motive for making the comments. The graduate student then came back and asked the participant if he or she would help the student by participating in another study. The dependent variable, in this case, is whether the participant agreed to help or not. In Jones' study, the hypothesized relationship was that praise would lead to cooperation, as Dale Carnegie suggested. However, the results aren't entirely in line with a simple explanation that praise leads others to help. Participants who thought that the graduate student had an ulterior motive for saying positive things were not more likely to help the student out. There is a relationship between cooperation and praise, but it seems to be conditional on the belief that the praise is genuine.

Muzafer Sherif et al.—Robbers' Cave (1954)

The story becomes more complicated when researchers look at the relationship from the other side. Jones looked at the effect of liking someone on cooperation—but what about the effect of cooperation on liking someone? A test of this relationship is the basis of one of the most famous experiments in social science history—Muzafer Sherif's Robbers' Cave study from 1954. In the study, Sherif sent 22 eleven- and twelve-year-old boys from middle-class families who did not previously know each other to a summer camp in Robbers' Cave State Park in Oklahoma. There, the camp counselors—who were really researchers—divided the boys into two groups, each unaware of the other. After the members of each group had some time to get to know one another, they were introduced to the other group and put into conflict-prone situations. Sherif observed that the mere presence of an outgroup—in this case, the other group of boys—led the boys to have hostility and negative beliefs about the other group and heightened their positive feelings toward their own group. Toward the end of the study, the groups were forced to work together, which resulted in the dissolution of these negative beliefs about the other group.

In the Robbers' Cave study, Sherif and his colleagues (1954) demonstrate that cooperation within the group led the boys to have more positive feelings about the people they were cooperating with and negative feelings about the group they were in conflict with. Liking someone may lead to collaboration, but collaboration also leads to liking.

In studies like these, the problem is one of **causality**: what's causing what. As mentioned previously, causality is generally clear in the physical sciences, but intricate causal relationships are more the rule than the exception in the social sciences. While Dale Carnegie and his devotees might think that people will like you if you praise them, social scientists know that the truth of the matter is far more complicated. In the social sciences, the goal of most research is to identify causality, to figure out what is leading to what. In the sort of social situations we encounter every day, it's impossible to figure out if liking is leading to cooperation or cooperation is leading to liking because people tend to like and cooperate with the same people: their friends. In this, friendship is what was previously referred to as a lurking variable, one that tends to go along with the other variables being examined and muddying the relationship between them. In Sherif's (1954) study, researchers were able to control for this lurking variable by setting the study in a summer camp where none of the boys knew each other, rather than at, say, a school, where there would be existing relationships and knowledge of the other group. By making the boys within a group collaborate or compete and then measuring how much they like one another, Sherif is able to get a better handle on the direction of causality.

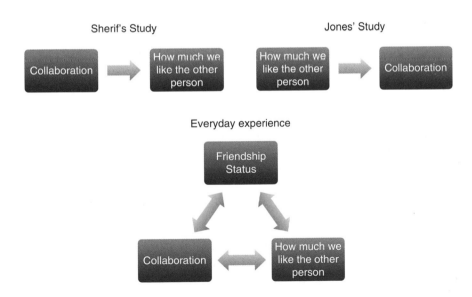

Causality: Correlation Does Not Mean Causation

Social scientists think through variables: dependent variables and independent variables. They look at the effects of the independent variable(s) on the dependent variable. However, a common mistake is to assume the independent and dependent variables have a cause–effect relationship. Oftentimes, scientists

Correlation

can show association or correlation. That means the independent and dependent variables go together, they are related, and there is a relationship. However, this does not mean that the dependent variable is a direct result of the independent variable.

To prove causality, researchers need to establish a few things. First, the independent variable has to precede the dependent variable. In order for A to cause B, A has to come before B in a time sequence.

Second, the researcher needs to make sure that there is no spuriousness. That means that the researcher needs to control for all other potential causes to establish that A is in fact the cause of B. Otherwise, it is possible that a third variable, C, causes both, making it seem as if A is causing B. For example, a researcher might find that people who are vegetarians (A) tend to weigh less (B) and conclude that vegetarianism causes weight loss. However, there could be a third lurking variable that the researchers are not measuring. It could be that people who don't eat meat are more environmentally conscious, and their lower weight could be due to the fact that they bike or walk more instead of driving. In this case, a third, hidden variable not accounted for in the research could be driving the results. If the researcher wants to prove causality—in this case, that the vegetarian diet, not any other factors, leads to the lower weight—the researcher needs to control for all possible explanations to isolate the effects of a vegetarian diet.

Finally, in order to establish causality, the researcher needs to start with theory. The theory will guide the direction of causality. As we see in the wheel of science, a good researcher is guided by established theories and paradigms. Existing research and theories will guide the researcher in establishing causality.

In the social sciences, causality arises almost exclusively from predictions based on theory. In experimental research (discussed in Chapter 9), researchers can most clearly determine causality, but even in experiments unobserved factors can contaminate the results. Similarly, it's often thought that time series analysis, a type of statistical analysis that allows researchers to show the order in which events occur, allows causality to be isolated. However, even time series analysis only gives researchers statistical evidence of what's called **Granger Causation**. This special type of causation refers to a situation in which A precedes B, and knowing A allows the researcher to predict B. Because the researcher knows the direction of the causality in time, it's clear that B can't be causing A. That certainly looks like causation, but there's always the possibility that A and B are both related to a third, unobserved factor. As always, the only way to be certain of causation is through careful research and thoughtful application of theory.

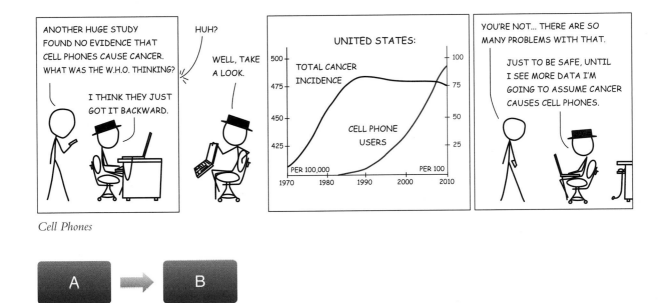

Cell Phones

TYPES OF VARIABLES AND LEVELS OF MEASUREMENT

Thinking in terms of independent and dependent variables, and using them to systematically ascertain cause and effect, is the essence of social science. However, not all variables are created equally. As discussed in Chapter 2, which deals with operationalization, the first task of social science researchers is to turn the somewhat nebulous concepts in which they're interested into something that can be measured, a process called *operationalization*. Once the variables are operationalized and measured, some of the biggest differences between the variables—and the ones that have the biggest impact on how those variables are treated once they're ready to be analyzed—are a function of the level of measurement.

Deciding on the appropriate level of measurement for a variable is a complicated decision for researchers. Some variables, like an individual's race, can only be measured at one level, while others, like income, age, or political party affiliation, can be measured at multiple levels. Ideally, a concept should be measured on the highest possible level, but sometimes asking questions that would allow for high-level measurements can lead to measurement error, refusal to answer, or flat-out lies.

The lowest level of measurement used in social sciences is the **nominal level**. Nominal variables have categories that don't carry any particular rank or order. Many of the characteristics that social scientists use most frequently (such as gender, race, religion, ethnicity, and marital status) are nominal-level variables. An indicator of marital status, for instance, might have the following categories:

Married
Single
Divorced
Widowed
Separated
Living as Married

Even if a researcher were to try and assign an order to these categories, it's not clear what that order would be. There's no underlying scale that's reflected in these categories—no natural order that they should be in. As important as these variables are, there winds up being very little that researchers can do with nominal variables; their main use in research is to group people together based on which category they fit in to.

One level up from nominal-level variables are **ordinal variables** (called this because they have an *order*). Ordinal variables have an order, or rank, to them, but the distance between the ranks varies. For instance, when surveys ask people how often they attend religious services, they often use a formulation such as this:

Never
Only for funerals, weddings, and similar special occasions
A few times a year
About once a month
Almost every week
Every week
More than once a week

There's no question that people who go to church "almost every week" go more often than people who go "about once a month," but how much more? The difference isn't clear from the question. A researcher could argue that there's not much of a difference between going to church "never" and going "only for funerals, weddings, and similar special occasions," but there is a big difference between going just for weddings and funerals and going "a few times a year." There's an order, but the difference between the categories isn't uniform. Ordinal variables can be made up of numbers as well as words. For instance, researchers could ask respondents how often they exercised in the past week:

0–2 times
3–4 times
5 or more times

Again, there's an order to the categories, but the difference between the categories isn't the same throughout. In constructing ordinal measures, researchers should ensure that the answer options are as balanced as possible and the intervals are approximately equally distributed.

The third level of measurement, **interval level** (called this because there is a set *interval* between categories), isn't used often in the social sciences; it is more common in the physical sciences. Interval-level variables are expressed in numbers and have an order but do not have a meaningful zero point. Because there's no meaningful zero point, researchers can't use interval-level variables to express differences in ratios. For instance, Fahrenheit temperature is an interval-level variable because 0 doesn't really mean anything. As such, it doesn't make sense to say that 50 degrees Fahrenheit is twice as hot at 25 degrees Fahrenheit, or that 100 degrees is twice as much as 50 degrees. Unlike ordinal-level variables, though, the difference between the categories is uniform: The difference between 50 and 55 is the same as the difference between 60 and 65 or 95 and 100. Because these types of variables are so rare in social science, they're often grouped together with the next level of measurement, *ratio level*.

Variables measured at the highest level of measurement, **ratio level**, are like interval variables but with a meaningful zero point, allowing researchers to draw conclusions about the ratios of responses. For example, researchers often ask respondents about their annual household income. If this data was collected as a whole number (as in "$52,762"), the result would be a ratio-level variable. The interval between values is set—one dollar is one dollar, no matter how many you have—and there's a meaningful zero point (there's something very meaningful about having no money). As such, researchers can say, for example, that someone who makes $100,000 a year makes twice as much as someone who makes $50,000 a year.

For researchers, there are clear advantages to collecting data on the ratio level. It's more detailed and specific, and some statistical techniques require interval- or ratio-level variables. However, there are also downsides. Respondents may refuse to answer specific questions about things such as income and age even though they are willing to provide a range in which their income or age would fall (resulting in an ordinal-level variable). With a variable like income, collecting data on the ratio level may also lead to error. Unless respondents have their tax return in front of them, they may be unable to tell a researcher what their income was last year down to the dollar.

When dealing with interval- and ratio-level variables, researchers also need to keep in mind whether the variable is **continuous** or **discrete**. A continuous measure is one that can take on any value, including fractions of a unit (like income, which can in theory be calculated down to the penny), while a discrete measure is one that is only measured in whole numbers. For instance, the number

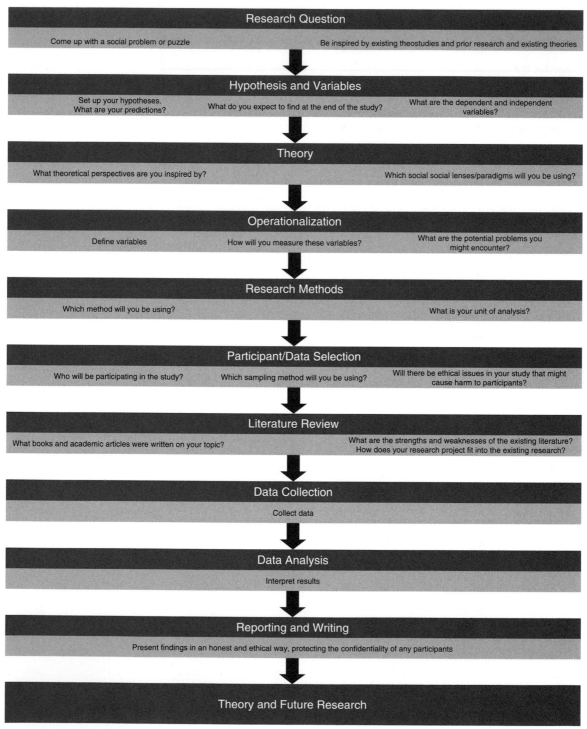

Research Question

Come up with a social problem or puzzle

Be inspired by existing theostudies and prior research and existing theories

Hypothesis and Variables

Set up your hypotheses.
What are your predictions?

What do you expect to find at the end of the study?

What are the dependent and independent variables?

Theory

What theoretical perspectives are you inspired by?

Which social social lenses/paradigms will you be using?

Operationalization

Define variables

How will you measure these variables?

What are the potential problems you might encounter?

Research Methods

Which method will you be using?

What is your unit of analysis?

Participant/Data Selection

Who will be participating in the study?

Which sampling method will you be using?

Will there be ethical issues in your study that might cause harm to participants?

Literature Review

What books and academic articles were written on your topic?

What are the strengths and weaknesses of the existing literature? How does your research project fit into the existing research?

Data Collection

Collect data

Data Analysis

Interpret results

Reporting and Writing

Present findings in an honest and ethical way, protecting the confidentiality of any participants

Theory and Future Research

Steps in Social Research

of children a respondent has is a ratio-level variable (it has a meaningful zero point), but people can't have 3.2 children.

SUMMARY

Researchers have found that human behavior is incredibly complicated, often driven by factors outside of our conscious awareness. In order to understand why people actually do what they do, social scientists think through dependent and independent variables. The dependent variables are the puzzles, the social problems. Their potential answers are the independent variables. Researchers look for causal links between the independent and dependent variables but must be careful to ensure that the relationships aren't spurious. The fact that two phenomena tend to go together doesn't mean that one is causing the other. The research process is further complicated by the fact that one dependent variable will almost always have many causes.

Because the idea of variables is so central to social science, researchers have to think through the characteristics of the variables they're measuring. Variables can be measured at different levels: nominal, ordinal, interval, and ratio. The level of measurement for a particular variable is determined by what's being measured and how the researchers decide to measure it. Generally, researchers strive to collect data and measure at the highest measurement levels possible. Often, though, researchers weigh the costs and benefits of measuring at each level. Variables can also be measured at the micro or macro level of analysis, looking at people individually or whole groups at a time.

Actually conducting the research is only the beginning of the process of social science research. Once the research is done, other researchers may test the same theories or models of behavior in different ways to see if the findings are generalizable. Others may even redo the same study to see if the results can be replicated.

Study and Review

Explain the difference between dependent and independent variables. Could something be both an independent and a dependent variable? Why or why not?

Why is it so important for researchers to isolate causality?

Why is monocausation such a problem for researchers?

Describe how a variable (such as age, income, or marital status) could be expressed as a nominal, ordinal, or interval/ratio variable.

Which is more important for researchers: replicability or generalizability? Why?

CHAPTER 2

Research Questions and Operationalization

Learning Objectives

- Be able to provide conceptual definitions for sociological concepts
- Be able to operationalize abstract concepts and measure them
- Be able to identify different forms of validity and understand what the potential threats to validity are
- Be able to describe internal validity and offer examples of this type of validity
- Be able to describe predictive validity and distinguish it from other forms of validity
- Be able to describe the concept of accuracy and offer techniques to create accurate measurement in research design
- Be able to describe the concept of reliability and offer techniques to create reliable measurement in research design
- Be able to describe the concept of precision and offer techniques to create reliable measurement in research design

MEASURING CONCEPTS

Anthony Greenwald, Debbie McGhee, and Jordan Schwartz— The Implicit Association Test (1998)

Starting in 1972, the General Social Survey, a national survey of social attitudes and behaviors generally carried out every other year, began asking respondents, "Do you think that there should be laws against marriages between Negroes and whites?" In the first year the question was asked, 37 percent of respondents said that there should be. By 1984, the question no longer used the word *Negro*, but 24 percent of respondents still said that such laws should exist (though they had been struck down by the Supreme Court in 1968). By the 2000 survey, the proportion of respondents saying that there should be laws against marriage between racial groups had dropped below 10 percent, and in 2002, the question was retired. Questions about allowing a member of another racial group to come to dinner, or if respondents would vote for an African American candidate for president, show similar trends.

Similar results from other national surveys might indicate to us that there is simply less racism, and fewer racists, in the United States than there used to be— even that racism is mostly extinct. However, it could also mean that people who hold racist beliefs recognize that their beliefs are socially undesirable and aren't willing to reveal their attitudes, even in an anonymous survey. Or, it could mean that people who hold racist attitudes no longer hold that *particular* racist attitude. They may think that African Americans are inferior to whites but don't think that there should be laws against intermarriage. It could also be a combination of all of these factors, and using questions like this, there's no way to tell.

The answer to why the proportion of respondents giving overtly racist responses to questions has decreased has implications for policy, politics, and society in general. If there really is almost no racism left in the country, it could mean that there's less need for Affirmative Action programs or scholarships to help African American students. But what if these questions aren't accurately measuring racism? Before we change social policies, we should try other ways of measuring racism. Greenwald, McGhee, and Schwartz (1998) set out to do just that, through a subconscious measure of racist views. Their measure, called the *implicit association test* (IAT), asks participants to categorize words that appear on a screen by pushing a button either on the left or on the right, corresponding with another word on the screen. So, in a control test, the words *pleasant* and *unpleasant* might be on the left and right of the screen, respectively, and a word such as *poison* might flash on the screen. The job of the participant would be to push the button on the right, indicating *poison* is *unpleasant*.

This test seems pretty easy, but it quickly gets more complicated. Let's say we add a second set of categories: names for women that might be more common among whites or African Americans. Now, the participant has to push the left button if the word that flashes on the screen is pleasant *or* a name associated more with African American women, and the right button if the word is unpleasant or a name associated more with white women (Sequence 3

Sequence	1		2		3		4		5	
Description	Initial Target-Concept Discrimination		Associated Attribute Discrimination		Initial Combined Task		Reversed Target-Concept Discrimination		Reversed Combined Task	
Task Instructions	Black	White	Pleasant	Unpleasant	Black or Pleasant	White or Unpleasant	White	Black	Black or Unpleasant	White or Pleasant
Sample Stimuli		MOLLY	rainbow		JADA		KATELYN			peace
	EBONY		honor		jackpot		EMMA		JASMIN	
	SHANICE			cancer		KATIE		TIARA	filth	
		AMY		grief		poison	ABIGAIL			JENNA
	NIA		gift			MADELINE		RAVEN		lucky
		CLAIRE		disaster	beauty			DEJA	KIARA	
		EMILY	happy		KIARA		CARLY		evil	
	AALIYAH			vile		mourn		IMANI		HEATHER

Based on Greenwald, McGhee and Schwartz, 1998

in the table above). Later in the study, the order is reversed: unpleasant or an African American name, and pleasant or a white name (Sequence 5 in the table). The idea is that we can determine an individual's uncontrollable, automatic response to racial groups by comparing the differences between Sequence 3 and Sequence 5.

Suppose that a respondent had an automatic, visceral negative response to the names associated with African Americans. She might have no trouble classifying the names (as in Sequences 1 and 4) or the words (as in Sequence 2), but she might have trouble doing both at the same time. In Sequence 3, she knows to push the left button when a pleasant word or an African American name comes up, but when the African American name comes up, her first impulse would be to press the right button, for unpleasant. She probably won't, but it may take her a moment to overcome this initial impulse and push the left button. When we compare the speed of her responses with Sequence 5, in which the left button is for pleasant words or white names, she would be much slower. Essentially, if you have an unconscious bias for or against African Americans, there will be a difference between your average response times on Sequences 3 and 5. Someone who takes a longer time on Sequence 3 than on Sequence 5 (as above) would be classified as having an unconscious bias against African Americans; someone who had a longer average time on Sequence 5 than Sequence 3 would be classified as having an unconscious bias in favor of African Americans.

Since its inception, the IAT has been available for anyone to take online (though the names have been replaced with photographs of faces to address concerns that the names reflected a subgroup of African Americans) and has been expanded to include a number of other tasks, but the results have been similar to what was found in Greenwald and his colleagues' (1998) initial study. About 70 percent of participants (and more, among whites) show an automatic preference for whites over African Americans. Perhaps more important, there is almost no relationship between what people say about other racial groups and their feelings toward them versus how they score on the IAT. The results of the IAT routinely upset the people who take it—they don't see themselves as racist, but the test tells them that they have an automatic preference against one group and in favor of another. If we take these results as our indication of racism, rather than the results of the questions about race from the General Social Survey mentioned earlier, we reach very different conclusions. Rather than being almost gone from America, racism is still an issue for 70 percent of Americans, at least in the sense measured by the IAT.

You can take the Implicit Association Test at https://implicit.harvard.edu

Conceptual Definition

This is why research design and **operationalization** is so important. Our conclusions about the prevalence of racism in American society are going to depend almost entirely on how we decide to measure it. Unlike natural scientists, who can directly measure things that they are studying, social scientists have a more difficult time. Things that natural scientists study, such as mass, pressure, and distance, are tangible and can easily be measured. In social sciences, oftentimes what we would like to study is not tangible. That is why researchers need to convert the abstract social concepts they would like to study to more concrete, tangible terms, so they can measure them. Since racism is a construct (an idea), it is not easily measured. In order to be able to measure racism, the first step is to define what racism is. We can imagine a continuum of what racism is: on one end would be individuals who knowingly carry out racist actions; on the other would be individuals who may have unconscious racist inclinations but go out of their way to ensure that they don't act on them, perhaps to the point of overcompensating and treating African Americans more favorably than whites. Any definition of racism would include the first group, but what about the second? An individual with a subconscious bias against African Americans may inadvertently sit farther away from African American job applicants in an interview and therefore be less likely to hire them. Is that individual a racist?

The step where the researcher defines the concept he or she wishes to study is called a *conceptual definition*. Conceptual definition is the process through which a scientist defines what he or she means by an abstract concept. When the researcher says "racism" and when the readers say "racism," they should be on the same page.

In the last chapter, we focused on theories and concepts, and our goal here is to transform those concepts into something that we can actually measure, a process called *operationalization*. Operationalization is the process through which researchers transform abstract concepts into concrete, tangible ones they can measure. In this case, researchers using the IAT are operationalizing racism in a very specific way (as such, they never refer to it as "racism," but as an "automatic preference" for one racial group over another), a way that may or may not correspond to what other researchers mean when they say, or research, racism. For instance, if we were interested in determining why police officers are more likely to shoot African American suspects than white suspects, the operationalization used in the IAT might make sense. In a split-second decision, when a police officer has to determine whether a suspect presents a threat or not, an automatic association between African Americans and danger, or threat, might make the difference between firing and not firing. On the other hand, if we were dealing with the question of why African American workers might be less likely to receive promotions than equally qualified white candidates, a different operationalization of racism (perhaps the holding of negative stereotypes about African Americans) would be appropriate.

The concepts that we're dealing with can potentially be manifested in the real world in a nearly infinite number of ways, and any of those ways can potentially be used as an operationalization of the concept. In this instance, racism has been operationalized as a difference in response times, but that doesn't make other operationalizations any less valid. The question we have to ask about our operationalization is how well it reflects the way that the concept works in the real world.

Another critical aspect of operationalization is the need for specificity about how the concept will be turned into something that we can measure. In the case of the IAT, automatic preferences for one racial group over another are measured by differences in the average response time between two of the sequences, controlling for the response time in the other sequences. (Their primary use is to figure out how quickly respondents can react to the words flashing on the screen under the best of circumstances—we'll talk more about this sort of experimental control in a later chapter.) It wouldn't be enough to say that respondents had an automatic preference for one group over another if they were "slow" in one of the sequences, or even if they were "faster" in another. How slow? How much faster? The operationalization has to answer these questions in the most detailed manner possible.

OPERATIONALIZATION: TRANSFORMING ABSTRACT CONCEPTS INTO MEASURABLE CONCEPTS

Michael Bittman, Paula England, Nancy Folbre, Liana Sayer, and George Matheson—Relative Income and Housework (2003)

Operationalization is not just an issue when researchers are measuring abstract concepts such as racism. Some concepts appear easier to measure. Think about the chores we perform at home. Compared to racism, time spent on household chores appears to be a more tangible, concrete concept, but is it?

In traditional households, where the husband worked and the wife stayed home to attend to child care and housework, it may have made sense for the wife to do all, or nearly all, of the chores around the house. However, the days in which this was the most common arrangement in most Western countries are long past. Today, most households contain two working adults, and it would make sense to assume that as women have entered the workforce, men have begun to do more chores around the house—but that doesn't seem to be the case. In fact, in households in which women earn more than their husbands, the women actually do *more* work around the house than they would if they earned less. The amount of housework done by husbands increases as the wife earns more money, peaking when they earn equal amounts, and declining when the wife starts to earn more.

The primary explanation for this behavior is based on how couples internalize society's expectations about gender: housework is perceived as women's domain, while earning money in work outside the home is perceived as the domain of men. As such, men who earn less money than their wives are subverting the societal expectations that they have internalized. The couple responds to this subversion by reverting to more traditional gender roles in other areas, like housework.

To test this model, Bittman, England, Folbre, Sayer, and Matheson (2003) looked at the 1992 Australian time use study, in which researchers asked the occupants of 4,000 randomly chosen households in Australia to keep a time diary for two days. In these time diaries, the respondents recorded their primary activity in five-minute increments throughout the day: when they were eating, sleeping, shopping, working, doing dishes, reading a book, whatever. For this study, the researchers ignored the responses of single people and minors (though they did treat cohabiting couples as being married), as well as the responses of retirees or any couple in which one of the members earned money without working (for instance, living off investments). They then went through the diaries looking for specific activities: cooking; doing dishes; doing laundry; cleaning (including tidying, dusting, scrubbing, and vacuuming); home and car maintenance; and lawn, yard, and pool care. They specifically did not include hours spent on child care or shopping. On average, husbands reported the equivalent of 11.0 hours of housework per week, while wives reported 23.3 hours per week.

After controlling for various factors like education and number of children (we'll talk about how to control for such factors in the discussion of regression analysis in Chapter 13), the researchers were able to determine the expected amount of time husbands and wives spent on housework based on the source of the couple's income. In cases where the husband earned all of the income, he was expected to do about 10 hours of chores around the house per week, while his wife was expected to do about 26 hours a week. When the husband and wife earned the same amount of money (as 13 percent of the respondents said that they did), the wife was expected to put in about 20.5 hours of housework, while the husband was expected to do about 10.5 hours per week. Finally, if the wife earned all of the money in the household, she was expected to do about 26 hours of housework per week, while the husband's contribution fell to about 9 hours. In short, a wife's contribution to housework declines as she makes more money, then starts going up again if she makes more than the husband does. Men's household work is pretty stable, rising as their wives make more money, then leveling out. Essentially, when women earn more, they can bargain within the relationship for less housework, but not for men to do more.

While we might agree that racism is a difficult concept to measure, it seems that housework should be easier. After all, there is an objective amount of housework that's done in every household: all we have to do is find a way to measure it. That doesn't mean, though, that there aren't definitional problems associated with housework. For instance, Bittman and his colleagues (2003) included lawn and garden care as housework but didn't include child care (mostly to enable easy comparisons with other studies carried out in the United States). Most researchers would probably agree that washing dishes or vacuuming are housework, but other activities could be questioned. Gardening might be a chore for some people, but it could be a form of relaxation for others. Not too many people enjoy doing laundry, but many people work on their cars for fun—and in this study, these activities would be counted equally as housework activities. Because the definition of housework is potentially so fuzzy, it is exceedingly important to specify exactly what we mean. Bittman and his colleagues provided a long list of the activities that they were looking for and made sure to defend their exclusion of other activities (like child care) that could potentially be included.

Even on a seemingly straightforward concept like house chores, researchers need detailed and operational definitions of what house chores are. We might think that we are referring to the same concepts when we say "house chores"; however, not everyone will be on the same page unless researchers define what they mean and how they operationalize each variable. Typically, researchers indicate in statements such as, "By *house chores*, I mean. . ." These operational definitions are very specific and work to inform readers how the researchers measure the concepts of interest. In this case, the operational definition lists which chores the researchers include in the list and which ones they do not. These definitions typically follow convention and theory; they are inspired by how previous scholars have defined the same concept, but the decisions are up to the researchers. Bittman and his colleagues (2003), for example, define *house chores* as follows: "Our major dependent variable is time spent in domestic work. More specifically, it includes food and drink preparation and meal cleanup; laundry, ironing, and clothes care; tidying, dusting, scrubbing, and vacuuming; paying bills and household management; lawn, yard, pool, and pet care; and home maintenance and car care. For comparability with the major U.S. studies, we excluded child care and shopping." These operational definitions clearly show the readers how the researchers measured the concept in their study. These definitions also enable replication of research findings. Researchers who want to retest the findings of Bittman's research team would have to use the same operational definition of housework or risk finding a difference when it was not really present.

In creating these operational definitions, the researchers have a vital role. Each decision of inclusion and exclusion could easily lead other researchers to call their results in to question. Hochschild (1989) points out that women report spending far more time than their husbands planning housework activities; the measure used by Bittman and his colleagues (2003) doesn't include that mental work. Similarly, in recent years, men have begun to place a far greater emphasis on fatherhood and childrearing activities than they did in the past. It's entirely possible that men who earn less than their wives spend more time with the kids but don't spend more time on the activities defined by Bittman and his colleagues' operationalization of housework. If child care or mental work were included in the operationalization, the results could potentially be different. One of the most important parts of any research paper is the way in which it defends the operationalization. It's not enough for Bittman and his colleagues to define exactly what goes into their operationalization of housework, they also have to explain why some activities were included and others were not. When possible, many researchers recalculate their results using slightly different operationalizations (for Bittman's work, this might mean including time spent on child care) to make sure that these differences don't have a dramatic impact on their overall findings.

Operationalization: How to Define "Chore"

Cleaning
Food preparation
Household organization
Fixing things inside
Fixing things outside
Lawn and garden
Car, tool, appliances
Household appliances
Caring for household members (children, general, educational, driving, pets, other adults)
Caring for non-household members (children, other adults, caring, helping, driving)
Shopping (for goods, food, gasoline, other)
Shopping for household services
Shopping for other services

VALIDITY

Researchers can run into many pitfalls when they operationalize abstract concepts. The most common ones are discussed next. The first, and most common, criticism of operationalization has to do with **construct validity**. We can think of the concepts that we're trying to measure in social science as unobserved variables: we know that there is a certain level of racism in people, or that men are doing a certain proportion of the chores in a household, but we can't directly measure it. All we can do is look at behaviors that we think are indicative of that unobserved true value, such as looking at answers to questions or response times or even direct observations of actions in a social situation. We should be careful not to confuse the concept with the specific manifestation of the concept that is actually being measured. Differences in automatic response times are not racism, and time journal reports of chores are not the same thing as the actual division of household labor. The question we have to ask is, "How well does our operationalization of the concept correspond to the concept we're trying to measure?" The extent to which it does is the construct validity—or just the **validity**—of the measure.

Face Validity

There are a number of types of validity, but they all deal with this same issue: how well our operationalization reflects the underlying concept that we're trying to measure. A typical starting point would be the question of **face validity**. Would an untrained observer perceive the relationship between the concept and the operationalization? In Bittman and his colleagues' (2003) study, we almost certainly have face validity. We want to measure the balance of household labor between spouses, and our measure gives us a self-report of the amount of time spent on various household labor activities. If we were instead measuring division of household labor based on the color of the cleaning tools—on the theory that men and women will buy different-colored brushes and gloves—we wouldn't have face validity. Face validity looks to see if the measurement at least appears to have something to do with what the researcher is trying to measure.

Content Validity

Another type of validity is **content validity**. Concepts that social scientists are trying to measure are often multifaceted. Content validity refers to whether or not the operationalization includes all-important aspects of the concept of interest. Explanations as to why, for instance, child care or mental chores are not included are necessary to establish the content validity of Bittman and his colleagues' (2003) measure. A measure of housework that failed to include some activities that are an important part of housework would lack content validity. Of course, since we can't directly observe the concepts being operationalized, there is always the possibility that we are missing some important part of a concept, which is why defending the particular observation used in a study is so important. While there are some statistical techniques—the most common being **factor analysis**—that can help in determining if different measurements belong to the same general concept, content analysis is best established through the thoughtful use of theory and careful reading of past research. Bittman and his colleagues' definition of household chores could be called into question, but it has the strong advantage of being in line with definitions used in the past. That doesn't necessarily make it right—just as there's no such thing as a "correct" operationalization—but at least the results can be compared with past findings.

External Validity

Bittman and his colleagues' (2003) study might also face some problems of **external validity**. External validity is the extent to which the results of a study can be generalized to other contexts. The data that Bittman and his colleagues used was gathered in Australia. While the authors make no claim that their results apply in other countries, we may well want to apply their results to explain the division of household chores in the United States—but would it be reasonable to do so? The case could be made that data collected in Australia, which has a culture of gender relations similar to that of the United States, could be generalized to the United States, while data gathered in India or Iran might not be. (Similarly, it would probably be inappropriate to apply data gathered in the United States to either of those countries.) Because Bittman's study collected real-world data, it has a leg up in terms of external validity relative to many other studies; at the very least, it can be applied to Australian households in 1992 (when the data was collected). Laboratory studies, even those that are designed to simulate real-world situations, may have a much more difficult time establishing their external validity.

CRITERION VALIDITY

John McConahay—The Modern Racism Scale (1983)

In many ways, the Supreme Court's decision in *Brown v. Board of Education* (1954) was only the start of the fight to desegregate American schools. After the decision, localities around the country began to take steps to delay, or even prevent, the racial integration of their schools. Some areas closed down their school system entirely to avoid integration. Others separated the areas in which African Americans and whites lived into separate school districts. Still others simply resorted to violence and intimidation of anyone trying to cross the color lines. In order to force schools into compliance with *Brown*, the Supreme Court gave lower federal courts increasing amounts of power to take control of the functions of school districts, allowing them to make budget decisions, draw district boundaries, or whatever else was necessary to create an integrated school system.

One of the most controversial policies adopted by federal courts in this era was the busing of students to schools other than the one closest to them in order to create integrated schools. So, African American students might be bused to suburban schools in predominantly white areas, and white students might be bused from those areas to predominantly African American urban schools. Such decisions faced enormous criticism in the white suburban communities that were affected. Not only were such decisions being made by unelected federal judges, but they had the result of sending their children to what they perceived to be worse schools. In Louisville, Kentucky, the uproar—which ran the gamut from protests and sit-ins to fire bombings—received national attention.

With few exceptions, though, critics of busing avoided even mentioning race as a factor; they talked about the importance of preserving neighborhood schools and the inconvenience to students who have to go long distances to school. Supporters of busing, however, charged that the opposition was based in racism. As discussed previously, by the early 1980s, there were relatively few Americans willing to express overtly racist views, so most people who opposed busing would do so on nonracial grounds, even if their real reason was a desire to keep African Americans and whites separate.

The question then becomes, "How do we determine how much of the opposition to busing is based on nonracial reasons, like preserving neighborhood schools, and how much is based on racism?" This distinction is important because it determines what the response of local governments to the sometimes-overwhelming opposition should be. If people are opposed because they think their children are being bused to worse schools, steps could be taken to improve the quality of the schools the students are being bused to. If people are opposed because of the inconvenience of long bus rides, steps could be taken to adjust the bus schedules to make things more convenient. If the opposition is based solely on racism, though, there's nothing that can be done to quell the objections—but those objections would rightly be seen as less legitimate than those based on nonracial grounds.

McConahay (1983) attempted to answer this question by looking at the relationship between how much individual whites had to lose from integration and busing and how much they opposed it. If it were the case that opposition was coming mostly from principled, nonracist reasons, then those individuals who had the most to lose (those who had children in school in the area and those who owned homes in the affected area) should be more opposed than those who had less at stake (because they didn't have children in school or rented, rather than owned, their homes, so they could move easily). McConahay carried out a face-to-face poll of 879 whites in Louisville, which lasted almost an hour and a half. While only 16 percent of whites said that they were opposed to school integration, 76 percent said that they were strongly opposed to busing. More than half of white participants said that there was no change that could be made to the busing program that would make it acceptable to them. Participants were asked questions to determine how much they would be affected by the busing program as well as two sets of questions that were intended to measure their racism.

The first set of racism questions was intended to measure what McConahay (1983) refers to as "old-fashioned" or "redneck" racism, the sort of overtly racist statements that were increasingly less socially acceptable. For instance, participants were asked if they would mind if an African American family with a similar education and income to their own moved in next door, and if African Americans were generally as smart as whites. In the second set of racism questions, participants were asked a series of questions that were later codified as the "Modern Racism Scale." McConahay defines *modern racism* as the belief that discrimination is no longer a problem, so the demands of African Americans are no longer justified; they are pushing too hard for special treatment. For the Modern Racism Scale, respondents would rate statements such as "It is easy to understand the anger of black people in America" and "Over the past few years the government and news media have shown more respect to blacks than they deserve." Respondents were also asked to rate their feelings toward African Americans using a feeling thermometer scale. On such scales, commonly used in survey research, respondents are asked to rate an individual or group on a 0-to-100 scale, where 0 represents the "coldest," or most disliked, and 100 represents the "warmest" feelings, or liking the most.

McConahay's (1983) analysis showed that self-interest had almost no relationship to whites' opposition to busing. It didn't matter if whites had kids in the district or family members who might be affected, or if they owned their homes rather than rented them. What mattered was how they responded to the racism questions. Individuals who gave more racist responses to the questions on the Modern Racism Scale and those who gave more racist responses on the old-fashioned racism scale were much more likely to oppose the busing program—whether they would be directly affected by it or not. While scores on both of the scales were able to predict how people would feel about the busing proposal, the analysis showed that they were distinct: people who scored high in one of the scales did not necessarily score high on the other. This indicates that some of the respondents showed up as racists on the Modern Racism Scale without showing up as racists on the old-fashioned racism scale—but they still opposed busing, whether they would be affected by it or not. To McConahay, this showed that the opposition to busing in the area around Louisville wasn't being driven by the concerns that were being voiced by opponents, but rather by racism, even if the racists had learned to hide their views.

The main advantage of the Modern Racism Scale is that it's nonreactive: people don't seem to change their answers based on the social situation. In McConahay's (1983) study, some respondents were approached by an African American interviewer, while others were approached by a white interviewer. Not surprising, those who were interviewed by an African American scored lower on the old-fashioned racism scale, but not on the Modern Racism Scale. This makes sense. You don't have to be a racist to agree with the items on the Modern Racism Scale. A political conservative who is against social welfare programs in general, not just those that relate to African Americans, would receive a high score on the scale whether he or she is racist or not. Unlike the questions on the old-fashioned racism scale, responses can be justified without resorting to racism. But this strength of the scale—maybe its most important strength—is also a problem from the perspective of face validity. McConahay's scale purports to be measuring racism, but it's also measuring conservative political views. Face validity asks if there is a clear and obvious relationship between the concept and the operationalization, and, in this case, even McConahay admits that this is a problem.

However, the lack of face validity doesn't mean that the Modern Racism Scale is invalid as a measure of racism. We simply need to evaluate it for other types of validity. By showing that scores on the scale have a significant impact on how people evaluate busing in Louisville, McConahay (1983) has established some external validity. We can move beyond this, though, by looking at **criterion validity**. Criterion validity is the extent to which the operationalization we're using has the same characteristics as other operationalizations that have been used in the past. To put it another way, are we measuring the same things that others have measured in the past? The Modern Racism Scale purports to measure racism, not just conservative political beliefs, and criterion validity allows us to determine if this is the case.

To evaluate criterion validity, we have to examine the relationship between the operationalization that we're using and other operationalizations that have been used in the past or that theory tells us are related to the concept. In this case, there are a number of behaviors that we have reason to believe are related to the concept of racism. Racists should score higher on the old-fashioned racism scale. Racists should give African Americans lower scores on the feeling thermometer scale. Racists should be less likely to hire African Americans in a job interview setting. It would be difficult to argue against classifying someone who did all of these things as a racist. As such, if people who do all of these things also score highly on the Modern Racism Scale, we can make the argument that people who score highly on the Modern Racism Scale are racists. In his study of anti-busing attitudes in Louisville and a number of follow-up papers, McConahay (1983) and other researchers were able to show that scores on the Modern Racism Scale are related to all of these behaviors and more. This is referred to as the multi-trait, multimethod approach to validity, and it gives us a great deal of confidence that we are measuring the concept that we're trying to get at.

INTERNAL VALIDITY

Peter Bearman and Hannah Bruckner—Do Virginity Pledges Work? (2001)

In 1993, church groups in the United States began an effort to discourage premarital sex by encouraging teenagers to take an abstinence pledge, in which they would promise not to have sex before marriage. Teenagers would also sometimes wear a ring to symbolize their commitment. These pledges have proven popular. Today, organizers of the various groups that encourage the abstinence promises claim more than 2.5 million pledgers worldwide. Proponents of the promises correctly point out that if teenagers don't have sex outside of marriage—and married people do the same—there would be no risk of sexually transmitted diseases (STDs) or of babies being born outside of wedlock. Not coincidentally, it would also mean that there would be little need for sex education in schools—the abolition of which was a goal of the same groups that sponsored the pledges. Critics contend that asking teens to completely refrain from sexual activity is unrealistic and that a lack of sex education may make them more likely to engage in risky sexual behaviors, and thus make them more likely to become pregnant or catch STDs. In addition, they argue that teens who make such a pledge and then have sex will feel worse about themselves afterward than if they hadn't taken a pledge.

As such, the efficacy of the abstinence pledges became a point of great contention among politicians, school boards, and churches, and a number of studies attempted to determine exactly what their effects were. At the time, the broadest of these studies was drawn from the National Longitudinal Study of Youth's Adolescent Health (NLSY). The NLSY is an enormous study of young people that includes questions on almost every conceivable topic: smoking, drinking, sex, work, self-esteem, friends, grades, religion, and family relationships, among many others. More than 90,000 participants were asked to complete a short form of the survey in their school, and the study did more in-depth surveys at the homes of about 20,000 participants. These same participants were then included in a follow-up study a year later, and the researchers were able to contact about 80 percent of them for the second survey. To reduce bias that might come from having teens discuss sensitive issues with a researcher, the participants in the home study listened to the questions on tape and put their answers on the response sheet themselves.

Bearman and Bruckner (2001) analyzed the relationship between abstinence promises and the age at which participants had sexual intercourse for the first time. To do this, they had to control for a number of other factors that might lead teenagers to have sex earlier or later. For instance, teenagers who participate in extracurricular activities have sex later than those who don't, and teenagers with strong ties to their parents have sex later than those who don't. Gender matters, too: the things that lead boys and girls to engage in sexual activity are very different. They also had to control for the size of the abstinence pledge movement in the participant's school. Previous research had shown that taking an abstinence pledge was a way of establishing a social identity, and like other social identities, it has the greatest impact when it makes people feel distinctive but within a group. If too few people take the pledge, it doesn't affect behavior as much because no one knows about the pledge. If too many people take it, it ceases to provide a distinctive identity. The researchers also looked at whether or not the teenagers used protection during sex, to test if pledging really did make teens more likely to engage in risky sexual behaviors.

The fact that there was a longitudinal element to the study—that they had data on participants at two time points—allowed Bearman and Bruckner (2001) to isolate cause and effect better than would be possible if there was just one time point. Essentially, they were able to look at participants who had taken the abstinence pledge before the first survey and see if they had sexual intercourse for the first time before the second survey. They could then compare the likelihood of having sex for teens who had and had not taken the pledge and see if there was any difference that wasn't accounted for by all of the other factors that were expected to have an impact.

As expected, the responses showed some differences between those who took the pledge and those who didn't. Pledgers tend to think their parents would disapprove of sex more than nonpledgers, to be more religious, to think that their parents like them better, and to get lower scores on standardized tests. Girls who take the pledge tend to come from families with a lower socioeconomic status and tend to date people who are embedded in their friend group (a factor which makes them less likely to have sex). The important effects, though, aren't the differences between people who did and did not make the pledge, but the differences that resulted from having made the pledge, which Bearman and Bruckner (2001) discovered. Controlling for all other factors that past research says should have an impact on the likelihood of having sexual intercourse, Bearman and Bruckner found that teens between about 13 and 15 years old who take an abstinence pledge tend to have sex later than those who don't take a pledge. There doesn't seem to be an effect on older or younger teens. Also, it only seems to matter in schools where about 5 to 30 percent of the other students have taken a pledge. Despite these qualifications, these results were seen as good news for supporters of the pledge movement. However, there were also findings that heartened opponents: students who took the pledge and then had sex were less likely to use contraception, though their self-esteem didn't seem to suffer as a result of having had sex.

The overall finding of Bearman and Bruckner (2001)—that teens who take an abstinence pledge tend to have sex later than teens who don't—has never really been in contention. Instead, questions about their results, and those of similar studies, relate to the causal mechanism of the differences. It's easy to show that there are differences between those who take the pledge and those who don't, but it's hard to establish the **internal validity** of these results. While the other types of validity that we've covered deal only with the operationalization, internal validity asks about the relationship, the cause and effect that the research is trying to establish. In this case, the researchers are arguing that taking an abstinence pledge results in a delay in the first time that teens have sexual intercourse. Internal validity asks us to evaluate whether it's actually the pledge that's leading to the delay.

Bearman and Bruckner (2001) have an advantage in this area because they have longitudinal data (information about the same participant at multiple points in time). Longitudinal data is important because it allows us to establish a temporal relationship. If we had a finding that showed that people with high self-esteem had higher incomes than those with low self-esteem, we could not be sure if people with higher self-esteem earn more or if earning more gives people higher self-esteem. On the other hand, if we were to find that taller people have higher incomes, we could be confident that height led to the increased income, as money very rarely makes people taller. Suppose Bearman and Bruckner had only collected one survey per participant. They would have had largely the same finding: teens who take an abstinence pledge are less likely to report having sex. However, without longitudinal data, it's possible that the cause and effect would be reversed: teens who hadn't had sexual intercourse could have reported having taken an abstinence pledge as a way of explaining why they hadn't had sex. In this study, the researchers only looked at participants who had not had sex as of the first survey and compared those who did and did not report having taken a pledge. Since no one in their analysis had yet had sexual intercourse, that lack can't explain any differences that showed up a year later.

Of course, there are also problems that come with longitudinal data—primarily the issue of *participant mortality*. Mortality refers to the loss in participants that almost necessarily comes with time: some move, some change their phone numbers, some refuse to take part in the follow-up surveys, some go to prison, and some even die (hence, the name). Since longitudinal data doesn't include participants who drop out of the survey, results could be biased if the participants who drop out are different from those who don't. For instance, if we were carrying out a longitudinal study of the long-term effects of adolescent drug use, only looking at those participants who stayed at the same address (and ignoring those who died or went to jail) could seriously alter our conclusions. In general, researchers deal with this problem by trying very hard to get follow-ups on as many of the participants as possible, sometimes making dozens of calls and sending dozens of letters to the participants and their families. If some participants still can't be reached, researchers determine if this is causing bias by looking at the characteristics of those who could be reached versus those who couldn't. If the two groups were about the same at the time of the first sample, researchers can be fairly certain that the mortality hasn't introduced bias. Even so, many researchers will make use of complex statistical techniques to try and correct for any possible difference, an approach that Bearman and Bruckner (2001) took advantage of.

A second threat to internal validity comes from **reactivity**. We'll discuss this in greater depth when we talk about interviews and writing survey questions, but the general idea is that the presence of a researcher or the act of answering questions on a survey can lead to differences that might be misattributed. In this case, knowing that they would have to answer questions—including questions about their sexual activity—again in a year's time might have led some of the teens who had made abstinence pledges to stick to their pledge. However, the study took some pains to limit the pressure on the participants to give socially desirable answers. Because the participants administered the survey to themselves and the researchers didn't know what the teens were saying, it's unlikely that knowing that they had to answer a survey had much of an impact on the teens' decision to have sexual intercourse.

The final major threat to internal validity is **selection bias**. Researchers are almost always comparing two or more groups; in this case, individuals who did and did not take an abstinence pledge. The fact that there are differences between the groups, though, doesn't mean that those differences are caused by the abstinence pledge. It could be that there were other differences between the two groups that led one group to be more likely to take the abstinence pledge, and these differences, not the pledge itself, led to the observed differences between the two groups. For instance, it is almost certainly the case that teens who are very religious are more likely to take an abstinence pledge, and those same teens are less likely to have premarital sex relative to teens who are less religious. However, in that case, it would be religious beliefs, not the abstinence pledge, that led to the difference in sexual behavior.

Researchers commonly deal with this problem by controlling for factors in a regression analysis. Regression analysis is discussed in detail later but basically allows researchers to correct for the effect of factors other than the factor of interest. So, when Bearman and Bruckner (2001) carried out their analysis, they were able to control for all of the other factors that they knew had an impact on the likelihood of a teen having sexual intercourse, such as religious beliefs, the views of parents, self-esteem, and being in a relationship. In experimental studies (covered in Chapter 9), researchers are able to deal with selection bias by randomly assigning participants to groups within a study. If the assignment is truly random, and there are enough people in each group, then there's no way that the observed effects can be the result of anything but the experimental treatment.

It's important to note, though, that regression analysis only allows researchers to control for factors that they know about and have been able to measure. If there is some other factor that they haven't thought of or weren't able to measure that led to the selection bias, then there is no way for regression analysis to account for it. This is exactly what critics of Bearman and Bruckner's (2001) work contend happened in the study. Janet Rosenbaum (2006), then at Stony Brook University, called into question many of Bearman and Bruckner's findings by controlling for attitudes about sex among the teens in the study. She argues that it's the teens' negative attitudes toward sex that led to both the virginity pledges and the delay in first sexual intercourse and that when you compare teens with negative attitudes toward sex who took the pledge with similar teens who didn't take the pledge, there's no significant difference in when they had sexual intercourse for the first time.

However, this isn't the only problem in Bearman and Bruckner's (2001) work. There's also an issue of content validity. As discussed in the study about housework and income, content validity asks if we are measuring all of the relevant aspects of the concept that we're interested in. If our operationalization deals with just one facet of the concept, it may lead us to inaccurate conclusions about the concept as a whole. You may have noticed that Bearman and Bruckner's study only deals with when teens have sexual intercourse for the first time. But, as they note, while intercourse may be the definition many of the teens use for losing virginity, it's far from the only form of sex. In a follow-up study, Bearman and Bruckner showed that teens who took abstinence pledges were slightly more likely to engage in other forms of sex than teens who hadn't taken a pledge. When all of the aspects of the concept (having premarital sex) are included, the differences between those who do and do not pledge are smaller than the initial study would lead us to believe.

Predictive Validity

Perhaps the strongest test of the validity of an operationalization is **predictive validity**. *Predictive validity* is the extent to which a measure can be used to predict behavior or scores on an accepted measure at a later time. For instance, if attitudes about sex when a respondent is 13 are correlated with the age of first sexual intercourse, the attitudinal measure would be considered to have predictive validity. Essentially, predictive validity is criterion validity with the added element of time, making it a stronger test (after all, predicting the future is a difficult business for a lot of reasons), but also leading to some confusion about the terms in the literature. Predictive and criterion validity are sometimes used interchangeably (in that scores on one operationalization *predict* scores on another operationalization taken at the same time), but the two are properly treated as separate concepts. After all, it's entirely possible for an operationalization to predict scores on another scale taken at the same time (criterion validity) but fail to predict behaviors or responses in the future (predictive validity). Of course, researchers can only test the predictive validity of their measures when they have multiple contacts with the same participants over a period of time. This sort of research is much more difficult to carry out than research that takes place only once but is often seen as more desirable because of the ability to test predictive validity.

Accuracy

In addition to validity, another concern with Bearman and Bruckner's (2001) findings has to do with the **accuracy** of their results. Accuracy deals with the question of how close the measurement used in our operationalization comes to the true value of that concept. Suppose we were measuring the weight of participants. Our accuracy would depend on how good the scale was: Is it accurate to within an ounce? A pound? Five pounds? If, instead, we were asking participants how much they weigh, our accuracy would depend not just on how good the scales they had at home were, but also on how recently they had weighed themselves and how much they remembered or lied about what the scale said. In Bearman and Bruckner's case, the measurement seems fairly straightforward. We've already established that the design of the study minimized incentives for the participants to lie, but there's also the possibility of misremembering. While it seems unlikely that they would forget whether or not they had sexual intercourse, many teens apparently forget whether or not they took an abstinence pledge. Rosenbaum (2006) showed that more than half of teens who took an abstinence pledge denied having done so in a follow-up study a year later. After five years, more than 80 percent denied having taken a pledge. If teens who have premarital sex after taking a pledge are more likely to forget or deny that they did so, then taking a pledge could appear to be far more effective than it really is. As researchers, we often take the accuracy of self-reports for granted, but with controversial or sensitive topics, this can cause serious problems, as the racism researchers discussed earlier found out some time ago.

RELIABILITY

Robert Levine—Pace of a City (1999)

It's common to refer to big cities as being "fast paced," with life seeming to move faster in large cities than in small towns, or faster in some regions or countries than in others. But what exactly does it mean to say that one city is "faster" than another? Are we talking about the speed at which people walk or drive? The amount of time it takes a waiter to visit a table or fill an order? The rate at which people speak?

In attempting to measure differences in the rate at which life moves in 31 different cities around the world, Robert Levine (1999), a professor of psychology at California State University, Fresno decided to look at a number of indicators that could be measured in any city: average walking speed in downtown areas, the speed at which post office workers were able to fulfill a request and give change, and the accuracy of public clocks. (If you aren't in a hurry to get somewhere, it doesn't matter if the clock is off by a few minutes.) Based on past research, Levine believed that cities with stronger economies and bigger populations and those in more individualistic cultures would be faster and that cities in hot climates or with cultures oriented around the general good, rather than the individual, would be slower.

Levine (1999) recruited students traveling back to their home countries on break to make the measurements, as well as psychologists and their students who volunteered to assist in the data collection effort, making sure that all were natives of the country (or able to pass as such) and were trained to make sure that they were taking measurements in the same way. To measure walking speed, Levine's assistants went to a flat, unobstructed area in the main business district of the city during main business hours on a clear summer day with significant foot traffic, but not so much as to prevent people from walking as quickly as they wanted to. They then timed how long it took 35 apparently healthy adult men and the same number of women, walking alone and not looking in the windows, to go 60 feet.

Similarly, the assistants went to a post office and handed the clerk a note written in the main language of the city, asking for a stamp with a small denomination, paid for with a bill that would require both paper and coins for change (for instance, in the United States, the assistant gave the clerk a five dollar bill in payment for one 32-cent stamp), and measured how long it took to get the stamp and the change. The assistant then did this at least eight times in different post offices around the city. Finally, the assistants walked into fifteen different downtown banks and noted how accurate the clocks inside were, compared to the time reported by the telephone company.

Once all of the data was collected, Levine (1999) combined the measures into an index—a single score that combined the walking speed, post office response time, and accuracy of bank clocks—and ranked the cities. Zurich, Dublin, Berlin, and Tokyo were the fastest; Rio de Janeiro, Jakarta, and Mexico City were the slowest. In Zurich, people took only about 11.8 seconds to walk 60 feet, compared with 16.8 seconds in Rio. Similarly, it took postal clerks in Berlin only about 17 seconds to give the stamps and make change, compared to 70 seconds in Mexico City. Bank clocks in Zurich were off by only about 20 seconds, while those in Jakarta were off by almost 3 minutes.

Far from being just a curiosity, or a confirmation that some cities do indeed run faster than others, Levine (1999) was able to show that people who live cities with a faster pace have a greater likelihood of dying from heart disease, and higher rates of smoking, but also seem to be happier, as measured through surveys carried out by other researchers.

Levine's (1999) research deals with many of the validity concerns that we've addressed in this chapter. For instance, he measures a number of markers of the pace of a city, in a number of different ways, which goes a long way toward establishing the content validity of his research. Because he's measuring the speed at which life moves in cities all around the world, he's certainly established some external validity, and since he's mostly measuring speed, his work has face validity as well. There may be some question about the internal validity of his findings (How can we be sure that it's living in a faster city that leads to greater heart disease or smoking, when it could be that people who tend to have high-stress jobs also tend to congregate in large cities with a fast pace?), but the work is generally sound, especially in the context of other research on the same topic.

One of the most striking aspects of this study, though, is the degree to which Levine (1999) specifies exactly how he and his researchers measure each aspect of the pace of the cities they're studying. By making certain that the measurements were being taken in the same way each time, and that they were carried out multiple times in each city, Levine was able to establish the **reliability** of his work. Reliability is the extent to which multiple measurements of the same operationalization will give the same results. For instance, in the post office, the researcher didn't ask for a stamp in the local language. He or she gave the teller a note asking for a specific type of stamp that was comparable across the countries covered and paid with a paper note large enough to require bills and coins in change. In measuring the walking pace, the researchers went to a comparable street in every city, at a comparable time, and measured the time to go the same distance without window shopping.

While we can try to increase the reliability of our measurements by standardizing the way in which we carry out the measurement as much as possible, the only way to be certain that our measure is reliable is by taking it multiple times, or in multiple ways. Our measurement is reliable to the extent that the different measurements give the same result. Levine (1999) made sure to have his researchers go to multiple banks and multiple post offices and collect data from each. Had he not done so, his research could have been left open to the criticism that he may have just gone to an especially slow post office, or to the one bank in Caracas that has an inaccurate clock. If he goes to ten banks in Caracas, or ten post offices in Jakarta, and all give about the same results, it's much harder to argue that his data is bad. This is generally referred to as the **test/retest method** of establishing reliability. McConahay (1983), for instance, could have established the reliability of his measure of modern racism by giving his participants the Modern Racism Scale a second time a few weeks after the initial data collection. If they answered the same way the second time, it would show the reliability of his measurement. However, this isn't always practical, for a number of reasons. The first is cost: tracking down all of the same people to ask them the same questions would generally more than double the cost of administering the survey and would introduce problems of **participant mortality**. In addition, taking part in the first administration might change responses to the second one. If McConahay's participants didn't initially realize that his survey was about racism, they might answer the questions differently the second time, when they knew what the questions were getting at. In Levine's work, it wouldn't make sense to approach the same post office clerk with a note multiple times, as he or she would almost certainly become quicker at getting the correct change and the stamp with each iteration. In either case, the fact that the participants learned from the first measurement would tend to artificially decrease the reliability of the measurement. On the other hand, participants may simply remember how they responded to questions the first time, and give the same answers again, which would artificially increase the reliability, making the measurement seem more reliable than it really is. If too much time passes, though, the views of the participant might actually change, meaning that the researcher wouldn't be measuring the same thing at both points in time, and the measure would appear less reliable.

All of this means that retesting to establish validity is a tricky business. Levine (1999) was able to do it by treating all postal clerks, all banks, and all individuals walking down the street without window shopping as being interchangeable; he was trying to measure the characteristics of a city, not of any individual. In most social science research, we don't have that option. Generally, retesting is most useful in the measurement of relatively stable traits, such as degree of racism or political values, rather than traits that might change before the administration of the retest, such as moods or vote intentions. The researcher also needs to balance the length of time before the second administration. Too long, and participants may change or no longer be available; too short, and they may remember previous responses. In general, the second measurement should be weeks, but not months, after the initial measurement.

To try and reduce these learning effects, researchers sometimes make use of an alternate form method. The alternate form method requires that the researcher randomly divide up the questions used in the operationalization into two parts: one part is used in the initial test and the second for the retest. As long as there is no systematic difference between the two parts (a requirement that should be satisfied by a sufficiently long questionnaire and random assignment of the questions into the two forms), the scores of participants on the two forms should be the same, providing proof of the scale's reliability.

Because of these problems with test/retest, researchers often opt for other means of establishing reliability, though all rely on the same logic. For instance, researchers might put two versions of the same scale on one questionnaire, in what's called a parallel forms approach, or **split–half method**. Using this approach, the measurement of one version of the scale is compared with the measurement of the other version. The measurements are reliable to the extent that they give the same results. Going again back to McConahay's (1983) Modern Racism Scale, he could have established reliability by including two scales of modern racism questions or randomly dividing the questions in a single scale into two comparison groups. In either case, he would compare the results in one scale with the results of the other, or the results of one half of the scale with the results of the other half.

Finally, researchers may try to establish reliability through the use of multiple observers or coders. This approach is most commonly taken when the operationalization contains some element of subjectivity. For instance, if we were measuring aggressive behavior on a playground or looking for political bias in newspaper headlines, different observers could reach different conclusions about the aggressiveness of an act or the implications of a headline. As researchers, we want to minimize these differences. Ideally, it shouldn't matter who is taking the measurements. This is another reason why Levine (1999) made sure to lay out so clearly how the walking speed was to be measured and how the researcher should pay for the stamp: anyone following the same guidelines should reach the same measurement. If he had failed to lay out the standards for the measurement very specifically, differences between cities might really be differences between the people making the observations. So, when possible, Levine used multiple researchers within the same city and checked their findings against each other. If the different observers provide largely the same measurements, we've established the intercoder or interreader (depending on the nature of the task) reliability of the measurement.

Precision

There's good reason for this sort of standardization and specificity in the measurement, and that's to ensure **precision** in the data collected. Precision means that the measurement is as specific as possible. In Levine's (1999) research, the time it takes to walk a certain distance can be measured in minutes or as "long" or "short." Even though both would be accurate, measuring it in minutes would be more precise. Even more precise would be to include second as well.

Precision is related to **accuracy** but isn't quite the same thing. Accuracy asks how close a measurement comes to the true value, so it's certainly possible to have a measurement that's accurate but not precise (different measurements giving different values that are all relatively close to the true value), or precise but not accurate (different measurements giving results similar to each other but not necessarily close to the true value). If a trade-off were necessary, it would be better to be accurate than precise (as it would be possible to average together a large number of accurate measurements in order to get a clear view of the true value), but an operationalization should ideally be both.

Think about this. As a researcher, you can measure the same concept on multiple levels. For example, suppose you're talking to a research participant who makes $32,250 per year and you want to find out about income. One option is to ask directly, "How much do you make?" This would be the most precise: the most specific information. Alternately, you might ask the same person how much he or she makes and ask the person to pick one of the following intervals: $0–$10,000; $11,000–$20,000; $21,000–$30,000; $31,000–$40,000; $41,000–$50,000; $51,000 and above. If the person picks $31,000–$40,000, then the information is still accurate—it is correct. The person does make between $31,000 and $40,000 per year. However, it is not as specific as knowing he or she makes $32,250. That is why using the highest level of measurement is important to increase the precision of the measurement.

Even though measuring on the ratio level instead of the ordinal level increases the precision of the measure, it might be problematic. People feel uncomfortable answering an income question directly. Even though measuring income on the ratio level is more precise, it has the potential to alienate respondents. While there's no correct level of precision, researchers generally try to get the most precise measure possible without creating too much reactivity.

Decisions about operationalization and measurement are some of the most important that we make as researchers in the social sciences. The task is made harder by the fact that there is no such thing as a perfect operationalization: concepts, by their nature, can never be directly measured. The best we can do is to be conscious of the various threats to the validity and reliability of our measure. By designing our research to minimize these threats, we can put doubts about our findings to rest and get as close as possible to the concepts that we're really interested in.

SUMMARY

Generally, social science researchers want to measure abstract concepts—like racism—that can't be directly observed in the real world. As a result, they need to find measures that relate to these concepts that can be directly observed, a process called *operationalization*. The way in which a concept is operationalized has enormous implications for the results of research. Researchers take great care to be very specific with the operationalization, creating a detailed operational definition that lays out exactly what is, and what is not, included in their version of the concept.

While there is no such thing as a perfect operationalization, some are more valid representations of the concept than others. To assess the quality of a particular operationalization, researchers look at several types of validity, ranging from the simple (like face validity) to the more complex (like criterion validity). There are a number of well-known threats to validity, like reactivity and selection bias, and good operationalization must avoid them. In addition to validity, researchers must also pay attention to the reliability and accuracy of their measures.

Study and Review

Which of the various operationalizations of racism described in the chapter has the greatest validity? Why?

What's the conceptual definition of racism used in the IAT?

Why is selection bias such a threat to internal validity?

Predictive validity is often thought of as the highest type of validity? Why?

Which is more important: that an operationalization be accurate or precise? Why?

Is a more precise measure more valid than a less precise one? Why or why not?

CHAPTER 3

Research Ethics

Learning Objectives

- Be able to describe the main principles of ethical research outlined in the Belmont Report
- Be able to understand and apply the basic principles of ethical research
- Be able to identify vulnerable subject pools and discuss techniques to work with vulnerable populations

LAUD HUMPHREYS—THE TEAROOM TRADE (1970)

Laud Humphreys, a student working on his doctorate in sociology at Washington University in St. Louis was interested in the little known phenomenon of the "tearoom trade": two men meeting at public restrooms to engage in sexual intercourse. While sex in a public place by itself raises interesting logistical questions (How do you approach a potential partner? How do you make sure not to get caught? How do the men know where to go?), Humphreys was also interested in the lives of these men outside of their sexual activities. At the time, homosexual acts were illegal in nearly every state, and it was common for the police to raid gay clubs and bars, arresting everyone inside. Gay men were openly and widely vilified. With all of this going on, who were these men engaging in sexual activity in public bathrooms?

Humphreys (1970) began his study of the tearoom trade by hanging out at rest areas where men were known to meet. There, Humphreys noted that the two men engaging in sex often needed a third person to watch the door, a position referred to as the "watchqueen." By offering to be the watchqueen, Humphreys had the opportunity to watch and take detailed notes on the sexual activity taking place. He would record the frequency, length, number of sexual partners, and types of sexual acts performed, as well as how often individual men came for sex, giving him very detailed information on what is generally a very private act.

However, to have a full understanding of what was going on, Humphreys wanted to go beyond knowing just about the sex lives of these men. As a (then closeted) gay man himself, he knew that gay men often didn't fit the stereotypes held by much of the public, so he set to examine the other aspects of these men's lives. Of course, he couldn't just ask to interview them: if revealed to be homosexual, these men could have been arrested. If their sexuality was exposed publically, they could lose their jobs, their social standing, their families—everything. So, he came up with a different strategy. Along with the other information about the men, he started recording their license plate numbers and was able to (illicitly) use this information to get their names and home addresses. Armed with this information, Humphreys (and some colleagues) posed as health surveyors and visited the families of these men at their homes, collecting information about their occupations, incomes, education, and other information he wouldn't otherwise have been able to obtain.

The findings of this research had enormous importance, not just for the study of homosexuality in the United States, but also to the gay rights movement. Humphreys (1970) showed that homosexuals were not depraved social outcasts that they had been portrayed as, but were often neighbors, husbands, fathers, and pillars of their community. Today, partially as a result of his work, laws banning homosexuality have been largely repealed, and with a few exceptions (sometimes involving politicians), police have stopped making raids on public bathrooms in search of homosexual behavior.

However, these results cannot excuse Humphreys' ethical lapses. The men Humphreys studied were not only engaged in illegal behavior that could have sent them to prison, but half of them were married, with wives and children who apparently knew nothing about their activities. Had the identities of the men ever come to light, the harm to them would have been immense and irrevocable. The invasions of privacy Humphreys carried out in the course of his work—finding these men and their families at home, tracking their license plate numbers—made such harms even more likely.

Of course, Humphreys felt that the potential benefits of the research—many of which came to pass—outweighed the potential harm to the participants. As a formerly closeted and married homosexual himself, Humphreys had an enormous personal stake in his work. But the fact that he thought the benefits outweighed the risks doesn't mean that the participants felt the same way; after all, it was their lives that would have been ruined. And they were never given the chance to make that decision. They had no idea that they were part of a study and had no way to consent to be a part of it, even if they wanted to.

Humphreys also lied to the participants in his study, posing as a voyeur and then having others pose as surveyors. While telling the truth may have made the research more difficult to carry out, one of the fundamental principles of ethics in every part of life, not just in research, is that we should tell the truth. Deception is sometimes allowable, but only under very specific circumstances.

Perhaps the most important thing to take away from Humphreys' (1970) work, though, is that he didn't set out to do anything bad; quite the opposite. He knew that many of the men involved in the tearoom trade were respected in society, but in order to get access to them, he had to pretend to be watching the door. And in order to find out where they lived, he had to track down their license plates. And in order to determine their place in the community, he had to talk to their families. It may be comforting to think that we, as researchers, would never make these sorts of judgment errors, but Humphrey's example is important because it shows how unethical situations can arise. It wasn't one choice of Humphrey's that rendered his research unethical; it was a chain of decisions that wound up having the potential to destroy lives. Because of these problems, Washington University eventually revoked Humphreys' doctorate.

The goal of this chapter is to demonstrate the protections that have been put into place over the past few decades to shield participants from potential harm and to discuss the factors that researchers need to take into account to ensure that their participants are giving true informed consent to participate in the study and that all of the potential harms to the participants are taken into account. We will look at studies in psychology, behavioral economics, sociology, medicine, and political science and examine how researchers in each met, or failed to meet, the ethical standards required of modern social science research.

You can take the human subjects tutorial and obtain your human subjects certificate at https://www.citiprogram.org

THE BELMONT REPORT

Looking back at Humphrey's (1970) research, it's easy to point out his ethical lapses. At the time, though, there was no standardized oversight of research involving people. Deciding what was, and what was not, ethical to do in the name of research was left up to the individual researchers, with departments sometimes providing guidance. While most of the research carried out under these conditions would pass today's ethical standards, a lot of it wouldn't.

Ethical lapses in scientific research first came to public attention after World War II, when the twisted experimentation Nazi scientists carried out on prisoners came to light. These experiments were more torture than actual science, and it was thought that nothing similar could happen in the United States. This changed in 1972, when a social worker named Peter Buxtun working for the U.S. Public Health Service leaked the existence of the Tuskegee Syphilis Study to a Washington newspaper. Starting in 1932, researchers working for the U.S. government enrolled 600 poor African American farmers from Alabama in a study of the progression of syphilis. About 400 of the farmers had the venereal disease when the study began (the other 200 served as a control group; we'll discuss control groups in Chapter 9), but the researchers didn't tell them that they had a contagious disease. Instead, they told them that they had "bad blood" and offered them free medical care, food, and burial insurance in return for their participation. This meant that these men continued to spread the disease to their sexual partners and even their children. This was bad, but it got worse. By the 1950s, syphilis could be successfully treated with penicillin: but the researchers opted to not treat the men in the study, nor even tell them that a treatment was available. The study continued until the 1970s, when Buxtun, having tried to stop the study through normal means, revealed it to the public. Within three months, the study was shut down, and Congress started working to make sure that nothing like this happened again.

Congressional efforts led to the National Research Act of 1974, which created a commission tasked with establishing:

> (i)   the boundaries between biomedical and behavioral research and the accepted and routine practice of medicine
> (ii) the role of assessment of risk–benefit criteria in the determination of the appropriateness of research involving human subjects
> (iii) appropriate guidelines for the selection of human subjects for participation in such research and
> (iv) the nature and definition of informed consent in various research settings

VOLUNTEERS NEEDED

FOR A SCIENTIFIC STUDY

INVESTIGATING WHETHER PEOPLE CAN DISTINGUISH BETWEEN SCIENTIFIC STUDIES AND KIDNEY-HARVESTING SCAMS.

(HEALTHY TYPE-O ADULTS ONLY)

TAKE ONE

Study

The result was the Belmont Report, which went into force in 1979. While the most prevalent examples of ethical lapses may come from medical studies, the Belmont Report, and the ethical principles it lays out, applies equally to all forms of research involving human participants. It outlines the core principles of ethical research—respect for persons, beneficence, and justice—and forms the basis for the ethics rules researchers follow today.

THE NO HARM RULE

Philip Zimbardo—The Stanford Prison Experiment (1971)

Professor Philip Zimbardo is the world's leading expert on the psychological origins of evil. He has studied murder, rape, child molestation, the abuses of Abu Ghraib prison in Iraq—all manner of depraved activities—to try and understand where these behaviors come from. At New York University, he studied the effects of deindividuation on how people treat each: people are more willing to harm others if they cannot see their faces or if their own identity is similarly concealed. For Zimbardo, these findings went a long way toward explaining the masked behavior of groups like the Ku Klux Klan, as well as why children so often hit costumed characters at Disneyland.

By 1971, Zimbardo was at Stanford University and had moved on to more abstract notions of deindividuation. In the same way that participants in his previous studies had been more willing to abuse masked people, he hypothesized that prison guards would be willing to abuse prisoners because they didn't see them as people, but rather as inmate numbers. If this were the case, it could explain, and potentially even provide an avenue for quelling, prison abuses and riots.

There was one problem: Zimbardo couldn't simply go in to a prison and study the behavior of guards there. First off, it doesn't seem likely that the California Department of Corrections would give him permission to go into a prison and document the abuses that weren't supposed to be going on in the first place. Second, even if he were able to document that guards in prisons deindividuated the prisoners and that it contributed to violence, it wouldn't prove anything about his underlying theory of deindividuation. In his previous studies in New York, he had shown that regular people were willing to commit violence against deindividuated victims; a finding about prison guards could be criticized as simply applying to the sorts of people who find work in prisons. Maybe people who chose to be prison guards were simply sadists who enjoyed hurting people, tended to deindividuate people as a coping mechanism, or had been psychologically scarred by years of working with inmates.

To do this right, Zimbardo (1971) decided to make his own prison. The set-up worked like this. He recruited 24 male undergraduates, all of whom had tested about average on personality tests and had no criminal record. For the week of Spring Break, the students agreed to be part of a prison simulation, held in the psychology building, in return for a cash payment. Zimbardo then randomly assigned half of them to be guards and half to be prisoners.

The students assigned to be guards were brought to the makeshift prison. Bars were placed on the doors of offices, and a broom closet was converted to solitary confinement. They were given uniforms resembling those of actual prison guards, complete with billy clubs and mirrored sunglasses. (The sunglasses are actually important. Because they hide the eyes, they make it harder for guards and prisoners to regard each other as individuals.) The students were given only rudimentary instructions: no physical violence, and don't let the prisoners escape.

At the same time, the students assigned to be prisoners were picked up by the actual Stanford police at home, in front of family and neighbors. They were told to come quietly and, upon arriving at the "prison," were dressed in humiliating smocks (think a hospital gown without underwear), bald caps, and ankle chains.

It took a bit less than a day for things to get out of hand. In the middle of the first night, the guards forced the prisoners out of bed for a headcount. In response, the prisoners mounted a riot the next day, barricading their cells and screaming at the guards. The guards, in return, sprayed the prisoners with fire extinguishers, began physical and sexual abuse reminiscent of the photographs at Abu Ghraib prison that Zimbardo would study years later, and forced prisoners to use a bucket instead of the bathrooms. The worst abuses came at night, when the guards believed (incorrectly) that they were hidden from the cameras set up by Zimbardo and his students.

Not surprising, some of the prisoners began pleading to be let out, to end the experiment. Zimbardo initially refused, only agreeing to let one of the most abused prisoners out after he seemed to be seriously ill. The abuse by the guards continued and seemed to break the spirit of the prisoners. After several more prisoners developed severe psychological or physiological reactions to the treatment and had to be freed, Zimbardo offered the others a deal: they could end the experiment if they wanted to, but they wouldn't get paid. The remaining seven prisoners stayed.

The study came to an end on the sixth day, when Zimbardo asked one of his graduate students, Christine Maslach (now Zimbardo's wife and romantically involved with him even then), to observe. As far as Zimbardo was concerned, the experiment had gone perfectly: the inhumane treatment of the prisoners showed that abuse of prison inmates came not from depraved individuals choosing to be guards, but rather by the roles of the situation. Upon seeing what was going on, Maslach, as might be expected, demanded that Zimbardo shut it down immediately, threatening to go to university administration if he refused. Zimbardo eventually relented and shut down the study the next day.

In one sense, Zimbardo was right. The study wound up being profoundly influential. Combined with Milgram's (1974) study on obedience to authority (discussed later in this chapter), it shapes how we understand the interplay of situation and behavior. Almost all of us are capable of inhumane behavior, it argues: as disgusting as the behavior is, in the same situation, you would probably do the same thing. Now, Zimbardo certainly knew that the "prisoners" involved in the study were suffering, and they were certainly worse off than they had expected to be when they signed up for the study, but he was able to justify continuing the experiment for two major reasons.

First, in Zimbardo's judgment, the harm to the participants in the study was outweighed by the benefit to science. The students assigned to be prisoners spent nearly a week being psychologically and physically abused, and the guards, after the experiment, may have come to an unwanted realization about themselves: most people would probably rather not think that they're capable of such behavior. However, if the results can be used to further our understanding of evil, if they could be used to prevent the abuse of thousands or tens of thousands of real prisoners in the future, we could make the argument, as Zimbardo must have, that their suffering was worth it.

Second, the prisoners had agreed to continue with the experiment. Remember, Zimbardo did offer them the opportunity to leave the study early (though they would forego their payment) and even offered one student a deal, in which he would avoid future physical abuse in return for working as a prisoner snitch. If they were really being hurt by the study, they could leave. The fact that they stayed meant that they were okay with what was going on. And, after all, they had volunteered to be part of the prison simulation.

Let's be clear. By today's standards, Zimbardo's (1971) Stanford Prison Experiment is *completely* unethical, and no university would allow it to be carried out today. The major reasons for that have to do with the **no harm rule**. A study using human subjects should not cause any physical or emotional harm to the subjects. Zimbardo's study caused long-lasting psychological—and even some physical—harm to the participants, and while the benefits to society resulting from the experiment may be great, that doesn't justify the harm he did to his participants. Now, all research involves some risk of harm to the participants (answering questions might lead to embarrassment, a study about racism might make a participant feel ashamed). The job of the researcher is to minimize any potential harm and ensure that whatever remains is balanced out with the potential benefit to society of the research.

Learn more about the Stanford Prison Experiment http://www.prisonexp.org/

INSTITUTIONAL REVIEW BOARDS (IRBS)

In Zimbardo's judgment, the benefits to science and humanity resulting from the study outweighed harm to the participants, but he isn't a neutral arbiter. Of course, he thinks that the work he's doing is important. Every researcher does. If researchers don't believe that the work they're doing is important to science and human progress, they probably wouldn't be doing it. It is for just that reason that we don't allow individual researchers to make the decision about whether the benefits of research outweigh the potential harms to participants. Rather, universities make use of **Institutional Review Boards** (IRBs) to, among other things, balance the potential harm and benefits of proposed research. These boards are typically made up of 12 members, some of whom are required to be outside of the university (so that they're not swayed by the benefit the research might bring to the institution) and some of whom must be outside of academic research altogether (these outside members, typically priests, ministers, or rabbis, are supposed to represent the conscience of the community).

By having outsiders weigh the costs and benefits of the study, it's thought that we can make problems like those seen in Zimbardo's (1971) study less likely. In

Zimbardo's study, the only real oversight came from Maslach, a student who was both under his control and romantically involved with him. Even though she was able to shut the study down, we can agree that more effective and disinterested oversight would be a good idea. The most important role of the IRB is to act in the interest of the participants, making certain that they don't suffer any undue harm. It is important to note that every research project does involve a certain level of harm to participants. These boards evaluate the level of potential harm and weigh these potential harms against the potential benefits of the study. A study that might cure a disease can justify more potential harm to participants than a study of musical interest. In both cases, the IRB makes sure that the potential harm to the participants is minimized and in line with the societal benefits of the research. Instead of the researcher, or principal investigators, who have a vested interest in the study weighing the costs and benefits, these decisions are made by impartial third parties, who ensure that no undue harm is done to the participants. This is an interactive process, more like a dialog than a judge's ruling. As such, the ethical responsibility is shared between the researcher and the IRB.

To learn more about the Institutional Review Boards, check out the U.S. Department of Health and Human Services website. Remember, the IRB is not responsible alone for ethical practices. The responsibility is shared between the researcher and the ethics board to ensure that a research is ethical.

http://www.hhs.gov

INFORMED CONSENT

With regard to prisoners agreeing to continue the experiment, Zimbardo, by today's standards, got it half right. All research participants have to give their **informed consent** before they are included in a study. Typically, this means reading a form that summarizes what the study will entail, all of the potential harms to them that might result, any benefits they might accrue as a result of participating, and who to contact if they have any questions (though there might be some question about whether or not the students in Zimbardo's [1971] study really knew what they were in for). Researchers sometimes make a distinction between consent and informed consent. Anyone can agree to be part of a study, but it's only informed consent if the individual knows exactly what to expect, is capable of understanding what's going to happen, and is competent to give that consent. Participants have to make the same calculation the IRB does, weighing the costs and benefits of participation in research. If they can't make that calculation, they can't provide informed consent. Minors, for instance, can't give informed consent because they're not considered competent; nor can individuals with mental illness, in most circumstances.

The form also has to tell potential participants that their informed consent is revocable at any time. This is the part that Zimbardo missed. The fact that participants choose to be in the study does not mean they have to stay until the end of the study. They always have the right to revoke their consent. This revocability means that any participant can leave the study at any time, without suffering any penalty as a result. So, if participants are offered, say, $10 for being part of a study, every participant who signs the consent form gets the $10—even if he or she decides to leave immediately afterward. The principle here is that no one should be asked to be part of a study that makes him or her feel uncomfortable in any way, and no one should feel pressured to continue an experiment because of some reward—money, extra credit in a class, or anything—that's at stake. Of course, there are other issues involved with giving participants money for their involvement in a study, which we'll talk about later. There's also the issue of when it's acceptable to leave things out of the informed consent forms, something that we'll address when we discuss deception.

Institutional Research Consent Form: Television News and Learning

To the Participant:

The purpose of this study is to investigate how different types of news broadcasts affect learning about politics, and how well that information becomes embedded in deep political knowledge and belief structures, often referred to as ideologies.

In this study, you will be asked to read and summarize three newspaper articles, as well as watch a television news program. No additional outside activities are required.

Your participation in this study does not carry any significant risks beyond the discomfort you may feel answering questions about political issues. If you would prefer not to answer any of the questions, you may do so with no penalty. All we ask is that you answer all of the questions that you feel comfortable answering honestly.

if you have any questions regarding the survey, please feel free to contact the principle investigator at the email address listed below. To preserve your anonymity, this sheet is the only place that your name will be recorded. No one, including the principal investigator, will be able to link your responses with you. You are free to withdraw from this study at any time without consequences. Your cooperation is very much appreciated.

After reading the above, I hereby voluntarily consent to participation in the study.

Print name: _____

Signature: _____

Date: _____

Experimenter: Dr. Dan Cassino

If you have any questions about the study, please contact Dr. Dan Cassino in the Department of Social Science and History, at dcassino@ ▮▮▮, or 973-▮▮▮▮▮. If you have any questions regarding your rights as a subject in this study, please contact Dr. ▮ ▮▮▮, Chair of the Institutional Review Board at 201-▮▮▮▮▮.

All participants must complete a consent form, witnessed by one of the researchers, prior to taking part in a study. They should be encouraged to read it fully and be given a copy for their records. The researcher should also keep a copy of it, to provide documentation of the number of participants in the study and that they all gave consent.

ANONYMITY AND CONFIDENTIALITY

Frank Marlowe—Ultimatums and Dictators in Tanzania (2004)

Economic theory has generated a large number of expectations about how people *should* behave under certain circumstances, and this set of expectations—often referred to as *rational choice theory* (discussed in detail in Chapter 4)—has informed many of the other disciplines in social science, including political science and psychology. In recent years, economists have started to test these theories in experimental settings to see how well their models explain actual behavior and if people diverge from them.

On large college campuses, it's fairly common for students to participate in such economic experiments to earn a few extra dollars, but there's something missing from this kind of study. Economists have been criticized for relying on the results of these student studies because the stakes involved are relatively low. It's possible that students playing for lunch money aren't sufficiently motivated to behave in the way that classic rational choice theory would suggest. If they were playing for hundreds, or thousands, of dollars, maybe they would act differently.

At the same time, economists and anthropologists have been exploring cultural differences in the way that individuals make economic decisions. If we want to talk about how *people* act in a certain situation, rather than how *Americans* act in a situation, researchers have to go around the world and have to include people from many cultures in their studies. Moreover, the farther removed from Western and American cultural norms the participants are, the more they tell us about what all people have in common versus what's determined by culture.

Florida State Anthropologist Frank Marlowe went to Tanzania to carry out economic experiments with individuals from the Hadza, one of the last societies of hunter-gatherers remaining in the world. Marlowe (2004) did his best to randomly assign participants to partner up and play one of two games—the ultimatum game or the dictator game—though random assignment is a tricky proposition in nomadic tribes, where people have a tendency to wander off.

Both games involve dividing money between two people. In the ultimatum game, the first player proposes a division, which the second player can then accept or reject. If the second player accepts the division, both players get whatever the first player proposed. If the second player rejects the division, no one gets anything. The dictator game is played the same way, except that the second player doesn't get the chance to reject the offer and has to accept whatever division the first player proposes.

According to classic rational choice theory, the first player in the ultimatum game should propose giving as little as possible to the second player, and the second player should accept it. After all, something—no matter how little—is better than nothing. Similarly, first players in the dictator game shouldn't give the second player anything, so they can keep all of the money for themselves. The extent to which people *don't* behave this way tells us about human rationality, and about cultural norms of generosity, especially important in a hunter-gatherer society, where a hunter may go weeks between big kills.

The Hadza were playing for relatively high stakes: 2,000 Tanzanian shillings. That's the equivalent of about $3, but for the the Hadza, who often don't have access to money at all, Marlowe calculated it to have the purchasing power of more than $250 in the United States. In some of the studies, Marlowe (2004) paid the players with beads of a roughly equivalent value. Among other things, this helped to make sure that all of the players understood the game, even if they didn't use money very often. (Generally, Hadza women have little contact with the outside world.)

Each of the players was paired with another anonymous player in the same camp. They had to be in the same camp to make sure that Marlowe could find both players after the game was over. He visited five camps, playing with almost all of the adults he encountered. All told, 196 Hadza adults played with Marlowe—about 20% of the total estimated population.

In the ultimatum game, the mean offer was 33 percent of the total amount. About a quarter of players offered less than 25% of the money, and about a quarter offered half of the money or more. This is very different from the results in the United States. In Los Angeles, the mean offer was 48 percent of the total amount. About 1 in 4 second players rejected the offers, meaning that no one got anything.

We would expect offers in the dictator game would be lower than in the ultimatum game. In the United States, the mean offer is about 20 percent. Among the Hadza, the mean offer was about 10 percent of the total amount of money. This seeming stinginess may be surprising, in light of how willing the Hadza seem to be to share food, such as big game and even berries. In their camps, individuals who don't share sometimes wind up ostracized, with no one willing to set up tents near them. Marlowe (2004) hypothesizes that the disconnect between food and money (or beads) may arise because paper bills, unlike dead giraffes, are easy to hide from the neighbors.

On the face of it, there doesn't seem to be anything unethical about Marlowe's (2004) work in Tanzania. The Hadza got money, Marlowe got his results, and everyone went home happy. But remember what we said at the beginning of the chapter. All research, no matter how innocuous it seems, carries some risk of harm, and in this case, there are some serious ethical issues to consider. First, there's nothing in Marlowe's description of his study about obtaining informed consent from his respondents, but that doesn't seem to be too serious, as any of them could have just walked away—and a lot of them apparently did.

A more serious issue arises from the effects of carrying out this study on so many individuals within Hadza society. At the time Marlowe (2004) carried out his work, there were estimated to be about 1,000 Hadza, and about 200 of them participated in the study. That means that, potentially, 20 percent of the population now has a substantial amount of money that the others don't. Does that lead to inflation within the camps? Could it lead to inequality within the normally egalitarian society? On this point, Marlowe worked to reduce potential problems by using beads, rather than cash, for half of the games. His actions show that he considered the potential problem, and it would be up to the IRB to determine if he had fully resolved it.

Another issue arises from **confidentiality**. Simply put, confidentiality means that no one should know how any particular individual responded in the study except for the researcher. The researcher knows the identity of the subjects, but in reporting, he or she will not disclose these identities. Typically, in publication and presentations, researchers use pseudonyms and change recognizable characteristics.

Closely related is **anonymity**. If a study is confidential, the researcher knows who the respondents are, and what they did in the study, but takes steps to ensure that no one else finds out the identity of the participants. If the study is anonymous, no one, including the researcher, knows who the participants are. In the best case scenario, even the fact that someone participated in the study is kept from others. Purely from a research design perspective, if participants suspect that their results may not be confidential, they may change their behavior to display more socially desirable traits, biasing the results of the study. Imagine, for instance, if the participants in Marlowe's (2004) study knew how all of the other people in their camp had played the games. They might try to appear more generous or might try and get back at someone that had been stingy or that they didn't like. So, lack of confidentiality can make the results of a study less useful. (We'll talk about this and related problems of reactivity in Chapter 6.)

But confidentiality is also an ethical issue because a lack of confidentiality can expose participants to harm on the basis of their participation. Marlowe (2004) tells us that sharing is necessary for survival among the Hadza, and those who are thought to be stingy or greedy can face severe social consequences. In a hunter-gatherer society, these consequences might be deadly. So, if confidentiality were breached in the Marlowe study, and everyone knew who had given low offers in the ultimatum and dictator games, those participants could be in real trouble.

In a perfect world, none of the Hadza would even know who had participated in Marlowe's (2004) study, much less what they had done. Logistically, it would have been very difficult for Marlowe to achieve this. The only way to find the people he was interested in was to go to the Hadza camps, and there were necessarily a number of people there who could see someone talking to the outsider with a truck and exchanging envelopes with him. Marlowe did take some steps to resolve this issue. He made sure that all of the transactions took place in sealed envelopes and made sure that no one knew who they were playing with. In fact, the only thing linking the people playing was that the proposer and the responder were in the same camp. (Remember, this was necessary because Marlowe might not have been able to find a particular individual again once he left the camp.) But this raises problems. In some of the camps Marlowe visited, there were less than 10 people present, and he played the games with all of them. If you were one of the people in that camp, wouldn't you want to know who had given you that lowball offer, who had refused to share in the dictator game? And if you knew it was one of the several people around you, wouldn't you look for the person who suddenly got more money, or more beads, than you did? While Marlowe had good reasons for working things the way he did, even the fact that people knew who his participants were may well have subjected them to harm. This is especially true in a case like this, where there is some physical evidence of how a participant played the game. Of course, these potential problems may well have been outweighed by the benefits of the study to the participants and to science—but it's something that an IRB would have to take into careful consideration.

COERCION

Finally, we have the most serious ethical issue arising from Marlowe's (2004) study, that of **monetary coercion**. In general, **coercion** refers to the ethical issues arising when an individual feels undue pressure to participate, or continue to participate, in a study. The pressure to participate in a study can arise when the subject is under the authority of the researchers. If the researcher is the subject's teacher, professor, or employer, the subject may feel pressure to participate because his or her grade, pay, or promotions will depend on the participation.

When people feel such pressure, for whatever reason, they're not really giving their informed consent, and they might be prone to start or continue to participate in the study regardless of whether or not they really want to. One of the best defenses against research that can harm the participants is that they can walk out, no strings attached. If, for whatever reason, participants don't feel as if they can do this, we have an ethical problem. So, for instance, a professor probably wouldn't be allowed to recruit participants for a study from his or her own class (at least not without providing for an alternative assignment), and a researcher wouldn't be allowed to carry out any kind of research on his or her own children. (A later example, that of neurologist Jay Giedd (1998), explores this issue.)

Monetary coercion is probably the most insidious form of this ethical problem. While it's relatively easy to put safeguards in place to ensure that there is no existing power relationship between the researcher and participant, and therefore limit the risk of coercion, the presence of money in a study can create a similar situation instantly. Suppose someone offered you $20 to participate in a study; the money might be nice to have, but you'd probably be okay with walking away from it if you didn't want to be a part of it. But what happens if someone offers you $200, or $2,000? You might not be as able to walk away as easily. In such a case, the amount of money being offered, in and of itself, creates a situation of coercion. (A similar case could be made for extra credit offered for participation in a school research study.)

In many cases, this sort of problem can be overcome through the revocability of informed consent. As noted before, a participant must be able to leave the study at any time and still collect whatever rewards were promised for completing the study. If the money will be given to participants at the end of the study, and a participant elects to leave halfway through, the participant will still get all of the money that he or she would have received if he or she had stayed the entire time. But this isn't foolproof. First of all, once a participant has signed the consent forms and agreed to be a part of a study, there is a great deal of social pressure to stay. There are plenty of instances where people remain in studies even if they are led to believe that their continued participation might lead to their own injury or death. In general, once people sign in, they tend to stick around. While this is generally a good thing for researchers—we don't want all of our participants leaving without completing the study—it means that we can't count on people leaving just because they're uncomfortable. Second, even the fact that people feel as if they have to sign the consent form, even if they would rather not, because they need the money presents an ethical problem. Informed consent isn't really consent if people feel as if they need to participate, for whatever reason. Third, in economic studies like Marlowe's (2004), there's no way to really give participants money if they walk away. If there's no set amount that they're supposed to receive, how would you know how much to give them? Moreover, for the participants, the whole point of the study is to maximize the amount of money that they take home. If they knew that they could get a certain amount—half the money or even all of it—by walking away, we'd be introducing another variable into the equation, making the results much more difficult and maybe even impossible to interpret.

How do we deal with monetary coercion? Prizes and money are offered in research projects to ensure participation and increase response rates, and most IRBs allow the use of such benefits. However, if money and prizes are offered, it is important that the researchers comply with the **opt-out rule**: if the subjects opt-out, they should still be eligible for the prize. Second, the best way to deal with this problem is to limit the amount of money that participants can earn through their participation. We don't have an ethical problem as long as the money that can be earned through participation is little enough that no one would feel that they had to participate. In Marlowe's (2004) study, the amount of money was pretty minimal by U.S. standards—2,000 Tanzanian Shillings is less than $5—but for a society with very little money, it had enormous buying power. There's no objective answer to whether or not that's enough to constitute coercion; we simply have to ask if it is so much that people would feel as if they had to participate. As a general rule, the money at stake should be enough to let participants buy a nice lunch, but not enough to buy a nice dinner, and certainly not enough to pay next month's rent. For a student sample in the United States, $250 would certainly be too much, and payouts should probably be less than about $30, though more could be acceptable if the study involved a great deal of time or effort on the part of the participants. If the sample in our study were Wall Street tycoons, $250 would probably be just fine. For the Hadza, in a study requiring very little time, it may be too much.

DECEPTION IN RESEARCH AND DEBRIEFING

Erich Goode—Personal Ad Deception (1996)

There has been an enormous amount of research in sociology on how men and women portray themselves to potential mates and which strategies tend to work best. In theory, a researcher could go to a bar and see who got hit on more, but that wouldn't necessarily tell us what we want to know. After all, how would you know what traits made one person more or less desirable than another?

Researchers have tried to resolve this issue by looking at personal ads. Unlike pick-up lines, personal ads are all in writing, making it easy for researchers to analyze the wording of a large number of ads, then determine which ones garnered the greatest number and quality of responses. So, it seems as if we have a relatively easy research design, with one big problem. How do you know how many responses an individual received to his or her ad? Several researchers have tried simply asking the people who placed the ads, but this hasn't worked out too well. In one case, only about 10 percent of the ad placers responded; after all, who would want to admit that no one responded?

Erich Goode (1996), a sociologist at Stony Brook University on Long Island, New York, approached the issue in a more direct way. He placed personal ads in four different newspapers and waited to see which ones would get the most responses. Two of the ads were men seeking women, and two were women seeking men. In one of the ads, the placer described himself or herself as being very attractive with a low-status job (a waitress, for women, or a cab driver, for men) or average looking with a high-status job (in both cases, a lawyer).

Based on the existing research, it was no surprise to Goode that the ads ostensibly placed by women received more than ten times as many responses as the ads ostensibly placed by men. Overall, 668 men responded to the attractive waitress, and 240 responded to the average looking lawyer; 79 responded to the two men's ads, combined. However, Goode was also interested in *how* people responded to the ads. He found that men were much more likely to be "blitzers," people who sent out responses to pretty much all of the ads in the hope that they'd get a date with one of them. He also found that there was a great deal of variance in the sexual references made in the responses. About 3 percent of the letters sent to the women's ads were explicitly sexual, while about a third of the letters sent to the cab driver included references that Goode calls "seemingly inappropriate at preliminary stages of the courtship process." One woman began her letter, "Dear sexy," explained that she liked "macho, domineering" men, and included a picture in a skimpy outfit.

Finally, Goode (1996) assembled a panel of ten men and ten women to evaluate the responses and determine which ones would be most likely to get a response from the fictional ad placer. The panelists were each shown ten of the responses, including pictures (if the respondent had included them), and asked to rate how likely the ad placer would be to respond, on a five-point scale. Overall, for the respondents to the ads placed by men, the panel said that about 60 percent of the respondents had a good chance of getting a date. Among the male respondents to the female ad placer, only about 34 percent were rated as being likely to get a date.

There are three glaring ethical issues arising from Goode's (1996) study. The first two arise from things that we've already talked about: informed consent and confidentiality. None of the respondents in Goode's study knew that they were part of a study, and they certainly didn't give their consent. Second is confidentiality. Goode received letters from respondents in which they talked, often in great detail, about what they were looking for in a respondent and what they liked in bed, and he also had photographs of some of these people. He passed on all of this information to a panel of outsiders. What if one of the panelists recognized a photograph or a letter sent by a friend? More than a few of the letters revealed that the writer was married and looking for a discreet affair. What if the spouse had been on the panel? In short, there was an enormous potential to harm the people who sent in letters and little effort made to limit it.

Goode's (1996) research also comes up as part of a debate about the role of **deception** in sociological research. Spurred on by the ethical abuses of Humphreys' (1970) Tea Room Trade study, sociologists began to debate whether it was ever acceptable to deceive individuals in order to find out what was really going on in their subculture. Some, led by Kai Erikson (1967, 1995) of Yale University, argued that it was never okay to enter a subculture under false pretenses, to convince people that you belonged somewhere that you really didn't (Erikson hadn't always been quite as scrupulous: as a graduate student, he had applied to be part of the team, led by Leon Festinger, that infiltrated a doomsday cult, a study discussed in Chapter 6. He was turned down.). Moreover, he argued, doing so might change the group that you were trying to study (as discussed in Chapter 6). Others, like Goode, argued that in cases like the one outlined above, deception was the only way to get an accurate idea of what was going on. As Goode points out, researchers had tried simply asking people who placed personal ads what their responses were like and hadn't gotten anywhere. Moreover, in some cases, like that of newspaper personal ads, the behavior wasn't entirely private. If people are doing something in public, they have to know that they might be observed by someone.

In this case, the deception came from the placing of the personal ad in the first place. Goode (1996) was pretending to be something that he was not—a waitress, a lawyer, or a cab driver—and it doesn't take a lot of ethics training to know that lying is generally a bad thing. However, Goode is right in saying that deception is sometimes necessary, and research ethics recognize that it is sometimes acceptable to lie to participants in a study, provided certain guidelines are met. First, deception is only acceptable if the study cannot be carried out any other way. If deception would simply make the study easier, it isn't acceptable. Second, the deception cannot put study participants at greater risk than they would be otherwise. In their initial consent form, participants have agreed to a certain amount of potential harm, and the deception cannot serve to increase it. If it does, the participants can't really give informed consent. Third, the deception has to be revealed to the participant as soon as possible, and the participant has to be thoroughly **debriefed**.

In the debriefing, the researcher tries to undo the effects of the deception on the individual. Debriefing is a process that takes place after the completion of the study, where the participants are informed about what the deception was and are told about the hypothesis and the findings of the study. They are also offered counseling services and are provided referrals if they experience any physical or emotional harm. In Goode's (1996) study, for instance, the researcher would have to reveal to the participants that they had been part of a study, tell them about the study, and try to mitigate any embarrassment or discomfort that resulted from it. Goode could have told them that their responses were typical of those received, so they didn't have anything to be embarrassed about, or that the panel had rated them as being very likely to get a date with the fictional ad placer, implying that they were desirable (even if none of this was actually true). The goal is to simply minimize harm. Finally, a proper debriefing would also include a written form of all of this information, as well as a number to contact if there were any other concerns.

Unfortunately, Goode (1996) didn't debrief the unwitting participants in his study at all. Rather, after the conclusion of the study, he placed an ad in a newspaper—one other than those that had contained the false ads—explaining the study and the results. We have no indication that any of his participants ever even saw it. Deception, in this case, might have been necessary, but Goode didn't do any of the things that would have made it ethical.

USE OF VULNERABLE POPULATIONS

Eric Kast—LSD and the Dying Patient (1966)

In the early 1960s, lysergic acid diethylamide (LSD) was gaining momentum as a wonder drug for psychiatric disorders. It was first synthesized in the 1930s from grain fungus (the same fungus that some have blamed for the Salem Witch trials), and the researchers hoped that it would work as a stimulant. However, there didn't seem to be any effects of the drug in animal trials, except for the animals seeming a bit "restless." It wasn't until five years later, when a researcher absorbed a bit through his skin and had mild hallucinations, that its psychoactive properties were discovered. (The same researcher, Albert Hofmann, took some intentionally a few days later and had the world's first "bad trip," convinced that he was possessed by a demon and that his furniture was threatening him.) Drug companies took note of its effects, and it was released for consumers in 1947 by Sandoz (now part of the company that makes Theraflu and Ex-Lax).

Researchers knew that it did something, but no one quite knew what it was good for. It was marketed to work for everything from schizophrenia to alcoholism, and some medical schools gave it to their students in order to help them understand a schizophrenic's world view. As part of this search for something that LSD would help, Eric Kast (1966), a doctor and researcher at the University of Chicago Medical School, arranged to give small amounts of the drug to patients dying in a local hospice. Permission was given by the hospice and the medical school to carry out the study, and patients were informed of the potential risks and benefits (at least, as many of the risks and benefits as were known at the time) and could decline to participate.

Eighty terminally ill patients, all with fewer than six months to live, opted in to the study, were given enough of the drug (100 micrograms) to trigger hallucinations, and were monitored for their responses. Participants worked with a therapist to relax and meditate before the administration of the dose (as researchers believed that this reduced the odds of a bad trip), and a researcher was on hand with chlorpromazine, a counter-agent to the LSD, in case the patients seemed frightened or wanted to stop. After the drug was administered, Kast (1966) followed up with interviews spaced over the following weeks. The majority of patients reported less anxiety about their medical condition, as well as less pain for up to several weeks afterward. Kast also called attention to "happy, oceanic" feelings that the patients reported experiencing for up to 12 days after their experience. These results led Kast to call for more research on the effectiveness of LSD and other hallucinogenic drugs for reducing pain among chronically ill patients—a call that went largely unanswered when LSD was banned by the U.S. government in 1968, primarily because of the rising recreational use of the drug.

Today, of course, it would be next to impossible to get permission to carry out a study using LSD. It is a Schedule I banned substance, so use or possession is a federal crime, and very few exceptions for research are given. While some psychologists might dispute the idea that it has no medical potential—a related drug, MDMA (also known as ecstasy), has been used in a therapy environment with some promising results in recent years—the risks of LSD use can be considerable. Some participants report anxiety or depression for a few days afterward, and a small number report persistent hallucinations (sometimes called flashbacks) that intrude on their daily lives, even after they stop taking the drug.

Are these potential side effects enough to render Kast's (1966) study unethical? Not necessarily. First off, Kast did everything he could to minimize the likelihood of these negative effects. Terrifying hallucinations sometimes happen while individuals are under the influence of LSD, but ensuring that patients are relaxed and in a calm environment seems to make these hallucinations less likely. Moreover, any participant who seemed to be having a negative experience while on the drug was immediately injected with a drug that would end the hallucinations. Second, while the long-term effects of LSD use might be troubling, Kast was working exclusively with participants who didn't have to worry about long-term effects, as they were expected to be dead within a few weeks or months. Because of the depression, pain, and other negative effects that their medical condition was (understandably) having on their lives, these participants had more to gain from LSD use than other patients and less to lose. It's entirely possible that, in this case, the potential benefits of the drug use outweighed the costs to the participants. As long as an outside body such as an IRB made this decision, and not Kast, the LSD use alone wouldn't make this study unethical.

However, there is another issue at stake: the use of **vulnerable subject populations**. An individual might be part of a vulnerable subject population for a number of reasons. First, the group to which the individual belongs might be less able than the average person to give informed consent. Children would fall into this category, as would individuals with mental illness. If someone cannot truly understand the costs and benefits of participating in the research, or can't make decisions about his or her own well-being, researchers need to take additional precautions before using the person in the study. For instance, in research involving children, researchers would generally have to obtain informed consent from the parents, then separate assent from the children themselves. They would probably have the parents observe the study so that they could stop the study if the children became uncomfortable.

Second, groups might be considered vulnerable subject populations because they may be subject to coercion: no matter what the researcher does, they may feel as if they have to participate in the research. Prisoners or residents of nursing homes might fall under this category, as would students in a professor's own class. In the case of prisoners or nursing home residents, the potential participants might feel that they would be punished in some way for not taking part in the study, even if they're assured that this isn't the case. People in these categories don't really have full control over their own lives, and if they can't really opt-out (or don't feel that they can), then they generally cannot be participants in a study.

Third, subject populations might be considered vulnerable if they face a larger degree of potential harm from participation than the average person. Pregnant women might fall into this category with regard to medical research, as might heart patients in any study that creates stress or anxiety in participants (as many political science and social psychology experiments do). Groups might also be considered vulnerable for this reason if they would face greater harm from a breach of confidentiality. So, for example, if you were doing a survey on sexual behavior among homosexuals, or any other subject that might expose participants to social stigma or legal problems, you would need to take extra care to preserve confidentiality. In such cases, researchers commonly avoid putting the actual names of participants in field notes or destroy any identifying information once the study is completed. That said, researchers should not simply decide to exclude such groups from research entirely. Many of the most important things that we want to know about are also things that might embarrass or endanger those who take part in them. Research on such vulnerable populations is important, but great care must be exercised.

In Kast's (1966) study, the hospice patients are very much a marginal case. Under intense amounts of psychological stress and, in many cases, physical pain, they may not have been able to give informed consent to participate in the study. They're also living in an institutional setting, and while they aren't prisoners, they might be excessively wary of doing anything that might upset the doctors and nurses that they depend on. Finally, the fact that they are dying might make them more likely to take risks that healthy people might not. As such, Kast was right to make use of a **multiple opt-in procedure**. That means that individuals or institutions other than the actual participant, as well as the actual participant, must both give their consent before the participant can take part in the study. In this case, that means that both the participant and the hospice administration must have agreed to allow participation. If either one declined, that participant could not be part of the study. Such procedures are most commonly used when research involves minors: both the parents and the minor have to independently agree to participate before the study can be carried out.

ANIMAL ETHICS

M. Keith Chen, Venkat Lakshminarayanan, Laurie R. Santos— Monkey Economics (2006)

Social scientists are typically most concerned with collecting data from human participants, and in much of the social sciences (unlike the natural sciences) animal studies are a thing of the past. Many researchers in psychology, and even sociology, still make use of animals, though, and the same ethical principles that apply to humans apply to this research as well. Animals may not be able to give informed consent, but they should be able to leave if they don't want to participate in an experiment. They may not be able to speak up in their own defense, but they shouldn't be subjected to any unnecessary harm as a result of research. Similarly, just as researchers wouldn't want to disrupt the Hazda society by introducing a large influx of new money, researchers wouldn't want their work to disrupt a hierarchy among wolves or primates or any other social animals. The challenges of working with animals are different, but the principles that guide ethical research remain the same, and understanding how ethical principles apply to animals can help us understand how they apply to human populations as well.

Chen is a behavioral economist at Harvard University (Lakshminarayanan and Santos are psychologists at Yale University), meaning that, unlike many economists, Chen goes beyond theorizing about how people should act and tests how they actually do act. Like most behavioral economists, much of his work has been shaped by the findings of Daniel Kahneman and Amos Tversky (1979, 1992, among many others). Kahneman won the Nobel Prize for their research into the biases people have that prevent them from acting rationally, a field now referred to as *prospect theory*. (Tversky was ineligible for the Nobel on account of being dead.) For instance, many supermarkets now give customers a small refund when they bring their own bags, something consumers seem to like. However, in the past, some supermarkets tested programs that would encourage customers to bring their own bags by charging them a small fee for using one of the store's bags, a program that consumers *hated*. What's interesting about this is that from an economic point of view, the two programs are identical. Not giving the store ten cents because you brought your own bag is the same thing as the store giving you ten cents because you brought your own bag, but people see one (in which the store gives you ten cents) as being desirable and the other as being detestable.

In the same way, gas stations have found out that consumers much prefer a "cash discount" to a "credit card surcharge," despite the fact that they're the exact same thing. (In one, consumers who pay with cash pay less for gas; in the other, consumers who use a credit card get charged more.) Laws in some states, like New York, even ban credit card surcharges while still allowing for the exact same thing through cash discounts. The reason is that one of the options is perceived as a gain, while the other is perceived as a loss, and even when they're the same thing, people think that there's a difference.

Chen and his colleagues (2006) researched, among other things, whether capuchin monkeys made the same mistake. To do so, they first trained the monkeys to understand that they could trade some money (silver coins with a hole in the middle) for a treat—grapes or Jell-O. The researchers were then able to demonstrate that the monkeys responded as economists would expect to changes in the prices of the grapes and Jell-O. When one got more expensive, they bought more of the other. It was only after they were sure that the monkeys fully understood money that they taught the monkeys to gamble.

For the gambling task, one monkey (of the seven who lived together in a room about the size of a one-bedroom apartment) at a time was brought into a separate holding cell. The monkey in the cell was then trained on two different gambles. In the first, the monkey got one grape, and then the researcher flipped a coin. If it was heads, the monkey got another grape. If it was tails, the monkey had to make do with just the first grape. In the second, the monkey got two grapes at the outset. If the coin came up heads, the monkey kept both grapes. If it came up tails, the researcher took one of the grapes. Once they had learned how the gambles worked, the monkeys vastly preferred the first gamble. Just like the credit card surcharge versus cash discount, the two gambles are the same: the monkey has a 50 percent chance of one grape and a 50 percent chance of two grapes. But just like humans, who like cash discounts, the monkeys prefer the gamble where they feel as if they're winning a second grape, rather than losing one.

This research is interesting enough, but Chen and his colleagues (2006) gained media attention for an instance in which the monkeys stole some of the money. The monkeys liked treats, and money was the way to get them, so it's no surprise that they would try to grab one or two extra coins. In one instance, though, rather than just grab a coin or two, one of the monkeys grabbed a whole tray of coins and threw them into the main enclosure, starting a chaotic scene in which all of the monkeys were grabbing the coins as fast as they could. It was during this chaos that Chen noticed one of the male monkeys having sex with a female monkey and then giving her a coin, which the female immediately turned in to get a grape. The researchers had, seemingly, created the first known instance of monkey prostitution and immediately took precautions to ensure that this never happened again.

The amount of animal research in social science has declined from its peak in the middle part of the century, when psychologists embracing the theoretical perspective of behaviorism and did extensive research on animals such as pigeons and pigs to learn the fundamental principles of learning and conditioning. Their research was guided by a radical response to Sigmund Freud, in which they held that the internal processes of people were simply irrelevant. It didn't matter what someone thought; it only mattered what the person did. For behaviorists, the main research questions involved how to get someone or something to carry out an action, whether it was learning a list of words or dancing the tango. The Freudians and the behaviorists have come to something of a truce in recent decades, as few researchers fully buy into either model, and animal research has moved largely into the realm of biology and medicine.

That doesn't mean that it doesn't happen, though. Sociologists study the group dynamics of fish, criminologists study aberrant behavior among primates, and political scientists look at leadership struggles and conflict resolution in troops of monkeys. Just as there's been a major shift in how researchers treat human participants in their studies, there's also been a shift in how animals must be treated. In some sense, the change in animal research has been even more dramatic. In the 1920s, a psychologist famously studied facial expressions by having his participants cut the heads off of mice. (Amazingly, most of the human participants consented to this grisly act.) Today, researchers who carry out work with animals need to ensure that the animals they use are kept in clean, sufficiently large enclosures and are as happy and well kept as they can be. The animals can't be subjected to any unnecessary discomfort or pain, and they must be given access to sufficient food, socialization, safety, and exercise to keep them physically and mentally fit.

> For more experiments with monkeys, check out http://www.anderson.ucla. edu/faculty_pages/keith.chen/datafilm.htm

For instance, a researcher doing work with mice would have to make certain that the cages the mice are kept in are cleaned regularly, that the mice are fed every day, and that they have an exercise wheel or similar apparatus. The mice would be weighed regularly to ensure that they're eating, and, if possible, they should be given some time to spend with other mice (taking into account that this is not something that all animals want or need). The capuchin monkeys in Chen and his colleagues' (2006) research were kept in a large enclosure with other monkeys to socialize with, and they participated in the economic studies to get extra treats, not their daily meals. In the case of higher animals, such as monkeys, the researchers have to make sure that they don't upset the social structure of the group. When the monkeys started trading the coins for sex—a dramatic shift in their society because mating rights are some of the main social controls in monkey troops—Chen and his colleagues had to make sure that it didn't happen again, even though it would have made for interesting research.

Just as for human participants, the harm to the monkeys (or the troop) has to be weighed against the potential benefit of the research, and the harm resulting from the introduction of prostitution would have been too great. Even when the research requires that the animal be killed, the death must be painless, and the researcher has to ensure that the animal doesn't have undue anxiety beforehand.

As with research on humans, any institution that houses work with animals has an IRB that oversees that work, often separate from the IRB for human research. The particular rules for animal research are generally much more detailed than the rules for human research, mostly because animals can't opt-out of the study or complain, so it's fully up to the IRB to ensure that everything is done correctly. These rules will vary by the animal being used but will typically specify how much food the animal is to receive by the weight of the animal, how much exercise and socialization is required, and what the acceptable ways of euthanizing the animal are. IRBs overseeing animal research, therefore, are much more likely to conduct site visits to make sure that everything in the lab is being done properly, something that's rare in most social science research.

In general, the more intelligent the animal is, the stricter the ethical requirements are. Experiments with worms or fruit flies have fewer restrictions than those with fish, birds, or mice. Work with primates is very closely monitored. Primate research has become controversial enough that some institutions have discontinued it in medical studies, or even completely. After all, if it's believed that some kinds of monkeys have emotional and mental states similar to those of humans, the same ethical rules that apply to humans would apply to them as well.

PUTTING IT ALL TOGETHER

Stanley Milgram—Obedience to Authority (1974)

Starting in 1961, Yale psychologist Stanley Milgram began recruiting participants to his lab with an offer of $4.50 for an hour's work. When they arrived, the participants were greeted by an experimenter dressed in a lab coat and another participant, who had apparently shown up first. The experimenter explained that they were going to participate in a study of learning, and they drew slips of paper to determine who would be the teacher and who would be the learner. The slip drawn by the second participant to arrive always said "teacher," and the two were separated into adjoining rooms, where they could not see each other. In some of the cases, the first participant (who had been assigned the role of "learner") mentioned that he had a heart condition.

Once in his or her room, the teacher was told that the purpose of the study was to see if people would learn better if they were given a painful, but not dangerous, electric shock when they gave an incorrect answer. The teacher's job was to read a list of word pairs (such as "Blue Cloud") over the intercom to the learner, then test how well the learner retained the pairs. The teacher would give the first word of the pair ("Blue"), and wait for the correct response ("Cloud"). If the learner gave an incorrect response, or no response at all, then the teacher was supposed to flip a switch on a console in front of him or her to provide an electric shock. Moreover, these shocks were to increase with every incorrect answer; once the teacher pushed the first switch (15 volts), it stayed up, and the next shock was supposed to be 30 volts, then 45, and so on. Along the top of the console were notations indicating that shocks of a certain level were dangerous, and shocks after that were just marked "XXX." The teacher was assured that the shocks weren't dangerous, just painful, and the experiment began. At first, the learner did pretty well, but he soon started missing more and more of the pairs. The voltage of the shocks increased, and it seemed that the learner was in more and more pain. After a time, the learner started banging on the wall, demanding to be let out.

At this point, many of the teachers hesitated. If they didn't want to continue, they were reassured by the experimenter, who told them that they needed to go on, that the experiment required it, that they had no choice in the matter, that the shocks wouldn't cause any permanent damage, and that the experimenter would take all of the responsibility. If the teacher refused to continue after the experimenter told him or her to continue four times, then the study was terminated. If the teacher went on, the shocks began to cause the learner to cry out and finally stop making any noise at all, even in response to the questions. In these cases, the teacher, especially when the learner mentioned a heart condition, thought that the learner had died.

Of course, no one was really dead. The learner was a confederate of the researcher, an actor playing a role. The actual participant was always the teacher,

Public Announcement

WE WILL PAY YOU $4.00 FOR
ONE HOUR OF YOUR TIME

Persons Needed for a Study of Memory

*We will pay five hundred New Haven men to help us complete a scientific study of memory and learning. The study is being done at Yale University.

*Each person who participates will be paid $4.00 (plus 50c carfare) for approximately 1 hour's time. We need you for only one hour: there are no further obligations. You may choose the time you would like to come (evenings, weekdays, or weekends).

*No special training, education, or experience is needed. We want:

Factory workers	Businessmen	Construction workers
City employees	Clerks	Salespeople
Laborers	Professional people	White-collar workers
Barbers	Telephone workers	Others

All persons must be between the ages of 20 and 50. High school and college students cannot be used.

*If you meet these qualifications, fill out the coupon below and mail it now to Professor Stanley Milgram, Department of Psychology, Yale University, New Haven. You will be notified later of the specific time and place of the study. We reserve the right to decline any application.

*You will be paid $4.00 (plus 50c carfare) as soon as you arrive at the laboratory.

- -

TO:
PROF. STANLEY MILGRAM, DEPARTMENT OF PSYCHOLOGY, YALE UNIVERSITY, NEW HAVEN, CONN. I want to take part in this study of memory and learning. I am between the ages of 20 and 50. I will be paid $4.00 (plus 50c carfare) if I participate.

NAME (Please Print) ....

ADDRESS ....

TELEPHONE NO. .... Best time to call you ....

AGE .... OCCUPATION .... SEX...........
CAN YOU COME:

WEEKDAYS .... EVENINGS ....WEEKENDS ....

and the actual purpose of the study was to see how far the teachers would go in shocking another person just because someone in a lab coat told them to. The learner was never hooked up to the shock generator, and all of his lines were scripted and were played back on tape. The participants in the study had no way of knowing this, and many exhibited fairly extreme emotional responses: laughing, crying, shouting at the learner to get the questions right. The scenario was certainly real to them. Only after the experiment was over were the participants debriefed and able to sit down with the "learner," to show that he hadn't been hurt.

Before he started the study, Milgram (1974) polled various experts for their guesses about how many people would go all the way to the end of the study, apparently shocking a man to death. No one predicted the actual result: that about two-thirds of teachers did so. Nor were his results an aberration. They've been replicated several times, for TV specials and in the laboratory as recently as 2009, all with similar results. In order to rule out the possibility that participants knew that the victim wasn't really receiving their shocks, one replication used a live cute, fluffy puppy, who received real shocks in full view of the teachers. The results were the same.

There is no question as to the ethics of Milgram's (1974) study. It's often used as an example of research that could not be carried out today without substantial changes. The problems with it are numerous. Most important, the majority of the participants in the study, for at least a time, thought that they had killed someone simply because an experimenter told them to. Deception is allowable—and is often necessary—in experiments, but that's because any damage done by the deception is undone by the **debriefing** process. In this case, there's no way to undo the damage wrought by the deception. The fact that the participants know that they didn't really kill someone is no protection against their knowledge that they would have killed an innocent person just because they were told to. It doesn't help that Milgram quite explicitly linked his results to the Holocaust. He wanted to find out why German soldiers were so willing to carry out atrocities, and he got his answer. For participants though, especially Jewish participants, that answer meant that they were the kind of people who would have carried out one of the most reprehensible acts in human history. Simply put, no debriefing can unring that bell.

The study was also carried out before the era of IRBs and consent forms, which means that the only person deciding that these harms to participants were justified by potential gains in scientific knowledge was Milgram himself. It's hard to make the argument that he was wrong, though recent replications have shown that the study could have been done in a way that didn't traumatize the participants. After all, it's one of the most widely cited studies in social science. It fundamentally changed the way that society looks at what seem to be evil acts, shifting the focus from the actions of bad individuals to the context that led to those acts (much like Zimbardo's [1971] prison study). So, while it's possible that the benefit to science and to society outweighed the harms to the participants, Milgram, or any researcher, isn't the one who should be making that decision. And when that decision is made, the rights and the dignity of the participants must be maintained. There's no evidence that Milgram was worried about his participants at all.

Researchers have to balance the knowledge gained by their studies with the potential for harm on the participants involved in them. While few of the studies social scientists carry out have the potential to put someone in physical or legal jeopardy (unlike some of the studies we've described in this chapter), every study has the potential to cause harm to the participants involved. Because of this, it is the responsibility of the researchers to think carefully about all of the possible harms that may arise from their work, take every possible step to reduce the likelihood of such harms occurring, and mitigate the effects of these harms if they should occur. Most important, researchers have to show respect for their participants as human beings, treating them with compassion and giving them as much information as possible in order to make sure that they know what they're agreeing to and that their participation is truly voluntary.

No one—not even researchers involved in what seem to be gross ethical violations—sets out to do something unethical. Rather, researchers face difficult problems in research design, and the unethical methods seem like the best way to approach the problem. This chapter began with Humphreys' (1970) research on the tearoom trade, work that had an impact on the civil rights of millions of Americans, but that probably could not have been carried out with the ethical standards most institutions now demand of researchers in the social sciences. All researchers believe that the work they do is of enormous importance to society and science alike. If it wasn't, they wouldn't bother. However, in the end, this is why the balance between costs and benefits has to be determined elsewhere, through the assessment of the IRB.

FURTHER CASE STUDIES

Jay Giedd—Picturing Alexandra (1999)

Giedd is one of the world's leading experts on the development of the brain during childhood and adolescence. He has scanned the brains of hundreds of minors with magnetic resonance imaging (MRI) scanners at the National Institute of Mental Health. Unlike X-rays or computed tomography scans, MRIs don't shoot radiation at the individual. Rather, they use a powerful magnet to excite certain particles within the individual and capture the protons released by these particles. While the machines may be noisy, they are safe for anyone being scanned, unless the person is claustrophobic (the tube in the machine can be very narrow) or has metal embedded somewhere (which can be ripped out by the powerful magnets).

Giedd (1999) was able to identify the structural features of brains that mark disorders and normal development by looking at the brains of adolescents of various ages and comparing the brains of adolescents with various disorders to the brains of typically developing minors. However, to really look at how an individual brain develops over the course of childhood and adolescence, Giedd needed a participant who would be available to come in for regular scans every few months for years, starting in early childhood and continuing through the teenage years. This would be an enormous commitment, but Giedd had the perfect participant: his young daughter, Alexandra. Starting when Alexandra was three years old (younger children probably wouldn't be able to keep still long enough for the scanner to work), Giedd brought her in to be scanned on a regular basis. By the time that she was eight, she had been scanned dozens of times and was comfortable enough with the process that she fell asleep inside of what she called "the noise machine."

The MRI scanner presents almost no potential for harm. Giedd wouldn't subject his daughter to it if it did, and the little girl doesn't mind participating. The benefits to having the first full portrait of how a brain develops throughout childhood could prove enormously important. Should the IRB approve of Giedd's continuing study of Alexandra? Why or why not?

Cengiz Erisen—Priming Opinion Change (2007)

Political psychologists have used the principle of subliminal priming to measure people's opinions for decades. Using computers, a participant is shown a word or image (the prime), which then disappears from the screen so quickly that the participant doesn't register that it was ever there. However, the word or image does have an effect on how the brain processes information that comes up just after the prime. If a participant has been primed with a positive word or image, the person is more likely to think of positive things, and less likely to think of negative things, for a short time afterward, and vice versa. However, the process generally requires some degree of deception: if participants know that they are being subliminally primed, it may confuse or mitigate the effects.

Cengiz Erisen (2007), while a graduate student at Stony Brook, was able to use this effect to change the thoughts that participants had in response to controversial political issues such as illegal immigration and gun control. Participants who were given a positive prime (in this case, a smiley face emoticon) were more likely to think of positive consequences of the issues. So, when asked, they would list more positive things about illegal immigration or gun control, with the opposite holding true for negative primes. At the end of the study, Erisen asked participants to rate how they felt about the issues, and not surprising, primed participants were more or less supportive of immigration or gun control, depending on the prime that they were exposed to. After the study is completed, each participant is fully debriefed, with the process explained and a phone number given in case of any questions. The results of the study are valuable for the insight they give.

While the effects of the priming have been shown to wear off relatively quickly, it has also been shown that once people make statements about their opinions (as participants in Erisen's [2007] study did), the stated opinions may be very long lasting. In effect, the participants' attitudes towards gun control and illegal immigration may have been changed by the study, even if only by a little bit, over the long term. What factors should the IRB consider in determining whether or not to approve the continuation of Erisen's work? What could be done to mitigate any potential harm to participants?

SUMMARY

Before 1979, researchers were largely on their own in deciding what constituted ethical research practices. This means that many of the most important studies in 20th-century social science failed to conform to the ethical standards to which researchers are now held. Many of these studies would be considered unethical because they subjected participants to an undue risk of harm, without giving them the facts necessary to decide whether or not they wanted to take these risks. Of course, all research carries some risk of harm to the participants. The job of the researchers, aided by the institutional review board, is to minimize these risks and balance them against the benefits to society provided by the research.

The fundamental premise of ethical research is the recognition that participants in a study are equal partners in the research and must be treated with respect. They must be told, in advance, exactly what to expect from the research experience (to the greatest extent possible) and debriefed after the research to answer any questions or concerns they may have. The participants should also feel that they are volunteering to participate in the study and aren't subject to any sort of coercion, including monetary coercion. Even if all of these conditions are met, the researcher still has the obligation to protect the confidentiality of the participants, and even their anonymity, when possible. Special care must be taken when dealing with participants who may not be able to fully understand the study or give fully informed consent, such as minors, vulnerable populations, and animals. If such participants must be used, multiple opt-in procedures may be needed.

Study and Review

How would Humphreys and Zimbardo have needed to adapt their studies to conform with modern ethics procedures?

The Bellmont Report was spurred by medical research. Does it make sense to apply these rules to social science research as well? Why or why not?

Given the ethical challenges arising from doing research with the Hadza, would it be reasonable to simply decide to not do research on the Hadza and similar societies worldwide? Why or why not?

Does it make sense to group prisoners, school children, and individuals with mental illness together as vulnerable subject populations? Why or why not?

Giedd's research would certainly be valuable to the study of developmental psychology. How could it be carried out in an ethical manner?

CHAPTER 4
Theory and Paradigms

Learning Objectives

- Be able to describe the role of theories in social sciences and research design
- Be able to summarize the historical progression of positivism in social sciences
- Be able to describe the dominant theories of social sciences and identify the types of research questions each theory asks
- Be able to explain the role of theory and the importance of being guided by a theoretical perspective in research design

THE IMPORTANCE OF THEORY

Theory is the basis of all real social science research. While it may seem as if researchers are just crunching numbers or doing interviews, their research is actually guided by motivating theories or paradigms. These theories tell researchers which questions to ask and which methodologies to use and guide them in creating their hypotheses. Theories generally don't make specific predictions about the outcome of a study, but rather work on the level of concepts. A relationship between two variables might be proven or disproven, but the theory itself cannot be proven or disproven—just that particular operationalization of that theory.

Since theories can't be proven wrong, they can't be proven right either. This is what researchers call *falsifiability*. As such, there's no such thing as a correct theory—theories are simply established ways of looking at the world. Any phenomenon in the world that social scientists are interested in can be studied through the lens of many theories, and the question is never which of these is the correct way of seeing that phenomenon, but rather, which theoretical perspective is the most useful in this circumstance. Researchers should never be tied to a particular theory; they should be flexible, adopting different theories based on which one is most useful for studying a particular phenomenon.

For instance, theories can be divided into micro- and macro-level theories. **Micro theories** focus on individuals and small groups, while **macro theories** focus on larger groups and institutions within society. Sigmund Freud's theories about the roots of psychosis are very much on the micro level, so it wouldn't make a lot of sense for researchers to use them to explain overall levels of mental illness in society (not that it hasn't been attempted). Similarly, Karl Marx's theories about class conflict are macro-level theories about the relationship between governments, corporations, and classes within society; they might not be useful in explaining the behavior of a particular individual. This is another way of saying that theories are often linked to a particular unit of analysis, and they may not work as well when applied to a different unit of analysis.

Every field has a set of dominant assumptions that shape the theories that researchers use. Social scientists refer to these overarching assumptions as *paradigms*. The classic example of a paradigm comes from physicist Thomas Kuhn's (1962) *Structure of Scientific Revolutions*. Kuhn demonstrates how paradigms work by discussing the transition between the Aristotelian paradigm that the sun went around the Earth, to the Copernican paradigm that the Earth goes around the sun. This shift in paradigms led researchers to ask very different questions about how the universe worked, and the same sorts of shifts occur in the social sciences as well. Researchers can choose the theories that they use to explain the world, but they're typically rooted in whatever paradigm is currently in use. The paradigms are big enough that researchers within a field typically don't even notice them. The social sciences today are fragmented enough that it's been argued that there isn't one dominant paradigm. Rather, there are several paradigms fighting for dominance, a fight which sometimes means that researchers from different fields can't understand each other easily.

This chapter gives examples of some of the dominant theories in modern social science and shows how these theories are used to shape research on various topics and across disciplines. It is by no means a complete listing of all of the theories in the social sciences, which would be a book on its own. It is designed to show how researchers apply theories and how those theories shape the hypotheses and methods that they use.

Rise of Positivism and Social Sciences

The basis for the way in which social scientists study the world is **positivism,** which can be seen as a very high-level paradigm. Positivism in the social sciences comes from the work of Auguste Comte (1868), a 19th-century French philosopher. Comte came of age during the French Revolution, and the revolution's upending of existing social relationships led him to advocate for the study of human behavior in the same way that natural scientists were studying the physical world. For Comte, positivism meant studying society and individuals using scientific evidence rather than relying on metaphysical, supernatural, or habitual explanations. He wanted to establish social science as a new disciple, where scientists could study the social world and their social environment in a scientific and systematic way.

One of Comte's most important followers was one of the first sociologists, Émile Durkheim. Durkheim (1897) argued that while individuals feel that they have agency (that they alone are determining their own behavior), their behavior is actually shaped by the rules and norms in the society around them. Most important, he didn't just opine about how this was the case; he used systematic data collection techniques to operationalize his concepts and test a model. Durkheim's most famous study is an examination of suicide rates in various countries over time. While the decision to commit suicide may seem to be intensely personal, Durkheim argued that it was shaped by society. For instance, he found that suicide rates increased in times of social stress, such as war, and decreased in times of general social cohesion. He famously found that suicide rates among Catholics were lower than those of Protestants, a difference he attributed to greater social control and increased social integration among Catholics. Even though some of his main findings have been disputed in recent years—it seems likely that Catholic areas have similar levels of suicide, but many suicides may have been purposefully misclassified as accidental deaths (mostly attributed to being crushed by a falling object) so that the victim could be buried in a Catholic cemetery—the paradigm he established, of individual behavior being the product of a complex interaction between the individual and society, remains. While there are important differences between the major theories in the various disciplines of social science, all of them, in some way, draw on this paradigm.

NATURE OR NURTURE? BIOLOGY OR SOCIETY?

Robert M. Sapolsky—The Trouble with Testosterone (1998)

Aggression, particularly among men, has long been a subject of inquiry among social scientists. What leads men to act out violently, and what can be done to minimize this behavior? In the 19th and early 20th centuries, alcohol was seen as a main culprit, as well as the development of various areas of the brain and the inclusion of "exciting" foods in men's diet. (Corn flakes were supposed to reduce aggression by virtue of being very, very bland.) More recent attention has hinged on some biological explanations, or the interaction of biological tendencies with social environments. Researchers have even found a strong relationship between men's levels of testosterone (a hormone found in higher amounts in men than in women that is related to many kinds of male sexual behaviors) and their levels of aggression.

This work on the effects of testosterone came into the public eye in the 1980s, when men with HIV were commonly given injections of testosterone in order to make up for depleted levels resulting from their illness. Rather than spacing out the injections of testosterone, some of these men received large doses all at once, presumably enough to get them through a week. These men experienced large spikes in their testosterone level and began reporting all sorts of uncharacteristic behaviors, such as picking fights with strangers. While it would certainly have been unethical to dose men with large amounts of testosterone in order to see what the effects would be, the medical treatment of these men led to what researchers call a *natural experiment* that seemed to show the critical role of testosterone in promoting male aggression. (We'll talk about natural experiments—also called *quasi-experiments*—in Chapter 9.)

As Sapolsky points out, once the negative side effects of large doses of testosterone were known, researchers couldn't very well continue with human studies, so they turned to animal analogues (in this case, monkeys). Male monkeys living in a hierarchical group were given testosterone injections, and researchers checked to see how increased levels of the hormone affected their behavior. So far, this seems like a purely biological, individual-level story—more testosterone in men leads to more aggression—but that's not what happened.

In this monkey troop, and ones like it, the male monkeys form a strict hierarchy. In a group of five monkeys, one (the alpha male) will be at the top, and all of the other males will show deference to him. Another (the Number 2 monkey) will be just below him, showing deference to the alpha, but dominating the three below, and so on. The testosterone injections did increase how much aggression the monkeys showed, but only within the confines of the established hierarchy. If the Number 3 monkey was given the injection, he would become much more aggressive to Numbers 4 and 5 but continue to show deference to the monkeys above him in the group.

Other research on the fluctuations of testosterone levels in men shows how much society shapes not just our behavior, but also our biology. Researchers have found that they can predict the outcome of a soccer match—the winner and even how close the match was—by measuring the testosterone levels of fans after the match. Supporters of the winning team show a spike in testosterone and cortisol levels, while fans of the losing team show a fall in these levels, with the increases and decreases proportional to the final score. Social roles influence men's hormone levels as well. It's been known for years that childbirth has an enormous effect on the mother's hormonal balance, but research by Lee Gettler and his colleagues (2011) has shown that it also affects men's biology. The studies found that engaging in child care activities such as feeding and changing diapers led to deceased testosterone levels, with the lowest levels coming among men who spent three or more hours a day taking care of their children. While there may be something of a selection effect—men with lower initial testosterone levels are more likely to take care of their children—the results show a steady decline among men who take care of children, regardless of their initial levels.

Biology and individual-level variance is important in explaining behavior, just as personal reasons are important for explaining why people in Durkheim's (1897) work committed suicide, but they aren't the only reasons. Humans (and monkeys) are social creatures, and our role in society shapes every aspect of our behavior. Modern theories in social science aim to figure out the relationship between the individual and society. Below, we will discuss some of the more frequently used theories in social sciences. These are the theories that most modern researchers in the social sciences use to guide their research; these theories focus on different concepts and different relationships between concepts.

STRUCTURAL FUNCTIONALISM

Structural functionalists look at the world and see order and function. For structural functionalists, society is like a biological organism: every component is there for a reason. If a social structure didn't serve a purpose, it would die out. Everything in society, no matter how irrational it may seem, is there because it serves a purpose, and together, these components create a more stable and cohesive society.

Many structural functionalists study rituals and patterns of interaction as ways of creating this social cohesion and stability. In modern society, rituals include rites of passage such as weddings, proms, bar mitzvahs, graduations, agreed-upon celebrations like holidays or birthdays, and the like. Structural functionalists also look at the role of institutions in society and the way that organizations such as schools, businesses, and the military work to socialize members of society and teach them the agreed-upon rules and customs. Structural functionalists would argue that when everyone knows the rules of the society and keeps to them, a society is more likely to remain stable and flourish.

Because of this, structural functionalists argue that even seemingly dysfunctional phenomena fulfill a social function. One of the earliest sociologists, Émile Durkheim (1895), argued that even crime has a social function in pulling society together. Every time someone commits a crime, the society gets together and reaffirms the rules of that society by publicly punishing that individual. In this view, societies punish criminals not because what they have done is inherently immoral—there are exceptions when almost any criminal act isn't a crime—but in order to reinforce the rules of that society. Modern structural functionalists might look at highly publicized criminal cases in America today, such as the case of Casey Anthony, a woman accused of murdering her daughter, or Scott Peterson, who was convicted of killing his wife and unborn child. These cases sparked intense national media coverage, and Durkheim would argue that the outrage vented at the accused individuals was a way for society to band together and reaffirm its own rules.

Kingsley Davis and Wilbert Moore—Some Principles of Stratification (1945)

While some people may look at economic inequality in society and see it as a problem that should be rectified through social policies or taxes, **structural functionalism** would look for the social benefits that arise from having some people on the bottom end of the spectrum and some people on the top. In a prominent *American Sociological Review* article, Kingsley Davis and Wilbert Moore (1945) argue that this sort of stratification is necessary because some positions within society are more pleasant, and others are more useful and more important or require different abilities, talents, knowledge, or experience. Social stratification is necessary, they argue, because it gives some people a reason to accept the more difficult, unpleasant tasks or those that require years of training or education. If there weren't financial and social rewards for people who agreed to take on high-stress jobs or jobs that required years of preparation, no one would do them. The people in these positions get more money and more respect because no one would bother trying to become a doctor, a judge, or a CEO if society didn't make it worth their while. This sort of structural functionalist view looks at seemingly disruptive, dysfunctional parts of society (like inequality) and sees something functional: order, unity and continuity.

It's easy to see how this sort of theory would translate into empirical research: researchers could look at the relationship between stress levels and pay or how education and training increases people's compensation. Alternately, researchers could look at the relationship between money and happiness, expecting that higher pay doesn't make people any happier because of the greater stress and unpleasantness that goes along with positions that pay more. Of course, this sort of inequality-accepting view has been widely criticized, leading researchers to show that the relationship between pay and stress, or between pay and the benefit that society receives from the worker, don't actually exist. They've also criticized structural functionalism for seeming to promote stability within society and excuse problems as being necessary. However, none of the criticisms or findings can actually refute the theory of structural functionalism; they can only show specific operationalizations in which the theory doesn't seem to hold.

Cele Otnes and Elizabeth Pleck—The Allure of the Lavish Wedding (2003)

Another seeming dysfunction of society comes from lavish weddings. According to survey data collected from couples using online wedding registries in 2011 (Reaney, 2012), the mean cost of an American wedding was more than $27,000: at the mean, couples spent about $5,000 on the engagement ring; $1,100 on the wedding gown; and $12,000 on the venue for the wedding. This mean figure represents more than half of the median income for an American household, so it certainly seems as if something is out of whack. (In some parts of the world, such as Syria and India, the relative cost of the ceremonies is even greater.) However, structural functionalists see order and utility in everything. Cele Otnes and Elizabeth Pleck (2003) explore the meaning of lavish wedding ceremonies in North America. While other researchers have criticized lavish spending on weddings as being no more than rampant consumerism (sociologist Chrys Ingraham (2009) has referred to the "wedding-industrial complex"), Otnes and Pleck show that these rituals create the possibility of escape and fantasy for many women: allowing them to be a princess for a day makes them more accepting of consumer culture in general and creates stronger links to the idea of romantic love and marriage. Lavish weddings may cost a lot, but Otnes and Pleck argue that the benefits society reaps from having them more than makes up for the cost.

Otnes and Pleck's (2003) study of weddings shows how structural functionalism can be applied to various "dysfunctions" within society and illustrates the general approach that structural functionalists take. Researchers from a different perspective might look at the negative effects all of the spending on weddings has on the lives of young couples, or look at the effects of wedding spending on marital happiness, but these elements just aren't important to structural functionalists.

These sorts of ideas are applied throughout the social sciences. In political science, for instance, it's easy to think of organized interest groups as being detrimental to society. Groups such as the National Rifle Association advocate for one narrow set of policies and are seemingly able to use money and political muscle to ensure that members of Congress do what they want. A structural functionalist, though, would look at the benefits that society accrues from the existence of organizations. In an influential 1984 article, for instance, Matthew McCubbins and Thomas Schwartz argued that such interest groups fulfilled a valuable function by working as information brokers for members of Congress, letting them know when something required their attention so that elected representatives could otherwise worry about more important things. Similarly, criminologists might typically think of prison gangs as being a problem, but researchers going back to the 1940s have argued that the presence of these groups within prison walls may actually help to preserve order.

CONFLICT THEORY

Conflict theory began as a critique of structural functionalism, especially with regard to social inequality. While structural functionalists look at the social world and see order, conflict theorists see competition between groups, with dominant groups within society using their position to repress others. Rather than seeing society as different elements working together harmoniously, conflict theory sees elements within society as being at war with one another, using social and political tools to try to get the upper hand.

Much of conflict theory was inspired by the theories of Karl Marx, who argued that society is defined by conflicts based on economic class. To support his position, he designed one of the first surveys about working conditions and argued that class inequality was a major social problem. This perspective has often led conflict theorists to argue for changes within society. Like structural functionalists, they believe that everything in society happens for a reason, but unlike structural functionalists, they don't think that those things benefit society as a whole.

While theories about class conflict and inequality are common, conflict theory also includes conflicts between other groups in society: those based on gender, race, religion, and so on. Researchers making use of conflict theory look at social phenomena by asking who benefits, and who is hurt, by them.

Jenny White—Money Makes Us Relatives (2004)

Family is generally seen as a site of love and support, and structural functionalist scholars see family relationships as being important to create and socialize new members of society. Conflict theorists, though, look at how family relationships can be used to exploit others and how families can be the site of dysfunction, oppression, and inequality. In her research, Jenny White (2004)—an anthropologist at Brown University—shows how family relationships are used to oppress women. Her book *Money Makes Us Relatives* looks at squatter neighborhoods in Istanbul, Turkey, and shows that female residents of these neighborhoods generally don't consider themselves to have real jobs, despite the fact that they work long hours subcontracting for the garment industry. Their labor isn't considered real work because they often aren't paid for it. Rather, their work is extracted by sometimes-distant relatives who pocket the proceeds.

In this context, the family is a site of economic exploitation, and familial ties become the mechanisms through which that exploitation takes place, with men making use of family obligations for economic gain at the expense of women. This sort of example very clearly shows how different theoretical perspectives can take very different conclusions away from the same phenomenon. Conflict theorists look at the underpaid women working for family members and see evidence of oppression, of men using their upper hand in society to keep another group down. Structural functionalists could look at the same relationships and see the benefits that accrue to the family and society, as the underpaying of women allows their male relatives to have profitable family-based small businesses.

FEMINIST THEORY

Feminist theory is a derivative of conflict theory but is differentiated because of its focus on understanding the world through the eyes of just one historically repressed group: women. Researchers working in feminist theory argue that separate theoretical constructs are necessary to study gender inequality because so much of the research in social science has been carried out by men and looks at the world through a male perspective. As Elizabeth Minnich, an advocate of curriculum reform in the United States argued:

> "To a stunning extent, the interests of one half of the human race have not been through history: men have not thought about them, and women have been kept ignorant. . . . If we adopt uncritically the framework, the tools, the scholarship created overwhelmingly by and for men, we have already excluded ourselves. . . . We are being forced to try to discover new intellectual constructs because many of those we have don't fit our experience and were never intended to." (Minnich 1977, p. 11)

Feminist theory argues that the male focus and authorship of so much research simultaneously obscures the perspective of women, whose problems and concerns aren't addressed by other theoretical perspectives, and ignores some behavior on the part of men. For instance, feminist theorists would argue that women's behavior becomes interesting to social science only when it's different from men's behavior, and it's only in recent years that there has even been a field of social sciences (masculinity studies) that examines men's behavior. In 1973, Pennsylvania State sociologist Jessie Bernard wrote that "practically all sociology to date has been of the male world."

Because these theories were dominated overwhelmingly by men, women's issues, lives, and ways of looking were excluded from many social sciences. Feminist scholars have shown that some findings generalize exclusively from men's experiences and assume these findings apply to women, when there is no research to support it. For instance, University of Chicago psychologist and sociologist George Herbert Mead (1934) studied how people form the image of the generalized other and argues that the roots of this understanding come from childhood games and sports, where children learn to define themselves in relationship to the other team. While this may seem like a neutral, broadly applicable statement, feminist scholar Janet Lever (1976) points out that it entirely ignores the ways in which girls play, which often don't include teams and opponents. What might look like a theory of humans is really a theory of men.

Paula England, Emily Fitzgibbons Shafer, and Alison C.K. Fogarthy—Hook-ups and Gender Equality (2007)

In addition to bringing to light previously neglected topics of inquiry such as sexual harassment, feminist theorists have looked for hidden gender inequalities in everyday life. Paula England and her colleagues (2007) focus on a familiar setting—a college campus—and explore how young people form intimate relationships. In particular, they study the social rules underlying casual sexual relationships, often described as "hook-ups."

From a male perspective, these hook-ups offer real benefits and give people more options. Before the sexual revolution of the 1960s and 1970s, premarital sex was taboo, and women who wanted a sexual relationship had limited options to pursue it; hook-ups seem like an expansion of sexual freedom. In a hook-up, young people can explore their sexual options without investing emotional or financial resources in a relationship or taking time away from hectic schedules to nurture a relationship.

However, England and her colleagues (2007) show that hook-ups are not nearly as beneficial for women as they are for men. Using qualitative interviews and online surveys, they were able to examine hook-ups from the perspective of the women involved and show the gender inequality in these relationships. First, there seem to be major differences in the rates of initiation. Just as in traditional dating, hook-ups were overwhelmingly initiated by men, meaning that while men were choosing from the pool of all available women, women were only choosing from the pool of men who had chosen them. Men also tended to enjoy the relationship much more than women did. Women were much more likely to want to turn the hook-up into a more meaningful relationship but were hesitant to initiate the "define-the-relationship" talk because they wanted to avoid the stereotype of women wanting commitment. The biggest gap in the hook-ups, though, was the respect gap: when students were asked if they experienced a decline in respect after the hook-up, 33 percent of men, but only 23 percent of women, said they respected their partners less after the hook-ups. Overall, though hook-ups provide some increased options for women, they tend to reinforce some existing stereotypes of women and serve to create further inequalities.

The research done by England and her colleagues (2007) on hook-ups demonstrates the importance of taking on the female perspective and examining social phenomena from both a male and a female point of view. For men, hook-ups allow people to have sexual relationships without significant emotional investment, but England and her colleagues show that the same does not hold for women. A relationship that offers increased sexual freedom to men does little to increase it among women, but it's only by researchers adopting the perspective of women that this becomes clear.

Such normalization of men extends even to biology. For instance, managers make generalizations about all workers based on men's bodies, so the prescribed length and frequency of bathroom breaks in work situations are generally based on men's needs and ignore the differences between women and men.

Pamela Stone—Why Women Really Leave Their Careers (2008)

In 2003, Lisa Belkin, the work-life columnist for *The New York Times*, published an article titled "The Opt-Out Revolution." In it, she argued that many high-powered female executives were leaving high-paying, high-stress careers to become stay-at-home mothers (intending to return to the workforce once their children were grown). The fact that women were choosing to stay at home meant that it wasn't really a social problem—rather, it was an expression of freedom, even of feminism.

In her research, Pamela Stone (2008)—a sociologist at Hunter College in New York City—explores why such women with high-level educational credentials and work experience actually leave high-paying, prestigious jobs. Stone conducted in-depth ethnographic interviews with 54 women in a variety of prestigious professions: law, medicine, business, publishing, and the like. Most of the participants were living in major metropolitan areas and were in their 30s and 40s: the exact women who were thought to be "opting-out."

In these interviews, Stone (2008) shows that these women do not really opt out of the workforce and for more traditional roles, but rather that they don't think they have a choice. Many of the women she studies experience the pull of motherhood and feel they need to be present for their small children. Doing so, however, is not compatible with high-power positions in the workplace, as the years where they would need to be with their children are the same years most critical to career advancement. With limited child care options, unsupportive spouses who are often nurturing their own careers, and bosses who offer more money only in exchange for more responsibility and more work, many women end up quitting their jobs. They aren't quitting because they have reverted to traditional values, but rather because they have no other options, no way to balance the demands placed on them by work with the demands society and their families place on them as mothers.

Quantitative methodologies can often tell researchers what is happening, but it's through qualitative methodologies that researchers can best understand *how* something is happening. In this case, quantitative research can show that many women in high-power positions leave them when they have children, but only qualitative research can show the process that leads to this. Because of this, feminist theory frequently employs qualitative methods and oral histories to incorporate women's untold stories and their unique perspectives. Indeed, one of the goals of feminist theory is to incorporate these excluded perspectives and recapture the points of view of women. This doesn't mean that feminist theorists ignore quantitative methodology, but rather that they believe it's necessary to go inside the numbers to see the perspective of women. As Dale Spender (1985) argues in *For the Record*, because women have typically been in historically subordinate positions, many historic accounts, archives, and statistics have been reported from the perspectives of men. The numbers may not lie, but they also may not tell the whole story.

Michael A. Messner and Jeffrey Montez de Oca—Beer and the Male Consumer as Loser (2005)

In addition to interviews, ethnographies, and observations, feminist scholars also make frequent use of content analysis of written or visual media (a technique discussed in detail in Chapter 8). Michael A. Messner and Jeffrey Montez de Oca (2005) study beer advertisements featured during sports media events as well as printed beer ads. In their content analysis, they find that the way male consumers are depicted has changed substantially over time. In the 1950s, beer advertisements would show men and women socializing together. Beer was depicted as a social lubricant to facilitate interactions. Later ads show that beer becomes a male drink to be enjoyed with other men in the absence of women. In recent years, they identify four distinct gendered stereotypes depicted in beer ads: losers, buddies, hotties, and bitches. The target consumer is a regular male, generally depicted as a "loser." He is surrounded by one or more "buddies," other men just like him. There is a bond between them, and often this bond is shown by the fact that they're drinking beer together. The role of women in these ads is much more problematic. Women are either depicted as attractive yet unattainable sexual objects ("hotties") who are admired by the losers and the buddies, or "bitches," who want to talk, share their feelings, or otherwise spoil the fun. These seemingly neutral beer ads show some of the popular assumptions and stereotypes about men and women. Their depiction of gender relations is important. The advertisers uncovered such stereotypes in society and replicated them. When people see these ads, they're inherently buying into and internalizing the potentially demeaning messages that they contain.

Research in feminist theory is not limited to the study of women. Just as women have been problematized (their differences from men have been treated as things that need to be explained), men's irrational or odd behavior has been ignored or treated as normal. Part of feminist research comes from studying men's behaviors and how society shapes these behaviors. Just as women learn to act like women, men have to learn to act like men. Sociologist R. W. Connell (1983) coined the term "hegemonic masculinity" to describe the dominant ways in which men are expected to show off their gender roles, and feminist scholars look at these roles and how society deals with men who violate them.

CRITICAL RACE THEORY

Feminist theory isn't the only area in which conflict theory has been applied to a specific disadvantaged group within society. One of the most widespread of these applications is **critical race theory**, which focuses on conflict and inequality among racial and ethnic groups. Critical race theory explores racism and racial inequality at different levels using a wide range of methods. Racial inequality can be studied from a macro perspective (looking at the differences in pay, educational opportunities, types of jobs, and health issues), but it can also be studied from a micro perspective (looking at the everyday experience of racial inequality and identifying the everyday mechanisms through which racial inequality persists).

Christopher Federico and James Sidanius—Racism and Affirmative Action Policies (2002)

Political psychologist James Sidanius is best known for his work on the social dominance orientation. He argues that a desire for social dominance is a personality trait that's present to varying degrees in everyone and that people's preferences for social policies are largely a function of this trait. Christopher Federico and Sidanius (2002) looked at people's opposition to Affirmative Action policies and how their opposition was related to their concerns about class and racial conflict. These views were assessed through a large-scale survey that asked about perceived conflict between groups. Respondents were asked to assess statements like "More good jobs for blacks means fewer good jobs for members of other groups." As discussed in Chapter 2, there's been an enormous debate about the role that racism plays in people's views of Affirmative Action policies, with many people arguing that opposition to policies that benefit African Americans is a function of principled conservatism, while others argue that it's driven by racism. In a series of studies, Federico and Sidanius showed that principled reasons for opposing Affirmative Action—such as the belief that people shouldn't be judged by the color of their skin—are mostly expressed by people who seek high levels of conflict and have high levels of education. People with lower levels of education support or oppose the Affirmative Action policies solely on the basis of perceived conflict between groups, while higher levels of education make people more able to hide these seemingly undesirable attitudes behind a veneer of principled considerations. They conclude that many of the principled objections to Affirmative Action are really driven by a tendency to see racial conflict and that people adopt them in order to sustain a situation in which their racial group has the upper hand.

Within conflict theory, there's room for groups to clash on the basis of gender, money, race, or any other distinction that society sees as being important at that time. These conflict theorists seek to explain a social phenomenon by examining who benefits and who loses. Conflict theory doesn't necessarily suppose that people are aware of these motivations. The men in White's (2004) study don't think of themselves as exploiting their female relatives any more than the whites in Federico and Sidanius' (2002) work think of themselves as trying to keep other racial groups down, but these conflicts shape society nonetheless. Sociologist Eric Hobsbawm (2010), for instance, argued that bandits in agrarian societies, ranging from Robin Hood to Billy the Kid, function as symbols of peasant resistance to ascending urban centers of power. The bandits themselves don't think of themselves as trying to overturn traditional power structures—they're in it for the money—but the function they serve within society is shaped by a class conflict.

SYMBOLIC INTERACTIONISM

Symbolic interactionism is a predominantly micro-level approach that focuses on intimate small-group interactions. Rather than focusing on large institutions, as structural functionalists and conflict theorists often do, symbolic interactionists look at the ways people interact with each other in small groups and how the behavior of individuals within these groups has symbolic importance. For instance, if a man is asked to do work around the house, this may be seen as an attack on his masculine identity, leading the man to resist doing housework, even when it makes sense for him to do it.

When researchers adopt this perspective, they look for the social meaning of everyday interactions. These actions, they believe, can only be properly understood within an individual's normal social environment. This view does a great deal to shape the sort of research that symbolic interactionists carry out. For instance, researchers operating within this theory would be much more likely to carry out ethnographic research, in which they observe how people behave under normal circumstances, than experimental research, in which participants' behavior might be studied in an artificial situation. Symbolic interactionists also make extensive use of in-depth interviews to try to understand how the participants in the phenomena they are studying make sense of their own worlds, rather than having the researchers impose their own views on them.

Arlie Russell Hochschild—Chore Wars (1989)

Arlie Russell Hochschild (1989), a sociologist at the University of California at Berkeley, examines how couples divide household chores. In particular, she is interested in why the division of these chores is such an issue of contention. She believes that arguments about the division of household labor aren't really about the chores themselves, but are instead about what the chores represent. Doing chores around the house is a way for people to demonstrate power in a relationship and respect for each other. When people ask their spouse to do the dishes, they're really asking, "Do you love me?" "Do you care about our family enough to put in the effort?" or "Do you respect me?" Arguments about these household chores, then, are about much more than the chores themselves; they are about the balance of power within the relationship. When men feel threatened in their gender roles, they may be less likely to do chores around the house, and their wives may actually start doing more chores around the house in order to make the men feel more secure in their masculinity.

There's no way that researchers would have known that these beliefs about gender roles may be driving the division of housework without actually interviewing couples about their relationship and observing how the couples acted in their own homes. If Hochschild (1989) had brought couples into the laboratory, it's unlikely that they would have behaved the same way in an artificial situation. It's only through ethnographic observation or in-depth interviews that researchers can see how people's actions reflect underlying meanings. This doesn't mean that researchers can't use quantitative techniques to do large-scale studies of how inequality within a relationship is reflected in the division of chores, but without the initial ethnographic and interview data, they would have no way to know to look for it.

> *Chore Wars* is an excellent documentary that tackles gender inequality in chores. You can see it at www.icarusfilms.com

Mary Laner and Nicole Ventrone—Dating Scripts Revisited (2000)

In addition to codified laws, societies also have unwritten rules. When the laws are written down, it's easy to follow them. Traffic rules, for instance, are written down so that everyone knows what side of the road to drive on and what the speed limit is. The unwritten rules of social interaction, though, can be much more difficult to pin down. Mary Laner and Nicole Ventrone (2000) look at the rules and norms of dating. Despite the fact that there aren't any written rules that tell people how they're supposed to behave on a date, people generally follow the same social script, just as surely as they follow the rules of the road. By examining actual first dates, Laner and Ventrone show that these rules have been so internalized by the participants that they're almost scripted, and these scripts can tell researchers a great deal about societal values. On first dates, for instance, men play a more active role (asking out, making plans, paying for the date), and women play a more passive role (waiting to be asked out, preparing for the date). Even though they don't actively think about it, every time people go on a date, they reinforce the rules and norms of their society. By studying these everyday interactions, even something as mundane as going on a date, researchers can uncover the unwritten rules of the society and uncover the biases within.

Arthur L. Beaman, Bonnel Klentz, Edward Diener, and Soren Svanum—Halloween Candy and the Looking Glass Self (1979)

Charles Horton Cooley (1902), a prominent symbolic interactionist, coined the term "looking glass self." He argues that individuals construct their ideas of self based on how they think others view them. This suggests that the very construct of self is created through interactions with other people and that by looking at themselves from the perspective of others, individuals define who they really are.

"In a very large and interesting class of cases the social reference takes the form of a somewhat definite imagination of how one's self—that is any idea he appropriates—appears in a particular mind, and the kind of self-feeling one has is determined by the attitude toward this attributed to that other mind. A social self of this sort might be called the reflected or looking glass self" (Cooley, 1902, p. 127).

The concept of the looking glass self has been used frequently in the more than 100 years since Cooley coined the term. Arthur L. Beaman and his colleagues (1979) used it in a study of self-consciousness and Halloween candy. One Halloween night, 363 children trick-or-treated at 18 different homes in Seattle, Washington, not knowing that they were part of a study. In each home, a large bowl containing bite-size candy was placed on a low table near the entryway. A festive backdrop was also placed in sight of the candy bowl with a small hole for viewing; behind the backdrop was an observer who would record the results of the study. There were several experimental conditions, but in each of them a woman would answer the door commenting on the children's costumes and inviting them in. She would then instruct the children to take only one piece of candy from the bowl and would excuse herself to another room.

The concept of the looking glass self comes in the form of a mirror placed directly behind the candy bowl in half of the houses so that children would see themselves as they were taking the candy. This forced them to see themselves as others would see them and therefore made older children much less likely to take extra candy. The same effect holds for adults, as well: Iowa State University psychologists Stacey M. Sentyrz and Brad Bushman (1998) show that participants confronted with a mirror ate a third fewer bagels than they otherwise would have.

The looking glass self is one of the most frequent ways in which researchers make use of symbolic interactionism. Participants in studies like these are forced to confront how they appear to others and, therefore, the symbolic consequences of their own actions.

RATIONAL CHOICE THEORY

The roots of **rational choice theory** can be found in economics and the idea of *homo economicus*, a completely rational decision maker who arrives at a decision by looking at all of the alternatives and their likely consequences, then choosing the one that leads to the best outcome. While it may have started in economics, the idea of individuals as rational actors has been enormously influential throughout the social sciences. Although most rational choice theorists don't think that people actually work through the consequences of all of their actions, they argue that people attempt to do so, so the rational outcome is the best aggregate prediction.

William H. Riker and Peter C. Ordeshook—Why do people vote? (1968)

While voting forms the basis of much of political science research—how people decide who to vote for, how candidates try to appeal to and mobilize voters—the act of voting is something of a paradox. All elections for federal office (House of Representatives, Senate, President) are plurality rules, winner-takes-all elections in which the candidate who gets the greatest number of votes gets the office, no matter if the candidate earned 51 percent of the votes or 99 percent. Because of this, the ballot cast by an individual voter only affects the outcome of the race if the race is so close that it can be decided by a single vote that turns the election from a tie into a one-vote win. However, the likelihood of this actually happening is exceedingly small: in fact, it's never actually happened. So, even in cases where voting is pretty easy, the relatively small amount of effort needed to learn about the candidates, register, go to the polling place, wait in line, and vote is still far more than any expected benefit that the voter could get from the act of voting. The likelihood of that vote actually mattering is just too small for it to ever be worthwhile.

Because of this, rational choice theorists in political science have long considered voting to be an entirely irrational act. If people were really rational, they wouldn't do it; but William H. Riker and Peter C. Ordeshook (1968) argue that these arguments leave out a critical element. While the material gain that voters may take away from casting a ballot is almost nonexistent, it could still be rational to vote if there's a benefit inherent in the act of voting. That is, if individuals like the act of voting so much that they would vote even if they knew that their preferred candidate would not win, it would be rational for them to vote even though it won't make a difference. Riker and Ordeshook refer to this as the "D" factor and attribute it to a sense of civic responsibility. There are some people who feel that they have a duty to vote, and this sense of duty is enough to motivate them to cast a ballot regardless of who wins. Provided this D factor is big enough—meaning that the citizen feels that voting is very important—voting actually becomes rational.

Riker and Ordeshook's contribution isn't just that people vote because they like voting or they feel they should vote—that's common sense—but that doing so is actually rational. In rational choice theory, individuals are expected to act in ways that maximize their utility and give them the greatest personal benefit, but there's no reason that such a benefit has to be entirely objective. It can, instead, be subjective—a benefit that only the individual enjoys. The main criticism of Riker and Ordeshook (1968) is that it changes the debate about the rationality of voting from an evaluation of the objective costs and benefits to an evaluation of how much people actually like voting—but that's not necessarily a bad thing. It means that when political scientists examine why some voters cast ballots and others don't, they focus on the factors that make voting seem more important or more enjoyable to individuals. Models of why individuals do things, such as the one created by Riker and Ordeshook, serve to guide future researchers in setting their research questions and hypotheses, which is the goal of any theory.

Julie Brines—The Exchange Theory of Housework (1993)

The division of housework between spouses has been fertile territory for social science research, and it's easy to see how symbolic interactionists such as Hochschild would come to study what housework "really" means. However, other scholars look at the same issue—the fact that women do far more housework than their husbands—and see a rational exchange. Before the 1980s, most married American women stayed home while their husbands worked outside of the home and brought home pay. In such a single-earner household, rational choice theory would expect that women would do nearly all of the housework. Asking the man to do the housework would be strange. If the husband had additional time, he could potentially use it to earn more money and better the family's financial situation. The traditional division of labor (the wife does nearly all of the housework) makes sense in a traditional household where the man earns nearly all of the income.

As married women increasingly joined the workforce, single-earner households became dual-earner households. A rational choice theory of housework would suppose that women would do less housework as their earnings rose relative to that of their husbands. The more money a wife earns, the more time a husband should spend on housework; if the two have equal salaries, they should both do about the same amount of housework. If the wife is the sole breadwinner in the family, the husband should do all of the housework. When researchers look at the division of household chores through this lens, it seems that the unequal division of labor within American households (women do far more housework than men) is driven by the unequal pay that men and women receive in the workplace. The United States has a significant gender wage gap, with women earning much less than men holding equivalent positions. This wage gap is exaggerated among women with children: mothers earn less than women without children, while fathers face no earnings penalty. Regardless of what the reasons for the wage gap are, as long as women earn less in the workplace, it's rational for them to do more around the home. Julie Brines (1993) argues that this sort of rational exchange characterizes most households; the exceptions are the relatively small number of households in which women earn more than their husbands. In those cases, a symbolic approach in which men assert their masculinity by doing less seems more predictive.

Brines' (1993) work on rational choice and housework illustrates another function of rational choice theory. If people are doing what rational choice theory expects of them, there really isn't anything for social scientists to explain. No one questions why people don't commit crimes when they're likely to get caught or buy a car that's a sensible price and makes sense for their family. People don't need reasons to do rational things. It's the job of social scientists to explain why people commit crimes when they'll probably get caught or buy an expensive sports car they can't afford. Rational choice theory, therefore, points researchers toward the interesting phenomena in society. There's nothing terribly interesting about women doing more housework when their husbands are the sole breadwinners, or doing less as their own income rises. What's interesting are the exceptions to that rule: the women who earn more than their husbands and still do most of the housework. Rational choice theory, then, tells researchers where to find those interesting cases.

In recent years, rational choice theorists have explored how people make decisions, given that people cannot be entirely rational. Complete rationality requires that individuals be able to understand all of the options in front of them, assign probabilities to each of them, and weigh the relative costs and benefits of each. This is fairly easy for a computer—one of the reasons that computers do so well at chess—but is difficult for humans because our brains just aren't set up for that. The recognition that these sort of calculations are difficult to carry out has led researchers to study limited rationality: how people make decisions without having all of the necessary information or without knowing the probabilities of various outcomes. So, it might be irrational to commit certain crimes (and rational to commit others), but criminals may well commit them anyway because they systematically underestimate the likelihood that they'll get caught. Based on these flawed perceptions of risk, the crime might be subjectively rational while remaining objectively irrational. Perhaps the most famous of these models is prospect theory, which won the Nobel Prize in economics for the work of Daniel Kahneman and Amos Tversky (1979, 1992). Prospect theory studies the biases inherent in how people treat probabilities and how this affects their decision making.

ETHNOMETHODOLOGY

Ethnomethodology was first introduced by UCLA sociologist Harold Garfinkel (1948), as an explanation for why there's so much order in society. While researchers tend to focus on why disorder arises, Garfinkel, who studied with the first generation of social psychologists, looked at the everyday experiences of people and how they create meaning and order in their lives.

Ethnomethodologists are interested in finding out where rules and norms of society come from and how people react when these rules are broken.

Ethnomethodologists often upset the order and break the rules on purpose to see how others will react; by seeing reactions to extraordinary situations, they can study the norms and rules that generally apply. For instance, an ethnomethdologist might enter an elevator and remain facing toward the back, rather than turning around like everyone else. What happens when one person breaks the rule? How do the others react? This technique of discovering unwritten rules by breaking them is called **breaching**.

John Darley and Bibb Latané—The Smoke-filled Room (1968)

Social psychologists John Darley and Bibb Latané (1969) make use of breaching methods in many of their collaborations (another example of their work can be found in Chapter 9). In one study, participants were asked to come to the laboratory to participate in a discussion of problems facing urban areas. Before going into the laboratory, though, the participants were asked to sit in a waiting room and fill out a questionnaire. Some of the participants were randomly assigned to sit in the waiting room alone; others were assigned to a condition in which there were two or three others in the room with them. Unbeknownst to the participants, the others in the room were confederates of the researchers.

While the participants filled out the questionnaire, smoke began to enter the room through a vent in the wall. When the participants were alone in the waiting room, they universally got up, looked around, and went out into the hallway to alert others to the seeming danger. However, ten of the participants weren't alone in the waiting room, and instead of jumping up, they looked around at the others. Since the others were confederates of the researchers and knew what was going on, they didn't react to the smoke at all; if the participant asked them about the smoke, they just shrugged and kept on filling out the questionnaire. Faced with this sort of social pressure, nine out of the ten participants assigned to be in the waiting room with others stayed there as the room filled completely with smoke, until it reached the point where the smoke interfered with breathing and the researchers stopped the study.

Darley and Latané (1968) use an extreme situation to demonstrate how reliant people are on social cues to define a situation. Even something as obvious as "leave a room if it's filling with smoke" stops being obvious if other people aren't doing it; despite the fact that their lives might be in danger, people don't want to go against the crowd.

In addition to rules and norms, ethnomethodology also studies power and roles. One of the basic assumptions of ethnomethodology is that social situations are constantly recreated, so people have to continue to create and recreate their role to themselves and to others. For instance, if someone is a class clown, or a good student, or any role, he or she has to constantly demonstrate this role, and ethnomethodology is partly the study of how they do so.

Ethnomethodologists look at everyday interactions and language to see how these roles are established and power emerges. How do individuals gain power in marriages? How do they gain power in friendships? Ethnomethodology posits that it's only by looking at everyday conversations and interactions that researchers can come to an understanding of the emergence of power and inequality. As such, analyzing the everyday and the mundane is central. One way they study the factors underlying these everyday interactions is through studies in which participants describe mundane events (ordering in a restaurant, watching a sporting event in a bar) as if they were doing it for the first time, examining the normally unobserved aspects of the actions. Doing so helps researchers using ethnomethodology to understand the social construction of reality in everyday life.

The Role of Theory

It may seem that the theories that have been discussed here aren't broadly applicable throughout the social sciences, but that isn't the case. For instance, rational choice theory was developed by economists, but it's used by political scientists, criminologists, and psychologists to explain individual behavior. It's even used on the macro level to explain why countries go to war with each other and how war can be avoided. Feminist theory—an offshoot of conflict theory that focuses on conflict and inequality based on gender—can be broadly applied in economics (Why do women make different spending decisions than men?), psychology (Why are men so much more likely to have unrealistic self-images?), criminology (Why do certain kinds of crime disproportionately target women?), or political science (Why are women in some countries more likely to vote for liberal parties?).

These theoretical perspectives are simply tools, and just as researchers adopt the research methods that are most appropriate for a particular research question, they should also adopt the theoretical perspective that best adds to their understanding of the topic. Even when researchers try to stick to a single theoretical perspective in their research—and there are plenty of scholars who think of themselves solely as ethnomethodologists or feminist scholars or conflict theorists—they can better understand the phenomenon they're studying by looking at it from one of the other perspectives. It's only by looking at these problems from a variety of angles, by triangulating their theoretical perspectives as well as their methods, that researchers can get a complete idea of what's going on in any issue of importance in the social sciences.

SUMMARY

Researchers derive their hypotheses from theories, all of which are embedded in overarching paradigms. The dominant paradigm in social science research today is interactionism, which posits that human behavior is the result of complex interactions between individual characteristics and the environment. Social scientists draw on a wide range of theories within this paradigm, from structural functionalism to rational choice theory.

Each of these theories makes predictions about the behavior of individual people or groups, but while the predictions of these theories can be tested, the theories themselves cannot. While theoretical perspectives fall in and out of favor among researchers in various disciplines, they can be applied across the social sciences. Rational choice theory might have originated among economists, but it's used widely in sociology, criminology, and political science. Conflict theory originated in sociology, but it is just as applicable in political science and criminology. The best researchers aren't tied to one theoretical perspective, but make use of whichever theories are most applicable for a given research project.

Study and Review

Why do researchers need theories at all?

Given that Durkheim's findings on suicide lacked validity, why is his research regarded as important?

How does feminist theory differ from some of the other theories discussed in this chapter?

Use the example of division of chores within a household to show how different theoretical perspectives look at the same phenomena in different ways.

CHAPTER 5
Literature Reviews

Learning Objectives

- Be able to describe the function of conducting literature reviews and summarizing prior research in original social research
- Be able to describe the logistics of the peer-review process and understand the rigorous process scholarly articles go through
- Be able to identify appropriate sources for a literature review
- Be able to learn new techniques to identify sources for a literature review
- Be able to use common online portals to identify academic sources for the literature review
- Develop techniques to read and comprehend research papers
- Be able to summarize the prior research and write a literature review

WHY LITERATURE REVIEWS?

A **literature review** is an overview of the existing work on the research question, found early in any research paper. Research is an ongoing process, with new research building on the existing research and engaging in a dialog with past work on the subject. The goal of any new research project is to build on the foundations of the existing research and move the discussion forward. As such, having a comprehensive literature review is vital to the quality of a research project. First, it shows the readers that the author is aware of the ongoing debates in the field. Second, the process of creating a literature review helps the researchers determine if their question has been answered already and, if it has, points to related areas in need of greater exploration. Finally, reviewing the existing research provides researchers with tools necessary to answer the research question at hand, helping them set hypotheses and determine appropriate methods.

Literature reviews in research papers consist of only academic sources. This means that newspaper articles, magazine articles, opinion pieces, and reviews have no place in a literature review. Popular magazines such as *Time*, *Newsweek*, *The Economist*, *The New Yorker*, or *The Atlantic* provide the public with news and opinions. While they can be helpful in guiding and inspiring research, they don't meet the level of quality necessary for inclusion in a research paper. These sources reflect the opinions of the authors and may include portions that resemble research papers, but they are not based on a rigorous social science approach. What differentiates such popular publications from literature review material is the **peer-review** process. Peer review refers to the review process that articles go through in order to be published in an academic journal.

The Peer-Review Process

When a research paper is completed, the authors submit it to an academic journal. The editor of that journal reviews the article to determine if it's suitable for publication: Does it deal with the questions that the journal is interested in? Are the writing and research techniques of suitable quality and rigor? Is the paper the right length for the journal? If the editor determines that the paper is suitable, he or she begins the **blind review** process by sending the paper to three anonymous reviewers. (Sometimes only two reviewers are used or, rarely, four or more.) The reviewers are experts in the field and do not have any relationship with any of the authors of the paper: they cannot be the author's family member, friend, advisor, professor, or coauthor. Ideally, the reviewers will not know who wrote the article they are reviewing. To make sure of this, the editor ensures that the reviewers only see blinded copies of the articles, ones that have the names of the authors and any identifying information removed. In this process, the reviewers don't know who the author is, and the authors don't know who the reviewers are. This is supposed to remove any bias and ensure that papers are judged solely on their own merits. Some journals go even farther and ensure that editors making decisions about the paper are also unaware of who the authors are, a system called **double-blind review**.

The expert reviewers aren't paid for their work and generally agree to volunteer their time in order to help the journal maintain its high standards and aid in the progress of their field. The editors of journals can't be experts in every field, so it's the job of the reviewers to read between the lines and determine if a paper's findings are credible, if the techniques are appropriate, and if the paper fills a need in the existing literature. The reviewers then recommend to the editor whether the paper should be published or not, or if it could be published with some revisions (what's often called a "revise and resubmit"). It's very rare for a paper to be accepted as is, and nearly every paper that's published has been revised with the help of the reviewers. Rejections are much more common than any other outcome; the best journals in the social sciences have very low **acceptance rates**, publishing fewer than 10 percent of the articles submitted to them. In addition to these recommendations, the reviewers offer constructive criticism. They don't just say that a paper should be rejected or revised; they explain exactly what the failings of the paper are and offer suggestions on how these issues can remedied.

Once the reviews have been submitted, the editor uses them to determine what should be done with the paper. He or she sends summaries of the reviewers' comments to the author. If the editor asks the author to revise and resubmit the paper, the revised version will typically be sent out to the same reviewers again to see if the author has adequately dealt with the issues raised in the reviews. This cycle can go on repeatedly, with the reviewers asking for more changes until the editor and the reviewers are satisfied with the article. The article then goes through copyediting to make sure the grammar and style are appropriate for the journal. Finally, the article is put in line to be published in an upcoming issue. The process is time consuming and rigorous, with articles typically appearing in print six to eighteen months after they were initially submitted. In recent years, some journals have moved online. They typically retain the peer-review process but publish the articles immediately upon acceptance in order to speed up the process and make the articles easily accessible to interested scholars. Time consuming as it is, the academic review process is generally considered worthwhile because it ensures that papers that appear in peer-reviewed journals meet the highest standards of quality.

SOURCES FOR LITERATURE REVIEWS

Scholarly Journal Articles

The primary source for literature review is journal articles that have gone through the blind review process described above. The articles that appear in scholarly journals are based on academic research and are not the opinions of the authors. The scholarly journals that publish these articles can be divided into three categories: general journals, topical journals, and methodological journals.

General journals seek to publish research from across an entire field, regardless of the subfield or methodology used. Examples might be *American Sociological Review*, *Social Problems*, *American Journal of Political Science*, or *Criminology*. Because they cover a variety of subfields and are often given to all members of major professional organizations, they have the widest readership of journals in their field. The fact that more people read these journals, and that the articles in them are therefore more likely to have an impact on the field, means that they are often considered to be the most desirable venues for publication.

Other journals are more specialized, focusing on a particular topic or a particular set of methodologies. Journals such as *Gender and Society*, *Political Psychology*, or *Punishment & Society* focus on subfields within their discipline, while journals such as *Ethnography* or *Public Opinion Quarterly* deal with specific methodologies. In addition, some journals only publish reviews of the recent academic books in the field (*Contemporary Sociology*), while others only publish literature reviews (*Annual Review of Sociology*, *Annual Review of Psychology*, *Annual Review of Anthropology*). Most scholarly journals publish a mix of peer-reviewed journal articles, book reviews, and shorter research reports. The majority of scholars consider the best journals to be those with the highest **impact factors**, which are determined by measuring how often articles from that journal are cited in later research. Published reports such as *Journal Citation Ratings* are assigned to each journal and show the rank of the journal in a certain field based on the number of citations.

Thomson Reuters publishes *Journal Citation Reports* based on the number of citations to determine the impact and the ranking of the journal.

thomsonreuters.com/products_services/science/science_products/a-z/ journal_citation_reports/#tab2

When researchers are searching for journal articles to build their literature review, they often begin by looking at the most important general journals in their field to see what's been published about their research question. Then, they typically move on to specialized journals that include their topic or their methodology in order to see what experts in their field have been publishing on the question.

Researchers should also be careful to look for recent articles. Since the review and publication process takes such a long time, research that was published two years ago might reflect data that was collected four or five years ago. Finding the most recent articles on a topic is of critical importance. Researchers can also look at the impact that individual articles have had. Just as the importance of a journal can be assessed by looking at how often its articles are cited, the impact of an individual article can be assessed by looking at how many times it has been cited since it was published. Today, this process is easy because websites such as Google Scholar keep track of how many times an article has been cited and where.

Scholarly papers are relatively short—typically twenty to twenty-five pages— but it would still take researchers a long time to read through all of the individual articles that seem relevant in order to figure out which ones are actually useful to their research question. This task is significantly aided, though, by the **abstracts** found at the start of nearly all social science articles. These abstracts lay out the findings, the theoretical background, and the methods of the study, allowing other researchers to quickly determine if the article is relevant or not. In many journals, these abstracts are followed by keywords, or individual terms that are designed to help researchers figure out what the article is about even more quickly.

This is an example of an abstract and keywords from Besen-Cassino, Yasemin. 2008. "Cost of Being a Girl." *National Women's Studies Association Journal* 20 (1): 146–160.

Abstract:

The gender wage gap is among the most persistent and durable characteristics of labor markets and women's lives. Despite differences in focus, almost all studies of the gender wage gap focus on the adult labor market; however, almost every teenager in the United States works before adulthood. Therefore, an overwhelming majority of the population experiences the labor market, and possibly the gender wage gap, well beforehand. This article focuses on the early labor market experiences of youth and analyzes the gender differentials in earning in the youth labor market. The findings show there are no gender differences in wages for twelve- to thirteen-year-old youths. However, we see the emergence of the gender wage gap around fourteen, which widens with age. The wage differential in the early labor market is explained mostly by occupational factors such as types of jobs in which boys and girls are employed. In this way, the "cost of being a girl" still remains.

Keywords: gender wage gap, youth employment, inequality

As noted before, there are now many journals that publish their articles solely online. As long as these journals maintain the same standards as print journals, there's no reason to treat them any differently than print journals, especially since they may have a shorter lag between article preparation and publication. However, researchers need to be careful with online journals, as many of them have lax standards for publication and exist only to charge researchers exorbitant fees for publication. Some of these nonscholarly journals even have names that ape the names of respected journals. While telling the difference between these journals and respectable journals can be difficult, clues can be found in the editorial board and the sponsors of the journal. If the journal is sponsored by a well-known professional or academic group (for instance, *Survey Practice* is a journal of the American Association for Public Opinion Research) or the editors are from well-known academic institutions, the journal is probably okay. If you don't recognize the sponsoring organizations or the affiliations of the editors, it's probably best to stay away from the journal.

Books

There are many advantages to using scholarly articles in the literature review. They are shorter, provide the most current findings, and have abstracts that make it easier to determine suitability without investing much time. Because of these advantages, the majority of a literature review is typically drawn from scholarly articles. Books take a long time to write, so by the time they are written and published, some of the information may be outdated. The limited amount of time a researcher has to build a literature review also means that he or she can only read so many books. The main advantage of using books is the depth and detail they can provide on a given topic. Books are useful for gaining very detailed information on a specific topic. However, unlike books that might be read for enjoyment, books used in a literature review do not need to be read in depth. A researcher may only be interested in one or two chapters or even in particular portions of a chapter. (This is part of the reason that book citations in a works cited, unlike article citations, typically include page numbers.) Reading the introduction and the conclusion and skimming through the figures and tables generally gives the researcher a good idea of what portions of the book are most relevant for the project at hand.

However, not all books are suitable for inclusion in a literature review; just as there are academic journals, there are academic publishers. Books based on opinions or not based on rigorous research are no more useful for a literature review than newspaper articles or magazine stories. Publishers affiliated with universities (such as Temple University Press, University of Chicago Press, or Duke University Press) are the most reliable source of quality research. Books submitted to these presses generally go through a rigorous review process, similar to that endured by academic articles. In addition to university presses, there are some reputable presses such as W. W. Norton that publish manuscripts based on research.

Websites

Although today's students often learn to start the research process by looking at online sources, material that's published purely online is of limited use in academic literature reviews. Some websites—many of which are discussed below—aggregate and provide access to articles and information published in other formats, such as government reports or back issues of journals. In some cases, journals may use their websites to provide access to articles that have been accepted for publication but not yet put into print.

The same features that make the Internet so useful (the democratization of content creation and access; the fact that people can post whatever they want, without any barriers to them doing so) also make it difficult for researchers to evaluate the credibility of information presented on websites. In general, websites associated with government agencies or well-known institutions (for example, the Gallup Poll or the Census Bureau) can be used as sources of data for analyses, and the official reports they post may be included in a literature review. Outside of these, though, researchers can't typically use the information posted on websites because there's no quality control to ensure that the information is reliable. An additional problem arises from the fact that, unlike printed material, websites can change rapidly. After a researcher accesses information from a website, that information can be taken down or altered by the administrator. The information may not be available for others who try to replicate the researcher's work. Because of this, when information from a website is used, the date of access needs to be noted, and the researcher should generally retain a copy of the data.

Government Documents and Policy Reports

There are some governmental and nongovernmental organizations that fund specialized research projects. The Bureau of Labor Statistics, for example, publishes short research projects called "Youth Employment" and "Report on the Youth Labor Force," and the U.S. Department of Labor publishes reports on the state of education in the United States. These research projects are generally heavy on numbers and light on analyses, but they are based on current research findings. These reports are often very specialized and are much shorter than a full-length article.

U.S. Department of Labor's (2000) "Report on the Youth Labor Force" is a great example of a specialized report.

www.bls.gov/opub/rylf/rylfhome.htm

Paper Presentations and Working Papers

Because of the difficulty of the peer-review process, researchers often present their findings to peers before submitting them to a journal. This may be done as a condition of funding (agencies who give researchers money may not want to wait months or years to see the result of that money) or as a way for researchers to get feedback on research findings from peers before submitting the paper to a journal.

Once a preliminary version of a paper is completed, scholars and organizations often post the papers online as working papers. Researchers also commonly present their findings at academic conferences and meetings. These academic conferences provide an opportunity for scholars to share their new findings and get valuable feedback to revise their research and prepare their manuscripts for publication. Many conferences make paper presentations publicly available, and some of them publish the papers as conference proceedings. Conference papers and working papers often include a warning that they should not be cited—and it's a good idea to take these warnings seriously. Because the papers have not been subject to peer review, their findings cannot be relied on. Researchers can still use the papers when preparing a literature review—by examining how the authors approach past findings in the field and the methods they use—but these articles should not be directly cited. If the research is of sufficient quality, it's most likely that the paper will eventually be published in a scholarly journal, and it can be used in the literature review once it has.

Dissertations

The guidelines for using working papers or conference presentations also apply to using dissertations. Doctoral dissertations are book-length manuscripts that Ph.D. students write at the end of their program of study. Many doctoral dissertations are eventually published in book form, but even those that are not are commonly made available by university libraries. While these dissertations may include the most recent data available, they have not been vetted by the peer-review process. As such, they should only be used indirectly and only cited with great caution. If a dissertation has great findings, it will almost certainly be published in book form or in scholarly articles before long.

Book Reviews

Academic journals often include a section reviewing recent academic books in the field. Book reviews are typically two to five pages and are written by experts in the field. Book reviews themselves reflect the opinions of the reviewers and are not based on research. However, they can be useful in identifying academic books that may be of interest. Since many book reviews offer a summary of the book, including the methods and the findings, researchers building a literature review can use them to determine if a book will be useful or not.

Research Notes

Full journal articles are generally around twenty-five pages long, but some research findings don't require that much space. In these cases, researchers can publish what are called research notes. Research notes are like other academic articles, but they often omit some of the theory-based sections of the paper, focusing instead on how the research was carried out and what the results were. Research notes are subject to the same sort of review as any other journal article and therefore can be included in the literature review.

Magazine and Newspaper Articles

The amount of time that it takes for papers and books to go through the peer-review process means that some information from them is dated by the time that they are published. This may make sources that don't have to go through such review tempting. Articles in newspapers or magazines almost always use very recent data and may appear in credible publications, but that does not mean that they are appropriate for a literature review. There's no guarantee that the research in the articles was highly rigorous, or that it would meet the standards of academic review. As such, these articles cannot be included in a literature review.

Overall, nearly all of the sources in the literature review of a research paper are journal articles. Since they are academic and are based on research, they have the advantage of being credible and short. For more in-depth information, academic books are also often included, but due to their length, a particular literature review will rarely cite more than one or two academic books.

FINDING SOURCES: THE BRANCHING METHOD

Academic journals are not of much interest to the general public, so finding articles from these journals is very different from finding materials that are marketed to nonacademics. Many magazines are available at bookstores and libraries or have their contents posted online for free, but academic journals aren't available that way.

Years ago, finding articles from journals meant going through paper copies of back issues or looking up keyword indices (published by each journal every year or so). Researchers often kept large personal libraries of journals to make it easier to find articles they might need later on. Today, smaller university libraries keep only limited numbers of paper copies of journals, as the archives of nearly any journal, going back decades, can be accessed online. Publishing a journal is not cheap, and the limited number of potential readers means that publishers charge a large fee to gain access to the information. For researchers, this means that online access can be very expensive if it's not done through a university library that has bought access to the journals in advance. If a university library has access to a journal, researchers affiliated with that university will typically be able to access articles from that journal, through one or more online portals, for free.

The existence of these online portals has dramatically altered the problems researchers face when looking for relevant pieces of their literature reviews. In the past, the problem was finding sources; now the most common problem is sifting through all of the possible articles to determine which are most relevant. Too broad a search may bring up too many articles that aren't useful; too narrow a search may exclude relevant articles. The best approach for finding relevant articles is the *branching method*. Most researchers find relevant articles and books this way, even if they've never been specifically trained in the method.

In the branching method, researchers begin by finding what's called a *seed article*. Using one of the major online portals (several are described below, but JStor's abstract search option is especially useful), researchers use keyword or abstract searches to identify one article that has a research question and theoretical perspective very similar to their own research. This is often a time-consuming process because different scholars describe the same phenomena with different terms. It's often best to start with a general search on a topic such as "youth labor," "recidivism," or "gun control," then manually look through the results to find the article that fits best.

In addition, the ideal seed article is also one that has been published recently, but not too recently. A good range would be between five and ten years ago. If a seed article has been published in just the past year or so, other scholars haven't had the chance to incorporate the findings into their own research. If it was published too long ago, the results and perspective may be outdated. Finally, seed articles should ideally be cited by other articles many times. Researchers want to be sure that their seed article is a good one, and while the number of times an article has been cited isn't a perfect measure of how good the article it is, it's the best metric available. If a paper has been cited many times, it's a sign that other experts in the field think it's worthwhile, or at least important. If a paper has been out for several years and hasn't been cited at all, there may be a reason for it. Because of this, articles from high impact rating journals are often the best seed articles.

Once researchers identify an appropriate seed article, they find more articles by branching up or branching down from that seed article. Branching down is simply a matter of reading the article and seeing which articles the seed article itself cites as being important or relevant. Researchers then look up these articles specifically and see which ones, if any, are relevant to their own paper. All of these articles will, necessarily, be older than the seed article, but if an older article or book is still discussed in the literature, it may be worthwhile to include it. After branching down, researchers use one of the online portals (for this, Google Scholar is currently best) to see which articles have cited the seed article. By looking at these more recent articles that list the seed article as relevant (branching up), researchers can often identify more books and articles that may be useful.

This process can help researchers uncover dozens of relevant articles and books to include in a literature review—but the process isn't over. By branching up and branching down from the initial seed article, researchers often find another article or two that's even closer to their research question and theoretical orientation. They then choose one of these to be the next seed article and repeat the process. The cycle of choosing a new seed article, branching up, branching down, and starting over again repeats until researchers don't find any new relevant material for the literature review.

COMMON ONLINE PORTALS

There are many specialized academic online portals, and university libraries may subscribe to all, just a few, or none of them. The most common online portals for discovering and gaining access to academic journals are discussed below, but anyone familiar with these portals should be able to navigate any others that they may encounter. In this section, we discuss the most common and available search engines. Different institutions, depending on their resources, use other online portals. Check with your institution's library to see which online search engines and portals are available.

JSTOR

Most university libraries buy at least some access to JSTOR for students and faculty members. JSTOR allows users to search for keywords or phrases within the title, text, or abstract of an article and gives users immediate access to the articles found (depending on the level of the subscription purchased by the library). Once found, the articles can be read or even downloaded as PDF files. JSTOR has some limitations. It has a limited number of articles in criminology and psychology (though its collection in most of the other social sciences is top-notch), and some journals don't make their most recent issues available through it. However, the sheer number of journals it contains, along with the ability to download articles and search article abstracts (which often results in more relevant results faster than other methods), makes it the first stop of many researchers. Users are advised, though, to use advanced search options to narrow down the fields and time periods before searching. JSTOR has begun allowing users who are not affiliated with university libraries to have limited access to a few journal articles per month. This may be useful, but it isn't really enough to build a literature review.

Google Scholar

A recent addition to the academic search world, Google Scholar builds on the fact that the Google search engine was originally designed by graduate students to help them find appropriate journal articles easier. Google Scholar catalogs far more articles than most of the other online portals, but that's not always a good thing because it includes unpublished papers, working papers, dissertations, nonscholarly books, and conference presentations that may not be suitable for inclusion in a literature review. The biggest innovation in Google Scholar, and one that's being quickly copied by competitors, is that users can click on a link next to each article to see all of the articles that have cited it, making it very easy to branch up. It also includes a citation guide for each article or book it finds, generating citations that match certain styles or can be imported into major citation management programs.

Google Scholar is free, which makes it easy for researchers to find relevant sources. However, it doesn't actually store any articles itself. Rather, it shows a link to articles only when those articles have been posted somewhere else, meaning that there's no access to the vast majority of articles that can be found through Google Scholar, and outside web pages may remove links that it posts. Because of this, Google Scholar is most useful when used in conjunction with other online portals such as JSTOR, which may allow researchers to gain access to the articles they find on Google Scholar.

EbscoHost

EbscoHost is another database that researchers can use to locate articles. Ebsco provides access to a wide range of publications, with availability depending on the subscription purchased; some of the articles that come up in a search might not be fully available, but the majority will be. Like Google Scholar, it includes sources that are not peer reviewed, so it is very important to limit searches to peer-reviewed articles. The Ebsco database is not limited to articles; through Ebsco e-books, researchers can access academic books in electronic format.

Lexis-Nexis

Lexis-Nexis is a database of legal documents, business documents, and patents. While it might not be helpful in identifying articles directly, it may be useful for scholars working on research involving legal decisions or business or who need to learn about individual court cases in depth.

Academic Libraries

Academic libraries, such as those found in universities, are equipped to provide information for a literature review. Many academic libraries subscribe to academic journals that publish peer-reviewed articles, and they make electronic subscriptions available to validated users through their websites. These websites are often very helpful in that they provide a list of the journals that the library has access to and the online portals that can be used to find them. In addition, some libraries still keep physical copies of academic journals in their periodicals section.

Most academic books are only available in the physical library. Online catalogs for books are most useful when researchers have already identified the book being sought; they can then use the title to look up the location of a physical copy of the book without too much effort. Many academic libraries offer **interlibrary loan** programs. Through these programs, researchers can borrow a desired book from another library if it isn't available at their library. However, books acquired in this way typically take a few days to arrive and can only be checked out for a limited amount of time.

RESEARCH READING: HOW TO READ A JOURNAL ARTICLE

Once researchers have found relevant articles for the literature review, they typically don't read each article in depth, at least not at first. Going through a large number of articles requires that researchers master the art of *research reading*, a way of finding relevant information as quickly as possible. Researchers have limited time and a large body of articles to review, so they need to identify the most relevant articles and not waste their limited time and resources on articles that are not useful to them.

Research reading is more than just skimming an article. It includes specific techniques that help researchers read a journal article effectively. The first step is to always read the abstract. The abstract summarizes the main methods and findings of the article. By reading the abstract, researchers get a general idea of the article's theoretical orientation, methodology, and findings. After determining that that article is relevant, researchers turn to the introduction. The introduction provides a bit more information about the paper and familiarizes researchers with the paper. After the introduction, many researchers go to the conclusion section at the end of the paper to identify the main findings of the paper. Together, these sections tell readers where the article fits in the ongoing dialog on the topic of interest and what the article contributes to the field. In general, this is enough to tell readers if it is worthwhile to continue reading the article. If the article isn't worthwhile, readers can skip to the next one. If, however, the paper still sounds interesting and relevant, researchers will read the entire paper from start to finish.

Reading a journal article is more challenging and more time consuming than reading a newspaper or magazine article, so it's important to go into it prepared.

Unlike opinion pieces, journal articles have complex methodologies, detailed tables and figures, and long descriptions of data collection and analyses. Therefore, reading these articles will require researchers' undivided attention. Often, the middle section of journal articles (which details methods, data analysis, and findings) overwhelms young researchers. However, this is the most important section of the paper because it describes the credibility of the findings and the discussion. It's no coincidence that most of the decisions a journal editor makes about whether to accept or reject an article come from the quality of the middle part of the paper.

The large number of articles that researchers go through means that it's difficult or impossible for them to keep track of all of the relevant articles without help. This help often comes in the form of an **annotated bibliography**, created by researchers as they read new articles or books. This annotated bibliography can take any form, from a spreadsheet to a word processing document, but many researchers still keep it in paper form, on the theory that writing the information by hand enhances memory of what's being written. Three-by-five index cards are often used for this purpose. On one side, researchers write bibliographic information about the article. The name of the article, authors, journal, volume number, and page numbers are included. On the other side, researchers include a short summary of the article and keywords. The same information should be included no matter what format is used. Having these summaries will help the researchers remember the articles and organize them later in the writing stage, and the keywords will help organize and identify common themes.

Front
Besen-Cassino, Yasemin (2008)
"Cost of Being a Girl"
National Women's Studies Association Journal
20(1):146–160.

Back
Keywords: gender wage gap, youth
employment, inequality
This article looks at the gender wage gap among 12–16
year-olds through quantitative analysis of NLSY data. The
findings show that 12–13 year-old boys and girls make the
same money, but the at 14–15 we see the emergence of the
gender wage gap which widens with age.

WRITING THE LITERATURE REVIEW

Tone and style

The aim of the literature review is to summarize the existing body of work to give the readers an idea of what has come before and where the current research fits. This section does not include any original data analysis or findings; it is just an overview of what others have done on the same topic. The literature review, however, isn't just a summary of what's been done. If researchers wanted that, they'd just print their annotated bibliographies. Instead, the literature review is the story of how the literature in the field has evolved over time and the ongoing discussion between researchers. Making this discussion clear requires that researchers carefully organize the literature review, without making it sound like a shopping list.

Organizing the Literature Review

The first paragraph of the literature review tells readers how the review will be organized. There are several ways to organize the literature review; the first is

According to the United States Department of Labor's *Report on the Youth Labor Force,* almost every American high-school student works at sometime (Herman 2000; see also Finch, et al. 1991; Greenberger and Steinberg 1986; Mortimer and Finch 1986; Paternoster, Bushway, Brame and Apel 2003; Schoenhals, Tienda and Schneider 1998; Steinberg and Dornbusch 1991). Thus, in the United States, the labor market experience of both men and women begins well before adult employment. Explanations of the gender wage gap cannot be complete if only adult employment is considered; rather, an understanding of the gap requires that we also examine the pay patterns of teenagers in the labor market. Furthermore, as Barbara Reskin and Irene Padavic demonstrate, "the younger the workers are, the more equal women's and men's pay" (1994, 107). Therefore, a study focusing on early employment patterns not only offers a more comprehensive understanding of the gender based wage differentials by including a previously excluded—yet substantial—portion of the labor force, but also provides the opportunity to trace the origins of the gender wage gap while allowing us to control for individual characteristics such as domestic and maternal duties.

Prior Research

A substantial body of research attempts to explain the difference in pay for men and women. Prior inquiries operate under two distinct strands: studies that focus on individual differences between men and women, and studies that focus on occupational differences between men and women.

The human capital/productivity approach focuses predominantly on the individual differences between men and women and attempts to explain the gender wage gap through individual differences which might result in lower productivity (Becker 1985, 1993; Bielby and Bielby 1988; Mincer 1962; Schultz 1960). In such explanations, the lower earnings of women are argued to be the result of lower productivity among women and are often associated with their domestic duties and childcare responsibilities, or by interruptions in employment due to these duties (Berk and Berk 1979; Hersch and Stratton 1997; Hochschild 1989; Mincer and Ofek 1982; Ross 1987; Waldfogel 1998).

Lower productivity of women has been associated with proposed differences in education and experience between men and women. Earlier studies have argued that different levels of formal education between men and women account for the gender wage gap, but this explanation has failed to explain fully the gender-based differences in earnings (England 1997; Tomaskovic-Devey 1993; Treiman and Hartmann 1981). However, many similar studies have shown that years of experience on the job accounts for a substantial portion of the gender wage gap. Due to women's

thematic organization, where researchers identify three or four major themes that emerge from the past research and base the literature review around them. In the example below, the researcher is looking at why teenagers work while still in high school and has identified several approaches from past research.

The themes in the literature on the gender wage gap are clear from the way this literature review is structured. The first set of literature arises from discussions of individual characteristics, such as differences in education, skills, and experience (called the *human capital approach*). The second approach, called *occupational segregation*, explains the wage gap through occupational differences. Women are concentrated in freelance, service-sector positions whereas men are concentrated in managerial positions. Finally, the third approach looks at the differences between men and women's values and what they care about at work. Each theme has subheadings. For example, under the human capital approach, the author discusses individual differences such as differences in education, work experience, and work interruption due to maternal and domestic duties.

Organizing through common themes is the most common method, but it isn't the only way to organize a literature review. Another popular approach is to organize the literature chronologically, from the earliest relevant studies to the most recent. Since the purpose of a literature review is to show readers the discussion that's been playing out between researchers in the field, it can be

---

PRIOR RESEARCH

A substantial body of research centers on youngsters' paid work during high school. In the latter half of the twentieth century, this research has progressed through three major phases and is now entering a fourth. In the first phase, prior to 1970, researchers paid almost no attention to students' paid work, and estimates of employment rates for 14- and 15-year-olds were low. Nevertheless, some studies from that era, as well as Ruhm's (1997) analyses of changes in employment rates from 1968 to 1988, suggest that youngsters' paid work was far more prevalent than commonly supposed. In the 1940s, for example, about 25 percent of whitemen in a national sample worked at age 14, and almost three-quarters worked at age 16 (Coleman 1984). Likewise, in the mid-1960s, 73 percent of males in the fourth to eighth grades did paid work in the greater Boston area (Engel, Marsden, and Woodsman 1968), and in the mid-1970s, 75 percent of seventh-graders did paid work outside the family in suburban and semirural New Jersey (Goldstein and Oldham 1979).

As it became technologically feasible, such isolated studies of youth work gave way to a second phase of research based on national samples. These studies left no doubt that youth work was exceedingly common. Shapiro (1979), for example, replicating results of Johnston and Bachman (1973), estimated that 62 percent of all high school students were in the labor force. D'Amico (1984) likewise reported that 70 to 85 percent of the National Longitudinal Survey of Youth 1978 sample of high school youth worked "sometime."

helpful to show how that discussion has changed over time, how those changes led to the state of the field today, and how the current research fits in. In the short excerpt below, Entwisle, Alexander and Olson (2000) organizes the existing research on teenage employment in this way. In the first phase, literature on teenage employment focused predominantly on establishing it as a social issue and a widespread practice. After establishing it as a widespread practice and an important topic of inquiry, the next decade concentrated on the advantages of working while still in school. These scholars argued that working has positive effects on academic progress and drop-out rates. The following decade focused more on the disadvantages of working and showed that working while in school negatively affects psychological development. Recent research evaluates the conditions under which work takes place as well as explores the self-selection effect.

Chronological organization is most useful when there has been a real progression of the research over time. When dealing with topics that are more fragmented, there may not be a central narrative or discussion, and in such cases a thematic organization may be more appropriate.

A less common technique for organizing a literature review is comparative. In a comparative literature review, studies on the same topic in different fields—or in different geographical contexts—are reviewed one after the other. There may be little or no connection between the strands of the comparative literature review until the end, when the researcher shows how the present research will bring together these disparate research agendas and add to the discussion of both.

No matter which method is used to organize the literature review, it is important to guide the readers by **signposting** throughout. Signposting is the technique used to remind readers of the review's organization. In a chronological literature review, the author should make repeated references to the period in which the discussed research took place. In a thematic literature review, the author should remind readers what theme is being discussed.

The end of the literature review sets the stage for the rest of the article by evaluating the state of current research, the positives and negatives in the past research, and the questions that still need to be answered. What areas were covered well in the previous articles? What gaps remain in the literature? What questions were omitted or need further work? Answering such questions will show readers how the current research fits into the existing dialog and how it adds to the state of the discipline.

CITATIONS

Throughout the literature review, and the rest of the article as well, researchers need to ensure that readers can easily identify every source mentioned. This is partly to allow them to read the articles discussed, if they care to, but also to give credit to past researchers for their ideas. There are two ways to give credit to the original authors. The first is to use direct quotation. Direct quotations are used when the original authors have expressed their idea in the best possible way; the current researchers can't find a way to say it better. In such cases, researchers use the exact words of the authors verbatim. Because the authors' exact words are being reproduced, quotation marks are used. For example:

> "Employers routinize work both to assure a uniform outcome and to make the organization less dependent on the skills of individual workers" (Leidner 1993, 24).

After the direct quote, researchers must give the last name of the author and the year in which the article or book was published. (*Note:* Giving the first name is generally frowned upon, as it can lead readers to subconsciously discount contributions made by female scholars.) These elements allow the reader to find the full information about the source in the **bibliography**. Since this particular quote is from a book, it also includes the page number from which it was taken. Articles are generally short enough that a particular page doesn't need to be mentioned.

Researchers do not commonly use direct quotes from a text to support their point. Instead, they use the idea. Researchers may want to express the idea more succinctly or in the context of other articles making a similar point, or perhaps the idea isn't found in one particular short quote. In these cases, researchers **paraphrase** the idea, summarizing it in their own words. Even though paraphrasing is not taking the direct words of the authors, researchers are still using the ideas of others and need to give credit. For example:

> The author argues that men in feminized jobs such as nursing experience great benefits in the workplace and are promoted faster than their female counterparts (Williams 1991).

Since the direct words of the author are not used, quotation marks are not necessary. However, citation information that allows the reader to easily find the original source in the bibliography is still present. In a well-balanced literature review, use of both quotes and paraphrases is important. Too many quotes listed one after another creates a choppy, stagnant read, while a few quotes sprinkled throughout can create interest. Therefore, it is important to create a balance between direct quotes and paraphrases.

PLAGIARISM

While intentional plagiarism is very rare in research papers—it's simply uncovered too easily to be worthwhile—incorrect use of citations can lead to unintentional plagiarism. The following passage is taken from Rosabeth Moss Kanter's (1977) *Men and Woman of the Corporation*.

> "The most distinguished advocate and the most distinguished critic of modern capitalism were in agreement on one essential point: the job makes the person. Adam Smith and Karl Marx both recognized the extent to which people's attitudes and behaviors take shape out of experiences they have in their work. If jobs "create" people, then the corporation is the quintessential people producer. It employs a large proportion of the labor force, and its practices often serve as models for the organization of other systems" (Kanter 1977, 3).

Let's consider how this text could be discussed in a literature review.

> ### Example 1:
> In today's society, corporations have taken on numerous roles. "If jobs 'create' people, then the corporation is the quintessential people producer" (Kanter 1977, 3)

This example is correct. The sentence used is directly taken from the text. Since Kanter's exact words are used, quotation marks are used, and a page number is included.

> ### Example 2:
> As both Marx and Adam Smith pointed out, people's identities in modern society are based on their work, meaning that corporations are, in a way, creating people.

This example is wrong. No direct quotes are taken from the text, but the central ideas are used without giving credit to them. The way to correct the problem would be to add a citation. A correct way would be:

> Today, many scholars agree that jobs are central to the identities of many workers. Since jobs are so important in people's self-definitions, identities, and their development, corporations have become essential in shaping people (Kanter 1977).

The literature review is much more than just a laundry list of what's come before. Rather, it sets the stage for the present research by showing readers the discussion among researchers on the topic and how the current article fits. As valuable as it is for the readers, though, the literature is a vital part of the overall research process. By looking back, researchers can see which approaches have proven fruitful in the past and what work still needs to be done. Doing this carefully and thoughtfully helps ensure that the research project will have a place in this larger discussion and be part of the material future researchers look at when putting together their studies.

Literature reviews are the foundation of every research project, and knowing how to build an effective literature review is a vital step in the research process. Literature reviews situate the new information and findings within the current literature and in the context of existing research. They help researchers build on existing knowledge while not reinventing the wheel. In the upcoming chapters, we will look at different methods social scientists use to collect data, including both qualitative and quantitative methods.

SUMMARY

Social science is an aggregative process in which current research is part of an ongoing conversation with prior findings. This means that researchers need to be aware—and show their readers that they are aware—of relevant past work in the field. While researchers are often motivated and informed by work in the popular press, literature reviews are limited to work that's been subject to the peer-review process. The most common source for these articles is peer-reviewed journal articles, though scholarly books and government reports may also be included.

Although there's no perfect way to find appropriate peer-reviewed publications, many researchers make use of the branching method, in which they look at the articles that cite, and are cited by, a single seed article. This process is repeated as many times as is necessary to achieve a sufficiently comprehensive literature review. In the past, this literature review process required combing through stacks of paper journals. Now, online portals such as JStor and Google Scholar make physical copies of journals largely unnecessary.

Even with these online tools, researchers often need to go through many journal articles to find the few that are relevant to the work that they're doing. As such, they need to be able to read the articles quickly and carefully—not just skimming, but identifying the relevant portions of an article and using them to decide if the rest of the article is worth the time. Abstracts and keywords can be especially useful in this process.

Because so much information is presented in literature reviews, researchers need to carefully consider the best way to organize and present the information, being especially careful to correctly cite research and avoid plagiarism.

Study and Review

Explain the importance of the peer-review process.

What characteristics are most important in finding a seed article?

Why should researchers pay attention to the impact factors of the journals they look at?

Under what circumstances would chronological or comparative literature reviews be more appropriate than thematic literature reviews?

CHAPTER 6

Qualitative Research I: Ethnographies

Learning Objectives

- Be able to identify the uses for qualitative research methods
- Be able to compare and contrast participant and nonparticipant observation and discuss the relative advantages and disadvantages of each method
- Be able to design an ethnographic study and identify components in an ethnographic study
- Be able to conduct systematic observations and record their findings
- Be able to identify advantages and disadvantages of ethnographies and discuss the types of research when ethnographies are suitable

INTRODUCTION TO ETHNOGRAPHY

Michael Moffatt—Coming of Age in New Jersey (1989)

Michael Moffatt (1989) started his career as an assistant professor at Rutgers University and was surrounded by young people every day. Despite that, he realized that he didn't know much about what sociologists call the "lived experience" of his students—what life was like from their perspective. He didn't share a culture, or sometimes even a vocabulary, with his students, but questionnaires and observation didn't seem likely to give him the insight he wanted. Moffatt says:

> "Conventional accounts of American college students rely on the anecdotal knowledge their professors have of them—a dubious source—or on questionnaires or structured or unstructured interviews. Questionnaires usually require the subjects to respond to predetermined topics, however; with students, they are about what adult investigators have decided should be relevant to youth in advance. Interviews give subjects a better chance to talk and think in their own terms. But interviews with adolescents, especially glib college adolescents, also encourage subjects to talk in their most formal adult-sounding ways. Participant observation on the other hand, amounts to hanging around with one's subjects for a long enough time to start hearing them in their more natural adolescent tones—very different ones and to start sensing their own priorities as they understand them." (Moffatt 1989, p. xv)

Moffatt (1989) argues that the only way to understand what life was really like for the college students he interacted with every day was to give up his own life as a college professor and enter the university as a college freshman. In this way, he believed that he would be able to see the world from their perspective, to come as close as he could to actually walking in their shoes. If he were simply to ask them about their experiences, the questions he asked or even his mere presence as a questioner or observer could bias their responses, so he conducted his research undercover. In doing so, Moffatt engaged in participant observation, probably the most drastic form of qualitative research that a social scientist can engage in and one that raises any number of logistical and ethical questions for researchers who use it. (These issues are discussed later in the chapter.)

Moffatt (1989) also gives a compelling justification for qualitative research in general. While qualitative research is widely used and respected in some branches of the social sciences, it has fallen out of favor in others, victim to an increasing emphasis on sophisticated quantitative methodologies. However, it's hard to imagine how a researcher could gain real insight into the lived experiences of students without engaging in some form of participant observation. Using surveys, researchers can find out a great deal about *what* people do, and using a well-constructed, theory-grounded model, they can learn something about *why* they do it. Qualitative research, however, tells researchers *how* people do things, and oftentimes, that can be the most important part of the puzzle.

Walking in their Shoes: Understanding the Perspective of the Participants

Yasemin Besen-Cassino—Hanging out with the Baristas (2013)

Yasemin Besen-Cassino (2013), a sociologist at Montclair State University, also studies young people in America, but instead of school, she is interested in another familiar part of teenagers' lives: work. Today, almost every teenager works some time during high school. At any given time, approximately two-thirds of American teenagers work. Many work long hours, in addition to their schoolwork, in demanding service-sector jobs that require minimum skill during odd shifts. Researchers have typically assumed that teenagers work for money. Why else would they willingly give up their free time to work for minimum wage in demanding jobs?

Over the years, researchers have developed scores of surveys and questionnaires to study the topic of youth employment, with their findings generally supporting their preconceived notions about young people's work: they do it for the money. Just as Moffatt (1989) was unable to separate himself from the focus of his research until he stepped into his participants' shoes, researchers studying teenage labor couldn't help but see the issue from their own perspectives. After all, adults know why *they* work—for money. And if young people don't need money to pay for mortgages or groceries, then they must be using it to support their conspicuous consumption habits—because they want more stuff! These notions persisted despite the fact that the actual patterns of young people's work are at odds with an economic explanation, as the teenage labor force in the United States consists of predominantly affluent teenagers. Teenagers coming from lower-income households—who presumably are more likely to need the money—are actually *less* likely to work.

This means that to understand what's really going on with young people, researchers need to take their participants' views into account. The perspectives of parents, educators, and employers have been studied, but the central actors have been left out of the study of youth employment. Only an **ethnography** of the workplace can accurately capture *why* young people do what they do. In her qualitative study, Besen-Cassino (2013) hung out at a local branch of a national coffee chain that mostly employs teenagers. (You'll notice that while you can probably guess it, the name of the specific coffee chain isn't mentioned, either in the papers she published or here—all a part of ensuring confidentiality, as discussed in Chapter 3.) There, she noticed that most of the workers came from the same type of affluent suburban families as many of the regular customers.

Closely observing the workers shift after shift (and coffee after coffee), Besen-Cassino (2013) saw that while the workers spent the money they earned on products in the store, they weren't working for the money, but rather for the social experience of being in the coffee shop. The entire time they worked, their friends—many of whom were also co-workers who were not on shift that day—gathered around where the coffee was served to gossip, make plans for the weekend, and talk about upcoming parties. After their shifts were over, the workers in turn stuck around the shop to chat with friends and other workers;

they took messages and notes for people who were expected to show up later. Many times, Besen-Cassino observed workers grabbing a mop to clean a spill or taking out the trash after their shifts were over. This is not the behavior of people who are just working for the money. Certainly, there aren't many adults who go back to work after their shift is over to carry out some of the worst tasks of the job without pay.

Besen-Cassino (2013) argues that the work is a way to overcome the social isolation of centerless suburbs. There simply isn't anywhere for these young people to congregate. (The suburbs, to use Donna Gaines' (1991) phrase, are a "teenage wasteland.") They see the schools (especially the local state university that many attend) as crowded and impersonal. As one student said, "No one notices if I miss a class or two." At work in the coffee shop, though, she's needed. Work functions as an alternative space for social interaction, almost like an afterschool club or team, except "not so lame." Even better, the young people's parents don't bother them about being at work.

From How to Why

But when Besen-Cassino (2013) asked the young people why they work, they almost uniformly told her that they do it for the money, and this tells us one of the main reasons why ethnography is important: we can't trust people's own statements about why they do what they do. There are a couple of reasons for this, but among them is the fact that people *don't know* why they do what they do.

We won't get too deep into the specifics, but cognitive psychologists have long demonstrated that the parts of the brain that make decisions about what to do are outside of our conscious awareness. To use a simple example, Benjamin Libet (2004) ran studies showing that when you move your arm, the signal from your brain to your muscles that allows for the movement happens about a quarter of a second before you are conscious of the decision to move. That is, you do something and only become aware of it afterward. Similarly, people's explanations for their actions don't reflect the real reasons, but rather are explanations after the fact for why they think someone would do that sort of thing. So, when a researcher asks participants why they do something, the individuals take what they know about themself and put together a plausible explanation for why they would do that. Think about it. How often do people say that they don't know why they did something? The explanation a person gives may be right—and it will certainly reflect why the person thinks that he or she is doing something— but it may also be wrong, as it was in the case of Besen-Cassino's (2013) baristas' explanations for why they work.

People can tell researchers about what they like, what they dislike, what they do, and how they do it, but they can't tell researchers why they do something. So, if social scientists want to find out why, they may take the route that Besen-Cassino (2013) did and take an in-depth look at how people do something. In the case of the baristas, Besen-Cassino was able to observe behaviors—such as working off the clock and socializing with the employees and customers at the coffee shop—that indicated the real reasons for the behavior.

Researchers can use **grounded theory** to determine what behaviors to look for. Developed by Barney Glaser and Anselm Strauss (1967 [2009]), grounded theory is a unique approach to data collection, almost the opposite of the scientific process outlined in Chapter 1. Rather than imposing preconceived notions on their study, researchers build their theories based on their interactions and observations. Grounded theory advocates entering the field with questions, not set theories. Theory emerges from the observations in the field.

The most important thing that ethnographers can do is to keep their eyes open. Most research methods we have discussed in the text so far—experiments or survey methodology, for example—start the data collection process with a very distinct hypothesis. Sometimes, if you are using qualitative methods, having such a rigid hypothesis might hurt your data collection. When researchers enter the field with a rigid hypothesis, they often find what they are looking for and end up interpreting everything they encounter in the field to prove that point. This doesn't mean that researchers enter the field with no hypotheses, but rather that hypotheses should be shaped by the findings. Researchers should be willing to revise their hypotheses to reflect what they are seeing, even if it isn't what they expected to see.

PARTICIPANT VERSUS NONPARTICIPANT RESEARCH

Researchers conducting ethnographies get to decide what their role will be. The first option is participant observation, where researchers fully immerse themselves in what they are studying, commonly referred to as the **field**. Researchers participate fully in the activities they are studying and take on all the tasks of the people that they are studying. The idea is to capture the participants' perspective, so walking in their shoes is a good way to see the world from their perspective. An example is Moffatt (1989), the professor who decided to live as one of his students for a year. To carry out his participant research, Moffatt gave up his daily routine to enroll in college and live on campus as a freshman for months without a break, actively participating in every aspect of the lives of his subjects. If the goal of the research is to see the world through the eyes of the people that the researcher is studying, there's no better way to do it. One of the biggest advantages of participant observation is that it helps researchers build **rapport** and gain trust. What better way to gain participants' trust than being one of them?

On the other hand, participant observation may get researchers *too* close to the people that they are living with. In such cases, researchers may lose the critical eye that makes ethnographic research valuable, in the same way that researchers who go into ethnographies with preconceived notions about what they're going to see lose sight of what's really going on. This is what researchers commonly refer to as **going native**.

Imagine being a part of a group for an extended period of time. You are required to dress like the group members, look like them, and do the tasks they do in their everyday lives. After all, the point of the participant observation is to capture the perspective of the participants in the study. Whether you are joining a cult or an environmentalist group or acting like a goth kid in school, after extended periods of immersion in the field, you might completely agree with your subjects because you are becoming one of them. Derek Freeman (1983) has criticized prominent anthropologist Margaret Mead's (1973) *Coming of Age in Samoa* on this basis. Largely regarded as one of the most important anthropological studies of the 20th century, *Coming of Age in Samoa* deals with the sexual maturation of teenage girls in the Pacific island nation. The girls and women Mead interviewed spoke about the openness of sexual experience on the island, leading her to argue that many of the sexual practices seen as "natural" in America and Europe were really cultural. Freeman argues that Mead became too close to the participants she interviewed and blindly accepted their stories about sexual experiences when she should have viewed the stories more critically. Had she followed up and really investigated, she would have found a very different story, he argues. Adding to this, while she was on her deathbed, one of Mead's participants admitted that she had made up much of what she had told the anthropologist. Getting too close to her participants seemingly compromised Mead's ability to critically examine what her participants were telling her; going native in this way led her to make critical errors in her research. As discussed later, participant observation also raises a number of serious ethical—and logistical—concerns.

Nonparticipant Observation

The alternative is **nonparticipant observation**. In nonparticipant observations—such as Besen-Cassino's (2013) study of the coffee shop—researchers observe the subjects but do not participate in the task. (For Besen-Cassino's research, participant observation would have involved taking a job at the coffee shop, just like the students she was observing.) Nonparticipant observation is not as involved as participant observation, but some researchers believe it provides a critical distance from the subjects.

Researchers who carry on participant research do their best to avoid getting too close to their subjects. They often take breaks after extended periods in the field. Some researchers do not start writing and making sense of their field experiences until after they take a break from the field. By creating these distances with time and space, they try to gain a critical distance from what they are studying.

This is, of course, easier said than done. On one hand, good researchers need to capture participants' authentic voices, no matter how different or unusual they might be. On the other hand, researchers need to be careful not to get too close to their participants in order to accurately recreate and recapture their perspectives. According to Patricia and Peter Adler (1999), many qualitative sociologists agree that a good researcher gets as close to his or her subjects as possible without going native. In some cases, it means that the researcher himself or herself will be a part of the narrative. In other cases, such as Carolyn Ellis' (1995) work on loss and grief, entitled *Final Negotiations*, the researcher uses his or her own experiences of death, loss, and chronic illness. This is referred to as **auto-ethnography**.

Sometimes, researchers can experience the opposite problem. Just as it is possible for researchers to get too close to the participants they are studying, it is also possible for researchers to become distant and alienated from their subjects. In some cases, they might have trouble identifying or empathizing with their subjects due to the subjects' unfavorable views. For his research, sociologist Richard Mitchell (2002) had to spend months living with antigovernment survivalists who frequently espoused offensive opinions. To effectively study them, he had to overcome his initial negative feelings, an experience common among researchers looking into marginalized groups. Like most researchers, he did his best to suppress and move past his feelings, leaving himself entirely out of the work.

This is part of ensuring replicability (as discussed in Chapter 1). With most research techniques, it shouldn't matter who carries out the analysis. The results should be the same. With ethnographies, though, researchers often discuss their role in the study and the personal obstacles that they had to deal with. As such, ethnographies often include what Patricia and Peter Adler (1999) refer to as "confessional tales." Alan Peshkin (1988) discusses the methodological issues he faced during his study of Bethany, a Christian fundamentalist community and school, in his book, *God's Choice.* He says:

> "I discovered, so to speak, that being Jewish would be the personal fact bearing most of my research. . . . They taught their children never to be close friends, marry, or go into business with someone like me. What they were expected to do with someone like me was to proselytize. . . . Bethany gored me." (Peshkin 1988, p. 14, quoted in Adler, 1987)

Part of the reaction that Peshkin's subjects had to him hinged on his religion. A researcher who isn't Jewish won't necessarily have the same experiences in Bethany that Peshkin did. Researchers looking to replicate Peshkin's work should take that into account. In addition, many ethnographers believe that honestly telling the reader about their experience requires that they insert themselves into the narrative. The reader can then decide for himself or herself whether there's bias in the narrative that the researcher produces.

REACTIVITY

Another potential problem qualitative researchers experience is the reaction of the subjects to the presence of the researcher. A researcher observing every move participants make and taking notes can wind up changing the very behavior that he or she is trying to study, thus tainting the entire exercise. This problem is broadly referred to as **reactivity**—that is, participants are "reacting" to the fact that they're being observed.

Reactivity can be positive or negative. **Positive reactivity** means that the presence of the researcher leads participants to exaggerate their activities in some way, leading the researcher to see things that wouldn't have happened if the participants had remained unobserved. The classic example of positive reactivity is the Hawthorne Effect, from research carried out by Henry A. Landsberger in 1955 in his analysis of experiments carried out at Hawthorne Works, a manufacturing facility outside of Chicago. The factory was understandably interested in increasing productivity and tried various manipulations to see what would do the trick. One of their first studies concluded that brighter lights were associated with higher levels of productivity, but Landsberger discovered that higher productivity rates were not due to lighting. Rather, they were due to the presence of the researchers at the work site. The fact that the corporation was paying attention to the employees resulted in a substantial (but short-lived) increase in productivity.

Negative reactivity means that the presence of the researcher leads participants to somehow mute their behaviors. This is a problem that Moffatt (1989) was especially worried about. Suppose that a student were sharing his dorm room with a professor who was taking notes on his every move. The student would understandably be on his best behavior. He wouldn't be acting naturally, and the researcher wouldn't be getting an accurate view of his life.

The good news about both forms of reactivity is that they tend to fade over time. No matter how intrusive the researchers might be, participants tend to get used to the researchers after a while. Keeping up a façade—being on one's best behavior or acting like someone else—is tough to do for a long period of time, and given enough time, people can get used to about anything. In a study concluding in 2010 (Saxbe, Repetti and Nishina 2008), researchers from UCLA spent months in the households of California families, tracking all of their movements at home, with graduate students filming hundreds of hours of footage and taking notes on every word. The researchers went so far as to collect saliva samples from the participants every hour or so in order to measure the presence of chemicals indicating stress responses. In sum, these people were being followed around by cameras in a house full of people taking notes on them while being asked to spit into vials—and even *they* seemed to get used to it after a while.

Leon Festinger, Henry Riecken, and Stanley Schachter—When the World Doesn't End (1956)

There's a long American tradition of predicting the end of the world. In 1843, a Baptist preacher named William Miller in upstate New York attracted thousands of followers and international attention with his prediction that Jesus would descend from heaven some time between March 21, 1843, and March 21, 1844. When the latter date rolled around, you might expect that Miller's followers would lose faith, but after a little recalculation, it was decided that the real date was some time later in the Spring of 1844. The date was moved again to October 22, 1844. Rather than become skeptical, the Millerites, as they were called, began believing more fervently, leading to what became referred to as "The Great Disappointment" when yet another date came and went.

The amazing thing about this is that, even then, Miller's followers didn't lose faith. Rather, they went on to found churches, including the modern Seventh-day Adventists. Somehow, a disconfirming event made people's beliefs in the event *even stronger*. For psychologist Leon Festinger (then at Stanford University) and his colleagues (1956), this was the ultimate expression of a theory called *cognitive dissonance*, in which people reshape their views of reality to match what they want to happen, with greater desires leading to greater reshaping. In December 1954, Festinger and his colleagues got the chance to test their theory when they read that a housewife from Michigan had received word from the Planet Clarion (through words that she wrote while in a trance-like state) that a flood was soon coming, and a group of followers had flocked to her home, where they would be rescued by a UFO.

Festinger and his colleagues (1956) decided that the best way to study what would happen when the flood and the UFO didn't come on the appointed day was to be there when it didn't happen. So, Festinger and a few others made the trek to join up with the true believers and managed to convince them that they, too, had been contacted by Clarion and been told to come. As might be expected, this was taken as great news, and they were quickly incorporated into the group.

Once inside the group, Festinger and his colleagues observed how the small group had developed a complicated belief structure to explain the reasons for the coming disaster and why the aliens would come to save them. On midnight (the appointed time) on the appointed day, nothing happened. The group decided that maybe the clock was off and waited another ten minutes. They made some attempt to explain why the UFO hadn't come for them (which was a major problem because the flood was expected the following morning). They mostly sat, shocked, until the housewife cum prophet was given another message via "automatic writing": the faith of the believers was so strong that God decided to call off the flood.

Before this time, the group had avoided any contact with nonbelievers—one of the reasons that Festinger's group had to lie to get in—but now, they called up newspapers, trying to spread the word about how they had saved the planet. Events that should have disconfirmed their belief, combined with the reinforcing presence of a group of similarly disappointed believers, led to even more fervent belief. Festinger and his colleagues (1956) received exactly the result they had expected, and they published a book about the event, *When Prophecy Fails*, that remains a classic of social psychology.

Deception in Ethnographies

Chapter 3 discussed guidelines for ethical research. But as Festinger and his colleagues' (1956) work shows, there are special considerations present in ethnographic studies. In a typical participant observation, the point is immersion in the field and walking in the participants' shoes—but what about the impact that the researchers' presence has on the people being observed? Festinger and his colleagues note how happy the small group was to meet others who had been contacted by Clarion. The researchers' presence reinforced the beliefs of the people that they were studying: if they hadn't shown up, maybe the failure of the prophecy would have led the participants to give up and go home. The researchers had a potentially life-changing effect on the people they were studying, and there was no informed consent or opportunity for the participants to opt-out of the research.

This is a common problem for researchers conducting participant observations. In order to avoid reactivity, they hide their identities from the people they're observing. This is, of course, a form of deception, but as discussed in Chapter 3, deception is allowable if there is no other way to carry out the research, and the researcher should reveal the deception as soon as is practical and give the participants the opportunity to retroactively opt-out of the study. In some cases, though, this is easier said than done.

Moffatt (1989) faced a particularly difficult instance of this dilemma. He was pretending to be a student in order to get more reliable information on college life. He could simply have asked these students questions as a professor, but the information the students would give to a professor would be much different from what they would tell their roommate. By enrolling in school and pretending to be a freshman, Moffatt established a rapport with his subjects. This is a crucial stage of the research process, where the subjects get to know the researcher and build trust. The better the rapport that the researcher establishes with his or her participants, the more comfortable they will feel and the more accurate and detailed information they will provide. As Moffatt said, "I thought I could operate more unobtrusively if they thought I was one of them. Then, I promised, I would come out and tell. . ." (1989, p. 20).

On one hand, researchers want to avoid reactivity effects; on the other hand, the longer researchers fail to reveal their identity, the longer they are engaged in deception. The length of deception is not only problematic for ethical reasons, but also for logistical reasons. The longer researchers wait to tell their subjects that they have been deceiving them, the more cheated the subjects will feel. This could potentially result in loss of rapport, loss of access to the group, and refusal to allow already-collected information to be used in future publications and presentations. So, when should researchers reveal themselves to the people being studied? Unfortunately, there are no hard-and-fast rules for this, and researchers have to use their best judgment. They should be far enough along in the process to have established a rapport, but not so far along that they have unnecessarily deceived participants. Ideally, though, when they engage in participant observation, they should work with a colleague staying outside of the group who can help to provide some perspective on the issue.

Another common ethical concern in ethnographic work involves issues of confidentiality. With face-to-face interviews, anonymity simply is not possible because the researchers know who their participants are. However, researchers can still ensure confidentiality. As discussed in Chapter 3, confidentiality means that the researchers can identify the participants' responses, but they promise not to identify the participants publicly. Typical methods of confidentiality involve changing the real names of the participants and using pseudonyms instead. The rule is that someone who is reading the findings should not be able to identify these individuals from the written text. However, even the use of pseudonyms might not be enough. Because ethnographies often describe their subjects in detail, they share very detailed information that could potentially make the subjects identifiable. Many researchers agree that names of places, stores, streets, or specific characteristics of the subjects could make them identifiable and potentially open them to embarrassment or worse, depending on the nature of the research. While a reader might be able to guess what coffee chain Besen-Cassino (2013) was spending time in, there's nothing in the published work that will give a hint about the towns where the work was carried out.

THE LOGISTICS OF ETHNOGRAPHY

Barbara Ehrenreich—Nickel and Dimed (2001)

In *Nickel and Dimed: On (Not) Getting By in America*, Barbara Ehrenreich (2001) demonstrates the difficulties of living on the minimum wage in the United States. To examine these issues firsthand, she gives up her job and takes minimum-wage jobs as a waitress in Florida, a maid in Maine, and an entry-level worker at Walmart in Minnesota. Although Ehrenreich was willing to give up her life for a year for the purposes of her research, she wasn't about to go in unprepared. Like most researchers undertaking participant ethnography, she entered the field with a list of rules that she would follow over the course of her study. Laying rules out at the beginning of the project makes it less likely that the researcher will have to abandon the rules or change the way that he or she is carrying out the study later. The first chapter of Ehrenreich's work lays out both her rules and her cheats.

Rules are pre-established guidelines to provide structure for the ethnography. In living on minimum wage, Ehrenreich (2001) first establishes that she is not going to use her own education, skills, and credentials to get jobs. In order to preserve the essence of the study, it is imperative that she does not use her own credentials (a Ph.D. in biology and extensive work experience), which would give her an enormous advantage over other minimum-wage workers. So, she fabricates a new resume for herself, omitting her education and work experience and claiming that she has been out of the workforce taking care of her children. Second, she sets out to do a good job in every job offered and will not be "sneaking off to read novels in the ladies room." Finally, she decides to take the cheapest accommodation—with acceptable levels of privacy and safety—that she can find in the area.

While having rules—and listing them for readers—is important, every good ethnographer needs *cheats* as well. Sticking to the rules all the time is not easy because a researcher is immersed in the field for extended periods of time. Researchers need some built-in cheats to ensure the quality of their ethnography. Just like the rules, the cheats are established before the researcher enters the field. The researcher has to decide what he or she cannot live without—what he or she absolutely needs to carry out this project. Every ethnographer will have different cheats. In order for Ehrenreich (2001) to carry out her project, she decided that she would not be homeless, live in a shelter, or sleep in her car. If her wages fell short of the rent that month, she would end the project early. She also did not want to go hungry, so if at any month she could not afford food, she would use her ATM card. Finally, she wanted to keep her car. In Key West, she drove her own car, and in other cities she used her own credit card to rent from Rent-a-Wreck.

Entering the field is never a clean or easy business. Upon entering the field, researchers realize that things do not go as planned: glitches and problems come with the territory. However, it is important to anticipate problems ahead of time and be open about them, turning a potential problem into a strength. Ehrenreich (2001) acknowledges all the times she broke her rules; even though she said she would not fall back on her own educational skills and credentials, in Florida she once got a job because of her basic knowledge of greeting customers in French and German in a touristy area. In Minnesota, she did not take the highest paying job available to her.

Entering the Field

As a researcher, entering the field is the most important part of an ethnography. After all, researchers often spend a year (in many cases, much longer than that) immersing themselves in a new world. First, it's necessary for researchers to define the group that they wish to study. This can be based on a place (as in Besen-Cassino's [2013] work in the coffee shop), a population (like the college freshmen Moffatt studied), or even an activity (as in Ehrenreich's [2001] study of the working poor). This definition is critical because it will shape everything about the work and answer many of the most important questions about what the researcher will do in the field. For instance, studying what goes on at a high school could be very different from studying a group of students at that school. In one, the researcher could be talking to students, teachers, administrators, counselors, coaches, or anyone at the school. In the other, the researcher would almost certainly have to follow the participants to their homes or anywhere else that they might decide to go. This sort of decision also plays a key role in what the researcher might find: the students might behave differently at home than at school, and a researcher who only saw them in the classroom would have no way of knowing.

Key Informants

Once a researcher has defined the group, he or she needs to recruit a **key informant**, a trusted individual within the group being studied through whom the researcher can gain access to other members of the group. This informant is especially important because his or her relationship with the researcher may mean that the informant can vouch for the researcher and overcome some of the initial resistance to his or her presence. (Of course, if the researcher isn't telling the participants about his or her role as a researcher just yet, this may not be necessary.) In addition, key informants can help the researcher with the vocabulary and social mores of the group that he or she is studying. However, researchers must also be careful to avoid relying too much on their key informant. In *Street Corner Society*, William Foote Whyte (1943) studied the Italian American youth culture in the 1940s, focusing on the illegal activities of "corner boys," whom he described as a "gang." Later, his methodology and findings were criticized when Marianne Boelen (1992), an Italian American immigrant, who replicated Whyte's study but reached entirely different conclusions. After reinterviewing Whyte's subjects, she found that these boys were not gang members; in their culture, men claimed the outside space while women occupied the indoor space, and this inside/outside division was not due to criminality, but gender. She argued that Whyte's erroneous conclusions were due to his overreliance on one key informant, who he referred to as "Doc."

One informant, though, does not an ethnography make. Most commonly, ethnographers make use of what's called a **snowball sample** (discussed further in Chapter 11). In snowball sampling (so called because the rate of growth in the sample corresponds to the size of the sample at that point, like a snowball rolling downhill), the key informant introduces the researcher to others within the group, who in turn refer the researcher to more people, and so on. This sort of sampling allows for a variety of perspectives on the group or place that the researcher is studying, while enabling the researcher to stay within the group or place.

In quantitative research, the size of the sample is of the utmost importance: a survey carried out on 1,000 people in a random sample is much more believable than one carried out on 100 people or administered to a nonrandom sample. Moreover, the assumptions underlying survey research allow researchers to leverage the size of a random sample to determine the approximate error rates associated with that sample. For example, political surveys might say that their results are accurate "plus or minus 3 percent." However, in ethnography, researchers don't have definite rules for determining how many people create a valid representation of the group. An ethnography in which the researcher spoke with twenty people could be just as valid as one in which the researcher spoke to a hundred. The key is to ensure that the sample fits the definition of the group that the researcher is studying. In a study of a sports team, the sample may need to include the coaches and the water boys. If researchers are studying what goes on at a school, they should make sure to incorporate the views of the substitute teachers or the custodial staff.

Rather than worry about the sample size, ethnographers are more likely to track how long they spent in the field with their subjects. Ethnography requires full immersion into the field and is most successful when the researcher spends extended periods of time with the subjects. Herbert Gans, one of the first sociologists to challenge the practice of razing "slums" to replace poor neighborhoods with what are now known as "projects," said that "ethnography is most successful when it becomes an all-encompassing 14- to 16- hours a day experience, with at least a year's full time fieldwork, and a good deal of additional time to analyze and think about the data" (1982 p. 416).

Fieldnotes

Once researchers have immersed themselves in the field, they have to turn their experiences into research material. There's no way for researchers to remember everything that they have experienced after spending months in the field, so they need to take notes. In addition, since ethnographic researchers use their experiences to draw conclusions about the reasons why their participants do the things they do, other researchers may want to look at their **fieldnotes** in order to see if the conclusions are valid.

Typically, researchers want to put down information as soon as they can, even while they're still in the field, if possible. Taking notes in the field may be impossible, especially if participants don't yet know about the research. (Festinger and his colleagues [1956] took turns going into other rooms to put down thoughts as soon as they could.) To speed up the process, many researchers make use of tape recorders, but it's necessary to exercise caution when doing so. Tape recorders are useful for recording impressions, as well as for recording interviews with participants, but researchers cannot, under any circumstances, record others without their full knowledge and permission. Doing so is not only unethical, but it is illegal in many states. Researchers must also remember to keep their note taking as unobtrusive as possible. If participants see someone scribbling down notes, they may stop whatever they're doing or try to give the researcher more of what he or she finds so interesting.

When taking fieldnotes—either on paper or on tape—it's important for researchers to record their impressions from all five senses, as well as their reaction to what they have experienced. Researchers must be sure to record the names of participants only by the pseudonyms that they've assigned to them. (Remember, at some point in the future others might want to see the notes, and researchers still need to maintain confidentiality.) In addition, there are a number of things that should always be included:

> When the observations were recorded
> Where the observations were recorded
> As many specific facts as possible
> Any specific phrases or vocabulary
> Notes to self about things to follow-up on
> The researcher's feelings about what's been observed
> Finally, there should be page numbers on the notes, so they can be kept in order

Examples of Fieldnotes

7:40 Another student starts his speech at the same time, speaking quietly while his partner reads along and checks his progress. It seems like many of the students are now out of the room. Teacher goes outside (to check on students?). Students get phone when it rings, teacher comes and takes it. Students go on practicing.

7:45 Teacher called in all of the students again. Made sure everyone had copies of the invitations. Teacher somewhat uncomfortable with my being here. Keeps looking at me. Teacher talked about expectations including having a prompter. Uses dry humor. seems pleasant and approachable. Treats the students as equals. First student goes.

> 7:50 Student doing very well and topic was interesting (from Black Like Me).
> Teacher doing some prompting. Student did awesome. Teacher told others that
> student "had thrown down the gauntlet and set the standard that the rest of
> you must meet." Switched to the group doing Macbeth. Students gave some
> feedback and suggestions to first student.
>
> 7:55 (Room is getting VERY hot. Fan is going, but doors are closed.)
> Shakespeare group goes. Group doing well. When they finish, teacher gives
> some feedback to them.
>
> 8:10 8th graders come in. Teacher introduces the 7th grade speakers to the
> 8th graders. Teacher gives me feedback that Subject F (although absent today)
> has already taken the initiative to practice. They had gone over it yesterday and
> she did a good job. Her topic is the "true" story of Humpty Dumpty. New
> group goes. Appears uncomfortable, and don't know lines as well as last group.
> Their topic, however, is "An Analysis of Scooby-Doo."

Once the researcher has made his or her notes, the notes should be put
somewhere with controlled access (a locked file cabinet, a safe), anywhere that
others won't be able to see or get to them and that the notes will be safe. After all,
until the notes are turned into computer files, a fire or even a rogue coffee spill
could wipe out weeks or months of work. Finally, researchers need to transcribe
fieldnotes into data form by typing them or hiring someone to do so.

STRUCTURED OBSERVATIONS

W. Andrew Harrell—Child Attractiveness and Parental Attention (2005)

W. Andrew Harrell (2005), a professor at the University of Alberta, has spent years
studying the risks to children that arise from everyday behaviors, such as the use
of shopping carts: more than 30,000 children are seriously injured in shopping
cart accidents every year in the United States and Canada. This isn't the flashiest
of research, but he made headlines in 2005 with a **structured observation** study
of when parents did, and did not, actually strap their children into shopping carts
while in a supermarket.

    With the consent of the management of fourteen different supermarkets,
teams of four researchers, posing as shoppers, stood by the doors until a child
between about two and five years old came into the store accompanied by
just one adult. For five minutes after the parent and child entered, two of the
researchers followed them around the store, recording the gender and approximate
age of the child, as well as rating the child on physical attractiveness (using a 1 to
10 scale). After the five minutes was over, the other two researchers followed the
parent and child around, recording whether or not the child was buckled into the
grocery cart and how often (if at all) the child was allowed to wander more than
ten feet away from the parent.

Over the course of 426 observations of parents and children, it became clear that more attractive children were much more likely to be buckled into the shopping carts. Thirteen percent of the most attractive children were strapped in, compared with just over one percent of the least attractive children. Less attractive children were also much more likely to be allowed to wander away from their parents.

Harrell (2005) attributed the difference in how parents treat attractive and unattractive children to evolutionary biology. Attractive children may be more likely to have offspring of their own, so it makes sense for parents to expend more effort protecting them. Other psychologists have argued that the findings are just another example of how attractive people wind up being treated better in all aspects of life; parents (subconsciously, in all likelihood) like the attractive children better and therefore pay more attention to them.

Harrell's (2005) research is similar to the other qualitative fieldwork that's been discussed so far, but there are some important differences. While most qualitative work is built from interviews and fieldnotes, Harrell and his colleagues didn't use either. Rather, they made use of a structured observation. In structured observation studies, researchers make a decision about what they will observe before going into the field. Once there, they record only those behaviors or characteristics that were previously decided upon. The researchers will often make use of checklists or worksheets for recording in lieu of standard fieldnotes. In Harrell's research, the first two researchers could have used a simple worksheet on which they recorded the attractiveness, age, and gender of the child, while the other two researchers could have simply recorded whether or not the child was strapped in and marked whenever the child wandered more than ten feet away.

Typically, the behaviors and characteristics listed on these sheets will be determined by looking at prior research on the topic, though researchers may also engage in a pilot study, where they undertake more casual observations to see what behaviors are interesting and frequent enough to warrant inclusion in the structured observation. Harrell has carried out studies of behavior in supermarkets for years, so this probably wasn't necessary for him. Less experienced researchers could have gone to supermarkets to make sure that parents sometimes let their kids wander off and do strap their kids in to shopping carts. If it turned out that all of the parents strapped their children into the grocery carts or that no parent ever let a child wander away, the structured observations would have been worthless. Some preliminary research is generally worthwhile.

There are some disadvantages to these sorts of structured observations. Primary among them is a lack of context and details. Since the researchers in these studies aren't collecting fieldnotes or carrying out interviews, all the information they have is what is written down on the sheet. If the researchers notice anything interesting once they're in the field, there's no way to capture it in the research, unless they want to rework the checklists or worksheets and start all over again. Structured observations also don't allow researchers to understand the lived experience of the behaviors that they're observing. It could be, for instance, that attractive children are more used to attention and get fussy if they're not attended to, or that parents think of unattractive children as being more independent. Harrell's (2005) research has been used to argue that parents like unattractive children less than attractive ones (though he makes no such claims about the emotional content of the behaviors), but there's no way to know about this aspect without doing interviews

On the other hand, structured observations greatly increase the reliability and replicability of qualitative research. They are considered to be more reliable because there's less room for variation between observers. If two researchers are sent into the same situation in a participant or nonparticipant observation, they may make note of entirely different things, all of which may be equally correct. In a structured observation, though, those two researchers would go into the situation with the same checklist or worksheet, and they would almost certainly wind up recording the same things. Structured observations are also more easily replicable than other qualitative research techniques. Suppose that a researcher wanted to **replicate** Moffatt's (1989) participant observation of college student behavior. He or she could go undercover in his or her own university, but there's no guarantee that the researcher would observe the same sorts of behaviors that Moffatt did. A researcher trying to replicate Harrell's (2005) study would have a much easier time. He or she could create a worksheet based on the same characteristics and behaviors, follow families in grocery stores, and compare the results to Harrell's study.

ADVANTAGES AND DISADVANTAGES OF ETHNOGRAPHIES

Ethnographies have many advantages. Most important, they allow researchers to get very rich and detailed information. In addition, ethnographies help researchers build grounded theories and capture the authentic perspectives of the subjects being studied. The particular methods allow the researchers to consider things they have not thought about. Finally, observations allow for the recording of nonverbal information.

However, ethnographies also have some disadvantages. First, they are very time consuming: observations are done over the course of a few months and even years. Participant observations require that researchers give up their everyday life to walk in someone else's shoes. After the completion of the data collection, transcribing, coding, and organizing fieldnotes is a very time consuming and labor intensive process.

Because ethnographies take such a long time, changes and do-overs are very difficult. If a researcher makes a mistake or wants to redo something after being immersed in the field as an undercover student for one year, it would not be a simple task. For similar reasons, replication of studies can also be challenging.

Being so close to the field and being so close to the subjects being studied has some advantages, such as getting a firsthand experience or inside knowledge. However, being so close to what is being studied could also be a disadvantage. Many ethnographers have to find ways to cope with the problem of going native: being too close to the subjects being studied and losing critical perspective.

In addition, ethnographies have been widely criticized for generalizability. One of the advantages of ethnography is the in-depth information it provides on a specific group or case. While the detail of information it can provide the researcher is certainly an advantage, it has also been criticized for its focus on very small, generally nonrepresentative groups. Unlike surveys that provide information on thousands of subjects, ethnographies focus on fewer cases. Because of that, many researchers argue that their conclusions might not be applicable to cases beyond the scope of the study.

Ethical Considerations

In qualitative methods, particularly in ethnographic studies, building rapport with the participants is essential. In order to gain rapport and potentially minimize reactivity effects, researchers often resort to deception. This could lead to potential ethical violations. In ethnographies and structured observations, the researchers collect very detailed information on participants. Due to the richness of the information, it is very important to ensure confidentiality. The researchers need to ensure that observational data collected cannot be traced back to the participants.

FURTHER CASE STUDIES

> Morgan Spurlock's "30 Days" is a series of ethnographies. In Minimum Wage, he tries to live on minimum wage for a month. In Off the Grid, two people try to live off the grid, in an environmentally conscious commune with minimum environmental impact. In binge drinking mom, a mother tries to binge drink for a month.

Richard Fenno—Congressional Homestyles (1978)

Much of the modern research on Congress deals with the incumbency advantage: once members of Congress get into office, they become almost impossible to beat. In most years, more than 95 percent of representatives who run for reelection win their seat again. A lot of this has to do with scaring off potential opponents by raising lots of money and making sure not to cast votes that would alienate voters. It's been much hypothesized, though, that the incumbency advantage also has a lot to do with how representatives deal with their constituents, by building personal relationships that may be able to overcome differences that may arise over policy.

However, there was very little research on what members of Congress actually do to build this support at home, and Richard Fenno (1978) decided to fill in this gap by following members of Congress on their trips home. In his words, he was "poking and soaking"—poking them to find out what was going on below the surface, and soaking in the experience. What he found was that members of Congress tended to divide the world into four types of people: the inner circle of advisors and family, the next circle of potential volunteers and donors, the next of supporters in the electorate, and then the rest of the people living in the district.

Fenno found that members of Congress have very different ways of relating with each of them, and these strategies shift over time.

Fenno (1978) found that members of Congress early in their careers worked largely on bringing people from the outer circles in, turning constituents into supporters and supporters into volunteers and donors. However, at some point most members of Congress stop this, fearing that expanding their base much more could serve to alienate their existing supporters. Essentially, once members of Congress are secure in their chances for reelection, they go in a consolidation mode, worrying more about holding on to the support that they have than changing the mind of anyone else.

He also found that members of Congress made certain to have a justification for all of their votes, just in case it was needed. They didn't know what votes their constituents would bring up, but the members knew that if they were asked why they voted a certain way on an issue that was assumed to be important to the person asking, they better have a good reason. Perhaps most important, Fenno (1978) found that even members who had been reelected for decades were insecure about their chances, almost always seeing a potential challenge five or ten years down the line.

Andre Lukacs, David Embrick, and Talmadge Wright— Emotion Work in World of Warcraft (2010)

Ethnographic research begins with a research question and a population that the researcher wishes to study, but there's no requirement that the population in question has to physically interact. The members only have to have some meaningful social interaction with each other. As far back as the 1980s, researchers looked at interactions between people on relatively primitive Internet message boards using ethnographic techniques, and the rise of virtual worlds has made this sort of research even more appealing. Today, the users of virtual spaces such as World of Warcraft and Second Life have interactions with each other that are potentially richer than the interactions that they have in the real world, making them a prime target for ethnographers. Research in these virtual worlds can often be easier than research in a real-world setting because researchers can much more easily disguise themselves in order to minimize reactivity, and participants in a virtual world may be much easier to track. No one knows if one player in World of Warcraft is taking frequent screenshots to record the action or saving all of the chat logs for future analysis. Fieldnotes are generally gathered in much the same way as in real-world ethnographies, though they're much less obtrusive because the participants can't see that the researcher is writing things down. The same distinction between participant and nonparticipant research, as well as the same ethical considerations, apply.

Andre Lukacs, David Embrick, and Talmadge Wright's (2010) research on players in World of Warcraft takes the form of participant observation. Working as a team, they played the game on both sides for more than 3,500 hours, interacting with other players, copying notable chat discussions (present on the screen in text form), recording conversations that took place over the players' microphones, and taking fieldnotes about the experiences within the game. The research question in their study had to do with the emotional work necessary to manage the challenges present at high levels of the game. In the game, players gain levels by completing sometimes dull tasks, generally on an individual level. Once players have reached the maximum level allowed in the game, though, the dynamic of the game changes. Challenges for players at the maximum level are too difficult to be undertaken by any individual player, so players form groups, called "guilds," which work in teams ranging from ten to twenty-five people to complete the challenges, normally referred to as "raids."

The question Lukacs, Embrick, and Wright (2010) deal with is how these groups are able to maintain themselves. Leading a raid requires members of the guild to coordinate the activities of the entire group and lead them through the entire raid, which can take anywhere from one to twelve hours. It's not just about numbers; the balance of the various character attributes has to be in place as well, so one person dropping out can be disastrous. In their ethnography, members of guilds talk about how they build their schedules in real life around when they need to be part of the raiding party; others do so just to be alternates for the raiding party, meaning that they will only be participating if someone else drops out. Players who show up without the necessary equipment to sustain themselves in the raid for several hours are belittled or even kicked out of the group, meaning the even the high-level players have to do their "dailies," completing tasks that they have probably already done in the past just to earn some in-game money to buy the supplies that they will need for the raid. Guild leaders monitor the time the members are putting in to make sure that they're doing enough. During the raid, communication over microphones is restricted to the leaders. Everyone else has to stay silent and is expected to remain at the keyboard except during designated break times. At the end of the raid, whatever "loot" is acquired is distributed by the leaders in accordance with predetermined rules. If this sounds like work, it's because it is. So how do guilds maintain leaders willing to put the work in and members willing to follow their orders?

Lukacs, Embrick, and Wright (2010) argue that the payoff for most of the players is camaraderie. By leading raids, players gain the respect of their peers. For nonleaders, joining in the raids is the only way to maintain ties with their friends within the guild. According to one player, "I just got a baby and was unable to make the raid times regularly. Kind of sucks—I had a lot of friends in the guild, but I cannot play with them, unless I make the raids." In essence, leaders are able to control access to a social group—the other members of the guild—by monitoring the behaviors of individuals within the group. As long as group members do what they're supposed to, in what really seems like work, they get to go on raids and have fun with their friends. If they slack off, though, they'll be cut off.

SUMMARY

In the abstract, ethnography seems like one of the simplest ways of carrying out social science research: the researcher closely observes the behavior of a group of people and takes notes on what he or she sees, experiences, and feels. In practice, though, ethnography, especially participant ethnography, is fraught with logistical concerns and ethical considerations. Ethnography almost always involves at least tacit deception, and it's easy for researchers to get overly involved with the people that they're researching.

Despite the difficulty involved with ethnographic work, it remains worthwhile because it enables researchers to understand the perspective of the people being studied, and by observing how people do what they do, researchers may be able to determine why they do it.

Because ethnographic researchers get so close to the participants they are observing, reactivity can be a real problem. The mere presence of a researcher carefully observing people and taking notes may well cause those people to act differently than they otherwise would.

When engaged in ethnography, researchers must take complete fieldnotes, which include all of the aspects of their experience in the field, including their own reactions to what they observed. As soon as possible after exiting the field, researchers turn these fieldnotes into more formal, structured notes. These notes are essentially the data from which the researcher will draw conclusions about the individuals and behaviors being observed, and they must be made available to other researchers who wish to examine or replicate the work.

In an effort to increase the replicability of their work, some researchers turn to structured observations, in which the fieldnotes are reduced to observations of specific, predefined behaviors. While ethnographic research is most commonly used in sociology and criminology, it has proven valuable in other fields, including political science and economics.

Study and Review

Was Moffat's (1989) research ethical? Why or why not?

Is deception a necessary element of participant ethnographies? Why or why not?

Compare the costs and benefits of carrying out participant, rather than nonparticipant, ethnography.

What can researchers do to minimize reactivity?

How do researchers prepare for the field?

Why might researchers favor structured observations over standard ethnographic techniques?

Notable Ethnographies

Klinenber, Eric. Heatwave: 2003. *A Social Autopsy of Disaster in Chicago.* University of Chicago Press.

Newman, Kathy. 2000. *No Shame in My Game: The Working Poor in the Inner-city.* Vintage Books.

Hays, Sharon. 2004. *Flat-Broke with Children: Women in the Age of Welfare Reform.* Oxford University Press.

Willis, Paul. 1982. *Learning to Labor: How Working-class Kids get Working-class Jobs.* Oxford University Press.

Gaines, Donna. 1998. *Teenage Wasteland: Suburbia's Dead-End Kids*. University of Chicago Press.

Eliasoph, Nina. *Avoiding Politics: How Americans Produce Apathy in Everyday Life*. Cambridge University Press.

Anderson, Elijah. 1999. *Code of the Street*. New York: Norton.

Bourgois, Phillippe. 1995. *In Search of Respect.* New York: Cambridge University Press.

Duneirer, Mitch. 1999. *Sidewalk*. New York: Farrar, Straus, and Giroux.

Kanter, Rosabeth Moss. 1993. *Men and Women of the Corporation*. New York: Basic Books.

Fine, Gary Alan. *Morel Tales*. 1998. Cambridge: MA: Havard University Press.

Hondegneu-Sotelo, Pierette. 2001. *Domestica*. Berkeley: University of California Press.

Karp, David. 1996. *Speaking of Sadness*. New York: Oxford University Press.

Miller, Jody. 2001. *One of the Guys*. New York: Oxford University Press.

Snow, David and Leon Anderson. 1993. *Down on their Luck*. Berkeley: University of California Press.

Hochschild, Arlie Russell and Anne Machung. 1989. *The Second Shift: Working Parents and the Revolution at Home*. New York: Viking Press.

Recommended Resources

Adler, Patricia A. and Peter Adler. 2003. "The Promise and Pitfalls of Going into the Field." *Contexts*. 2(2):41–47.

Atkinson, Paul, Amanda Coffey, Sara Delamont, John Lofland, and Lyn Lofland. 2001. *Handbook of Ethnography*. Thousand Oaks, CA: Sage Publications.

Charmaz, Kathy. "Grounded Theory: Objectivist and Constructivist Methods." 2000. *Handbook of Quantitative Research*, edited by Norman Denzin and Yvonna Lincoln. Thousand Oaks, CA: Sage Publications.

Denzin, Norman K. and Yvonna Lincoln. 2000. *Handbook Of Qualitative Research*. Thousand Oaks, CA: Sage Publications.

Glaser, Barney and Anselm Strauss. 1967. "The Discovery of the Grounded Theory." *Strategies for Qualitative Research*. Chicago: Aldine Publishing Company.

Harris, Scott R. 2008. "Constructionism in Sociology." Chapter 12 in the *Handbook of Constructionist Research*, edited by J.A. Holstein and J.F. Gubrium. New York: Guilford Publications.

Holstein, James A. and James F. Gubrium. 1995. *The Active Interview*. Thousand Oaks, CA: Sage Publications.

Lofland, John and Lyn Lofland. 1995. *Analyzing Social Settings*. Belmont, CA: Wadworth. 3rd edition.

Oakley, Ann. 2001. "Interviewing Women: A Contradiction in Terms." In the *American Tradition of Qualitative Research vol III* eds. Norman Denzin and Yvonna Lincoln. Thousand Oaks, CA: Sage Publications.

Weiss, Robert S. 1994. *Learning from Strangers: The Art and Method of Qualitative Interview Studies.* New York: Free Press.

Weiss, Robert. 2004. "In their Own Words: Making the Most of Qualitative Interviews." *Contexts*. 3(4):44–51.

CHAPTER 7

Qualitative Research II: Interviews and Focus Groups

Learning Objectives

- Be able to discuss why researchers use in-depth interviews and what types of research questions would most benefit from in-depth interviews
- Be able to comprehend the structure of in-depth interviews and design in-depth interviews
- Be able to discuss the importance of and identify the key points in interviewer training
- Be able to understand the use of specialized software in transcribing in-depth interviews and discuss the potential advantages and disadvantages
- Be able to identify the advantages and disadvantages of using in-depth interviews
- Be able to identify the purpose of focus groups and identify the conditions under which focus groups are the optimal research method
- Be able to design and identify the components of a focus group design
- Be able to identify advantages and disadvantages of using focus groups

IN-DEPTH QUALITATIVE INTERVIEWS

In Chapter 6, we discussed ethnographies. The rich observations collected during participant or nonparticipant observations are often supplemented with in-depth, qualitative interviews. The **in-depth interview** is a flexible, semi-structured, and conversational technique for asking mostly open-ended questions; it is used predominantly in qualitative research. Survey research typically uses more structured questions, with defined options; the difference is analogous to the difference between ethnographies and structured observations, such as W. Andrew Harrell's (2005) study of attractive children in shopping carts (as described in Chapter 6). Chapter 10 will discuss writing the questionnaires used in survey research.

The goals of the two types of interviews are very different. In survey research, the goal is to collect standardized responses from a large group of people; the aim of qualitative interviews is to get very detailed, in-depth information on a more limited, and probably not representative, group of people. Rather than ask about *what* people do or think, qualitative interviews tend to ask about the details of what happened, how it happened, and how the respondent felt throughout. This information allows researchers to form what Princeton University anthropologist Clifford Geertz (1973) called a "thick description" of experiences, processes, and events, which can allow researchers to capture certain social phenomena in ways that other techniques simply cannot.

Eran Shor and Dalit Simchai—Incest Avoidance in Kibbutzim (2009)

The examples in Chapter 6 generally tackle questions that couldn't be answered with other methods: surveys wouldn't tell researchers much about why students actually work in bad jobs because students generally just say that they work for the money. Similarly, Moffatt (1989) couldn't have answered his questions about the daily lives of students with any other method. However, qualitative research can also be used to supplement, or even challenge, the findings of other techniques. In their research on sexual relations within Israeli kibbutzim, Eran Shor, a sociologist at McGill University, and Dalit Simchai of the University of Haifa, challenged long-standing findings from quantitative analyses.

More than one hundred years ago, Finnish sociologist Edward Westermarck (1934) argued that incest avoidance—the aversion to sexual relationships with siblings—was a biological safeguard against the sorts of developmental defects that could arise from incest. He knew of cases where siblings who had been separated at birth married, so he argued that it must be a function of who the individuals live with in early childhood. He suggested that if two children are raised together for a significant period of time before about age eight, they would not experience any sexual attraction toward one another. This idea has faced some significant challenges over the past 120 years, most notably from Sigmund Freud's theories, which place a desire for incest at the heart of almost all family relations. For a Freudian, the avoidance of incest would have to be structural: people want to have sexual relations with their relatives, but society and the superego prevent them from doing so. As Freud's theories of human behavior began to lose their sway, sociologists began empirically testing whether people raised in close contact actually did avoid sexual contact.

Some of the strongest evidence in support of Westermarck's claims came from studies in the early 1970s of people raised in Israeli kibbutzim: collective farms in which children were raised communally. Children raised in these kibbutzim were educated along with other children of the same age throughout the day and would only see their parents for a few hours in the evening, even sleeping in the children's area with their peers. Anthropologist Joseph Shepher (1971) studied the married couples who met in the kibbutzim. Of nearly 3,000 couples from more than 200 kibbutzim (almost all of the couples who grew up in the communal arrangements), only 14 came from the same peer group, and none of those 14 had been in the same group for the first six years of their lives. Other work on arranged marriages in Taiwan, some of which involve the bride moving in with the future husband's family at a very young age, seemed to bear out these findings. The couples who lived together as children were more likely to get divorced and had fewer children.

However, as Shor and Simchai (2009) point out, the fact that people who live together as children are less likely to get married doesn't necessarily mean that there's a biological aversion mechanism at work. It could mean that the people are simply less sexually attracted to one another or even that there are structural barriers preventing them from getting married. Shor and Simchai began the process of actually interviewing people who had grown up in the kibbutzim to find out whether or not they were sexually attracted to others whom they had been raised with. The researchers carried out sixty interviews with people who had grown up in kibbutzim, with each interview lasting from one to two hours. The researchers made sure not to reveal the purpose of the study or their hypotheses to the participants until the end of the interviews to avoid contaminating the participants' answers. There is also the potential problem that the participants misremember, or even forget, some of the events that happened in their youth. (For some of the participants, the time in the kibbutz was fifty years before.) If that's the case, though, the participants would probably underreport socially undesirable behaviors, rather than overreport them. There were strict rules against sexual contact with other members of their peer groups, so participants would be more likely to lie about following the rules than breaking them. It makes sense to believe the people who say that they were sexually attracted to others in their peer group in the kibbutz, even knowing that some of the participants who were sexually attracted to their peers will deny it.

The researchers initially contacted the participants via telephone, then excluded anyone who had left the kibbutz for a long time during childhood. During the face-to-face interviews, the researchers asked general questions such as "What feelings did you have toward boys/girls within your group?" In response to these questions, Shor and Simchai (2009) say that participants talked at length about the other members of the group, including their sexual feelings toward them. In some of the interviews, the participants didn't give enough information for the researchers to determine if they had any sexual attraction to other members of their group or not. In those cases, the researchers pushed the participants a little more, though they were still careful not to reveal what their hypotheses were.

More than half of the participants (53 percent) reported either strong or moderate sexual attraction toward the others in their peer group, with 43 percent saying that they were indifferent toward them. The researchers illustrate this indifference by quoting one of their participants, who said, "It is very different from what I feel toward my brothers. With them the idea of sex clearly incites feelings of aversion. With my peers it was simply something that did not cross my mind." Many said that they were attracted to one of their peers and indifferent toward the rest. Others reported that they were initially attracted to one or more of their peers, with the attraction fading over time. As another participant said:

> "We didn't think, 'Just a minute, they are like our sisters.' It was part of the intimacy and closeness, and there was also sexual excitement involved, because it was convenient and we knew it was not going anywhere . . . There were half-incidental touches, and it was not a secret. It was in the open and with consent. But it was also clear to everyone that it is not going to be fully consummated." (Shor and Simchai 2009)

It seems that the people who grew up in the kibbutzim were attracted to each other, but sexual relationships were socially unacceptable; therefore, they didn't get married. Shor and Simchai (2009) illustrate this point by quoting another participant, who said,

> "I loved him very much, and was also very much attracted to him. We became a couple, but it was never consummated, because it was highly unorthodox at the time. I really wanted to consummate our love physically, and so did he, but I never let it happen. I was afraid that something awful is going to happen if we do." (Shor and Simchai 2009)

In addition, a number of participants reported that they suppressed the feelings because they were forbidden. The few participants who wound up dating someone from their group reported that outsiders thought it was strange that they would do so; they were told there was something wrong with it.

These findings have important implications for the study of incest avoidance. It doesn't seem as if there is an innate, biological aversion to sexual relationships, as Westermarck (1934) and many others have suggested. Rather, it seems that participants were sexually attracted to their peers (boys more than girls), and many consummated that relationship in secret. However, there was immense social pressure, especially on the girls, to avoid these relationships: a social, rather than a biological, explanation for the lack of marriages seems likely.

In this case, the hypotheses of past researchers were making claims about the internal states of the individuals in the kibbutzim—that they experienced aversion to sexual relationships with their peers—without really bothering to ask the individuals about their feelings. By asking people about their feelings, rather than just assuming, Shor and Simchai (2009) called into question the mechanism by which humans avoid incest. Once again, we see the importance of understanding the lived experience of the participants being studied. There are caveats here, of course. We know that people aren't very good about telling us why they chose to do, or not do, something. As such, the interviews Shor and Simchai carried out don't really tell us why the people growing up in the kibbutzim didn't marry their peers. We can, however, generally trust what they say about their behaviors: in this case, sexual relationships and feelings of attraction toward peers. While this doesn't fully answer the question of how incest avoidance among humans works, it does give us some clues, at least to how it *doesn't* work. Perhaps most important, this research improves our understanding of human families and sexuality, and the research simply could not have been conducted in any other way. Analysis of marriage rates, no matter how sophisticated, doesn't tell us why people do or do not get married. An ethnography of the kibbutzim wouldn't tell us much about people's inner states, even if such an ethnography were possible or ethical. By simply talking to people, Shor and Simchai were able to find out more than researchers using any other technique.

CAPTURING THE VOICES OF THE UNDERPRIVILEGED

Qualitative interviews are especially useful in capturing the perspectives and experiences of less privileged members of society. With most members of society, we can find out something about their experiences by looking at public records or media reports, but these sources don't cover everyone.

Eric Klinenberg—Heat Wave (2003)

In July 1995, Chicago experienced the worst heat wave in the city's recorded history, with temperatures of 106 degrees Fahrenheit and a heat index (a measure which takes humidity into account) of more than 125 degrees Fahrenheit. It was so hot that the streets buckled, and people opened more than 3,000 fire hydrants to try to cool down, causing a loss of water pressure for much of the city. It was so hot that fire departments hosed down children riding in school buses. You might think that air conditioning would help, but many of the city's poor simply didn't have air conditioners (ACs), and within a day or so, there weren't any ACs to buy. Even those who had ACs weren't necessarily better off. Since everyone was using them, power failures were rampant. Such intense heat causes vulnerable people's immune systems to shut down, leading to death. Hospitals—and morgues—were soon overwhelmed, and paramedics who found someone in need of medical help sometimes drove for hours looking for a hospital that could take the patient. The heat wave was only predicted to last for a few days, but it stretched on for a week. By the end of that week, more than 500 people—and perhaps as many as 700— had died as a result.

Klinenberg, a sociologist at NYU, used a combination of archival research and in-depth interviews to try and uncover why these deaths were spread so unevenly throughout the city. For instance, most of the victims were elderly, but men were far more likely to die than women, and African Americans were more likely to die than whites. Hispanics, while no better off financially than African Americans, and, on average, in worse health, were far less likely to die:

while Hispanics account for a quarter of Chicago's population, they were only 2 percent of deaths.

Eric Klinenberg's (2003) interviews reveal that the deaths weren't caused by the heat nearly as much as social isolation. Elderly women were less likely to die because they kept up social relationships: someone called, visited, got them to a cooling center or hospital, or invited them to an air-conditioned house. Elderly Hispanics were less likely to die because they lived in parts of Chicago with more of a street life (not because of tighter familial relationships, as many at the time suggested). If their apartments were too hot, they could walk somewhere close by. Elderly African Americans, on the other hand, tended to live in areas where the streets were deserted, where stores had given up. If no one came to get them, they had nowhere to go. Many of them died locked in their own apartments, afraid to go outside. The killer, Klinenberg argues, wasn't the weather; it was social and geographical isolation.

It's easy to think that today, with advanced telecommunication technologies, people's lives are basically open books, but Klinenberg (2003) shows that this really isn't the case. There were whole groups of people shut inside of their own apartments, dying in the heat, and the outside world had no way of knowing that they were even there. When researchers can't rely on official sources to give them insight into these marginalized members of society, in-depth interviews may be the best way to go.

STRUCTURING THE INTERVIEW

When carrying out surveys (as discussed in detail in Chapter 10), interviewers are supposed to stick to the wording of the script exactly and are provided with detailed directions to cover any contingencies. This is necessary since the aim of surveys is to get comparable information from a large number of different respondents. However, the aim of in-depth interviews is quite the opposite. Instead of gathering short but comparable information on a large body of respondents, in-depth interviews try to elicit detailed information from a few respondents. As such, in-depth interviews don't start with a set of carefully worded, closed-ended questions. Rather, they use a list of open-ended questions so respondents aren't constrained by the answers that the researcher is expecting. For instance, a political survey might ask respondents which issue in an upcoming election is most important to them and give a few options to choose from. A researcher in an in-depth interview might ask the same question, but rather than listing the options, the researcher would allow the respondents to give whatever responses they wanted. The point of an in-depth interview is to be as conversational as possible. Instead of having an interviewer and a respondent, qualitative interviews should be like two people taking and exploring a topic. Like participants in ethnographies, participants in interviews may initially be reluctant to open up. The more the interview seems like a conversation—and the more comfortable it is—the sooner the participants will open up.

For this purpose, interviewers employ two central tools: **probes** and **follow-up questions**. Probes are typically used to get the respondent to talk and elaborate a little more on the issue. In some cases, respondents may be shy or are not as talkative as the researcher would like. Probes can be used in those circumstances to get respondents to talk more and provide more data. Researchers commonly use probes such as:

> Could you tell me more?
> Would you give me an example?
> Can you elaborate on that idea?
> Would you explain what you mean by that?
> Could you explain that? I don't think I understand what you mean by...
> Could you talk some more about...

Probes can also be used to remedy the opposite problem. Sometimes respondents are very talkative and go off topic. Probes can be used to get these respondents back on track without offending them or introducing unneeded artificiality into the interview.

> Could you come back to the point you mentioned about...
> Could I stop you for a second?

In addition to probes, follow-up questions are essential when designing a qualitative interview. They are good alternatives to probes; interviewers ask respondents to share more information through a series of more specific questions. Especially when they follow "yes/no" questions, follow-up questions give respondents the opportunity to walk interviewers through a process or explain some points in greater detail.

The order of questions is also important to maintain the conversational tone of the interview. When ordering questions, researchers generally start with easier questions and build up to more difficult, personal questions. As the interview goes on, participants generally become more comfortable and should be more willing to answer questions about sensitive topics. In addition, asking people about sensitive topics at the beginning of an interview can lead them to quickly cancel the interview. Even if the interview is canceled once sensitive questions begin, it's better if it occurs at the end of the interview than at the beginning.

In terms of the phrasing of questions, many qualitative scholars agree that the wording and phrasing should not be completely rigid and predetermined. Researchers should feel free to change the way that a particular question is phrased in order to make it better fit the interview up to that point or the respondent. As long as the information elicited by the question is the same, it really doesn't matter how the question is asked. In contrast, it would be disastrous to adopt such an approach in survey research, where every respondent must get the same set of questions. In interviews, though, researchers can use guidelines when determining how to phrase their questions.

Most important, researchers should rely on concrete observations rather than vague generalizations. By doing so, researchers get responses that are both more accurate and more specific. A researcher could elicit responses that are more useful by asking, "What did you do last Saturday?" versus "What do you do in your leisure time?" In response to the leisure time question, respondents might give the researcher a socially desirable answer and say what they think will make them look good in the eyes of the interviewer. Even if they aren't intentionally lying, respondents may decide that what they did last weekend, or most weekends,

---

The following excerpt is from a study on retirement. The researcher shows how to concert a raw interview into a written report.

Interview

Interviewer: What are your days like?

Respondent: Very quiet and uneventful.

Interviewer: Like yesterday, what, how did yesterday work? Maybe start in the morning.

Respondent: Well, I, I got up, had some breakfast I went out, ah, went out for about three or four hours and did a bit of window shopping, a little Christmas shopping. I got back around noon time or so. Ah, I had lunch, watched the news then just puttered around the house. Then I usually go to bed around 9 or 10 o'clock. I had supper and watched television for a while and then I usually go to bed. But, like I said, very unexciting, very uneventful.

Interviewer: If you wanted to describe a really boring hour and get across what it felt like and what was going on.

Respondent: Well I don't have a problem with that. I, ah, I can sit down and do absolutely nothing for an hour. And it does not bother me. I enjoy a chance to relax and not have the pressure of having to do something.

Report

Puttering is a relaxed way of moving through a attract one's day. engaging in activities as they attract one's attention, undertaking nothing that demands energy and concentration. The dishes need doing, so why not do them now? It's nice out, so a bit of gardening might be enjoyable. It's noontime, it's time for a sandwich and the news on television. Later, the magazines need to be picked up and room straightened. There is time for a bit of reading. Email may be checked, or an hour taken to organize the attic. Nothing has special urgency.

Retirees seem not to be bored by puttering. There is always something to fill time with, and the puttering is regularly interrupted by an activity to attend to, a hobby to pursue, a walk or a bit of shopping or coffee with a friend. Mr. Oldsten was among the many respondents who liked taking it easy. He had been the purchasing director for a high tech company, job that was frequently stressful. His wife was still employed and so he spent most of the day alone.

Source: Weiss, Robert S. 2004. "In their Own Word: Making the Most of Qualitative Interviews." *Contexts. Vol. 3. No. 4: 44–51.*

isn't representative of what they "really" do. By asking about last Saturday instead, the researcher is likely to get closer to what the respondent really does over the weekend. If what they did last Saturday wasn't typical, the respondent will likely explain why it isn't. Asking specific, concrete questions gets the researchers closer to the lived experience of the respondent, which is, after all, the goal of qualitative research.

In the excerpt above, note how the interviewer goes from a relatively vague question—"What are your days like?" to a very specific one, "How did yesterday work? Start in the morning." The latter question elicits a much longer, more detailed answer—one that gets the researcher much closer to what the respondent's life is really like.

Also, bear in mind that interviews are not a substitute for the sort of ethnographic observations that were discussed in the last chapter. As in an ethnography, researchers carrying out interviews must make sure to use all of their senses, as well as their observations of their own feelings about the person being interviewed and the environment where the interview takes place. These informal fieldnotes are often just as important as the interviews, so researchers should try to take as many notes as possible. Some researchers are worried about taking too many notes; others worry about the opposite. When in doubt, more notes are always better than fewer notes. A researcher can always decide later not to use some of the notes, but he or she may not know until the end of the research what topics will, and will not, prove to be important. These fieldnotes are helpful in understanding and interpreting the interviews.

INTERVIEW LOGISTICS

Interviewer Training

It isn't always possible for a single researcher to carry out all of the interviews personally. There might be too many respondents for one person to deal with, or the interviewer might be worried about reactivity arising from the gender or race of the interviewer, necessitating interviewers from various backgrounds. The researcher might be interested in talking to respondents in different cities or different continents. Whatever the reason, researchers sometimes need to train others in how to conduct in-depth interviews. Since in-depth interviews are conversational in tone and more interactive, the training of interviewers is crucial. Also, the sort of training that interviewers need to successfully carry out in-depth interviews is the same that novice researchers need to carry out their own interviews.

The key skill interviewers need to carry out qualitative interviews is the ability to keep the conversation going, to ensure that the interview is able to hit all of the topics of interest. First, the role of the interviewer is to establish rapport with the participants. If the rapport is not strong, respondents won't be willing to divulge the sort of detailed or sensitive information that makes these interviews worthwhile. In addition, the interviewers should be trained to practice active listening to provide follow-up questions as well as probes to get the interview back on track, if necessary. Oftentimes in a conversation people are more focused on what they're going to say next than what the person in front of them is actually saying. Having an ordered list of topics and questions means that the interviewer doesn't have to worry about the next question and can engage fully in what's being said. This can be difficult, especially when the interview veers into controversial topics, but it is especially important when dealing with sensitive areas.

When doing these interviews, researchers can be tempted to express agreement with the respondent. This can help the conversational tone and build rapport, but, unfortunately, it can also introduce bias into the findings. Although disagreeing with respondents can lead to problems of reactivity in the findings, agreeing with them can be just as harmful.

The best way to train interviewers in these techniques is through practice. Mock interviews, often with people pretending to be uncooperative, can be useful. Other researchers monitor these interviews and offer pointers. It can also be helpful for novice interviewers to observe more experienced interviewers in the field and discuss their techniques before going into interviews alone.

Transcription Software

Once the interview process is complete, researchers need to transcribe the interviews. **Transcription** refers to the process of converting audio files to written ones. Though audio recording makes it easy to record interviews, transferring audio-recordings into written documents is often time consuming. Transcription can be done manually. There are also many companies that provide professional transcription services, often for a significant fee.

In recent years, computer-assisted transcription has become a useful tool for researchers as well. As recently as ten years ago, computer transcription was bad enough to be basically worthless for researchers, but some products (the best known of which is Nuance's Dragon) are now available for around $100 and can be of significant help in transcription. In some cases, they're even accompanied by smartphone apps, which can carry out many of the same functions anywhere there's a wireless connection. Such software isn't a panacea, though. Most are voice dependent, meaning that researchers often end up reading and recording the interviews again, in their own voices, before using the software. In addition, the software needs to be monitored during the transcription process so that the researcher can correct any errors the computer makes. Still, programs like these can significantly reduce the amount of time that it takes to transcribe interviews, for much less than it would take to hire an outside professional transcription service.

Coding

After the interviews are transcribed and are written in text form, the next step is coding. **Coding** refers to the systematic process of categorizing the findings. First, the researcher determines the **coding categories.** Coding categories are the words or concepts that the researcher is looking for in interviews. For example, in Besen-Cassino's (2014) in-depth interviews with young baristas, she wanted to find out why they worked, particularly their nonmonetary reasons for working. As such, some of the coding categories were money, discounts, meeting new people, seeing friends, and fashionability of the brands. The process for determining coding categories is much the same as the process for creating a dictionary in content analysis, as described in Chapter 8.

Researchers can also make use of software that automates this sort of coding. Packages such as Dedoose or MAXQDA can look for patterns in interviews and even link the interviews with other data that's been collected about respondents. For instance, they could tell a researcher if certain responses are more prevalent among women or if respondents who make one sort of response often make a related one as well. These packages have also become much less expensive in recent years. While they aren't a replacement for careful data analysis, they can make that analysis easier.

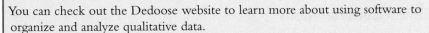

You can check out the Dedoose website to learn more about using software to organize and analyze qualitative data.

www.dedoose.com

You can check out MAXQDA and take free online tutorials to learn how to use the software to organize and tabulate qualitative data.

www.maxqda.com

ADVANTAGES AND DISADVANTAGES

In-depth interviews provide very rich, detailed information. Because they consist of open-ended questions, they allow researchers the chance to uncover information that doesn't fit into preconceived categories. These interviews are also the best way to understand the everyday experience of participants, especially individuals whose lives aren't included in public narratives.

As we saw in the kibbutz example, there are many research projects for which observational data just does not suffice. During in-depth interviews, participants can walk interviewers through their reasoning, describe a process, or elaborate further on a topic. Since the tone of the interview is conversational, the researcher can go back and ask for clarification. It is also advantageous because carrying out interviews is relatively inexpensive. While specialized software and equipment can be useful, it's far from necessary, and anyone with a recorder and a computer can do a good job of interviewing.

Unfortunately, getting detailed information is time consuming. In-depth interviews often take a very long time: several hours per interview. Also, since the tone of in-depth interviews is conversational, the interviews could easily get off topic, leaving the researcher with information he or she is not necessarily interested in.

The biggest challenge for researchers pursuing in-depth interviews is building rapport with participants so that participants feel comfortable enough to speak candidly. As such, in-depth interviews are used in conjunction with ethnographies. During an ethnography, researchers spend long hours with the participants; this establishes the rapport that allows them to effectively conduct the in-depth interviews.

Finally, in-depth interviews are not generally designed to be representative of a population. Because researchers will rarely talk to a random sample of people, the responses that they record can't necessarily be applied to people not included in the sample. Even if all participants in Shor and Simchai's (2009) research said that they had been attracted to others within their kibbutz, it wouldn't mean that all people are attracted this way. These interviews can't tell us about the wider population, but they can tell us about processes—about how things work—and that's often just as valuable.

Ethical Considerations

In-depth interviews gather a large amount of information from each participant, and since the researcher is conducting the interviews face-to-face, participants cannot be anonymous. The researcher knows who gave the information and has to take careful steps to protect the identities of the respondents. For instance, the real names of respondents should be replaced with pseudonyms, even in the audio or video recordings and fieldnotes created by the researcher. To further protect the identities of the respondents, the researcher should be careful to avoid revealing too much detail in any publicly available version of the data or results and should make sure to destroy recordings once transcription is complete.

FOCUS GROUPS

A **focus group** is a qualitative technique in which a group of participants is asked to discuss an issue together. As with in-depth interviews, researchers using focus groups strive to create a conversational tone, one that's reflective of the actual social dynamics underlying an issue. In-depth interviews try to uncover the lived experience of one individual, including things that particular respondent wouldn't want to share publicly. Focus groups, on the other hand, try to uncover the social dynamics of a topic, to see how people talk or think about issues in a group context.

Erica Chito Childs—Black Women and Interracial Relationships (2005)

While the rate of interracial marriages has increased significantly over the past few decades, marriages between African Americans and whites remain relatively rare. As of the 2000 census, 1.2 percent of all marriages in the United States were between whites and Asians. Only 0.06 percent of marriages were between whites and African Americans, and about 70 percent of these were between African American men and white women. This raises two interesting issues. First, within the African American community, the lack of eligible men is seen as a real problem, so why don't more African American women marry men from different racial backgrounds? Second, given that eligible men are seen as a scarce resource within the African American community, how does the African American community view men who choose to marry outside of their race?

Media portrayals of African American women show them as intransigently against interracial relationships, blaming white women for stealing the best men and the African American men for falling for it. Spike Lee movies, however, aren't research, and Erica Chito Childs (2005) set out to analyze how African American women actually viewed these relationships.

To do so, she convened focus groups of African American women at three different American universities, as well as carried out in-depth, semi-structured interviews with four African American women who were married to white men, with each interview lasting two to three hours. The focus groups consisted of between seven and twelve women. Childs (2005) began each session by having the participants introduce themselves and give a little background about themselves before she described the rules for the focus group. In focus groups, participants are typically told that the goal of the group is to facilitate discussion about a topic, that all of their ideas are valid and important, that their identities will be kept entirely confidential, and that they should be respectful of each other's views and opinions. Generally, participants then sign a consent form before beginning the discussion, including notification that the discussions will be recorded.

In Childs' (2005) focus groups, she began by prompting the women to discuss any experiences that they had with interracial relationships, their views of such relationships, and how they perceived the views of the African American community on such relationships. Participants also asked Childs (who is of Portuguese descent) why she was interested in the issue, leading her to disclose that she is married to an African American man and has mixed-race children.

None of the women in the focus groups admitted that they were involved in an interracial relationship (given their rarity, this was likely true), and Childs (2005) reports a consensus among the groups that such relationships were problematic, with participants saying things like "Blacks just like to see other Blacks, especially Black men who are successful, to stay Black, to be with a Black woman," and that they "would be uncomfortable knowing someone who dated a white person because whites just don't understand Blacks." They also said that their families and friends wouldn't support or understand a decision to be in a relationship with a white man.

According to the women in the focus groups, much of this opposition is based on the continuing problem of racism. If white people are biased against African Americans, why in the world would an African American want to be in a relationship with a white person? As such, the women in the focus groups tended to argue that African American men who chose to be with white women were, in some way, less tied to their communities than other African Americans. As one woman said, "Black men who are with white women are also usually submerged in white culture and have white friends." Another said, "Black guys who act white do tend to date white girls." A choice to be in a relationship with white women, in their view, is a betrayal. The men aren't just choosing to be with a white woman; they're rejecting African American women and the larger African American community. "It's dating outside of your race for a purpose," one woman said. "Black guys want their laundry done, homework done, food cooked, guys tell Black women off because they won't do their shit." African American men, according to the focus groups, "feel that white girls are easier, sexually loose, and on the flip side that Black women are too aggressive, too controlling, have an attitude."

Of interest, the women seemed far more accepting of African American women dating white men, saying things like "When I see a Black girl with a white guy, I think it must be love; he must be doing something right for her to cross over like that," and "A Black woman with a white man can go further, and there's not the same idea that she's going to desert the African-American community." They also told Childs (2005) that skin color had a different meaning for African American men and women: women with darker skin are less desirable, but skin tone doesn't matter for men.

The women Childs (2005) talked to in her interviews told her that they felt the same sorts of pressures against their relationships that the women in the focus groups had discussed. They said that their families had reservations about the relationships, mostly on the basis of the belief that whites were racist. They reported that other African American women had been hostile toward their relationships and even acknowledged that they had felt that they were selling out their own community.

Childs (2005) concludes that much of the media portrayal of African American women's views of interracial relationships are accurate: they do oppose these relationships and have very negative views of individuals who engage in them. These views, however, seem to be more focused on the effects of the relationship on the community, rather than the impact of the relationships on them personally.

Most of the time, when researchers want to study the views of members of a subpopulation, they make use of surveys, but this wasn't possible or desirable in Childs' (2005) case. A survey would have been very difficult to carry out because the population of African Americans married to whites is small, and contacting enough of them for a reasonable sample would be cost prohibitive, even if such a sample could be obtained. When researchers can't obtain a large, random sample of a population, they often turn to in-depth interviews in order to at least gather very detailed information about a smaller, nonrandom group, as Childs did. So why, then, would Childs go to the trouble of supplementing her in-depth interviews with a series of focus groups?

WHY FOCUS GROUPS?

Focus groups are similar to semi-structured interviews but are carried out in a group context. Just as in semi-structured interviews, the researcher (in focus groups, the researcher is sometimes referred to as a **moderator** or *facilitator*) comes in with a series of questions that are designed to prompt discussion in the group. The goal of these questions is to get the participants to talk and interact with each other as much as possible. During the course of the focus group, the job of the researcher is twofold. First, the researcher has to ensure that no individual in the focus group dominates the discussion and that every member of the group contributes to the discussion. Generally, researchers avoid cutting anyone off in the discussion, but they do cut in to ask for a different participant's input. Second, the researcher must try to keep the discussion on track to the greatest extent possible. Focus group discussions are semi-structured, not structured, interviews, so it's acceptable for participants to take the discussion in a direction other than what the researcher had originally anticipated. However, the researcher has to bring the group back from such tangents if the participants get too far away from the questions or time is an issue. The researcher has to make sure that the group gets through all of the questions before time runs out. Oftentimes, the prompts used by the researcher involve asking a general question, then asking participants to comment on what the other participants said.

In Childs' (2005) focus groups, the questions were about general topics: asking participants if they had ever been in or known someone in an interracial relationship, asking how they felt about other women engaging in these relationships. Once one of the participants responded to these questions, Childs would move the conversation around the room and bring in any participants who hadn't commented. If one of the participants said something especially interesting, she would ask others for their response to it. In a semi-structured interview, when a participant makes an interesting comment, the researcher asks him or her to expand on it. In a focus group, when a participant makes an interesting comment, the researcher asks someone else to expand on it.

The problem with focus groups is that participants may feel much greater pressure to conform to societal expectations than they would in an individual interview. In an interview, the participant may be worried, even subconsciously, about what the researcher wants to hear, and it's the job of the researcher to make the participant feel more at ease and minimize any reactivity. In a focus group, putting participants at ease is much more difficult because they are talking to a group of their peers. Therefore, if a researcher wants to know what an individual thinks, focus groups are not the way to go. However, if the researcher wants to know the opinions of a particular community, focus groups are often appropriate. Childs' (2005) research question wasn't about what the individual African American women thought about interracial relationships. She wanted to understand how the African American community treated women in interracial relationships. If she had been given a choice between knowing views that the women had but were afraid to express in front of their peers and hearing things that they would say in a group but didn't actually believe, she would prefer the latter. This isn't always the case, but when it is, focus groups may be the best way to go.

As in any qualitative research, reactivity can be a problem, as it was for Childs (2005). In her focus groups, she tells us that participants asked her why she—an apparently white woman—was asking a room full of African American women about interracial relationships. This is potentially a problem in interviews as well, but focus groups often lead to a more pronounced "us versus them" dynamic. Participants in an interview setting may have reservations about the researcher, but the researcher has enough one-to-one interaction to be able to assuage these concerns. In a focus group, there isn't nearly as much individual interaction, and there's the added dynamic of the participants in the group bonding with each other, potentially in opposition to the researcher. To avoid such issues, the researcher should attempt to identify with the group as much as possible by using words such as *we* and *us*, rather than oppositional terms such as *you*. In addition, the researcher should try to be as demographically similar to the group as possible: a woman probably wouldn't be the best choice to run a focus group of men, or an African American to run a focus group of whites. Childs was able to overcome these issues and get the women in her focus group to open up despite their demographic differences (especially relevant when the discussion is about race), but she may have had an easier time if she had been African American herself.

FOCUS GROUP COMPOSITION

Any focus group is only going to be as useful as the individuals who are brought into it. While in-depth interviews might strive to find representative individuals—respondents whose experiences mirror that of the larger population—the composition of focus groups is generally much more deliberate. Since the goal of a focus group is to look at how issues play out in a social context, it's important that the group be composed to look something like society. If an issue is controversial, a focus group that is entirely on one side of it isn't going to be very informative; on the other hand, a focus group made of people who are at each other's throats won't tell the researcher very much either.

Maggie Evans and Colleagues—Parents' Perspectives on Immunizations (2001)

In the past 20 years, the percentage of parents who are immunizing their children against childhood diseases such as measles, mumps, and rubella has fallen dramatically. Not too long ago, these diseases were unheard of in wealthy nations, but the decline in immunizations has led to a resurgence in these illnesses. Perhaps more important, public health researchers are worried about herd immunity—as long as a certain proportion of a population is immunized against a disease, it's okay if some people aren't because the disease won't be able to spread. If too many people aren't immunized, the whole population is at risk, sometimes even those who have received the vaccine.

As this trend began to take hold in the late 1990s, researchers such as Maggie Evans, a researcher at the University of Bristol, and her colleagues tried to find out why more parents were refusing immunizations. To do so, they held six focus groups, with four to nine participants in each. Because they wanted young parents—the type of people who are making decisions about immunizations—

Evans and her colleagues (2001) provided child care for the hour or two that each discussion lasted. This is actually an important step: researchers using focus groups always try to make the participants feel comfortable, providing informal settings, snacks, and whatever participants need to feel at ease. For young parents, not having children running around is crucial. Evans and her colleagues recruited the parents from community groups in two English towns and made sure to include individuals from a variety of socioeconomic backgrounds.

Evans and her colleagues (2001) divided individuals into focus groups based on their vaccination decisions: three of the groups were composed of participants who had vaccinated their children, and three were composed of participants who had not. This is not because society was split about evenly on the subject—the vast majority of parents still vaccinate their children—but rather to ensure that participants would speak freely.

In each focus group, the researchers had a moderator and an assistant. The focus groups were semi-structured, with the moderator asking a series of open-ended questions to the group, making sure that everyone responded and also allowing participants to talk about any related issues that were important to them. Once the focus groups were completed, the researchers transcribed the recordings and began examining the transcripts, defining various themes as they went. (This process of emergent coding is described in detail in the Chapter 8.) They then had various members of the research team independently analyze the transcripts according to these themes and made sure that everyone found the same things in the transcripts.

Once the analysis was done, the researchers compared the statements of immunizing and nonimmunizing parents to find any differences in their statements on the various themes. They found that nonimmunizing parents understood that their children were at risk for contracting a disease but felt that nothing too bad would happen and that having childhood diseases was somehow good for the children. They also found that both sets of parents tended to distrust government reports on the subject and that they felt that doctors were unwilling to talk to them about the subject.

The researchers concluded that since parents felt they couldn't get trusted information from the government, and couldn't talk to their doctors about immunizations, they were turning to less reputable sources—mostly online—that were giving them the false idea that there was a real scientific controversy about vaccines, especially the MMR (measles, mumps and rubella) vaccine that some celebrities have claimed is linked to autism. To fix this, they recommend opening lines of communication and having government reports and flyers that take the issue seriously and report on the actual benefits and risks of these vaccines.

In order to find out why people were refusing to vaccinate their children, Evans and her colleagues (2001) had to balance two major concerns when populating their focus groups. First, they needed to ensure that all participants felt comfortable discussing their views on a difficult issue. They created separate focus groups for parents who had or had not vaccinated their children. If the groups had been mixed, it's likely that each group of parents would have spent the focus group defending their decisions and potentially challenging the decisions of the other group. In the real world, parents don't generally know whether other parents have vaccinated their children, so putting people into a situation where they do know this information may artificially create conflict. That's a fine strategy for *Jerry Springer*, but not so good for social science research. Because the groups were separated, participants did not have to defend their decisions. Many of the parents expressed regret or said that they had been bullied into their vaccination decision. Because they knew that everyone in the group had made the same decision, they didn't worry about being judged.

Second, Evans and her colleagues (2001) needed the focus groups to represent a cross-section of society. While these focus groups weren't intended to be representative of the whole British population in the same way that a survey is, the researchers wanted to have some idea of whether socioeconomic status, education, and other factors mattered in how parents made decisions about vaccinations. If the researchers had selected participants through a random process, it's likely that the small groups wouldn't have included participants from all walks of life. Researchers can't simply trust that their focus groups will look like the population they're trying to study (as they often do in survey research), but must actively construct such groups. Often this means seeking out participants through community groups or schools rather than simply offering money, which tends to attract poorer people. To achieve diversity within a focus group, it's best to use a combination of recruitment techniques.

Typically, focus groups consist of five to twelve people. Having fewer participants can allow one or two strong personalities to dominate the discussion. Having more participants makes it too easy for some individuals to get away without contributing to the discussion. It's also important to ensure that there aren't any preexisting power relationships within the focus group. It wouldn't be appropriate to have an employer and employee in a group together, or a teacher and student, or generally even people who know each other well. Focus groups require participants to openly state their opinions and engage with the opinions of others. Any relationship that might make participants less likely to do so is undesirable. Of course, some degree of inequality often arises during the focus group. Some participants talk more than others or have stronger opinions. These sorts of inequalities, though, can be remedied by an active moderator who makes sure that everyone's opinion is heard and that no one dominates the conversation.

ADVANTAGES AND DISADVANTAGES OF FOCUS GROUPS

Focus groups allow researchers to collect data from a group of participants. Compared to individual interviews, focus groups save time, and, in some ways, the two techniques are designed to do the same thing: let participants explain their decisions and views and walk the researchers through the process. Focus groups, however, add in a social element and can thus help researchers understand not only how participants feel about an issue, but also how they portray themselves and their decisions publically. This social aspect is why the technique is used so often by market researchers to test products and by political analysts to test political candidates and messages.

The group setting, however, can also leave some participants feeling intimidated. In some cases, especially when they're expressing what they perceive to be unpopular opinions, participants may be willing to talk in a confidential interview but not in a focus group. Furthermore, some of the opinions expressed in a group discussion might not accurately reflect individual opinions. Since the participants are artificially brought together, some of the opinions they express are context based and wouldn't necessarily be aired if the participants were alone. The social aspect that makes focus groups valuable to researchers can also distort what individual participants say. If an individual feels marginalized within the focus group, he or she may become more aggressive or defensive than would otherwise happen. If the participant feels that he or she is in accord with the other participants, he or she may exaggerate views that seem desirable to the group. Furthermore, focus groups tend to display a **polarization effect**, in which participants express more extreme opinions than they would in individual settings. While it is the job of the moderator to minimize these group effects, it's impossible to fully do so. Researchers should be careful not to conflate the views expressed in the focus group with participants' opinions outside of that context.

Ethical Concerns

Focus groups aren't as ethically problematic as some other research techniques, but they do raise a unique set of concerns. First, participants are being asked to express opinions in front of other people, and this may include unpopular views. Participants might reasonably be worried that they'll be judged for airing certain views (and the moderator may well be pressuring them to make those views known), so it's the job of the researcher to minimize any potential social consequences from the focus group. This means making sure that focus group members don't know each other, and it often means ensuring that everyone in a particular focus group is on the same side of an issue, as in the research that Evans and her colleagues (2001) carried out.

A second ethical concern arises from the fact that focus groups are typically video-recorded to allow the researcher to record any nonverbal communications (frowns, crossed arms, rolled eyes) and to make sure that statements are attributed to the correct participant. While this is useful, it also means that researchers need to be extra cautious to protect confidentiality. Of course, when reporting their findings, researchers change the names and all identifying characteristics of the participants, but they also need to ensure that no one outside the research team has access to the videos and that the videos are destroyed when the analysis is over.

Finally, since focus groups can be so time consuming and typically require that participants travel to a certain place at a certain time (in-depth interviews, in contrast, are generally scheduled for whenever the participant is available, near or in the participant's home), researchers often give participants prizes or honoraria. Offering small prizes or honoraria often helps increase response rates, but researchers should be certain to follow the guidelines for monetary coercion discussed previously. These issues can be minimized by keeping the honoraria and prizes small and making sure that participants know that they can leave at any time and still receive their full payment.

SUMMARY

While ethnographic research and focus groups can give researchers some traction in understanding the lived experience of the people they're studying, it's sometimes necessary to actually talk to people. This need is clearest when the research involves questions about things that happened in the past; internal states, which can't be directly observed; or the experiences of the underprivileged, which can't always be found in official records or public accounts.

When talking with participants, researchers make use of semi-structured interview techniques. Most of the questions are predefined, but there's room to explore certain topics in greater depth. Researchers also need to make judicious use of prompts and follow-up questions to get all of the relevant information and to keep the interview on track.

As valuable as interviews can be, researchers may be interested in the social dynamics of phenomena: how people act when they're in a group. In these situations, researchers often turn to focus group research, in which a facilitator or moderator conducts interviews in a group setting, making sure that everyone in the group contributes and no one individual dominates the discussion. When carrying out focus groups, researchers also have to be careful to avoid groupings that may lead to undue conflict or make individuals less likely to speak their minds.

Study and Review

Different research techniques often lead to different conclusions. Why did Shor and Simchai's (2009) conclusions about incest avoidance (and Klinenberg's [2003] work on the Chicago heat wave) differ so much from that of other researchers?

Under what circumstances can we trust the statements that individuals make during in-depth interviews?

Why is transcription of interviews necessary?

Why couldn't Childs (or Evans and her colleagues) have carried out their research with in-depth interviews?

CHAPTER 8
Content Analysis

Learning Objectives

- Be able to discuss the purpose of content analysis and identify research questions that require content analysis
- Be able to identify potential issues of validity in content analysis
- Be able to explain why content analysis is useful for the analysis of historical data
- Be able to explain the circumstances under which content analysis can be ethically problematic
- Be able to summarize the advantages and disadvantages of content analysis

STUDYING STATEMENTS

Steven E. Finkel and John G. Geer—The Effects of Attack Advertising (1998)

The research techniques discussed thus far use the responses of individuals—either directly or indirectly—as the source of their data, but not all research does this. Many research questions can be better answered by looking at communications: Internet postings, magazine or newspaper articles, photographs, diaries, or any way in which people transmit information to one another. These communications can be analyzed to reveal information about the people who made them or about society in general. The systematic study of these communications for research purposes is called **content analysis**, and while it may seem easier to carry out than many other types of research, its validity relies almost entirely on the care with which the analysis is done. Content analysis is unique in the sense that it is the only research technique in this book that does not collect information directly from people in the way that in-depth interviews, surveys, experiments all do. However, many research questions focus on media or other recorded information. Do cartoons promote aggressive acts? Is there a racial bias in the models used in advertising? How do newspapers frame gun laws? These questions cannot be answered by in-depth interviews, questions, or experiments. The only method that allows researchers to study recorded communications is content analysis. These recorded communications can come from a wide range of sources. Researchers can study any kind of communication: newspapers, television, online sources, magazines, novels, diaries, textbooks, historic documents, cartoons, television shows, movies, videogames, children's toys, literature, and poems. This chapter explores how content analysis is used to examine these sources and systematically analyze them.

One of the most fiercely debated questions in modern political science has been the effect of negative political advertising. Almost since candidates began using television ads in the 1950s, they've used negative ads to smear their opponents. Public opinion polls have shown that voters don't like these ads, and many candidates have claimed that they won't use them (often giving that promise up before the campaign ends). However unpopular these ads are, though, political strategists apparently think that they work because campaigns keep on using them. These strategists believe that negative ads will work by reducing voter turnout. Some people who would have voted for a candidate, they think, will see the negative ads and decide against voting for the candidate targeted in the ad. Alternately, some people who aren't paying much attention to the election might see a barrage of negative ads, decide that they don't want to have anything to do with the upcoming election, and stay at home on Election Day. These effects, if real, would be troubling because they would mean that some candidates could wind up benefiting from something that impairs democracy. Ideally, we want everyone to vote, so a process that drives down turnout is a bad thing. This model seems plausible. Since Presidential campaigns started using negative ads in the 1960s, overall voter turnout has generally been lower than in past decades.

The strongest findings in support of what's called the *demobilization hypothesis* (the expectation that negative ads will reduce voter turnout) come from research carried out by political scientists Stephen Ansolabehere, Shanto Iyengar, and their colleagues (1994) in a series of laboratory experiments and field studies. When participants in the laboratory are shown negative ads, they say that they're less likely to vote in an upcoming election. When they're shown positive ads, they report that they are more likely to vote. However, its clear that lab experiments aren't really the best way to carry out a study like this because of potential problems with external validity: if the ads aren't for real candidates, then participants in the study may respond to them differently than they would ads in a real campaign. Even if the ads are for real candidates, the laboratory setting itself might make people pay more attention to the ads than they would otherwise— and therefore magnify the effects of the ads. Moreover, who cares if the negative ads affect what people say they're going to do immediately after participating in an experiment? What really matters is what they actually do: vote or not.

Because of potential problems like this, Ansolabehere and his colleagues (1994) followed the experimental studies with analyses of actual turnout in the 1992 California State Senate elections. They found that State Senate races in which there was more negative coverage of the candidates in the media had lower turnout than those in which there was more positive coverage of the candidates. This appears to be strong evidence, but there's a problem. Ansolabehere and his colleagues just looked at the media coverage of the candidates, not the actual ads that the candidates ran, so the results don't necessarily tell us anything about the effects of ads. A candidate who was attacked left and right in the media may not have run – or been the target of – a negative ad. Second, the researchers looked at a very limited sample of ads: only State Senate races, only in California, and only in 1992. If that place and time are weird in any way, the researchers would have no way of knowing.

To get a broader view of the question of demobilization, Steven E. Finkel and John G. Geer (1998) use an archive of political advertising at the University of Oklahoma that contains the most complete collection of Presidential political ads available, dating back to 1960. They then analyze the contents of each advertisement, breaking each one down into individual statements, along the lines of "My opponent's policies led to increased inflation." For each statement, the researchers record who made the ad, whether the statement was negative or positive (this one would be negative), and what the topic was (in this case, inflation). To ensure that the statements are coded correctly, they have multiple researchers look at each statement independently and make sure that everyone agrees on how the statements should be coded. They then use all of the statements to create a score for negativity in the campaign. Next, they check to see if that score has any relationship to actual turnout in the Presidential election, either on the macro level (national voter turnout) or the micro level (individual decisions to vote or not vote). Unlike Ansolabehere and his colleagues (1994), Finkel and Geer (1998) find no effect of negative advertising on voter turnout in these Presidential elections. While some negative ads might lower turnout, Finkel and Geer argue that others might actually serve to increase turnout by making contrasts between the candidates more obvious or making people feel better about the candidate they've chosen by making the other candidate seem worse.

While it might seem as if the researchers are just disagreeing, there are good reasons why Finkel and Geer's (1998) findings about the effects of negative campaign ads might be more credible than those of Ansolabehere and his colleagues (1994). First off, Finkel and Geer use the ads themselves and can pinpoint exactly how negative the ads are. This is by no means a quick or easy process. Content analysis of this kind takes an enormous amount of effort to do correctly, but there's simply no other way to determine how positive or negative a campaign really is. Second, Finkel and Geer aren't limited to a set of races in one state at one time. Rather, they can use all of the Presidential elections since 1960, so if one year is unusual (and 1960, for instance, is an oddly positive year for ads), it doesn't throw off their results. Finally, Finkel and Geer's use of content analysis means that they're working with real-world ads and the real-world people who saw those ads. There's no question of the external validity of their research.

The type of research Finkel and Geer (1998) carried out (content analysis) has seen a significant resurgence recently, mostly because computers have made it relatively easy. Before modern computers and the availability of so many public records in electronic format, content analysis required a lot of time and resources. Today, the process can be quick, cheap, and easy. Content analysis was a popular technique in the early days of social science research, but it fell out of favor during the middle of the twentieth century, when behaviorism—the belief that internal states are irrelevant and only behaviors are worthy of analysis—held sway. Even after behaviorism largely died out, content analysis seemed less rigorous to many researchers than other, more quantitative approaches. Recent technological innovations have allowed content analysis to achieve the quantitative rigor demanded by modern social science.

Why Content Analysis?

Compared to most of the techniques discussed in other chapters, the results of content analysis may seem less compelling. Instead of measuring behaviors or attitudes, researchers are simply looking at what people say or write. How do researchers know if the results will be useful? Why bother with it at all?

First, language is important. By looking at what individuals say or write, researchers can examine subjective experiences and intentions in a way that may be impossible with other methods. Much of the research in the social sciences deals with how individuals socialize, communicate, persuade, or stereotype others—all things that can be measured indirectly with surveys or experiments but directly with content analysis.

Second, content analysis allows researchers to test hypotheses that other methods may not be able to. Carried out properly, analysis of an individual's speech can reveal far more about the inner thoughts and cognitive processes of that individual than the person may realize or intend to reveal. It can even tell about the impact of cultural norms on how an individual thinks, acts, and treats others, a process that's largely opaque to the individual.

Third, content analysis allows researchers to study participants who are unavailable or unwilling to be part of a study. There's no way to assess the effect of past campaign ads on voters without content analysis: the voters who the ads were designed to reach have grown older and possibly died. Similarly, content analysis has been used to look at the speeches of politicians currently in office. Maybe these studies could be done through an experiment, but it's unlikely that elected office holders would submit to research that could potentially lead to embarrassing results (though some political scientists had success in securing detailed interviews with members of parliament in newly democratized states in Eastern Europe in the early 1990s), or that they would have the time to be part of such a study even if they were willing. In many cases, content analysis of an individual's communications can be carried out decades after the fact, or even after they have died.

The real concern about content analysis is typically not its applicability but how well it's carried out. A sloppy content analysis—one that doesn't carefully define what's being coded, how it's being coded, or how the items were selected—doesn't tell us anything about the subject being addressed. Finkel and Geer (1998), like most researchers employing content analysis, used multiple coders and carefully trained them to ensure that all of them scored the same statements the exact same way. Researchers generally have to develop detailed guides for the **coding**, which tell the coders exactly what to look for in the statements. They also have to prepare a number of example passages for the coders to practice on, both to make certain that the coders are scoring the passages the way the researchers intended and to ensure that the coders are giving similar scores to the selected passages. If a large number of passages are being scored, the researchers should monitor the scores awarded by the coders to make sure that none of coders are trending much higher or lower than the other coders. If one or more of the coders are awarding scores that are too high or too low, the researchers can step in with additional training. Finally, if possible, many of the passages should be scored by several of the coders so that the researchers can measure how well the coders agree, a process we'll discuss shortly.

All of these procedures have the same goal: to remove as much subjectivity from the coding process as possible. Ideally, it shouldn't matter who scored the passage or when. Anyone receiving the same training and looking at the same passage should come to the same conclusion. This not only provides for replicability in the study (that is, any other researcher can follow the same steps and get the same results) but also provides evidence that the results of the content analysis are not a function of the individual coders, but rather of characteristics of the statement itself.

CONTENT ANALYSIS AND VALIDITY

Stan Weeber and Daniel Rodeheaver—Why Do People Join Militias? (2003)

Before the researcher can even begin the coding process, he or she first has to find the source of the data that will be used in the content analysis. For most research in the social sciences, the data is created with the research questions in mind. Survey researchers design and administer surveys; qualitative researchers visit the sites of the ethnographies they want to carry out. For the most part, though, researchers in content analysis must rely on existing data and generally sources that were never designed for analysis. As such, there are no clear boundaries on what constitutes useful data, and researchers must be very careful about determining the validity of the data that they make use of.

Stan Weeber and Daniel Rodeheaver (2003) faced such a challenge in their look into the American militia movement. The militia movement contains any number of separate, independent quasi-military groups operating outside of law enforcement or the military, who hold a strong belief that the government is illegitimate. The reasons for the perceived illegitimacy vary. Some militias believe that the government in Washington has been taken over by a world government seeking to destroy American independence; others believe it's being run by a Jewish cabal. The movement seemed to peak in the early 1990s with a series of armed stand-offs between militia groups and law enforcement agencies. Almost all of the engagements ended badly. The bombing of the Oklahoma City federal building by militia sympathizer Timothy McVeigh finally discredited the movement, but it has made a resurgence in recent years, especially after the election of Barack Obama.

From a sociological and political standpoint, these groups are interesting, but research on them has been limited for a number of reasons. Most important, they're secretive. If you believe that the government is out to get you, you probably wouldn't welcome a researcher who brings surveys or asks to conduct interviews. Researchers who carry out observations through less obtrusive means, such as participant ethnography, face real physical danger when they reveal their role as researchers. As a result, there are a number of unanswered basic questions about militias; for instance, why someone would choose to join such a group. Marxist theories would hold that militias are a form of lower-class resistance to capitalism, but the rhetoric of militia groups doesn't seem to support this theory. A resource mobilization approach would hold that militia members should expect some material gain from their membership, but this doesn't seem to match the goals or membership of the movement either.

Weeber and Rodeheaver (2003) argue that it makes more sense to study militias within the context of Neil Smelser's (1964) work on social movements. According to Smelser, social movements are the result of structural strain—combined with an existing belief system about who should be blamed for the strain and what should be done about it—and some sort of precipitating event that leads individuals to conclude that action is necessary. The difference between the models is important because they lead to different conclusions, not just about why the militias were formed in the first place, but also what can be done to mitigate the harm they cause and stop them from forming in the future.

To test the application of Smelser's (1964) model to militias, Weeber and Rodeheaver (2003) developed a strict functional definition of what constitutes a militia. They then downloaded the Usenet postings of these groups from a three-year period. From the Usenet postings, they were able to conclusively identify

171 members (all but one by name) as members of one of twenty-eight different militias scattered across the United States, most of them with large numbers of postings on the public web forums. The large number of postings bolsters the case that these users actually were militia members and not just people pretending to be part of the movement. It also means that the researchers could use all of the postings from one militia member to build an overall picture of that individual and see if the findings match Smelser's model. All told, Weeber and Rodeheaver downloaded 6,285 online documents, even though they only wound up using about 20 percent of these for their actual analyses. The rest didn't seem relevant to the hypotheses (discussion of survivalist techniques, meeting places, the relative quality of various weapons and explosives, and so on).

Weeber and Rodeheaver's (2003) functional definition of a *militia*

1. Puts combat scenarios/skills and weaponry plans into (at least) mock action
2. Has an identifiable territory in which members reside
3. Bases organizational philosophy on antigovernment rhetoric
4. Develops plans in case of government provocation
5. Considers extreme measures such as bombings and kidnappings
6. Considers using criminal means to acquire weapons and explosives

---

After downloading all of the relevant postings, Weeber and Rodeheaver (2003) converted the postings to Microsoft Word files. They then used text analysis software to identify postings with their key words and used the chunks of messages associated with those key words to find the postings that were relevant to their research questions. (We'll talk more about key words and dictionaries in content analysis later in the chapter.) Following Smelser's (1964) model, they looked for evidence of structural strain, a generalized belief system, and precipitating events.

While the researchers identified a number of different strains reported by the militia members, almost two-thirds of the strains mentioned had to do with the U.S. federal government, specifically fear that the government had become, or was becoming, oppressive or like the Soviet or Nazi states. However, the findings were not as clear-cut for the generalized belief systems. Of the 110 messages that included discussion of belief systems, only a few mentioned the "New World Order." Some mentioned alternate theories like the "Zionist Occupational Government," and others didn't seem to fit into a generalized framework at all.

The militia members showed more unanimity on what precipitating events led to their radicalization. More than three-quarters mentioned the firefights at Waco and Ruby Ridge, both incidents in which federal law enforcement used seemingly disproportionate firepower in response to armed groups, resulting in significant loss of life.

Weeber and Rodeheaver (2003) argue that the fact that the postings generally conform to Smelser's (1964) model gives insight into why these movements happen in the first place and how they can be prevented or mitigated. If structural strains and false beliefs about the American government are a necessary ingredient in the rise of militias, then greater transparency in government, especially among local law enforcement, may be able to help. If violent precipitating events have such an impact on how people view the government, then it may be in the best interest of law enforcement to avoid violent showdowns that can lead to radicalization.

> Experts who have been watching such developments say all this is leading one place—to the establishment of a genuine national police force. You can see it in the way the FBI now routinely interferes in local law enforcement affairs. You can also see it in the plans of big-government architects . . . who [have] urged that Treasury Department police agencies . . . be placed under the control of the Justice Department.

> I am scared that we are becoming a police state a la Nazi Germany or Stalinist Russia. I do not want to be slave labor, (post 238)

> I was . . . outraged when government forces firebombed an inner city neighborhood of Philadelphia in 1985, killing 11 . . . and then there are the countless murders and cover-ups by "law enforcement" that have become common-place in my community.

> the bulk of the . . . militias of the various United States have formed a grass roots response to . . . government-sponsored terrorism as well as the continued degradation of our constitutional rights at the hands of the current federal administration, (post 31)

The conclusions of Weeber and Rodeheaver's (2003) research are only valid to the extent that we believe that the researchers are analyzing the statements of actual militia members, that those militia members are generally representative of the movement as a whole, and that the militia members are telling us what they really think. The general anonymity of Internet postings can make it hard to determine validity. In Finkel and Geer's (1998) study, this wasn't an issue, as the advertising archive recorded *all* of the political ads shown, and there's no way that something that was never shown on television could have been included, as it never would have been taped in the first place. Weeber and Rodeheaver's (2003) situation, though, is much more typical: researchers don't have a comprehensive data source and may not be able to conclusively identify the individuals behind the communications being analyzed.

In such cases, there are a few guidelines that researchers can follow to ensure the greatest possible validity of their dataset. First, content analysis should generally avoid strategic communications. The goal of content analysis in the social sciences is normally to determine something about the underlying characteristics of the communicators, rather than the communications themselves. Researchers want to know *why* people join militias, not what members of militias say about why they joined. Weeber and Rodeheaver (2003) were generally able to overcome this problem by focusing on Usenet discussions, which group members used to communicate with each other rather than the outside world. Researchers probably wouldn't be able to tell much about militia members by looking solely at the statements that they made to the press or outsiders about their activities. In strategic communications, the individual making the statement is trying to make the listener believe or understand something. Individuals avoid topics that might make a listener suspicious or make the speaker seem strange. If the militia members were making statements to the general public, they probably wouldn't include anything about the New World Order or the Zionist government, regardless of how important they think these topics are. This is not to say that strategic communications are not interesting, but study of these communications generally falls under the rubric of communications research, rather than sociological, political, or psychological studies.

There is some evidence of bias in the Usenet posts that Weeber and Rodeheaver (2003) analyzed. Researchers who have conducted interviews with militia members have reported that many members point to specific personal events as critical to their antigovernment beliefs. For instance, they may have had their house foreclosed or lost custody of their children, and there are very few mentions of this sort of personal precipitating event in Weeber and Rodeheaver's data. This raises the possibility of self-presentation in the messages they analyzed, similar to the negative reactivity found in qualitative research. This gap wasn't especially problematic for Weeber and Rodeheaver because they were concerned with structural, rather than personal, explanations for militia formation, but it does point out the potential problems with content analysis of existing communications. Ideally, the fewer people who were intended to read the communication, the more valid the communication is as a representation of the individual making it. This helps to explain the long-standing interest among social scientists and historians in people's personal diaries. Researchers analyzing politicians might find rehearsed and scripted stump speeches less revealing than personal communications to constituents or spontaneous answers to questions.

Researchers should also work to ensure the representativeness of the individuals whose communications they are analyzing. Although it's almost impossible to get a simple random sample of individuals for content analysis as can be done for a survey, researchers should do everything possible to ensure that the communications being analyzed don't paint an overly biased view of the larger group being analyzed. In most cases, researchers will only be able to obtain communication from a subset of the whole population of interest. The results of the content analysis, then, are only applicable to the whole group to the extent that the sample from which the communications were taken is representative of the whole group. For their militia research, Weeber and Rodeheaver (2003) have to make the case that Usenet is a common form of communication among militia members, that it does not require any great technical knowledge or equipment, and that it can be assumed to be a valid representation of the movement.

Their analysis would be less valid if they were using communication that is less widespread, such as short-wave radio or fax chains. The best way to check on the representativeness of the sample is to match the characteristics of the sample with the demographics of the group being studied: more than 90 percent of the Usenet postings were from men, a figure that corresponds pretty well to the gender make-up of the militias. If only 70 percent of the Usenet postings were from men, it would be a sign that the postings weren't valid as a sample of the movement as a whole.

Finally, researchers in content analysis should generally begin with the largest possible universe of data and narrow the analysis down from there. Weeber and Rodeheaver (2003) were interested in the views of militia members, but they didn't examine all of the discussions from the militia Usenet boards. Rather, they narrowed their analysis down to those groups that they could verify were actual militias, and then down to the individuals who posted frequently enough to be conclusively identified as actual militia members. In this sort of process, the goal of the researcher is to strike a balance between the representativeness of the final sample and the certainty with which communications can be identified as valid representations of the group being studied. The final sample should be narrowed down enough to remove any communications from individuals who aren't actually members of the group, or who are making purely strategic communications, but not so much that the sample becomes nonrepresentative of the group being studied.

DICTIONARIES AND REPLICATION

Charis Kubrin—The Code of Gangsta Rap (2005)

Once researchers have determined an appropriate source for the communications to be analyzed, the next step is to build up a **dictionary**. In content analysis, the dictionary is the guide to coders to let them know how to classify the communications. Remember, one of the goals of content analysis is to ensure replicability: anyone who looks at the same communications with the same dictionary should come to the same conclusions as the researchers did. Also, having a clear dictionary ensures transparency in the content analysis. If a researcher draws a conclusion based on content analysis, readers and other researchers should be able to see exactly what factors led to that conclusion, and the dictionary is a big part of this process. Finally, this set of written guidelines helps researchers ensure that the way they code communications doesn't shift over time.

Gangsta rap, a subgenre of rap music that first gained prominence among California-based performers in the early 1990s, has been seen as problematic by the law enforcement community and even Congress. Earlier forms of rap music had political and social messages about life in African American communities, but gangsta rap has a strong focus on violence and criminality. Criticism of it has focused on the extent to which it glamorizes violence and the degradation of women.

Charis Kubrin (2005), a professor of Criminology at George Washington University, argues that the function of gangsta rap is to provide a context within which listeners can understand the violence that goes on in their neighborhoods, particularly through the communication of a "street code." This code is a set of beliefs about when violence is acceptable and how that violence should be understood. Based on previous ethnographic work, Kubrin broke down the street code into six themes: respect, violence, material wealth, violent retaliation, and nihilism. She looked for these themes in all of the rap albums that went platinum (sold over a million copies) between 1992 and 2000. She explains that she looked at all of the albums, rather than just the gangsta rap albums, because albums often contain tracks from various genres. She excluded compilations and soundtracks. She says that she ended the analysis in 2000 because the genre became much more commercialized and therefore more divorced from the experience of individuals.

This netted a total of 130 albums and around 2,000 tracks, of which Kubrin (2005) randomly selected one-third for coding. After reviewing about 350 songs, though, Kubrin didn't find any new aspects of the street code in the lyrics. She listened to another 53 songs, then terminated the coding. In the first stage of the coding, she listened to a song in its entirety while reading the lyrics. She then listened to the song again, coding each line for the presence of one of the six themes of the street code. She allowed each line to have more than one theme if necessary. When she was unsure of the meaning of a phrase, she consulted online rap and hip-hop dictionaries to determine the meaning. This allowed her to match the themes of the street code with categories in the songs. The validity of the research, though, depends on the confidence we have in these **coding categories**.

After the initial coding, Kubrin (2005) brought in another researcher to code a subset of the songs in the same way. The other coder looked at sixty-four of the songs. The results of the two codings were compared; Kubrin and the other coder agreed about the presence of the themes in a given song between 70 and 88 percent of the time.

Three of the elements of the street code (respect, violence, and material wealth) were mentioned in the majority of the songs, with violent retribution, nihilism, and objectification mentioned in 35, 25, and 22 percent of the songs, respectively. Songs that featured themes of respect often had the message that disrespect is grounds for violence. Moreover, the rapper often noted that if he failed to retaliate for a lack of respect, he would lose face in the eyes of those around him. Lyrics such as these are an attempt to communicate what constitutes acceptable behavior, list consequences for violations of this code of behavior, and give examples of what's happened in the past to people who violated the code. The violence, according to the lyrics of the songs, is justified by the actions of the victim.

Note that Kubrin (2005) isn't arguing that the stories told by the rappers reflect the real experiences of the rappers, or even real experiences on the streets that the rappers may or may not have actually come from. It's enough to show that there is a code of behavior and that the songs are communicating this code of behavior. Even if the songs exaggerate, there are real consequences to their messages. As Kubrin notes, witnesses to crimes in inner city neighborhoods often refuse to come forward to identify the criminals or tell the police what happened. This may be understandable in the face of entire songs about how talking to the police is a serious offense that justifies killing the "snitch."

> The following songs express the necessity of violent retribution. You can easily find their lyrics online.
> Ice Cube, "Ask About Me."
> Juvenile, "Guerilla"
> 2Pac, "Only Fear of Death"

Kubrin's (2005) findings about gangsta rap reflect some of the negative views that are popularly held about the medium. It does frequently portray violence—and portrays that violence as justifiable, even in response to relatively small slights. On the other hand, objectification and degradation of women was encountered much less than outside observers might otherwise expect, with only about one in four of the songs sampled mentioning it. However, these findings are only valid to the extent that we believe that the songs were coded properly. There is some prima facie evidence that Kubrin's codings hold up because the second coder agreed with her codings most of the time, though the level of concurrence isn't quite as high as we might like. (We'll talk about intercoder reliability later in the chapter.)

If all we had to work with were general descriptions of the categories without any sort of dictionary, it's not clear if we would be able to code the lyrics and come to the same conclusions that Kubrin (2005) did. For instance, take the last theme in the street code: nihilism. Traditionally, nihilism refers to a philosophy that in some way negates the meaningful aspects of life and existence. It's unlikely that the rappers in Kubrin's dataset are quoting Immanuel Kant or nineteenth-century Russian novelists, so the reference would almost certainly have to be indirect: something about meaninglessness. But without a more complete definition, coding would be difficult or impossible. In the box are four songs used in Kubrin's published papers on the topic. Find the lyrics online. Without a functional definition of nihilism, which songs would you code as nihilistic?

> Nihilism or not? Find the lyrics to these songs online, then decide if they reflect nihilism.
> 2Pac, "Only God Can Judge Me"
> Notorious B.I.G., "Ready to Die"
> C-Murder, "How Many"

Once we have a dictionary with a functional definition of nihilism to guide the coding, we can easily identify how the passages should be coded. Kubrin's (2005) functional definition of nihilism is that the lyrics must evoke a "bleak outlook on life, perceived or real sense of powerlessness, frustration and despair, fear of death or dying and resignation or acceptance of death."

In the first song, 2Pac mentions death and potentially a fear of dying (if he doesn't kill the other man first), but he doesn't express a sense of powerlessness, frustration, despair, or resignation that death is inevitable. On the contrary, he can avoid death if he takes action. Parts Notorious B.I.G.'s "Ready to Die" would certainly be coded as showing nihilism: he's ready to die, can't be saved, and as close to acceptance of death as could be imagined. In other parts of the song, he shows a bleak outlook, not because of powerlessness or fear of death, but because he's about to shoot someone at point-blank range. In the C-Murder song, the rapper says that he never had a choice about being a criminal, that he got advice about killing from his father, and that he keeps an extra clip of ammunition so he can shoot more people—but never that he's helpless, despairing, or resigned.

This is why having a dictionary with functional definitions of the terms we're looking for in the coding is so important. Without a detailed definition of what *nihilism* looks like in these songs, there's no way that we could get agreement from multiple coders about what does or does not constitute it.

Arriving at these definitions can be time consuming, and there are essentially three ways to do it. The first is to adopt definitions that have been used by other researchers in the past. This is most useful in cases where there have been past content analyses of the same types of communications. It's rare, though, to have a past analysis of the same types of communications for which the functional definitions would be useful for testing a new set of hypotheses. The second way is using *a priori definitions*: creating functional definitions for the terms based on past research and what the researcher expects to find in the communications. These a priori definitions are set before the researcher actually looks at any of the data to be coded. Finally, researchers can build their definitions while going through the dataset based on what they actually observe in the communications—a strategy called *emergent coding*. This last strategy carries some dangers because researchers are more likely, even inadvertently, to build the definitions so that the data will better fit the hypotheses. In order to avoid this problem, researchers generally take precautions. Most important, they build the definitions from a *sample* of the data, rather than the entire dataset—a practice called *pilot coding*. That way, if there is bias in the definitions, that bias only applies to a subset of the data. Second, they make sure to base their definitions, whenever possible, on the functional definitions used by past researchers, as in the first strategy, even if these definitions are only used as a baseline. Finally, researchers should make sure to include the full definitions in the paper so that others can evaluate if the definitions are biased or not.

COMPUTERIZED CONTENT ANALYSIS

Sara Binzer Hobolt and Robert Klemmemsen—Public Opinion and Policy: Which Comes First? (2005)

All of the content analysis research that's been discussed so far has been carried out by individuals sorting through large amounts of data to find the elements in the communications that are significant for the hypotheses being tested. Some, like Weeber and Rodeheaver (2003), used computers at the start of their analysis to winnow down the amount of information that they would have to look through, but at the end of the day, humans did the reading. Until recently, this was probably the easiest way to carry out a content analysis: getting text into a computer was time consuming and tedious (Mosteller and Wallace [1964], discussed later in the chapter, needed punch cards to read all of their texts), and teaching a computer to do a search of that text required a degree in computer science. With the advent of the personal computer and the Internet, though, these problems have largely been overcome. Enormous amounts of research material are now available on the web, and anyone can use a program as basic as Microsoft Word to search for individual words or phrases in a document. As we've seen, though, content analysis generally requires that researchers do far more than simply count the number of words that show up in a communication. Rather, they need to see how these words are used in context. For individuals interested in carrying out content analysis using computers, there are many programs offering keyword-in-context analysis, or **KWIC**.

The most basic of these programs allows researchers to list keywords and select a set of documents to search. The program then generates a report showing the frequency of these keywords in each document and a sentence or two around each usage. Researchers can use this information in one of two ways. First, like Weeber and Rodeheaver (2003), they can use these reports to determine which documents are most likely to contain information relevant to their hypotheses— essentially using the KWIC search as a sieve to get rid of irrelevant data. Second, researchers can use the KWIC report as data in and of itself, using the frequency of the words within the various communications as a way to test hypotheses. This approach requires that researchers pay more attention to the keywords they establish for the search, generally through pilot coding, but it can make it possible to use far more communications than if humans had to read them.

Sara Binzer Hobolt and Robert Klemmemsen (2005) use the second approach in their study of the effect of public opinion on governmental priorities. This relationship seems simple: the public (as measured by public opinion polls) demands for the government to do something, and government officials respond by doing what the public wants. This simple relationship, however, is complicated by the fact that political leaders actively try to shape public opinion through speeches and ads. This question of causality—Is A causing B, or is B causing A?— can be resolved through the inclusion of a temporal element in the research. If the researcher can show that the shift in public opinion occurred first, followed by the shift in the positions of political leaders weeks or months later, he or she can prove that public opinion is driving the leaders' positions, and not the other way around.

To test this, Hobolt and Klemmemsen (2005) looked at the responses of Danish and British citizens to a "most important problem," or MIP, question. In the MIP question, which is widely used in political surveys around the world, respondents are asked to name the one issue that they feel is the most important problem facing the country at the time. This is an open-ended question, meaning that the respondents can say whatever they want, rather than being constrained by the categories set up by the survey. Hobolt and Klemmemsen recoded those responses into one of ten categories (for example, employment, environment, and foreign affairs).

The dependent variable in their model is the content of the annual speeches opening up the parliaments of the United Kingdom and Denmark. In both cases, the speech is written by the Prime Minister and his cabinet (though in the United Kingdom it's delivered by the Queen) and reflects the policies that the government in power hopes to get passed that year. The more important an issue is to the government, the more often it should be mentioned in that speech. So, if the political leaders are responding to public opinion, they should talk about the things that their citizens mentioned in earlier MIP questions. To test this hypothesis, though, Hobolt and Klemmemsen (2005) needed to carry out a content analysis of the speeches to determine the relative frequency of the various categories from the MIP. Because they looked at a large number of documents, they made use of computer analysis of the speeches. To start, they built a dictionary similar to the dictionaries used by researchers in more traditional content analysis. The major difference was that instead of building a specific functional definition for each term that they were interested in, they had to build a list of words that represented that term in the opening speeches. For example, they coded an opening speech as paying attention to "taxation" when the speech mentioned taxes, VAT (Value Added Tax, a kind of national sales tax used in European countries), public expenditure, budget, or other related terms. "Economics" was coded when the speech made reference to inflation, interest rates, trade, growth, or competitiveness. Of course, these sorts of terms show up in almost every speech; the key is the relative frequency with which they are mentioned. Economic terms might be mentioned in the opening speeches in both countries each year, but they'll be mentioned more some years than others, relative to the other terms the researchers are interested in.

To determine causality, Hobolt and Klemmemsen (2005) looked at the relationship between the two series of data: how many people mentioned a problem as the most important in that country and how much that term was mentioned in the opening speech. They then checked to see whether changes in public opinion moved before the opening speeches, or vice versa with a lagged regression model (a statistical technique that tries to establish Granger causation, as discussed in an earlier chapter). Their results show that in both countries the data is best explained by a model in which the opening speech is determined by the policy priorities of the public in the previous year (rather than the other way around or a longer lag in which the speech reflects what the public wanted two or three years ago). The Danish government seemed more responsive to the public's priorities than the British government—a difference the researchers attribute to differences in the way the governments are structured—and the responsiveness seemed lower in foreign affairs than in domestic policy. They caution that there may be a difference between what the governments try to do (as laid out in the opening speeches) and what they actually do, but the main finding remains that the public seems to be driving the government, rather than the other way around.

It would have been much more difficult for Hobolt and Klemmemsen (2005) to carry out their analysis without computer assistance. The key to their findings was the relatively small differences in the frequency of mentions of various terms between years. Traditional content analysis is well suited for finding the presence of a theme in a communication—as in Kubrin's (2005) work on rap lyrics—but it is not well suited for measuring the frequency with which that theme appears. A researcher may be able to code the presence of nihilism in a song but would not be able to code the relative frequency of nihilism. Is one song more nihilistic than another? How much more?

In addition, Hobolt and Klemmemsen's (2005) work required that they code *all* of the opening speeches, not just a sample of them. In traditional content analysis, the researcher only needs to code enough communications to be sure that there aren't any patterns being missed. Recall how Kubrin (2005) went through 350 songs, then stopped after not encountering anything new in the next 50 or so tracks. Hobolt and Klemmemsen needed the relative frequency of every set of terms in every year for their analysis, so a traditional content analysis (even if it was feasible) would have taken a great deal more time and effort.

The content analysis software that Hobolt and Klemmemsen (2005) used was relatively basic. The researcher can see when the keywords are used, and the context in which they are used, in order to make sure that the particular usage is relevant. For instance, one of the opening speeches might say, "The war is taxing our national resolve." Although the word *taxing* normally denotes a mention of economics, this is clearly a statement about foreign policy, and the researchers would only know this from seeing the word in context. There are also a number of much more sophisticated content analysis programs available. These programs often have predefined categories that may be of interest to researchers: self-centered versus group-centered language, passive versus active language, and so on. However, while it may seem that these programs would make a researcher's life much easier, caution should be exercised. In many cases, the dictionary that defines usage of these categories is proprietary. It's owned by the software company, and the users don't have access to it. If a researcher doesn't know how the program came to a conclusion about the frequency of a certain category, there's no way to check the results, and other researchers may be understandably skeptical.

CONTEXT UNITS

Linda M. Blum and Nena F. Stracuzzi—The Gendering of Prozac (2004)

The use of KWIC or a more sophisticated content analysis program involves a trade-off in the size of the **context unit** used in the research. Context units are the largest element of a communication that can be used to make a decision about coding. For instance, Kubrin's (2005) research coded each verse of a song to make a decision, while Finkel and Geer (1998) looked at individual sentences. If a rapper had a nihilistic outlook in the song as a whole, but one that couldn't be traced to any particular verse, the song wouldn't be coded as nihilistic. Computerized content analysis almost always relies on very small context units, on the level of a few words at most, and this can limit the types of hypotheses that can be tested. Neither Kubrin nor Finkel and Geer could have carried out their analyses with individual words as context units, but Hobolt and Klemmemsen (2005) *couldn't* have carried out their work with larger context units. The decision about what size context units to use is an important part of creating a dictionary for the context analysis, and researchers need to consider what works best with their hypotheses—and perhaps even carry out some pilot coding—before making a determination.

Linda M. Blum, a sociologist at Northeastern University, and Nena F. Stracuzzi, a sociologist at the University of New Hampshire, carried out a content analysis of eighty-three articles in large-circulation magazines between 1987 and 2000 that dealt with Prozac. When introduced in 1987, the antidepressant Prozac and similar drugs (collectively known as *selective serotonin reuptake inhibitors*, or SSRIs) quickly achieved widespread acceptance and even pop culture status, with bestselling books such as *Prozac Nation* (2002) and *Prozac Diary* (2011). Many feminist scholars, though, are wary of the gender content used to market and sell drugs. In the past, "hysteria" was used as a diagnosis for women who were unhappy. The word even comes from the Latin word for uterus. By definition, a man *can't* be hysterical. Later, Valium was portrayed as a drug women could take to repress their emotions and become more like men, therefore making them more successful in the workplace. In more recent years, drugs have been approved and sold for premenstrual dysphoric disorder (antidepressants to be used by women before their periods). Feminist theories refer to this as *heteronormativity,* or the medicalization of women. The differences between women's bodies and men's bodies are viewed as problems to be fixed, and if women don't fit into the roles society wants for them, medicine is used to make them fit. From such a perspective, Prozac could be seen as problematic. It could be that modern women have very good reasons to be unhappy with relationships, work, or their role in society, but instead of trying to fix the underlying causes, society medicates women so that they don't get upset about these problems.

To test this theory as applied to Prozac, it is necessary to actually see if Prozac is presented and discussed in a gendered manner. To do so, Blum and Stracuzzi (2004) used online indices to find articles in print magazines that discussed Prozac between 1987 (when Prozac was introduced) and 2000 (when the data was collected), yielding 149 articles. They then sorted out those articles that weren't focused on health or appeared in publications with a circulation of less than 100,000, leaving 83 for the analysis. Blum and Stracuzzi developed an a priori dictionary based on what they expected to find, then individually coded each of the articles. They compared their results to make sure that they were coding in about the same way.

Few of the articles analyzed mentioned that women were more likely to use Prozac than men, and the vast majority of the articles discussed the causes of depression in biological terms (talking about neurons misfiring) rather than more gendered talk about family relationships. Most of the articles even used gender-neutral terms such as *Americans* and *users* to describe the people taking Prozac. However, when the articles used narratives to describe the effects of Prozac on people's lives, the stories were highly gendered. Of the thirty-nine articles that had personal stories of Prozac users or pictures of them, thirty represented more women than men, and the testimonials were almost entirely from women, with a focus on women in gendered occupations, such as teachers and day care workers. In most cases, the only men mentioned or pictured in the articles were the doctors prescribing the drug and the pharmacists dispensing it. More gendering was found in the discussion of the uses of Prozac. Articles discussed how it was used to treat anorexia, bulimia, and PMS and to aid in weight loss. These disorders (save PMS) might be theoretically gender neutral, but in practice all of them disproportionately refer to women rather than men, and none of them were actually U.S. Food and Drug Administration (FDA)-approved uses for the drug at the time. (The FDA approved the use of Prozac for PMS in 2001.)

The results of their analysis, then, are mixed. While the need for Prozac is generally discussed in biological, gender-neutral terms, the people using the drug are portrayed as women—often women who have too many feminine traits and need biological help to adopt more masculine traits in the home or workplace. Prozac isn't nearly as gendered as Valium was in previous years, but it's still far from being discussed in gender-neutral terms.

Blum and Stracuzzi's (2004) analysis makes use of relatively large context units. While there were some elements of the articles that were coded on the level of individual words—as in the gendering of terms used to describe the users of Prozac—other elements were coded from large sections of the article. Coding at the word or sentence level can't determine the portrayal of more women than men as users of Prozac and the gendering of the stories about the users of Prozac. That doesn't mean that these elements aren't present in the articles or that the conclusions relying on them are any less valid. Indeed, these elements may be the only way to test the hypotheses. Rather, a different methodology than content analyses looking only at words or phrases is necessary.

The size of the context unit used in a study necessarily represents a trade-off. On one hand, larger context units may enable the researcher to create functional definitions that are closer to the actual concepts that they wish to measure. It may be possible to create a dictionary that measures gendered portrayal on the level of words and phrases, but such a functional definition may leave out important elements of what the researchers are trying to test. On the other hand, smaller context units tend to make coding easier and increase the replicability of the study. With very large context units, the functional definitions almost necessarily become less specific. Very small context units may be individual words that the researcher is looking for; very large ones are more conceptual. As such, there's less question about the presence of very small context units. When a dictionary is defined at the level of individual words, there's no discussion about whether the word is there or not. When a dictionary is defined at the level of concepts, there's more room for disagreement. The size of the context unit also affects the replicability of the study for the same reason. If researchers can list exactly which words they were looking for in a communication, another researcher can easily look for the same words. However, two researchers may interpret the definition of a concept in different ways.

Finally, the question of whether to use large or small context units also depends on whether the researcher is looking for manifest or latent content in the communication being analyzed. **Manifest content** is the actual content or the structure of the content in the communication: What words are used? How complex are the ideas being expressed? Analyses of political ad negativity or Hobolt and Klemmemsen's (2005) work on the opening speeches in parliament are examples of analyses of manifest content. In both cases, the research question involves the words that are used or some other aspect of the communication in and of itself. Such research is not particularly concerned with the messages underlying the communication, what's commonly referred to as subtext or, in the terminology of content analysis, **latent content**. Studies of latent content look not at what the communication says, but what it actually means in the context of the society in which it was produced. For example, Kubrin (2005) was looking not at the words or phrases used by the rappers, but rather at how the lyrics communicated various themes of the street code. Blum and Stracuzzi (2004) weren't as interested in what words were used to describe Prozac users as they were interested in how gendered the portrayals were. Manifest communication is generally studied through relatively small context units, while the study of latent communication generally requires larger ones.

INTERRATER RELIABILITY

Mikayla Hughes, Kelly Morrison, and Kelli Jean K. Asada—The Rules of Friends with Benefits Relationships (2005)

Perhaps because content analyses with larger context units are more subject to interpretation, Blum and Stracuzzi (2004) made sure that they coded all of the articles in their analysis separately and then compared the results to make sure that they were both coding the same way. Like most researchers, they reported the level of agreement between the coders as a way for readers to assess the reliability of their dictionary and, in a very real way, the overall research. Low levels of agreement between the coders may indicate vague or unreliable functional definitions or codings that are overly susceptible to who is doing the coding, rather than what's actually present in the communication.

As noted before, this is less of a problem for content analyses of manifest content and analyses with small context units, but the level of agreement between the coders is an important diagnostic in any coding that requires humans to actually read the communications in question. For research relying exclusively on KWIC software or other computerized content analyses, agreement is probably unnecessary. If the computer is giving you different answers at different times of the day, the problem generally isn't one of reliability, but of programming.

Mikayla Hughes, a professor of communication at University of California, Davis, worked with colleagues to carry out interviews of 143 heterosexual students, asking them about their attitudes toward relationships and including a series of open-ended questions about any friends-with-benefits (FWB) relationships that they were, or had been, involved in. For the purposes of the study, FWB relationships were defined as "an opposite sex friend that you have, who you also have sexual activity with (this can include sexual intercourse, but can also include other types of sexual activity.) This is NOT someone you describe as your boyfriend/girlfriend" (p. 54). All of the participants, whether they had engaged in a FWB relationship or not, were then asked to list three rules that should apply to such relationships.

The open-ended questions were first broken down into distinct ideas: the context units used in this analysis. In an example given by Hughes and her colleagues (2005), a male participant wrote that he was part of a FWB relationship because he "liked other girls as well, and did not want to be tied down." This was broken into two separate ideas: he liked other girls, and he did not want to be tied down. Each statement was split into context units by two of the three researchers, and the results were compared for each statement. To make sure that the researchers were splitting the statements in the same way, the results were compared. The researchers found that the statements had been split in the same way in 85 percent of the cases. Once the statements had been broken down into the context units, the researchers began pilot coding the ideas. They began by grouping the ideas into categories, adding categories when they encountered an idea that didn't fit into any of the existing ones. The three researchers then began using the resulting categories to code the data. They met to discuss the difficulties they were facing in categorization and refined the categories together to make sure that they were all on the same page. They went through this process a total of three times before having each of the ideas coded independently by two of the researchers. Then, to make certain that there was no bias in the codings, they trained two undergraduate research assistants in the coding process, had them code one-fifth of the ideas, and checked the results the undergraduates got against their own. In all cases, the measures of intercoder reliability—the tests that

Type of rule	Example	Percent mentioning
Emotional rules	"Don't let your heart get involved or in the way"	56%
Communication rules	"No calls the next day"	41%
Sex rules	"Don't be a fool; wrap your tool"	33%
Friendship rules	"You have to spend time together not getting freaky"	23%
Secrecy rules	"Don't tell anyone else"	22%
Permanence rules	"Enjoy it while you can as it is not going to last forever"	17%
Negotiate rules	"Make sure each person is clear on what the relationship is"	8%

measure how similarly different coders categorize the same responses—showed that the results would have been about the same no matter who was applying the dictionary.

The rules on how to maintain FWB relationships were broken down into seven categories (plus a category for miscellaneous statements that didn't fit any of the other categories), and the researchers looked at how characteristics of the participants affected the types of rules they mentioned. For instance, participants who had never actually engaged in a FWB relationship were much more likely to mention secrecy rules than those who had engaged in such a relationship (55 percent of the sample, though Hughes and her colleagues [2005] don't make any claim as to the representativeness of their participants). There didn't seem to be any real differences between men and women in the rules that they thought should apply to the relationship. These sorts of results indicate that FWB relationships are different from the casual sex relationships that other researchers had previously looked at. Past research had indicated that women tended to use these relationships as stepping stones into committed relationships, but this did not seem to be the case among Hughes and her colleagues' participants. Similarly, previous research indicated that people tended to keep such relationships secret in order to avoid social consequences from engaging in what was considered to be aberrant behavior. However, while people who had never engaged in FWB relationships seemed to think secrecy was important, 84 percent of those who had been in one said that they had told a friend about it.

Many researchers find it tempting to do their own content analysis. After all, grant money can be hard to come by in the social sciences, and training and hiring others to do the coding can be expensive. However, having just one coder is almost always problematic. Hughes and her colleagues (2005) had the various ideas listed by the participants read at least three times during pilot coding and at least two more times during the final coding—and this is far from overkill. In any type of research, validity is one of the most important concerns, and the main way to establish the validity of content analysis is through measures of intercoder reliability. In general, these measures require two or more coders to look at the same context unit, and they give an indication of how often the readers come to the same conclusion about how that context unit should be coded. A high level of intercoder reliability indicates that context units are being given the same codes no matter who the coder is, while a low level indicates that the coding is subjective, depending on who is doing the coding.

Unfortunately, there's no one fully agreed-upon technique for measuring intercoder reliability (also called **interrater reliability**). The most common measures, though, are percent agreement and **Cohen's Kappa** (used by Hughes and her colleagues 2005). Both are relatively simple to calculate. Percent agreement is simply the total number of cases that were coded in the same way by two raters, divided by the total number cases coded. If the coding was carried out by more than two raters, the figure can be calculated for each pair of readers, then averaged; if the different pairs coded different numbers of cases, the average would be weighed by the number of cases in each pair. For example, suppose that two coders individually coded the same 200 context units. If 150 of them were coded the same way, the percent agreement would be 75 percent. If 180 were coded the same way, the percent agreement would be 90 percent. For three coders (A, B, and C), the percent agreement would be the number of context units agreed on by A and B, divided by the number of context units coded by both A and B. We would then do the same for the other two combinations of coders (A and C, and B and C). Next, we would divide the total number of agreements by the total number of context units coded by all of the combinations (the number coded by A and B, plus the number coded by A and C, plus the number coded by B and C).

> In a context analysis, there were 150 context units to be coded.
> A and B coded all of them, and C was brought in as an outside check, coding just 30.
> Therefore, there were 150 context units coded by both A and B, 30 coded by A and C, and 30 coded by B and C.
> A and B coded 128 of the context units the same way.
> Of the 30 coded by A and C, there was agreement on 25.
> Of the 30 coded by B and C, there was agreement on 18.
> The percent agreement would be:
>
> (Cases agreed on by A and B + Cases agreed on by A and C + Cases agreed on by B and C)/(Cases coded by A and B + Cases coded by A and C + Cases coded by B and C)
>
> $(128+25+18)/(150+30+30) = .814$, or 81.4%

While percent agreement is pretty straightforward, there's a problem. Different coders will have some agreement just by chance. Suppose that two coders are sorting context units into two categories. Even if the process was totally random, they'd agree half of the time, and they'd have a percent agreement of 50 percent. Cohen's Kappa is a way of resolving this problem, giving us the percent agreement between two coders while accounting for random chance.

As useful as it is, Cohen's Kappa can't be used in all circumstances. First, it requires that the categories be mutually exclusive and exhaustive. That is, every context unit must fit in to one, and only one, category. Second, the coding must be independent. The researchers must be looking at the context units on their own, even if they're going to be comparing their results afterward.

To calculate Cohen's Kappa, it is necessary to first break down how each coder categorized the context units. For instance, suppose that we have two coders breaking down context units into three categories: emotional, communication, and friendship. Coder A coded 49 percent of the responses as being in the emotional category, 35 percent in the communication category, and 16 percent in the friendship category. While A coded 49 percent of the responses as being in the emotional category (the bottom left "marginal total"), only 41 percent of A's responses were also coded as emotional by B (the number in the top left of the table). The remainder were coded by B as being in the communication category (5 percent of A's total responses, in the middle left of the

		Coder A			
		Emotional	Communication	Friendship	**Marginal total**
Coder B	Emotional	0.41	0.11	0.03	**0.55**
	Communication	0.05	0.23	0.04	**0.32**
	Friendship	0.03	0.01	0.09	**0.13**
	Marginal total	**0.49**	**0.35**	**0.16**	**1.00**

table) or friendship category (3 percent of A's total responses, in the bottom left of the table about the marginal total). Similarly, 13 percent of the context units that B coded were in the friendship category (the marginal total on the right near the bottom), but only 9 percent of B's total responses were coded by B *and* A as being in friendship (the number in the bottom right).

Based on these figures, it would be fairly easy to calculate the percent agreement: it would just be the sum of the diagonal. The two coders agreed on 41 percent of the context units as being in the emotional category, 23 percent as being in the communication category, and 9 percent as being in the friendship category, giving a percent agreement of (41 + 23 + 9 =) 73 percent. Some of that is certainly due to chance, but how much? It may be tempting to say that since there are three categories, each category should get one-third of each of the context units, but that's not quite right. After all, since there were a lot fewer context units put into the friendship category, there would be a lot fewer agreements just by chance than there would be in a category with a lot of context units, like emotional.

Still, figuring out the expected number of chance agreements is pretty simple: it's simply the product of the two marginals for that cell. So, the expected number of chance agreements in which both coders categorized a content item as emotional would be the marginal total of emotional for A (.49, on the bottom left) times the marginal total of emotional for B (.55, on the top right), or .27. Just based on the number of responses that were categorized as emotional by both coders, it would be expected that they would agree on a context unit being emotional in 27 percent of the total cases coded.

Again reading down the diagonal, the expected number of agreements just due to chance is .27 (from the top left) plus .11 (from the middle) plus .02 (from the bottom right), totaling .40. It would be expected that the coders would agree on 40 percent of the cases just by chance. This puts their actual level of agreement,

		Coder A			
		Emotional	Communication	Friendship	**Marginal total**
Coder B	Emotional	.55 × .49 = .27	.55 × .35 = .19	.55 × .16 = .09	**0.55**
	Communication	.32 × .49 = .16	.32 × .35 = .11	.32 × .16 = .05	**0.32**
	Friendship	.13 × .49 = .06	.13 × .35 = .05	.13 × .16 = .02	**0.13**
	Marginal total	**0.49**	**0.35**	**0.16**	**1.00**

73 percent, in context. Once we have these figures, Cohen's Kappa is simply the percent agreement, minus the expected agreement due to change, divided by the total amount of percentage agreement that wouldn't be due to chance. In this case, it would be $(.73 - .40)/(1 - .40) = .55$.

$$\text{Cohen's Kappa} = \frac{(\text{Percent Agreement} - \text{Agreement by Chance})}{(1 - \text{Agreement by Chance})}$$

Once the Cohen's Kappa has been determined, it's necessary to interpret it. Kappa can be as high as 1, or as low as -1. Zero doesn't really mean that there isn't any agreement, but rather that the agreement between the coders is no better than would be expected from chance. So, zero would be a pretty poor Kappa, and 1 would be a very good one, but what about the values in the middle? In general, a Kappa of .6 or better is acceptable, and greater than .8 is considered good.

If the Kappa is too low—as it seems to be in the example—researchers should go back to the dictionary to adjust the definitions, retrain the coders, or both. Training in general, and retraining if necessary, should follow the same steps laid out in Hughes and her colleagues' (2005) research: the researchers code a series of context units, compare their codings, discuss the differences, adjust the definitions if necessary to create consensus about a coding, then go back and repeat the process until all of the coders agree on how to apply the definitions to the communications being analyzed.

This sort of training, which is necessary to refine the definitions, shows again why multiple coders are important. Not only are measurements of coder agreement, like Cohen's Kappa, the main measure of the validity of content analysis, but without other coders, there's no way to tell how to refine the dictionary.

ANALYSIS OF HISTORICAL DATA

Francesca Cancian and Steven Gordon—The Changing Meaning of Marriage (1988)

Content analysis has become especially important to feminist research. One of the main tenets of feminist research is that while sex may be biological, the roles assigned to the sexes, and the meaning of those roles, is socially determined. These social roles are reproduced not only in the behavior of individuals and groups within society, but also in mass media. The analysis of media portrayals of gender roles—largely carried out through content analysis—allows feminist researchers to study how society is shaping women's lives.

Francesca Cancian and Steven Gordon's (1998) research looks at how marriage was represented in major magazines between 1900 and 1979. The perception at the time was that magazine articles in the early part of the century told women to repress their emotions, especially anger, and subsume themselves entirely in their marriage. Cancian and Gordon quote a *Ladies Home Journal* article from 1940, which tells women that the most important rule of a happy marriage is "to please the one I have chosen." Conflict was something to be avoided at all costs, no matter what the husband did. A 1957 article advised women, "What may seem to an unimaginative, inhibited woman like brutality is often pure intensity of want because her husband finds her unbearably attractive. Most women—if they know this—can find a great joy themselves in their husband's violent need of them" (quoted in Cancian and Gordon, p. 321). In case it wasn't clear, this article is essentially telling women that if their husband wanted to forcibly rape them, they should be flattered. Even as late as 1967, *Reader's Digest* was telling women that it was okay for their husbands to flirt with other women because it made them feel attractive, but that women should probably avoid flirting with men outside of marriage because their husbands were likely to get jealous.

By the 1970s, though, it seemed as though the tone had shifted. Women were advised that true intimacy came from sharing all of their emotions with their husbands. A 1973 *Reader's Digest* article told women that "how a husband or wife sees a situation can make all the difference between making a marital problem out of it, or turning it into an opportunity to express love" (quoted in Cancian and Gordon, 1988, p. 316).

To try to quantify this shift, Cancian and Gordon (1988) carried out a content analysis on a sample of articles from each of the eight decades studied. The authors went through high circulation women's and general interest magazines throughout the century and found articles about marriage or that offered marital advice. They then coded the dominant messages in the articles—using the whole article as a context unit—according to what it said about marriage in six categories. The researchers randomly selected sixteen articles from each of the decades to code, then refined the dictionary and recoded until they had 85 percent agreement. These refinements included dropping a seventh category, which described the role men should take in the relationship, because it turned out to be almost exactly the same as their sixth coding category.

1. Is love presented as self-sacrifice and compromise, or self-fulfillment and self-expression?
2. Is love identified with routine and maturity or romance, passion, and impulse?
3. Is sex presented as important in marriage or not?
4. Are expressions of anger and disagreement good or bad for a marriage?
5. Should wives communicate openly about problems or keep up a cheerful, harmonious front?
6. Does the article endorse traditional feminine roles, with women responsible for feelings and family relationships, while remaining sexually passive?

Cancian and Gordon (1988) note that in many cases, the articles are actually coded as having messages on both sides of a single category. For example, one article tells how a wife refused to go with her husband to meet his boss at a country club because she had a prior engagement, but then she went with him on another occasion because "a girl wants to feel that she's helping" (quoted in Cancian and Gordon, p. 325).

While the results show that the magazine articles moved away from more traditional views of marriage (a good marriage depends on a woman's self-sacrifice, obedience, and acceptance of traditional roles), the trend was inconsistent. Things got much less traditional by the 1930s, went back to old roles by the 1950s, then made a dramatic shift in the last decade studied. This pattern—with peaks in "modern" views of emotions, family, and marriage in the 1920s and 1970s—gets some outside validation from other research in sociology and women's studies that show dramatic shifts in Americans' overall attitudes during these periods.

However, their results also show that while the overall trend has been toward increasing rejection of traditional views of love and marriage, this hasn't occurred in all categories. Over the course of the century, the impact of Sigmund Freud and psychoanalysis led women's magazines to be less likely to tell women to repress their emotions and more likely to tell them to pay attention to sex. At the same time, though, many of the psychiatrists quoted in the magazines told women that their place was in the home, and articles throughout the century were equally likely to tell women that it was their job to regulate emotions within the home. If a husband is angry or frustrated, it's the wife's job to calm him down or build him up. If the wife is angry, it's her job to calm down before (maybe) discussing whatever the problem is with her husband.

In addition to telling us how the norms about marriage that were communicated through these large-circulation magazines shifted over eighty years, Cancian and Gordon's (1988) results also tell us how changes in society were reflected in views of marriage. In periods of generally more traditional social views, such as the 1930s and 1950s, women were counseled to obey their husbands and repress their own views. In more liberated periods, like the 1920s and 1970s, women were told to express themselves, take on less gendered roles in the household, and expect that their husbands do the same.

It's difficult to see how Cancian and Gordon's (1988) research questions could have been answered other than through content analysis. Perhaps researchers could find out how people view marriage today through public opinion surveys or in-depth interviews, but even then the results would apply only to the modern day. Moreover, questions about highly personal topics such as sex and marriage are subject to very large demand and desirability effects: respondents to surveys and participants in interviews want to tell researchers what they want to hear and want to present themselves in a positive fashion. As such, they would almost certainly not tell the researcher about their own experience of marriage, but rather about what the participant thinks society says marriage *should* be like. Content analysis therefore gives researchers a direct line into what society is saying about marriage, rather than the indirect version offered by most participants in studies. The content analysis also allows researchers to look at how society has changed. It's impossible to interview people in the 1910s about their marriages, but researchers can see what mainstream media sources in the 1910s were saying about what marriage should be.

ETHICAL CONCERNS

David Snowdon et al.—Predicting Alzheimer's 50 Years Early (1996)

It may seem as though content analysis is less likely to lead to ethical complications than many of the other forms of research. Because researchers are typically looking at communications that have already been made public, there's not generally any need to obtain informed consent from the people who made the communication in the first place. It isn't as though Kubrin (2005) needed to get permission from the Wu-Tang Clan in order to analyze their lyrics or link examples of the street code found in their music. By releasing the material publicly, the rappers made the material available for public consumption and can't claim to have any expectation of privacy. Of course, in cases where the researchers carry out content analysis on interviews that they have carried out themselves (like Shor and Simchai's [2009] work on incest aversion in kibbutzim, discussed in the Chapter 7), normal rules about getting informed consent and protecting confidentiality apply. This lack of ethical complications is often seen as one of the selling points of content analysis; researchers often aren't even required to get Institutional Review Board (IRB) approval for content analyses of publicly available works. This is based on the understanding that a researcher carrying out content analysis is looking at the characteristics of a communication, and the communication, unlike a person, doesn't have any rights that need to be protected. When Kubrin (2005) was looking for examples of the street code in rap lyrics, she wasn't claiming that 2Pac or C-Murder endorsed retributive violence, but rather that the lyrics endorsed it. As such, she was doing research on the song, not on the individual, and normal rules about informed consent and confidentiality simply weren't applicable.

In some cases, though, content analysis research can be ethically fraught. While many researchers—like Kubrin (2005)—are looking for the underlying meanings of a communication, others use a communication to determine something about the individual who made the communication in the first place. An example of this sort of content analysis can be found in the work of David Snowdon and his colleagues (1996), who along with other researchers, were looking to answer some of the most puzzling findings about Alzheimer's disease. Alzheimer's, a crippling neurological disease that leads to a steep decline in cognitive function and memory, eventually resulting in death, has a biological basis—victims develop tangles and plaques in the affected areas of their brains—but it seems that education reduces the likelihood that an individual will develop at least the outward signs of Alzheimer's. It's possible that this relationship is due to confounding factors, such as the fact that less educated people in the United States tend to have worse diets or drink more alcohol, but it could also be due to factors that lead people to have more education. If that's the case, and we can identify these factors, we should be able to predict the onset of Alzheimer's well before any symptoms show up.

To look for these factors, Snowdon and his colleagues (1996) made use of a unique dataset known as the Nun Study. In the early 1990s, a group of over

500 elderly nuns in the North-Central United States consented to annual tests of physical and mental function, to give researchers access to their records at the convent, and to donate their brains for study after their death. This dataset has been used by a number of researchers to study facets of aging because the nuns constitute a perfect research group. They all have about the same lifestyle, with relatively low levels of stress and no smoking or drinking, and all of them lived in just about the same environment. These similarities remove many of the confounding variables that could otherwise call into question results from the general public. If we wanted to determine the effects of education, or some other measure of cognitive ability, on the likelihood of developing Alzheimer's, we would have to contend with the fact that people with less education drink more alcohol and have fattier diets. How could we be sure that the differences were due to education and not the other factors that tend to go along with it? None of the nuns drank, smoked, got married, or had children. They all had about the same diet and the same access to healthcare. For this study, Snowdon and his colleagues (2005) looked at a subset of the nuns who had joined a particular group of nuns in the 1930s and had submitted handwritten biographies before taking their vows. These biographies were supposed to be about a page long and detail the facts of their lives before coming to the convent, as well as their reasons for wanting to take on religious orders. It was important that the biographies were handwritten—the few nuns who had typed biographies were excluded from the study—so that the researchers could be sure that the nuns wrote the papers themselves.

In each biography, trained coders looked at the last ten sentences and measured their grammatical complexity (the simplicity or complexity of the structure of the sentences) and their idea density (how many ideas were expressed in each sentence). They then tested the relationship between the characteristics of these biographies, written when the women were in their early 20s, and their cognitive function in old age. The brains of the nuns who had died were tested for physical signs of Alzheimer's.

For instance, the researchers give examples of two nuns from the study. In her biography, Sister A writes that she "was born in Eau Claire, Wisconsin on May 24, 1913, and was baptized in St. James church," a statement with an idea density of 3.9, and a grammatical complexity score of 0. Sister B writes that she is "wandering about in 'Dove's Lane' waiting, yet only three more weeks, to follow in the footprints of my Spouse, bound to him by the Holy Vows. . ." (both quoted in Snowdon et al., p. 35). Sister B's sentence has 9.1 ideas, and grammatical complexity score of 7.

The results showed that the idea density—but not the grammatical complexity—of the biographies that the nuns had written as young women strongly predicted Alzheimer's and cognitive function in later life. Essentially, it seems that the complexity of thoughts either offered some protection against Alzheimer's or led the nuns to be able to continue normal functioning despite the disease. Among the nuns who had died, the relationship between physical signs of Alzheimer's and the idea complexity in their biographies was even stronger: 90 percent of those with Alzheimer's had low idea density in their 20s, compared with only 13 percent of those without Alzheimer's.

To begin with, it should be stressed that it seems as though Snowdon and his colleagues (2005) have covered their ethical bases in this research. They carried out the content analysis only on the biographical essays of nuns who agreed to be part of the study and knew that the study was about the onset of dementia and Alzheimer's. There may be some question as to whether nuns who were already in the early stages of dementia when the study began—and there seems to have been some—could give informed consent, but it seems unlikely that the researchers would have used data from these women if they had not been sufficiently lucid to know what they were getting into, especially since part of the research involved the donation of organs for research purposes after death.

We can also be fairly certain that Snowdon and his colleagues (2005) didn't tell the nuns who were part of the study how their biographies were scored and what this meant for their risk of falling prey to Alzheimer's disease. First, it would be unethical to give such potentially damaging information to people without their full consent and without providing follow-up counseling sessions. Second, giving people such information would also tend to bias the results of further research on this group, as nuns who knew that they were, or were not, more likely to suffer from the disease would almost certainly act differently than they would have if they hadn't had such information.

When researchers carry out content analysis with the intent of uncovering information about the individuals who created the communication being analyzed (rather than information about the communication itself), they should ensure that the individuals give their informed consent and are fully aware of any potential harms arising from the study. Snowdon and his colleagues' (2005) study may be an extreme example, but there are any number of other studies in which an analysis of writing might reveal someone to be sexist, racist, harboring negative feelings toward loved ones, or the victim of a traumatic event in childhood. These may be uncomfortable truths, and, ethically, the researcher may not be able to reveal the results of the analyses to the individual participant, at least without clearance from the IRB and appropriate follow-up measures to ensure that there aren't any lasting consequences from the revelation.

What can researchers do when the text is written by someone who is already dead? The ability to carry out research on people who are deceased or otherwise unavailable for interviews or other techniques is one of the advantages of content analysis. However, it also raises some important ethical questions. Xuan Le, a researcher in computer science at the University of Toronto, analyzed the works of several deceased mystery authors, most notably Agatha Christie. Christie's later novels, written in the few years before she died, are of notably lower quality than those that she wrote in her prime. One of them in particular, *Elephants Can Remember*, involves a main character who is losing her memory, and neither the character nor the author seems to be able to keep the plot straight. It was thought that Christie suffered from Alzheimer's disease or some related form of dementia, but both Christie and her family denied it.

Le and her colleagues (2011) carried out a quantitative content analysis of the works of Christie and two other female British mystery writers (one of whom was still alive and writing at almost 90, and the other who was known to have had Alzheimer's), and found a significant decline in the complexity of sentences used by Christie and the author who was known to have had Alzheimer's (Iris Murdoch), with the complexity declining well before any outward signs of Alzheimer's were present. In Christie's work, the decline is striking, with the complexity of her sentences declining precipitously, even as her use of indefinite nouns (such as *the thing*) climbed, both patterns that have been seen in the analyses of known Alzheimer's patients. Just as the nuns who later developed the disease showed signs of it when writing in their early 20s, the authors who suffered from Alzheimer's showed signs of it in their writing years before. Christie and her family certainly knew that there was something wrong before she died, but they apparently did not want it publicly revealed. Is it ethical to overturn such a decision after she dies? The analysis included a living author, P.D. James, who showed no signs of precipitous decline in her work, but what if the analysis had shown that she was developing Alzheimer's disease or that she would develop it in upcoming years? Would it still be ethical to publish the research?

In a case where the content analysis may reveal potentially sensitive information about someone who is still alive, the individual whose communications are being analyzed should be treated as though he or she were a participant in any other form of research. Ideally, full, informed consent should be obtained; at the very least, the individual should grant permission for the analysis to be carried out or the individual's name to be published. For instance, Le and her colleagues (2011) should probably have gained James' consent before carrying out an analysis of her writing and should probably have changed her name in order to protect her confidentiality if the results were potentially troubling.

In the case of the analysis of a deceased individual's communications, there is of course no way to obtain informed consent, but the researcher should be conscious of the privacy of the recently deceased's relatives. If Christie's family did not want her Alzheimer's disease known, and members of the family who made that decision are still alive, their wishes should generally be respected, whatever their reasons. This is not to say that it would not be appropriate to carry out an analysis of her works, but perhaps the research should respect the confidentiality of the recently deceased.

In terms of ethical considerations, content analysis is one of the easiest research methods to deal with. Because principal investigators are not dealing with human subjects, but rather using recorded material, they are not required to apply to their IRBs for approval before starting their research projects. Because content analysis uses secondary data, which already exists in recorded material, it does not use human subjects. Therefore, with content analysis, there is no potential harm to human subjects. In recent years, however, researchers have started to debate the potential harm in content analysis. Content analysis does not directly deal with human subjects, but it might indirectly cause potential harm by violating their privacy. Think about the study of Christie's novels. Based on the content analysis of her novels, the researchers concluded that Christie might have had Alzheimer's disease. Given that the author is deceased, what are the ethical obligations of the researcher? It is certainly possible to uncover something during content analysis that the author might be trying to keep private. Therefore, even though we do not typically think of content analysis as potentially harming human subjects, it is important to keep in mind that individuals potentially can be harmed. Researchers still need to be cautious of issues of privacy.

ADVANTAGES AND DISADVANTAGES OF CONTENT ANALYSIS

Content analysis has many advantages. Unlike many other techniques we studied in this book, content analysis is the only technique that does not directly deal with people. In-depth interviews, surveys, and experiments all focus on the individual participant or respondent: asking questions; recording the participant's reactions, behavior, attitudes, or values. Content analysis, however, systematically studies patterns in printed or visual media. There are some research questions that can only be answered with this method. Do cartoons use aggressive messages? Do advertisements use more white models than African American models? Do presidential speeches use religious messages? These are not questions researchers can answer by directly asking individual people. If researchers want to capture the nonliving portion of culture, content analysis provides them with the tools to systematically analyze it.

Content analysis is especially useful in women and gender studies. Many feminist scholars argue that historical reports are biased because they come from the perspective of men. Using historic artifacts, diaries, letters, and women's narratives, many feminist scholars conduct content analysis to capture the perspectives of women. Women's perspectives have historically been marginalized; content analysis sheds light on these untold stories.

Content analysis is also an **unobtrusive measure**, meaning the method itself does not interfere with the content of what is being studied or the participants in the study. In many studies, the researcher and the research design could potentially influence the content of what is being studied. Even the mere presence of the researcher, in some cases, might influence the way participants behave and alter the outcome of the study, as we see in the Hawthorne effect. With content analysis, this is not the case. The researcher cannot alter the results of the study because he or she is not directly interacting with the content. The cartoons, advertisements, movies, newspaper articles, presidential speeches, and novels that are being studied have already been completed.

Compared to some of the other methods we studied in this book, content analysis saves time and money. Methods such as large-scale surveys (for example, the General Social Survey, World Values Study, and American National Election Study) collect information from thousands of respondents. In some cases (for example, World Values Study and Luxembourg Income Study), questionnaires are distributed to respondents overseas. Such large-scale surveys require large staff to oversee data collection, coding, and analysis as well as expensive computer equipment to collect, store, and analyze data. In addition to monetary costs, data collection and analysis is very time consuming. For example, ethnographic studies are very lengthy. Many researchers give up their lives to do what their subjects do for extended periods of time. Michael Moffatt (1989) enrolled in college as a freshman; Barbara Ehrenreich (2001) worked several minimum-wage jobs. Doing such participant observations is very time consuming. Conducting in-depth interviews that last a few hours and then transcribing and coding these interviews also takes a very long time. Compared to these methods, content analysis requires little money and time. Therefore, this method is suitable for many student researchers and younger researchers, who have limited resources.

Because content analysis does not require a lot of investment, studies using this method are easier to replicate. If a researcher believes he or she has made a mistake, it is relatively easy to go back and replicate the study. Even for reliability purposes, replicating such studies is relatively easy. This is not the case for many other methods. If the researcher makes a mistake on a question on a large-scale survey, it is very costly to go back to potentially thousands of respondents. Alternately, if an ethnographer would like to replicate a study such as Moffatt's (1989) *Coming of Age in New Jersey*, he or she would have to enroll in college. Therefore, in studies using content analysis, replications are much easier, and there is more freedom for do-overs.

Overall, content analysis has many benefits; however, it also has been criticized for a range of shortcomings. It allows researchers to study systematically recorded material; however, not everything is recorded, and the researchers are limited to recorded material only. Available recorded material sheds light on important sources of inequality, especially in women and gender studies. However, many important portions of women's lives have not been historically documented. Therefore, there might be great inequality regarding what is recorded and what is not. Men's perspectives, views, and experiences have been recorded historically, and women's have not been recorded in the same level. Therefore, content analysis is limited to what has been recorded. Such omissions call for more oral histories and accounts to capture these nonrecorded perspectives and experiences.

Although content analysis is more economical in terms of money and time, it is more likely to get misused. Content analysis is a strong method if used systematically and designed well, but designing a systematic content analysis may take time. Therefore, while it is not as time consuming as some other methods, content analysis takes time to develop intensive and excellent examples.

Content analysis is also criticized due to potential issues of validity. Is the researcher studying what he or she set out to study? Since content analysis is limited to recorded media, it is important that the conclusions pertain to recorded media only. If a researcher is conducting a content analysis of violence in cartoons, he or she can claim that there is violence in media representations. However, the conclusions are limited to media representations. The researcher cannot use content analysis to claim that the cartoons cause children to be violent, for example.

This method has also been criticized because of potential issues of reliability. Since researchers have the power to operationalize and decide on coding categories (for example, which acts they will code as aggressive), there might be a subjective element. This means that if the coding categories are not comprehensive enough or if the concept is not operationalized well, then the results will not be the same when replicated.

ADDITIONAL EXAMPLES

Bill Hu, Thomas McInish, and Li Zeng—When Do Stock Spam Emails Work? (2010)

Email has proven popular as a way to attempt to scam unwary recipients, and one of the more popular scams involves pump-and-dump stock schemes. In a pump-and-dump scheme, criminals buy large amounts of cheap stock in a company, then try to enlist other investors to buy stock in the same company. As more people buy the stock, the price goes up; once it's risen enough, the criminals sell off their stock, taking a profit while dramatically decreasing the price of the stock for their victims, who are left holding mostly worthless shares. It's a simple scheme, but it seems to work. Researchers have found that the criminals behind these schemes can expect about a 4 percent return on their investment within a couple of days, far better than the return from a normal investment.

What makes this sort of fraud interesting is that it requires the cooperation of the victim. This sort of fraud is potentially more enticing for potential victims than other email scams like fake Nigerian royalty asking for money because there is the opportunity for victims to make money. Even if the victims know that they are being enlisted in a pump-and-dump scheme, as long as the stock price actually does go up and they sell before the criminals dump their shares, they may still turn a profit. This sort of activity is of interest to experts in finance who want to understand fluctuations in stock prices resulting from these scams, as well as criminologists who want to understand how criminals are able to recruit otherwise innocent civilians to help further their illegal activity. The recipients of these pump-and-dump emails almost certainly know that they are scams and almost certainly know that they are illegal, but they participate anyway. What makes them do so?

Bill Hu and his colleagues (2010) analyzed the content of over 40,000 spam emails and identified 580 distinct spam campaigns touting various stocks. They then looked at the actual fluctuations in the prices of those stocks during the spam campaigns to determine which messages actually worked to drive up the stock prices. Initially, they analyzed the content of just 50 of the messages in an exploratory content analysis to determine what content to look for. They then integrated this information into the existing literature on what makes people read spam emails in order to determine which characteristics of the emails they should code. They came up with five characteristics that could be related to the success of the messages: the inclusion of a target price (which could serve as a signal to victims telling them when to sell), the length of the message, whether it masqueraded as a research report, whether it hinted at some sort of inside information, and whether the touted company was based in the United States or not.

The researchers then used regression analysis to determine the relative effectiveness of these characteristics in actually driving up the price of the stock. First, they found that spam with a short-term target price served to drive up the price; second, they found that touting U.S. companies had a much greater effect than touting international companies.

These results lend credence to the idea that victims of pump-and-dump scams are willing victims in their own fraud. The fact that they are allured by a short-term target price (which both gives them some clue as to when the spammers are going to sell and may let them get out before the spammers do), but not a long-term target price (which would encourage them to hold on to a stock for the long term), indicates that they don't actually *believe* that there's something good about the company. Rather, they think that they can make a quick profit along with the scammers and leave others holding the bag.

Frederick Mosteller and David Wallace—Who Wrote the Federalist Papers? (1964)

After the Constitution was written, the United States engaged in fierce debate over whether or not the new document should be ratified. It was, after all, written largely in secret and represented a huge shift of power from individual states to a new federal government. Opponents felt that it could potentially lead to the sorts of tyranny that the Americans had only recently fought against in the Revolutionary War; supporters argued that it would make the country stronger and that the government was sufficiently constrained that it could not become tyrannical. While the State of New York debated whether or not to ratify the Constitution, a series of articles was published in New York newspapers in support of the document, all of them signed with the pen name "Publius," after Publius Valerius Publicola, one of the founders of the Roman Republic. The articles were actually written by a team of three men: James Madison, John Jay, and Alexander Hamilton. Collectively, these articles became known as the Federalist Papers, and they are very important documents about the intentions of the founders.

It wasn't clear, however, who wrote which of the essays, and the authors, who had a falling out in later years, released conflicting lists of which ones they had written. Of the eighty-five essays, fifty-one were attributed to Hamilton, fourteen to Madison, and five to Jay. That leaves fifteen with disputed or unclear authorship. Madison claimed to have written all of these disputed documents, but historians generally agreed that this was unlikely. Hamilton and Madison had similar enough writing styles that scholars were unable to distinguish between their essays, but Frederick Mosteller and David Wallace (1964), both mathematicians, realized that it would be possible to distinguish between the two of them based on their use of individual words. First, they went through a subset of writings that were known to have been written by Hamilton and Madison, and from those texts, they built up a set of words that were highly discriminatory; that is, they were used very frequently by one of the men and not frequently by the other. They then validated this list by analyzing another set of texts that were known to have been written by either Hamilton or Madison, to make sure that the word frequency could correctly determine which of the men had written each of the known articles. Finally, they turned to the disputed Federalist papers, looking for the frequency of the various words while being sure to ignore any words that actually had to do with the content of the essay. (Remember, they were looking to match the style of the writer, not the topic on which the author was writing.) They analyzed the word frequency counts using the best technology available at the time—computers run off of punch cards—and came to the conclusion that all fifteen of the disputed articles had, in fact, been written by Madison, just as he had claimed.

Janet S. Fink and Linda Jean Kensicki—How Sports Magazines Deal with Women Athletes (2002)

After the 1996 Olympics, in which American women took home gold medals in basketball, and gymnastics, and around the time of American women's victory in the Soccer World Cup, there was optimism among feminists that female athletes would begin to be appreciated as athletes, rather than as mothers or sex symbols. As discussed previously, researchers in women's studies have often used content analysis as a way to measure societal views of women's roles, so it's natural that Janet S. Fink and Linda Jean Kensicki (2002) would turn to sports magazines (specifically *Sports Illustrated* and *Sports Illustrated for Women*) to see if there really was a shift in how female athletes were viewed. They note that while even the existence of magazines about women's sports may mean more coverage of women athletes, that doesn't mean that the coverage is becoming less gendered. If the women in the magazines are still being portrayed in traditionally gendered roles, coverage may even be getting worse.

Fink and Kensicki (2002) looked for a few markers to tell them about the gendering of women in the magazines. They looked at the content of the articles to see whether the articles about women focused less on sports and more on other aspects of the women's lives than similar articles about men. They also looked at the photographs to see if women were portrayed in active poses less often than men.

The analysis of photographs, graphics, and other nonwritten materials largely follows the same rules as the analysis of written communications. Coders need to agree on context units and functional definitions in order to build up a dictionary, code independently, check the results, and refine until there is sufficient agreement between coders. Fink and Kensicki (2002) took categorizes from existing research to put the photographs into four categories: athletic action (in athletic apparel and engaged in sports activity), dressed but poised and pretty (in athletic apparel, but not engaged in a sports activity), nonsports setting (not in athletic apparel and not engaged in sports activity), and pornographic/sexually suggestive (dressed provocatively or photographed in a way that focuses solely on sexual attributes). Photos that contained both men and women were coded separately for each gender, and photos that only depicted nonhumans (such as shoes or horses) were not included in the analysis. They also developed nine categories for content analysis of the articles, ranging from sports struggle articles to personal health articles to fashion articles. After the two authors coded the photos and articles, they trained a graduate student to do the same and tested the reliability of the three: percent agreement was greater than .9 (90 percent), and Scott's Pi, a figure similar to Cohen's Kappa, was calculated to be around .8.

In *Sports Illustrated* (SI) the researchers found that only about 10 percent of the photos were of female athletes. While the vast majority of stories about women in *SI* were about sports, articles about women were much more likely to be about personal issues than were articles about male athletes. Fifty-five percent of the photos of women in *SI* were categorized as nonsports setting, and 46 percent were athletic action. The other two categories comprised less than 1 percent of the photos each. In contrast, 66 percent of the pictures of male athletes were athletic action shots, and only 25 percent were coded as nonsports setting.

Things were better, though, in *Sports Illustrated for Women* (SIW). Most of the photos of women athletes in SIW were athletic action shots (56 percent), and only 24 percent were nonsports setting. Another 19 percent fell into the "poised and pretty" category.

> Jean Killburn's documentary, "Killing Us Softly 4," shows gender bias in the media representations of women, especially in advertisements.

Fink and Kensicki (2002) argue that these results—especially in SI, the largest circulating sports magazine in the world—show the marginalization of women athletes. As they note, SI doesn't have much coverage of women athletes, but it had room for nude pictures of Olympic athletes Amy Van Dyken and Marie-Jose Perec and ten pages of coverage about the possibility that the owner of the Lakers could turn the team over to his daughter, a former *Playboy* model (including a full page picture of the daughter naked, with basketballs covering her breasts). Some solace could be taken from the high proportion of articles in SI dealing with athletic activity. Though there weren't many articles about women, most (80 percent) dealt with women's athletic activities. Upon further inspection, though, Fink and Kensicki found that two-thirds of these articles were about sports that were traditionally viewed as being appropriate for women, such as ice skating, gymnastics, softball, or tennis, rather than soccer or basketball, despite the presence of professional leagues for women in these sports. While SI and SIW cover women athletes, they conclude, they do so in a way that serves to maintain the gender status quo.

> For the use and application of content analysis in women and gender studies, check out *Feminist Methods in Social Research* by Shulamit Reinharz (1992). It was published by Oxford University Press.

SUMMARY

Content analysis analyzes communications, allowing researchers to understand the characteristics of what's being said or written, as well as draw conclusions about the person or people who made the communication. This is especially valuable when individuals are unavailable to the researcher directly, for whatever reason. However, these conclusions are only as good as the care with which the content analysis is done. Researchers need to define clear dictionaries that define exactly what characteristics lead to a certain categorization and ensure that all coders involved in the research are coding the communications in the same way. Unlike some other research techniques, in which validity can be rather subjective, there are mathematically defined ways in which some aspects of the validity of a content analysis can be measured. Cohen's Kappa is the most common of these, and research with a high score on this or similar measures has a strong claim on validity.

Content analysis has experienced resurgence in recent years because computers have made it possible to carry out KWIC analyses using the tools available on most computers. There are also a number of more sophisticated content analysis programs that can carry out analyses of video or audio, though there are always concerns that the researcher doesn't fully control the coding dictionaries used in these programs. These programs are also most useful when the researcher is interested in very small context units, which may not be appropriate for all analyses.

Study and Review

Why might validity be a greater concern for content analysis than for other research techniques?

What can researchers do to establish the validity of research with large context units?

Under what circumstances is computerized content analysis most useful?

Does a high Cohen's Kappa mean that research is valid? Why or why not?

Why is content analysis so often used in feminist research?

CHAPTER 9

Experiments

Learning Objectives

- Be able to identify the features of classic experimental designs
- Be able to compare blind and double-blind experiments
- Be able to identify the features of natural experiments
- Be able to identify major threats to the internal validity of experiments
- Be able to explain the major advantages and disadvantages of experimental research designs

ISOLATING CAUSALITY

Claude M. Steele and Joshua Aronson—Stereotype Threat and Test Scores (1995)

No matter how carefully planned and carried out most research is, the results are descriptive or correlational. Descriptive results tell researchers *what* is happening: how many people are dying in a war, the characteristics of teens who work while in school. Correlational results tell researchers about the relationships *between* different variables: racists are more likely to be opposed to busing policies; people who take virginity pledges have sexual intercourse later than those who don't. What these findings don't tell researchers is *why* these things happen; that piece of the puzzle has to be filled in by theory. The only way that researchers can determine the cause of a relationship is through a carefully conducted experiment. Other methods can explain how two variables go together or associated, but they do not clarify cause and effect. Even time series studies can, at best, show Granger Causation. For this reason, experiments are considered the gold standard of social science research—but researchers must be extremely careful or the results of the experiments won't be valid.

The testing gap between African American and white students has been present since the beginning of the use of standardized tests in education. African American students do considerably worse on tests such as the SAT than white students, and researchers have posited a number of theories to explain why this is the case. Some have pointed to bias in the questions, some have argued for worse preparation, and some have even controversially argued that genetic factors play a role. Claude M. Steele and Joshua Aronson (1995), though, find an explanation in research on stereotype threat. Past research in social psychology has shown that when individuals are the only members of a group with a characteristic—for example, the only woman or the only African American—they tend to do worse on a task. The idea is that they're so busy worrying about representing their group badly in front of others that they aren't able to fully concentrate on the task at hand. Steele and Aronson thought that a similar effect could be reducing the test scores of African American students. If African Americans thought that the test was measuring intelligence, they would be worried about fulfilling negative stereotypes about the intelligence of African Americans and thus perform poorly on the test.

However, this is not a hypothesis that we could test by looking at people's test scores. If someone performs badly on a test, how would you know that it was because of stereotype threat and not because of poor preparation? Similarly, the hypothesis couldn't be directly tested by interviewing test takers. They may not be aware of the role of stereotype threat in their scores, and they wouldn't have any way of measuring how much of an impact the stereotype threat had.

Steele and Aronson (1995) tackled the question by offering 114 Stanford undergraduates (some white and some African American) $10 each to participate in a psychology experiment. The students were asked beforehand to provide their SAT verbal scores and their interest in verbal-oriented classes. When they came to the lab, all of the students were given the same exact instructions by an experimenter. He told them that they would spend the next half hour working on a set of questions in the same format as the SAT verbal section, that the questions were very difficult, and that they shouldn't expect to get very many of them right. Half of the participants, selected randomly, were then told that the test was designed to measure the effects of "various personal factors involved in performance on problems requiring reading and verbal reasoning abilities" and that it was a "genuine test of your verbal abilities and limitations so that we might better understand the factors involved in both" (p. 405). The other half of the participants were told that the study was to measure "psychological factors involved in solving verbal problems" and that the questions were supposed to give "even highly verbal people ... a mental challenge" (p. 405). The participants were also asked try hard, even though no one was assessing their ability.

After tabulating the results of the test and running a number of additional studies to clarify the results, Steele and Aronson (1995) found that the difference in instructions had a large effect on the performance of African American students on the test but no effect on the performance of white students. Of the thirty questions—which were designed to be difficult to solve—white students answered about twelve correctly, regardless of the instructions. When African American students were told that the test was about "factors involved in solving verbal problems," they scored the same as the white students, getting about twelve correct. However, when they were told that the test was a measure of their "verbal abilities and limitations," they only answered about nine of the questions correctly. These differences hold up even when Steele and Aronson accounted for the actual SAT scores of the students.

In a later study, Steele, along with Steven Spencer and Diane Quinn (1998), replicated these findings for women taking the math section of the GRE. One group of women was randomly assigned to a condition in which they were reminded that there are performance differences on mathematical tests based on gender: men generally do better on these tests. In the other group, the women were told that men and women score about equally well on the test. When the women were told that there was a gap in test scores between men and women, they did worse on the test. Their anxiety about confirming the stereotype led

women to do worse on the test, at least partially confirming the stereotype that they were worried about.

CLASSICAL EXPERIMENTAL DESIGN

In a **classical experimental design**, participants (though much of the literature in experimental research still refers to them as "subjects") are divided into two groups: the **experimental group** and the **control group**. The only difference between these two groups is that the experimental group receives the stimulus and the control group does not. The **stimulus** is whatever the researchers are studying, such as a new cholesterol drug, an experimental method to teach math, or a new workshop to decrease prejudice. For the workshop to decrease prejudice, the stimulus that the researchers are testing is stereotype threat. They create stereotype threat by calling the test a measure of intelligence. The stereotype threat is only administered to the experimental group; the control group does not receive any stereotype threat.

The researchers are trying to prove that the stereotype threat results in a decrease of scores. To establish a base level of achievement, ideally both the experimental group and the control group should take a standardized test to establish their base-level scores. This is called a **pretest**. After the pretest, the experimental group is presented with a stereotype threat (the stimulus), and the control group isn't. Afterward, to capture the effects of the stereotype threat, both groups are given **posttests** to see whether or not stereotype threat had an effect.

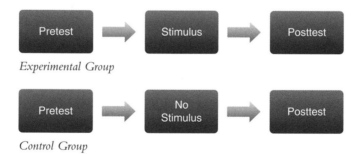

Experimental Group

Control Group

THE IMPORTANCE OF GROUP ASSIGNMENTS

Results like those found by Steele and Aronson (1995) are the reason that experiments are viewed as the most powerful form of research in the social sciences, the gold standard of evidence. Unlike analyses of things that have happened in the past or what individuals tell researchers, experiments allow researchers to determine causality, or why something happens. In Steele and Aronson's experiment, it's impossible to argue that the difference between the African American and white test scores is the result of differences in preparation or education because the participants were randomly placed into the groups. If Steele and Aronson had put all of the people who showed up first into the group that was told that the test wasn't about intelligence, and all of the people who showed up late into the group that was told that the test *was* about intelligence, then the results could have been the result of characteristics of the individuals. Maybe better, more motivated students are more likely to show up on time and do well on the test. The same could be said if the students in the two groups were drawn from different colleges or had different majors—but they weren't. The students were placed into groups randomly, so the only difference between the two groups was the instructions that they were given. If the randomization was carried out properly, and the two groups were essentially identical at the start of the experiment but had different results at the end of it, the difference has to be the result of the condition the groups were placed in. In this case, the difference in the instructions caused African American students to do worse on the test.

This is not to say that there isn't a bias in the test caused by the questions or any other factor, but it proves as definitively as social science can that the scores of African American students are depressed when the students believe that the tests are a measure of intelligence. This information, combined with the results about the underperformance of women on a math test when they are told that women do worse on the test, makes a strong case for the stereotype threat explanation. Women don't do worse on a verbal test when they are told that it is a test of ability because there's no stereotype that women are bad at verbal skills, just as in prior research African Americans didn't do worse on tests that were described as a measure of hand–eye coordination. These groups only do worse on tests when they are worried about confirming a stereotype.

Participant Selection

Experimental results are only valid when the experiments are carried out properly. The two most important factors are random assignment and control of the environment. **Random assignment** of participants into the various experimental conditions, often called *cells*, ensures that the groups were equivalent before the experiment begins. Any nonrandomness in this process—such as sorting participants based on the time that they came in the lab, by the day the study is carried out, or by the lab assistant who greets the participant—introduces a potential confound into the experimental results. A **confound** is something aside from the experimental condition that separates the groups, making it impossible for researchers to be sure that any differences between the groups at the end of the study are the result of what cell they were in, rather than the confound.

Control of the environment is necessary for the same reason. The only difference between the environments that the participants experience throughout the study should be the experimental manipulation: in this case, the instructions. In order to be sure that any differences are caused by the instructions (and only the instructions), the researchers must ensure that everything else about the experiment is identical, regardless of which cell the participant is in. For instance, if participants from the two conditions are put into different rooms, one room could be noisier or colder or have a bright wall color—a confound. This lurking variable—instead of the independent variable—may affect the dependent variable, a result that researchers called *spurious*. A less obvious confound could arise from the expectations of the experimenter. If the experimenter knows which participants are in which cell, he or she may treat the individuals differently. Even if such differences are unconscious, they could still have an impact on how participants react in the experiment, confounding the results. Note that in Steele and Aronson's (1995) study participants in both conditions received instructions that were the same, down to being about the same length, except for the critical phrases of the experimental manipulation. Even something as small as the complexity of the instructions or the amount of time spent reading them could be a confound.

Random Assignment

The easiest way to avoid a confound based on the groups to which participants are assigned is through random assignment. In random assignment, the researcher uses a random process—the role of a die, a number generated randomly by a computer—to determine the experimental cell into which the participant is placed. Ideally, the researcher shouldn't even know the cell to which the individual is assigned.

Having a random process doesn't eliminate the possibility of systematic differences between the experimental and control groups. For instance, in Steele and Aronson's (1995) study, it's possible that only some students are vulnerable to stereotype threat, and those students could have happened to be assigned to the stereotype threat condition. While this is possible, it doesn't seem very likely—especially as the size of the sample increases. If Steele and Aronson only had a few people in each experimental cell, this might be a plausible explanation; given their fairly large sample size, this doesn't seem very likely.

Random assignment also means that experimental cells may well end up with a different number of participants in each cell. While it's possible that there will be an equal number of participants randomly assigned to each condition, it's not likely, and this can cause some concerns. What if one condition gets very few participants? The only way to resolve this issue is by increasing the sample size. The bigger the sample size, the less likely that any cells will be too underpopulated.

Finally, it's important to note that the random assignment process must be fully random. It wouldn't be enough to, for instance, assign the first participant to the control condition, the second to the experimental condition, the third to the control, and so on. Suppose that friends were coming in pairs or that the first person to come in each day was a good student who showed up early. Similarly, assigning participants based on the hour or the day they entered the lab might lead to some systematic differences between the groups. True random assignment may be more difficult than these techniques, but it is necessary.

Matched Groups

While random assignment is generally considered the best way to avoid systematic bias in the participant assignment, it isn't always feasible. For instance, if an experimental treatment is very expensive or the pool of potential participants is very small, there may not be enough participants to make random assignment work. Psychological studies examining new techniques for counseling, educational studies looking for better ways to instruct a classroom, or medical studies that require expensive imaging equipment such as functional magnetic resonance imaging all face these sorts of limitations. If random assignment would result in having only a few participants in each condition, the risk of systematic bias may be large enough to justify forgoing random assignment altogether and using a matched group assignment instead.

In matched group assignments, participants are paired according to any characteristics that the researchers believe might cause systematic bias in the results. For instance, Steele and Aronson (1995) might have been worried about systematic bias resulting from gender and SAT scores. In that case, they would ensure that the control and experimental groups had equal numbers of men and women, equal distributions of SAT scores, and so on. Some researchers go so far as to match up individual participants on all of the characteristics of interest. So, if the researchers had access to two women with the same (or very similar) SAT scores, they would ensure that one went into the control condition and the other into the experimental condition.

This is a perfectly acceptable technique if the researchers have controlled for all the factors that could lead to systematic biases in the results of the study. However, it may be very difficult to control for *all* of these factors, and there's always the chance that there is some characteristic leading people to react differently to the stimulus that the researchers simply haven't considered. True random assignment is generally preferable, but if it isn't possible for whatever reason, careful use of matched groups assignment is an acceptable alternative.

Systematic Bias: Falling Cats

Eliminating systematic bias is vital because it ensures that the results of the experiment can be generalized to the larger population. Without it, it's impossible to be certain that any differences found at the end of the experiment are actually due to the stimulus and not some preexisting difference between the groups.

To understand why this is important, consider the example of cats falling out of windows. Conventional wisdom is that cats always land on their feet, but this isn't necessarily true when cats fall out of high-rise apartment buildings. To look at the issue, a group of veterinarians in New York City tracked the mortality rates of cats falling from different heights. Of course, the veterinarians didn't throw the cats out windows. This was a natural experiment dealing with cats that had fallen out of windows of various heights, presumably while chasing birds in the summertime, when their owners had left windows open. (We'll discuss natural experiments later in the chapter.) Common sense might suggest that the higher the floor the cats fell from, the less likely they would be to survive, but the veterinarians found a bizarre twist to this explanation. Cats that fell from the first five floors of a building didn't suffer too much injury, but cats that fell from the sixth through the tenth floors typically suffered worse injuries than cats that fell from higher floors (above the tenth). This suggests that cats are safer falling from the fifteenth floor than the sixth, a result that needs explanation. The veterinarians suggested that since cats falling from any significant height reach the same speed (terminal velocity), the difference comes from the cats having time to orient themselves, relax their muscles, and prepare for impact.

This seems like an interesting finding and has become part of popular lore about cats, but astrophysicist Neil DeGrasse Tyson, Director of the Hayden Planetarium in New York, has publicly disputed it (in Abumrad and Krulwich 2010). He argues that the results arise from a selection effect. Yes, the cats that fell from higher stories and were brought to veterinarians suffered less injury, but not all cats are brought to veterinarians. If a cat dies on impact, the owner isn't going to bother bringing it to the veterinarian. It could be that all cats that fall from above five stories have about the same risk of injury, as they're all falling at the same speed, but that a lot of the cats falling from higher stories just aren't part of the sample the veterinarians were studying. This bias might mean that the results of the analysis are only valid for the group studied—cats brought to veterinarians—and not the larger population of cats falling from buildings in general. The question could be resolved through a random cat-dropping experiment, but ethical concerns make such a study unlikely.

THE IMPORTANCE OF PROPER EXPERIMENTAL DESIGN

Gráinne M. Fitzsimons, Tanya L. Chartrand and Gavan J. Fitzsimons—Does Apple Make You Think Different? (2008)

It's impossible to overstate the importance of random assignment to experimental conditions for researchers carrying out experiments. Any failure of randomization means that the results could potentially be explained by differences between the groups before the experiment was begun, raising doubts about the validity of the study.

Gráinne M. Fitzsimons, Tanya J. Chartrand, and Gavan J. Fitzsimons (2008) looked at how the brain processes brands through the use of **subliminal priming**. In a subliminal priming task, participants are asked to look at part of a screen, where they can see a sequence of letters or a picture, referred to as the "forward mask." Then, participants may see a flash, which is quickly replaced by the "backward mask," often the same sequence of letters or picture that participants were looking at previously. What the participants don't know is that the flash, lasting ten to thirty milliseconds, was actually another word or picture, shown quickly enough that their brain was able to process it, but too quickly for it to come into conscious awareness. Essentially, the participants are thinking about something but don't know that they're thinking about it.

In Fitzsimons, Chartrand, and Fitzsimons' (2008) work, the subliminal primes were corporate logos from two different companies: Apple and IBM. Before beginning the experiment, the researcher carried out a pilot study on the logos to see how they were perceived. The participants in the pilot study liked both of the logos about equally, but, as the researchers had supposed, thought that the

Apple logo represented creativity better than the IBM logo (not that IBM was seen as uncreative—on average, it was placed right in the middle of the scale). Three hundred forty-one students participated in the main study, with each group coming from a different section of the same class, held at the same time on different days. Normally, the use of entire classes could represent a confound, but the researchers report that the students were assigned to the different sections randomly. To make sure that the groups didn't vary from each other, the researchers had all of the students complete a demographic questionnaire and checked that all of the important characteristics of the two groups were about the same.

Once participants had signed consent forms, they were asked to watch the screen. They were subliminally primed repeatedly with one of the logos while carrying out a simple arithmetic task. (The forward and backward masks were numbers between one and thirteen, and the participants were asked to add all of the numbers that they had seen.) After the priming, the students were randomly assigned to a further experimental condition. Half of the participants received a workbook that asked them to complete a menial task (crossing out all of the instances of the letter *e* in a dense engineering text, which took about five minutes), followed by an "unusual uses" task. The other half of the participants were asked to immediately do the "unusual uses" task. In the unusual uses test, participants were asked to come up with as many unusual uses for a common object as they can; for instance, using a paperclip to hold paper together isn't unusual, but using it as an earring or as handcuffs for a mouse would be. It's generally unclear how long the effects of subliminal priming last, so the researchers included the menial task as a delay, to see if the effects of the Apple or IBM logos would last more than a few minutes.

After finishing the unusual uses task, the participants filled out a debriefing sheet, in which they were asked whether or not they had seen the logos and what effect the logos may have had on their unusual uses task performance. After everyone had finished, one of the researchers explained the purposes of the study to the participants.

In the analysis of the unusual uses task, the researchers found that those participants who had been primed with the Apple logo generated more ideas for unusual uses (an average of 8.14 uses) than those who had been primed with the IBM logo (an average of 6.17 uses). They also had coders rate the creativity of the various uses listed and found that participants who had been primed with the Apple logo generated more creative ideas than those who had been primed with the IBM logo.

Because of potential problems with this study, Fitzsimons, Chartrand, and Fitzsimons (2008) replicated it under different conditions. For the replication study, they recruited seventy-three participants from the campus, paying each of them $20 for their participation. These participants were told that they were part of a study on "spatio-temporal ordering"; essentially, they were asked to look at three randomly ordered pictures on a computer screen and place them in an order that made narrative sense, or told a story. Each participant ordered four sets of photos before the experimental manipulation occurred. In the fifth series, about one-third of the participants viewed a series that included a picture of an IBM computer with the logo visible, about one-third viewed the same series but with a picture of an Apple computer with the logo visible, and the remaining third had a series of pictures without a computer in them. Afterward, the participants completed the same unusual uses task that participants in the previous study had, but in a different format from the spatio-temporal ordering task to make it seem as if there was no connection between the tasks.

In the second experiment, the pictures of the computers served as a superliminal prime, meaning that participants saw the logos but were unaware of the influence of the logos on their behavior. Once again, participants who had been exposed to the Apple logo gave more unusual uses for the object than participants who had been exposed to the IBM logo or hadn't been exposed to either logo. Also, the responses of the participants exposed to the Apple logo were rated as being more creative than the responses of those in the other experimental conditions.

Fitzsimons, Chartrand, and Fitzsimons' (2008) findings are fascinating. People tend to think of creativity as an inborn trait (something people either have or don't have), so the idea that someone's creativity (at least as operationalized in an unusual uses task) can be increased through mere exposure to a corporate logo is shocking. Moreover, the differences between the groups reported in the first study were substantial: a bit more than eight responses for the group primed with the Apple logo versus a bit more than six responses for the group primed with the IBM logo. Still, the researchers found it necessary to do a version of the study again to correct what could be perceived as problems in the first study.

The first of these problems was a lack of complete randomization in assignment. In the first study, the participants were students in a large lecture hall. They were all watching a screen in the front of the room at the same time. As such, all of the students in the room at that time were necessarily getting the same prime; the students in the other section, the next day, got the other prime. Now, Fitzsimons, Chartrand, and Fitzsimons (2008) make a good case that the classes represented random assignment. All of the students were randomly placed into one section or the other, and the two sections met at the same hour, in the same room, just one day apart. There's no reason to expect that one of these groups was more creative than the other going into the task, so why did the experiment need to be redone?

Even if the measurable characteristics of the two classrooms full of students were identical, there were almost certainly some differences between the first group and the second group other than the experimental manipulation. The weather may very well have been different from one day to another, and that could have affected the mood of the participants. Studies have also shown that people tend to have better moods on certain days of the week than on others. The difference between Wednesday and Thursday may be small, but it still could be consequential, and the difference between Thursday and Friday could be quite large. Perhaps students in one of the groups were more likely to have just taken a test or stayed up late studying for one. There's no evidence that any of these potential confounds occurred, but there's also no way that Fitzsimons, Chartrand, and Fitzsimons (2008) can show that they *didn't* occur. The differences in performance on the unusual uses task in the first study were probably the result of the priming, but without full randomization, there's no way to be certain. In the second study, this issue was corrected by randomly assigning participants to a condition when they began the study. It's unlikely that there were systematic differences between participants in the two groups of the first study, but there's no way that there were systematic differences between participants in the second study. Some participants may have just taken a test or may have been in a bad mood, but all participants were equally likely to be in any of the experimental conditions.

In the first study, Fitzsimons, Chartrand, and Fitzsimons (2008) made use of a 2 × 2 experimental design. There were two conditions (IBM vs. Apple, and delay vs. no delay), and participants were randomly assigned to one of the four resulting cells. About half of the participants who were primed with an Apple logo were delayed before doing the unusual uses task, and so on. In the second study, Fitzsimons, Chartrand, and Fitzsimons got rid of the delay (it didn't seem to make a difference) and introduced a third condition, the control group, making the second study a 3 × 1 experimental design with a total of just three cells (IBM, Apple, or control). In the first study, participants were primed with either the Apple logo or the IBM logo, but everyone was primed with something. The problem with an experimental design like this is that it's possible—though there's certainly no evidence for this—that the act of priming people has some impact on their performance on the unusual uses task. Maybe all of the participants would have given ten unusual uses if they hadn't been primed. It doesn't seem likely, but there's nothing in the experimental design that precludes it. A second problem with the experimental design is that it's not clear what direction the results are going in. Fitzsimons, Chartrand, and Fitzsimons argue that exposure to the Apple logo is making participants give more unusual uses, but all that the study shows is that the participants give more uses than individuals exposed to the IBM logo. An equally valid interpretation of this is that the Apple logo has no impact on the number of unusual uses listed, but the IBM logo decreases it.

The introduction of a control group resolves both of these issues. Since the control group isn't exposed to any prime at all, the study can show if exposure to a prime—regardless of what the prime is—has an impact on the number of unusual uses listed. If it does, both of the primed conditions will do worse than the control condition. Second, the control condition allows the researchers to show that exposure to the Apple logo not only leads to participants listing more unusual uses than participants exposed to the IBM logo, but also listing more uses than participants would if they had not been exposed to a logo at all. This is what the results from the second study show pretty clearly: participants in the IBM condition and those in the control condition scored almost exactly the same.

STIMULUS PRETESTING

Samuel R. Sommers and Michael I. Norton—Race and Jury Challenges (2007)

Samuel R. Sommers and Michael I. Norton (2007), both professors of business at Harvard University, were looking at the use of preemptory (pronounced "per-emp-tory", for some reason) challenges by lawyers in jury cases. Before a trial starts, lawyers on both sides are allowed to dismiss a certain number of potential jurors who they think might be unfair to their side without having to give an explanation. Lawyers are not allowed to dismiss a juror solely because of the race of the juror, but there's a great deal of suspicion that lawyers do just that. It's very hard to prove that racism is going on, however, because lawyers generally don't have to say why they dismissed a juror, and if they are asked, they're unlikely to reveal that it was because of race.

The goal of Sommers and Norton's (2007) study was to determine if race actually was a factor in the dismissal of jurors. They did this by setting up a trial scenario, complete with prospective jurors. The participants in the study—which consisted of three different groups, including undergraduate students, advanced law students, and practicing attorneys—were asked to decide which of two jurors they would challenge if they were a prosecutor.

Each participant was presented with a scenario in which the defendant (whose race was not specified) allegedly beat a homeowner (a twenty-four-year-old African American male) with a blunt object after being caught in the middle of a burglary. The victim couldn't identify the attacker, so the case against the defendant relied on DNA evidence and hair and footprint analysis. The participants were then shown the profiles of two jurors, along with a picture of each, and told that they had one challenge left and had to decide which of these jurors they would remove. Finally, they were asked to explain why they had decided to remove that particular juror.

> ### Juror 1
>
> A forty-three-year-old married male with no previous jury experience. He was a journalist who, several years earlier, had written articles about police misconduct.
>
> ### Juror 2
>
> A forty-year-old divorced male who had served on two previous juries. He was an advertising executive with little scientific background who stated during *voir dire* that he was skeptical of statistics because they are easily manipulated.

The researchers had pilot tested a number of profiles to find these two, which were perceived as being equally hostile to the prosecution in the case. Absent any other information, the participants should have been equally likely to challenge the jurors. However, there was more information—a picture of each juror—and this is where the experimental manipulation came in. For half of the participants, Juror 1 was pictured as African American and Juror 2 as white; for the other half of the participants, the race of the jurors was reversed.

Overall, about two-thirds of the sample chose to challenge Juror 1, but they were far more likely to challenge the African American juror than the white juror.

When Juror 1 was African American, almost 80 percent of participants challenged. When he was white, only 53 percent of participants did so. Similarly, about half of participants challenged Juror 2 when he was African American, and only about a quarter did so when he was white.

Sommers and Norton (2007) also looked at how the justifications given by the participants changed based on the race of the jurors. Very few of the participants (about 7 percent) said that they had made their challenge based on race. When Juror 1 was African American, 73 percent of participants said that his experience with police misconduct was the main reason for challenging him, compared with just 49 percent of the time when he was white. When Juror 2 was white, 23 percent of participants said that his skepticism about statistics was the main reason for challenging him; when he was African American, 48 percent did so.

The results of Sommers and Norton's (2007) research are troubling. They show the ineffectiveness of the process set up by the Supreme Court in getting rid of race-based jury challenges. The results show that participants—including practicing attorneys with trial experience—take race into account when challenging jurors, and they almost always have a race-neutral explanation for having done so.

The validity of Sommers and Norton's (2007) findings, though, like those of Fitzsimons, Chartrand, and Fitzsimons (2008), are bolstered by their pilot testing of experimental materials. **Pilot testing** refers to the process of collecting data about experimental materials before the experiment, to ensure that they function the way that the researchers intend. In the logo priming study, the researchers had a group of students comparable to the students who were later part of the experiment rate the logos of various companies to see which ones were viewed as more creative, which ones were more or less liked, and various other criteria. As a result, the researchers were able to pick logos that were viewed as being about the same on everything except creativity. If it had been the case that the Apple logo was well liked while the IBM logo was not, the difference could have been due to positive feelings toward Apple, rather than increased creativity.

Similarly, Sommers and Norton (2007) tested a large number of juror profiles on a sample similar to the sample that they would actually use in the study, and they only used the two profiles that were rated as being the most similar by their pilot testing group. The goal of this pilot study was to ensure that the participants in the actual experiment would be about equally likely to choose either of the prospective jurors and that any differences would be the result of the profile's race. It's clear that this pilot testing was not entirely effective (participants in the study were more likely to challenge Juror 1 regardless of his race), but it was effective enough. If it were the case that Juror 1 had been challenged 90 percent of the time, it would be hard to tell if that number went up when he was African American because there isn't much room for it to increase. Similarly, if one of the prospective jurors had only been challenged 10 percent of the time, it would be difficult to know if being white reduced his likelihood of being challenged. In this case, a failure to pilot test could have led to the results of the study being completely invalid.

DESIGNS TO CONTROL FOR PARTICIPANT PRETESTING

David P. Redlawsk—Shortcuts and Accurate Voting (2002)

Once researchers have carried out pilot studies to ensure that their experimental materials will work the way that they are supposed to, it becomes necessary to design the actual experiment. In a classic experimental design, participants begin with a pretest. The pretest of the participants is used to measure whatever characteristics interest the researchers, followed by the stimulus (or lack of stimulus, in the control condition), and ending with a posttest. The researchers can then estimate the effect of the experimental stimulus by looking for differences in the amount of change between the pretest and the posttest in the experimental versus the control group. If the experimental manipulation worked, there should be greater change in the experimental group than in the control group.

David P. Redlawsk (2002)—now the director of the Eagleton Poll at Rutgers University—follows this structure. In his study, participants begin by filling out a political attitudes questionnaire that asks about their demographic characteristics and political views, determines their level of political knowledge, and gages the importance of various political issues to them. Afterward, they practice using what Redlawsk calls a "dynamic information board" to collect information about the candidates in a mock election. The information board is supposed to simulate a real election by allowing participants to click on headlines to get positive or negative information about one candidate or another. However, the amount of information participants could get was limited. Clicking on one item meant ignoring some others. The participants had 20 minutes to gather information from the dynamic information board before making a choice about which candidate to vote for, and were interrupted with campaign ads or polls while they were trying to get the information. Since this was all done on computer, Redlawsk was able to track exactly what information the participants looked at, how much time they spent on it, and what impact this seemed to have on their vote choice.

At this point, the experimental stimulus begins. Half of the participants are told that after making their vote choice they'll have to list everything that they know about each of the six candidates in the election. The other participants aren't told this. The purpose of this instruction is to create an accuracy motivation in the participants who are told that they'll have to justify their choice. People do not like to look like idiots, so participants who are told that they'll have to explain why they supported one candidate over the others should go out of their way to collect lots of information about the candidates to be able to explain their decision. Those who don't know that they'll have to explain their choice are expected to gather enough information to decide who they like and then ignore any information that would lead them to change their minds. Voters who don't pay as much attention to the information, though, still are able to vote correctly (the same way that they would have if they had all of the information) most of the time.

Redlawsk's (2002) study makes use of both experimental and control groups, as in a classic experimental design, so his results show that there is a significant difference in the amount of information participants look for when they're trying to be as accurate as possible and when they're just trying to make a decision. He is able to rely on a large body of research in political psychology to show that voters, most of the time, are acting like the participants who aren't given the accuracy motivation. There is, however, a key difference between most voters and the participants in Redlawsk's study: the pretest. While a pretest may be vital to establish differences between the experimental and control groups, it may also work as a confound. Remember, all of the participants in Redlawsk's study filled out a long questionnaire about their political beliefs and the factors that led to their voting decisions in previous elections, and it could be argued that the act of filling out such a survey makes participants in both the experimental and control conditions more likely to think about their views and how to apply them, and perhaps more likely to seek out information. Now, this issue doesn't reduce the validity of Redlawsk's results: if participants in the control condition were seeking out more information than they would have otherwise, it would have reduced the size of the difference between the control and experimental conditions, so all it means is that the effects could actually be larger than what Redlawsk found. Still, the bias introduced by the mere act of filling out the pretest could be a significant problem, and researchers often use a variant on the classic experimental design in order to deal with it.

Solomon Three Group Design

This variant is the **Solomon Three Group Design**, first discussed by psychologist Richard L. Solomon in 1949. In it, researchers make use of a second control group. Unlike the first control group, which gets the pre- and posttests but not the stimulus, the second control group gets the stimulus and the posttest,

Classic Experimental Design			
Experimental Group	Pretest	Stimulus	Posttest
Control Group	Pretest		Posttest
Solomon Three Group Design			
Experimental Group	Pretest	Stimulus	Posttest
Control Group 1	Pretest		Posttest
Control Group 2		Stimulus	Posttest
Solomon Four Group Design			
Experimental Group	Pretest	Stimulus	Posttest
Control Group 1	Pretest		Posttest
Control Group 2		Stimulus	Posttest
Control Group 3			Posttest

but not the pretest. The additional control group allows researchers to estimate the effects of the pretest by looking at the differences in the posttest results of the experimental group and the second control group.

Suppose that the pretest doesn't have any effect at all. If this were the case, the second control group and the experimental group should have the same results on the posttest. In Redlawsk's (2002) study, this would be represented by a group of participants who were told that they would have to list everything they knew about the candidates (the experimental stimulus), but who were never given a pretest. If the pretest had an effect, this group of participants would perform differently from the experimental group. If the pretest didn't have any effect, the groups would perform about the same.

Solomon Four Group Design

The same logic can be extended into what's seen as the highest standard of experimental designs, the **Solomon Four Group Design**. This design is similar to the Solomon Three Group Design, save that another control group has been added. This control group receives only the posttest. The scores from this group on the posttest can be used to estimate what the results of the other groups would have been if they hadn't participated in the study at all. There are a number of reasons why this could be a problem. Many studies, like Redlawsk's (2002), require a great deal of mental energy, and by the end of the study, participants could be tired, which would affect their scores on the posttest. If the study takes place over a long period of time, events in the outside world or even aging could have an impact on the responses of participants. However, there's no way to know how these external factors affect the responses of participants in the Solomon Three Group Design or the classic experimental design because they happen equally to all of the participants. The calculation of the effects in the Solomon Four Group Design seems as if it could be tricky because there aren't any pretest scores for the third control group. However, as long as there is random assignment of participants into groups, researchers can assume that the pretest scores of the third control group would have been about the same as the average of the groups that did take the pretest. As such, the effects of external factors such as tiredness or events in the outside world would be estimated by looking at the difference between the posttest scores of the third group and the experimental group, after taking into account any effect of the pretest (as in the Solomon Three Group Design).

If Redlawsk (2002) had wanted to carry out a Solomon Four Group Design, some of his participants would have been randomly assigned to go home, or wait in a lounge watching TV, and come back only when it was time for everyone to take the posttest. He could have safely assumed that this group started off like everyone else in the study and therefore been able to use their scores to control for the influence of all the outside effects on the posttest scores.

The Solomon Four Group Design is seen as the gold standard of designs for good reason. It accounts for many of the factors that may corrupt the results of the experiment, from bias on the pretests to outside events that researchers don't have any control over. However, it's not used very often in modern social science because it's highly inefficient. It requires two additional control groups, so if all of the groups are the same size (though they don't have to be, it can make the math trickier if they aren't), it requires twice as many participants—and therefore twice as much time, effort, and money—as classic experimental designs. Researchers tend to make use of the Solomon Three and Four Group Designs only when they are worried about the impact of pretest effects (in the case of the Three Group) or external events (as in the Four Group). If these are expected to be a factor (for example, if the posttest is weeks or months after the pretest or if the pretest involves questions about sensitive topics), it makes sense to use one of these designs. If these issues don't seem as if they're going to be a problem, the additional control groups are probably unnecessary.

MY HOBBY:

SNEAKING INTO EXPERIMENTS AND
GIVING LSD TO THE CONTROL GROUP

How Many Participants Are Needed?

The question remains, though: How many participants does an experimental study actually need? There are two ways to answer the question. The first is that the sample size necessary to obtain valid results is a function of the expected magnitude of the results, how much variance there is in those results, the statistical certainty with which the researcher wants to establish those results, and the number of cells in the study. The calculations using these variables to arrive at an optimum sample size is called *power analysis*, and the basics are pretty simple. If an experimental manipulation is expected to have a large effect on the participants, a smaller size is probably okay. An experimental manipulation with a highly variable outcome (that affects some participants a great deal and others not very much) requires more participants. An experimenter who wants to achieve 99 percent statistical certainty in the results needs more participants than one who wants to achieve only 95 percent certainty. Finally, the more cells that are used, the more participants are needed. Of course, many of the figures that go into these calculations are guesswork. It's unlikely that a researcher knows how big the effect of an experimental manipulation will be or how variable those effects will be before actually doing the study. The only way a researcher would know that is if the study had been carried out a number of times before under similar circumstances, and if that's the case, what's the point of doing it again? So, the second answer is that researchers carrying out experiments generally insist on a minimum of twenty participants per cell in the experiment, with more if the experimental manipulation is relatively subtle. A Solomon Four Group Design would generally require at least eighty participants. For a more complicated experimental design, such as a $3 \times 2 \times 2$ factorial design (discussed later in the chapter), a minimum of about 240 participants would be needed to find the desired results.

FILLER TASKS

Michele Alexander and Terri Fisher—Fake Lie Detectors and Sex Lives (2003)

In all of the experimental designs that have been discussed, some of the participants skip parts of the study. For instance, in the classic experimental design, the control group doesn't get the experimental stimulus—but that doesn't mean that participants go straight from pretest to posttest. It's vital that participants in the control group (or groups) have as similar an experience to the experimental group as possible. This means that researchers in experimental studies frequently make use of filler tasks. These filler tasks are designed to have content similar to the stimulus and take as much time as the stimulus but not actually have an impact on the posttest.

Michele Alexander and Terri Fisher's (2003) study gives a good example of why this is necessary. Alexander and Fisher are psychologists who study the difference between the sexual behaviors reported by heterosexual men and women. For instance, in surveys of sexual behavior, heterosexual men report having more sexual partners than heterosexual women, report having more sex than heterosexual women, and report having their first sexual encounter earlier than heterosexual women. These results persist even when the surveys are completely anonymous, but it seems very unlikely. If the heterosexual men are only having sex with women, then the average number of sexual partners and sexual acts among men and women should be exactly the same. The size of the differences implies that someone is lying on these surveys, and Alexander and Fisher designed a study to find out if that's the case.

For their study, they made use of the bogus pipeline, an experimental technique in which participants think that they've been hooked up to a lie detector. Actually hooking participants up to a lie detector would almost certainly be unethical, but there's nothing necessarily unethical about making them *think* that someone will know if they're not telling the truth.

After pilot testing to make sure that participants believed that the nonfunctional lie detector was working, Alexander and Fisher (2003) divided their participants (college undergraduates getting course credit) into three groups. All of the groups were taken to individual rooms for the study and didn't interact with other participants. The first group watched a video showing a student talking to a professor. Next, these participants were shown the "lie detector"; were told how it worked; and had electrodes attached to their hands, forearms, and neck. They were given a demonstration of the lie detector, in which they gave a false response and a true response to a simple question and were shown that there was a difference in the output of the machine. They were also told that the machine would be able to pick up lies, even in written responses. After that, the participants were asked to fill out a questionnaire about their sexual history while they were attached to the nonfunctional lie detector. They were left alone to complete the questionnaire in private and put the questionnaire into a locked box as they left.

The second group was brought into the room and attached to the polygraph in the same way, but instead of filling out the questionnaire, participants watched the video and rated the degree of sexual interest displayed by the student and professor. They were then disconnected from the lie detector. They filled out their questionnaire alone and put it into the locked box.

The final group was never attached to the polygraph, but participants were told that they would hand their questionnaire to the research assistant sitting outside of the room, ostensibly making them fear that a peer would see what they had said. Of course, this didn't actually happen, and after participants watched the video and filled out the questionnaire, they were instructed to put the survey into the same locked box as everyone else.

Which of the conditions had a significant effect on what the participants said about their sex lives? Men who were put into the third group—in which they were told the research assistant would see the results—reported more sexual partners than women in the same group; however, there weren't any differences between men and women in the other conditions. Similarly, while men reported more liberal sexual attitudes in all of the conditions, the biggest difference was when they thought they would have to give the questionnaire to someone directly. Based on these results, Alexander and Fisher (2003) conclude that many of the reported differences between men and women's sexual behaviors based on surveys are the result of men and women trying to conform to what they perceive as socially appropriate sexual roles. Women downplay how much sex they have and how much they like it, and men pretend to have more.

In this study, the filler task was watching the video while attached to the fake lie detector. Having the second group (the control group) engage in this task served two purposes for Alexander and Fisher's (2003) research. First, it made sure that participants in the first (experimental) and second (control) groups were in the room for the same amount of time. It's possible that just sitting in a small room can affect how people answer questions on surveys, and if one group is in the room longer, this could be a confound. Second, the filler task eliminated any change in responses due to participants having electrodes attached to their hands and neck. By making sure that participants in both groups watched the video and were attached to the lie detector at some point, Alexander and Fisher (2003) ensured that any differences between the groups were solely the result of being hooked up to the fake lie detector while filling out the questionnaire.

Although this study seems to follow the classic experimental design (one experimental and one control group), it has an additional group. The third group, which was told that participants would have to hand the questionnaire to the research assistant, wasn't a second control group, as in a Solomon Three Group Design, but a second experimental group. There's nothing terribly unusual about this. Most experimental studies use more than two groups, and this is referred to as a *factorial design*. In this case, participants were randomly assigned to one of three groups, which is referred to as a 3 × 1 design. If the participants had also been randomly assigned to work with a research assistant who was the same gender or the opposite gender, the study would use a 3 × 2 design, with the three main conditions (control, bogus pipeline, threat of exposure) crossed with two gender conditions (same gender, opposite gender), for a total of 6 cells.

Although Alexander and Fisher (2003) took steps to ensure that all of the conditions of the experiment were the same for participants regardless of which condition they were assigned to, they didn't worry about making sure that the experimenter dealing with the participants treated everyone equally. That's not to say that they didn't take any steps: the experimenters were trained to hook the fake polygraph up to everyone in the exact same way and give the same instructions, but there was no way for the researchers to hide the conditions from the experimenters or the participants. The experimenters necessarily knew which condition each participant was in; after all, the procedures were very different. The participants didn't know what was happening to the other participants, but if they chose to compare notes, they would have been able to determine which group they were in. This potential problem is referred to as *contamination*, and it occurs when participants from different conditions discuss the study, allowing them to potentially figure out the research question, the hypotheses, and what group they were assigned to.

Contamination wasn't too much of a problem in Alexander and Fisher's (2003) study because their study focused on differences that resulted from how the participants were treated. There's a potential problem if the experimenters who hooked up the participants in the control condition did a sloppier job than they did in the experimental condition, but, again, this is the sort of problem training can correct. In other research, though, the failure to blind or double-blind the study can lead to real problems.

BLIND AND DOUBLE-BLIND STUDIES

Jack van Honk and Dennis J.L.G. Schutter—Testosterone and Emotion Recognition (2007)

Jack van Honk and Dennis Schutter's (2007) research on the effect of testosterone on the recognition of emotions shows why this precaution is sometimes necessary. Laboratory studies, mostly on rodents, have shown that higher levels of testosterone lead to more aggressive social behaviors. This seems to be the case among humans as well because men who are given testosterone as part of medical treatments report more aggressive behaviors, even fights, immediately after getting a shot of the hormone. However, there hasn't been much research on human participants—it is difficult to carry out ethically—and there's almost no research that explains how testosterone works. What does testosterone do to people that causes them to engage in aggressive behavior?

One explanation is that testosterone reduces people's ability to recognize emotions in facial expressions. If someone doesn't know when he or she is making someone else angry, the person may be more likely to find himself or herself in a conflict. To test this hypothesis, van Honk and Schutter (2007) recruited sixteen women ages nineteen to twenty-six years, all of whom were taking birth control pills (which regulate their hormone levels throughout the month). The researchers paid the women 45 Euros (about $60) for their participation. The women came in for the study twice, two days apart, and each time they were given a pill that dissolved under their tongues. A few minutes after taking the pill, the participants were asked to look at pictures of actors to determine what emotion they were portraying.

The experimental manipulation in the study was the actual contents of the pill. One of the times that each woman came in, the pill contained half a milligram of testosterone, along with water and ethanol. The other time, the pill contained everything but the testosterone; this pill, commonly referred to as a *placebo*, had no actual effects. Neither the women nor the researchers knew whether the women were getting the testosterone pill or the placebo that day.

Results of the study showed that when women were given the testosterone pill, they did a worse job at recognizing angry faces; the faces had to be angrier before the women recognized the emotion being portrayed. Van Honk and Schutter (2007) argue that this gives some indication as to why higher levels of testosterone may lead people to be more aggressive. These individuals just don't realize that people are getting angry with them. The results also parallel differences between men and women—men, who have generally higher levels of testosterone than women, are much worse at recognizing facial emotions. The extra dose of testosterone made the women in the study act just a little bit more like men.

The research on the effect of testosterone on the facial recognition of emotions is a good example of why it's sometimes necessary to make studies blind or even double-blind. In a **blinded study**, participants don't know what condition they've been assigned to. In a **double-blind study**, neither the participant nor any of the experimenters know what condition the participant has been assigned to. The goal of blinding or double-blinding research is the same as for many of the experimental procedures that have been discussed: to ensure that everything about the experiment except for the actual stimulus is the same for participants in the experimental and control groups. Any difference in how participants in the two groups are treated could be a confound, and the way the experimenters treat their participants is no different. In van Honk and Schutter's (2007) research, if the experimenters had known that a participant had just received a dose of testosterone, they might have, even subconsciously, treated the participant differently from one who had just received a placebo. This difference in treatment could lead participants to act differently during the posttest of looking at facial expressions and could therefore destroy the validity of the findings.

A related problem is *experimenter expectancy*, in which researchers not only inadvertently reveal which group participants are in but also hint at the hypotheses. As discussed in Chapter 10, participants in a study constantly try to figure out what the person asking questions wants them to say, so if they think they know what the researcher is trying to prove, they may act differently in order to give the "correct" answer.

To eliminate this bias, researchers make use of a double-blind experimental design. In a double-blind experimental design, neither the researcher nor the participants know which condition the participant is assigned to. If the researcher does not know which group is taking the experimental drug and which group is taking the placebo, the researcher cannot treat the groups differently.

Even in double-blind studies, it is possible for the participants to figure out what the hypothesis is. The wording of the questions, the information about the research project, and even the research design itself could potentially reveal to the participants what the study is about. Once they discover what the researcher's hypothesis is, many participants try to "prove the hypothesis." The tendency of participants to please the researcher and help the researcher prove the hypotheses is referred to as *demand characteristic*. To avoid this, introductory sections of studies tell the participants what the study is generally about, but they leave out the specific hypotheses. In some cases, deception is used to avoid this potential threat to internal validity.

Similarly, participants who think that they've just been given a pill containing testosterone would almost certainly act differently from those who don't think this, even though the pill may not contain active ingredients. This difference is called the *placebo effect*—the tendency of people to perceive the expected effects of a treatment even when the treatment is ineffective. So, giving people pills that contain a purported antidepressant will make them feel happier, even if the pills are merely cornstarch. As such, if participants know which condition they're in—whether the study involves giving participants pills or exposing them to subliminal primes—they are likely to act differently than they would otherwise, and this change could serve as a confound on the experimental results.

MANIPULATION CHECKS

Eric Stice, Diane Spangler, and W. Stewart Agras—The Effect of Seventeen Magazine on Body Image (2001)

Large numbers of laboratory experiments have shown that women—especially adolescent women—tend to have worse body images after they're exposed to media representations of idealized women. In some studies, it's been shown that just watching a half hour of television shows and advertising leads women to overestimate the size of their waist and hips relative to women who did not watch television. This research, though, faces some of the problems of external validity that bedevil much experimental research. Even if these effects pertain to a laboratory setting, do they work in the outside world as well? If they do happen in the outside world, how long do they last? After all, if watching television makes women feel worse about themselves or perceive themselves as fatter for five minutes afterward, it's not nearly as important as it would be if women had worse body images for days or weeks afterward.

To try to resolve these concerns, Eric Stice, Diane Spangler, and W. Stewart Agras (2001) carried out an experiment outside of the laboratory. These sorts of studies, called **field experiments**, are discussed in more detail later in the chapter, but they generally represent an effort to improve the external validity of experiments by applying experimental methods outside of a completely controlled environment. For their study, Stice, Spangler, and Agras sent a consent letter to the parents of girls at two private schools in San Francisco, California, vaguely explaining that they were doing research on the "development of adolescent physical and mental health" and giving parents the opportunity to opt their children out of the study if they liked. Nearly all of the parents agreed, giving the researchers a sample size of 219 participants between thirteen and seventeen years old. The researchers went to the schools, where the girls filled out surveys that asked about their body image, perceived pressure to be thin, how much they were dieting, and an index of bulimia-related behaviors.

The experimental manipulation, which the researchers didn't even recognize was an experimental manipulation until after they began the study, was the pay-off for filling out these surveys. Forty-five percent of the girls who filled out the surveys (randomly assigned) were rewarded with a subscription to *Seventeen*, and about 5 percent were sent a gift certificate to a book and music store. The gift certificates were used so that the girls wouldn't recognize that the research was linked to the magazine and to create a second control group. Half of the girls in the study did not receive an incentive. *Seventeen* was chosen because it was the most popular magazine targeted toward adolescent girls and because previous research had shown that it featured ultra-thin models more than other, similar magazines. The researchers carried out follow-up studies (repeating the survey ten and twenty months after the first survey) and looked for differences between the girls who had received *Seventeen* and those who had not.

Their results did not show any main effect of receiving the magazines on the girls' body images, dieting behavior, or bulimia. On average, girls who received the magazine weren't any different on these scales than the girls who didn't receive the magazine. Their results did show some conditional effects, meaning that while receiving the magazine didn't affect everyone in the group, it did have an effect on girls who had certain traits at the start of the study. Getting *Seventeen* led girls who didn't have much social support—strong connections and communication networks with parents and their peers—to be less satisfied with their bodies, more likely to diet, and more likely to show symptoms of bulimia. Similarly, girls who started out (in the initial survey) dissatisfied with their body and felt pressure to be thin were sadder on later surveys if they received the magazine than if they did not.

These conditional results make sense. Girls who have strong social support may be more able to resist the negative effects of being exposed to idealized body images, and girls who have negative body images to begin with may be more likely to compare themselves with the images in the magazine and therefore feel bad about themselves.

Stice, Spangler, and Agras' (2001) work is important because it brought experiments on the effect of media exposure on body images out of the laboratory and into the real world. This increase in external validity, though, leads to problems in control. Namely, their research is only valid to the extent that the girls who got the subscriptions to *Seventeen* actually read the magazine. If the research had been carried out in a lab, Stice and his colleagues could have made certain that the girls assigned to the *Seventeen* condition read the magazine. But since the girls got the magazine at home and could have read it, given it to a sibling, or thrown it directly into the recycling bin, the researchers had to carry out tests to see how effective their experimental manipulation actually was. These sorts of follow-up studies are called *manipulation checks*. They are questions or observations taken after the experiment to determine whether participants assigned to the experimental condition received the intended stimulus. For instance, in Alexander and Fisher's (2003) research using the bogus pipeline (fake lie detector) technique, the manipulation was that some participants thought that the researchers would know if they were lying. A manipulation check would ask participants if they knew, or suspected, that the apparatus wasn't really a functional lie detector. In a study of subliminal priming, a manipulation check includes asking if participants saw the words that were supposed to have flashed too quickly to be recognized. For Stice, Spangler, and Agras, the manipulation check needed to determine whether or not the participants who were randomly assigned to get a subscription to *Seventeen* actually looked at the magazine.

To assess this, Stice, Spangler, and Agras (2001) included questions on the three surveys that asked participants about how much time they had spent reading *Seventeen*, *Cosmopolitan*, *Glamour*, and *Mademoiselle* each month. The inclusion of the other magazines in the questions served two purposes. First, it helped make sure that participants didn't link the magazine with the surveys. Remember, the participants thought that the magazine subscription was just a reward for filling out the surveys; they didn't know that it was supposed to have an impact on them. If they had known that they were supposed to be acting differently because they were getting the magazine, this could have created a confound.

Normally, giving participants indications of what the study is about isn't a problem in manipulation checks, but that's because manipulation checks normally take place after the posttest—after all of the data has been collected. In this case, because the manipulation check took place over the course of the experiment, it had to be disguised. Second, including the other magazines in the manipulation check helped weed out some alternate explanations for the results. It could have been the case that receiving the subscription to *Seventeen* simply led participants to stop reading another magazine portraying equally bad body images. If that had been the case, participants in the experimental group wouldn't have had any greater exposure to media portrayals of women than participants in the control group: another potential confound. By showing that the time spent looking at other magazines didn't decrease, Stice, Spangler, and Agras can rule out this potential problem. The results of the manipulation check showed that girls who received the subscription spent, on average, about twenty-one hours reading *Seventeen* over the course of the fifteen-month subscription, while girls who didn't receive the magazine averaged about fifteen hours over the same time period. This six-hour increase in the amount of exposure to the magazine may not seem like much when spread over more than a year, but it's far more than participants in a laboratory study are exposed to media sources.

FIELD EXPERIMENTS

Lawrence Katz, Jeffrey Kling, and Jeffrey Liebman—Moving to Opportunity (2001)

Researchers have long known that children born into poor neighborhoods wind up much worse off than children in richer areas on a variety of measures, including education, health, and criminality. This may not seem surprising. People who are poor do worse on these measures as well, and the people living in poor neighborhoods tend to be, well, poor. However, these results seem to hold up even when researchers control for most of the things that should predict these outcomes. That is, on average, if there are two families with the same background, structure, and income, one is in a poor neighborhood and one is in a better neighborhood, the children growing up in the better neighborhood will wind up doing better. So if it isn't absent fathers, the parents' education, or low income, why do the kids from the poor neighborhoods wind up doing worse? Some researchers have concluded that the neighborhood itself has an effect: kids who grow up around areas that have more poor people, more crime, and more high school dropouts might be more likely to drop out of school and commit crimes themselves.

To look at the effect of the neighborhood, Lawrence Katz, Jeffrey Kling, and Jeffrey Liebman (2001), economists at Harvard University, worked with the U.S. Department of Housing and Urban Development to set up a large-scale field experiment, with the goal of seeing whether taking poor families out of poor neighborhoods would actually have an impact. In the study, families living in federally subsidized housing in areas with a poverty rate greater than 40 percent were eligible to apply for housing vouchers that would potentially get them into a better neighborhood. Of the families that applied, one-third received a voucher that they could use to move anywhere they liked, with the voucher covering all of their rent over 30 percent of their income. One-third of the families didn't receive any additional aid. The final one-third were given the same sort of vouchers as the first group, but their vouchers could only be used in neighborhoods with poverty rates below 10 percent. To help them find suitable apartments and adjust to the new neighborhood once they got there, the families were given free counseling by a local nonprofit group. Several years later, Katz, Kling, and Liebman followed up with all of the families who had initially enrolled in the study, through both surveys and in-depth interviews, to see if the change in neighborhoods had made any difference.

In some respects, the families who moved to the better neighborhoods were better off than those who were in the control groups. Compared to the two control groups, children who moved to the wealthier areas were much healthier, with far fewer injuries and greatly reduced rates of asthma. They also were much less likely to report having been the victims of criminal activity. The adults were much less likely to report being depressed and were both healthier and happier. However, the children didn't do any better in school. Their test scores had about the same amount of improvement as the children who didn't move, and the children who moved were just as likely to get into trouble with the law as those who didn't move. Although the adults were happier, they were not more likely to have a job or make more money.

Results of the moving-to-opportunity study were discouraging: spending the extra money to get poor families out of depressed areas and into better areas didn't pay off. The families didn't do any better financially, so the question is whether the additional happiness of the adults and the additional safety of the children are worth the cost. Of course, the real test will come years from now, when it will be possible to track the results of the random assignment decades after the families moved.

Kees Keizer, S. Lindenberg, and L. Steg—Testing the Broken Windows Hypothesis (2008)

In criminology research, the Broken Windows Hypothesis, first put forward by James Q. Wilson and George Kelling in the early 1980s, is one of the most influential theories of criminal behavior for modern policing. Wilson and Kelling argued that relatively small markers of tolerance of criminal behavior, such as graffiti or broken windows, lead people to feel more comfortable carrying out further, and more serious, criminal activities. The theory proved popular among city governments and police departments, who began to focus on preventing minor crimes (vandalism, toll jumping on subways) in the hopes of preventing larger crimes. In New York, Mayor Rudy Giuliani began a zero tolerance campaign for petty crimes, a campaign which corresponded with a dramatic and long-lasting decrease in the rates of both major and minor crimes. Critics charged that these reductions were more the result of demographic and economic trends than the increased policing. As real estate became more expensive in New York City, criminals increasingly took to other nearby cities. As the unemployment rate fell, people got jobs instead of turning to crime. Critics also claimed that the arrests largely targeted poor men from minority groups. Moreover, the fact that serious crimes happen in the same places that minor crimes do doesn't mean that one causes the other. It could simply be that there are other factors that lead to both types of crimes.

To untangle this question of causality, Kees Keizer, S. Lindenberg, and L. Steg (2008), researchers at the University of Groningen in the Netherlands, carried out a series of field experiments. In each experiment, they arranged a location in two ways: with signs of minor criminal activity and without. They secretly observed the location to see how the behavior of people in the area changed. For instance, they left cash visible in an envelope in a mailbox. In one condition, there was graffiti on the mailbox; in the other, there wasn't. They found that when there was graffiti on the mailbox, people were much more likely to take the money. Similarly, they left a flyer on a bicycle available for people to borrow while going around town. (Such municipal bicycle programs are common in European cities.) In one condition, there was litter on the ground near the bicycle; in the other, there wasn't. When there was already litter on the ground, people were much more likely to simply throw the flyer on the ground, rather than pick it up and take it to a trashcan.

Keizer, Lindenberg, and Steg's (2008) field experiments have been cited as some of the strongest evidence for the Broken Windows Hypothesis. Nonexperimental studies may be unable to sort out cause and effect, but experimental studies do not have this problem. As long as the only difference between the conditions is the presence or absence of signs of minor criminal activity, researchers can be confident that any differences in the actions of the people in the study are caused by the experimental condition.

These sorts of field experiments have been used widely in political science research, largely because they have the benefit of the relative causal certainty of an experiment without the external validity issues that often plague experiments. However, there are still some problems with running such an experiment. First, most experiments take place in a lab not only for the sake of convenience, but also to allow the researcher to maintain control. Experiments only work to the extent that the researcher can ensure that everything in the environment of the participant is the same save for the experimental manipulation, and this is very difficult to do in a field experiment. For instance, in Keizer, Lindenberg, and Steg's (2008) field experiments it would be necessary to carry out the experiments many times over the course of a number of days to make sure that the results of the two conditions of the experiment were equally likely to take place at various times of the day and in various weather conditions. It's entirely possible that people are more likely to take some money from a mailbox or throw a flyer on the ground when it's nighttime, when there are fewer people around, or when it's cloudy or rainy. If any of these conditions, or any number of others, coincide with the assignment of the experimental condition, the results of the study would be invalid. Moreover, any of these situations could happen solely by chance, necessitating a larger number of runs of the experiment than would typically be needed in a more controlled laboratory experiment.

There are also a number of potential ethical problems arising from field experiments. By their nature, field experiments involve members of the public—people who haven't volunteered to be part of a study and almost certainly haven't given their informed consent. In general, of course, it wouldn't be ethical to run experiments under such conditions, but field experiments are ethical provided that they adhere to certain conditions. First, the experimental manipulation must come as close as possible to harmlessness. There is no such thing as a completely harmless experiment, but field studies come as close as they can. Unlike most studies, field experiments involve activities that individuals may very well have engaged in anyway. The people borrowing the bicycle in Keizer, Lindenberg, and Steg's (2008) experiment were going to borrow the bicycle anyway. The only harm added by the researchers was the increased probability of throwing a piece of paper on the ground. Although there is some potential for harm from this action (someone could see the person throwing the paper and think less of him or her, a police officer happening by could arrest the person for littering), the odds of any harm happening are pretty remote. In many studies, the potential for harm results from negative self-revelations: people find out things about themselves that they would rather not know, as in Milgram's (1974) obedience to authority studies or Zimbardo's (1971) prison experiment, discussed in Chapter 3. In a field experiment, though, if people never know that they were part of an experiment, they never find out that they did anything wrong or undesirable. In studies such as those carried out by Keizer, Lindenberg, and Steg (2008), the people involved probably never think about their actions again.

Second, researchers in field experiments must take great care to preserve confidentiality. The people involved in Keizer, Lindenberg, and Steg's (2008) field experiments were largely protected from harm by the fact that they didn't know that they were part of a study. This is scant protection, though, if their identities are compromised in any way. No one wants other people to know that they took money from a mailbox because they thought that they wouldn't get caught. There's potential for harm if people find out who took the money and who didn't. If identities could possibly be revealed, the research almost certainly is unethical.

DECEPTION IN EXPERIMENTS

Solomon Asch—Peer Pressure and Vision Tests (1955)

Solomon Asch, a psychologist at Swarthmore College, was interested in studying conformity. However, while other researchers studied the willingness of participants to follow the instructions of an authority figure, such as a scientist in a lab coat, Asch's (1955) research focused on the effects of peer pressure. He was particularly interested in finding out how far people would go to avoid being out of step with the people around them.

This research agenda resulted in a series of famous studies in social psychology. In one, 123 participants (all men) were told that they would be participating in a vision test. (This wouldn't have been seen as unusual at the time; psychologists in the 1950s often carried out studies of perception.) When the participants arrived, they were seated in a room with five to seven others, and the group was shown two cards. On one of the cards was a set of three lines, labeled A, B, and C. On the other was a reference line. The people in the room were asked a series of questions about the length of the reference line, including how long it was relative to the three lines on the other card. The answers were pretty obvious, and in the first few trials, all of the people in the room gave the correct answer out loud, with the participant giving his answer either last or next to last. For instance, for the example shown, the participant and the others in the room were asked which of the lines was the same length as the reference line, with the correct answer being C. In the experimental condition, after a few trials, though, the other people in the room, who answered before the participant, started giving wrong answers, saying that the reference line was the same length as A or B. Aside from the participant, everyone in the room was a confederate of the experimenter, paid to give these wrong responses; Asch (1955) was studying the responses of just the one participant. Of the eighteen total trials, the confederates unanimously gave incorrect answers in twelve. The question was whether the participants would ignore the obvious input of their own senses and go along with the group.

Five percent of the participants always went along with the group, and 75 percent went along with the group at least once. Overall, the participants in the experimental condition ignored their own senses and went along with the group about 37 percent of the time. In the control group, participants were surrounded by others who gave the correct answer. They gave incorrect answers less than 1 percent of the time. (In these cases, they apparently didn't know which line matched, or had become bored with the study and gave a wrong answer out of inattention.)

In variations of the study, Asch (1955) was able to show that group size mattered: participants were willing to ignore one or two wrong answers, but they were much more likely to go along with the crowd when there were more than three confederates giving the wrong answer. Similarly, if there is even one other individual in the group who gives the right answer, the participant is likely to avoid giving in to the crowd. Finally, when participants write their answers down, rather than state them publicly, there's much less pressure to conform to the group.

In Asch's (1955) study, like Stice, Spangler, and Agras' (2001) work, a manipulation check would have been an important part of analyzing the effects of the experimental manipulation. In Asch's research, this manipulation check would involve asking the participants if they knew that the other people in the room were confederates or if they realized that the point of the experiment was to see if they would stick to their guns in the face of peer pressure. If a participant had figured the study out, Asch would have been justified in removing that participant's results from the study; the experimental manipulation didn't work, so that participant isn't a fair test of the hypotheses.

Asch's (1955) study would also require another step after the posttest. Modern ethics would almost certainly require Asch to debrief his participants.

This debriefing, discussed previously in Chapter 3, would explain the design and purpose of the study to participants. Video of a later version of Asch's study is available, and it shows the participants in the experimental condition squinting at the lines, leaning forward to study the lines more closely, laughing inappropriately when they realize that everyone is giving another answer, and even showing signs of real emotional distress. The decision of whether to trust their own eyesight or to go along with the group was obviously a very stressful one for the participants in the study, and it's easy to imagine that they could suffer some harm if no one told them what had happened. If participants were let out without a debriefing, they could go for vision or neurological checks to find out what was wrong with them. In this case, the debriefing would take the form of a pamphlet or a discussion with the experimenter explaining that the other individuals in the group were confederates of the experimenter and that the participant really was seeing things correctly. Participants who resisted peer pressure would be told that they were less susceptible to group dynamics than others, and those who went along with the group would be told that most people went along with the group at least some of the time, so they shouldn't feel bad or different because of their responses. This last step in the debriefing, in which participants are told that their results are normal or even better than most people, is necessary to avoid unnecessarily harming participants' self-esteem, regardless of what the participants actually did in the study.

Debriefing is necessary in experimental studies more frequently than in other studies because experiments so often rely on deception. Had participants in almost any of the studies discussed in this chapter known about the purpose of the experiment, the results would have been thrown off. Think what would happen if Alexander and Fisher's (2003) participants knew that the lie detector wasn't real or if Sommers and Norton's (2007) participants knew that the researchers were looking to see if they would kick the African American man off the jury. Lying to participants constitutes harm and should be avoided whenever possible. When it isn't possible to avoid deception, though, it's necessary to remedy that harm through the debriefing process. This debriefing is the last step in any experiment; after the participants know exactly what the study was about, and their role in it, it's generally impossible to collect any more valid data.

EXTERNAL VALIDITY OF EXPERIMENTS

John Darley and Bibb Latané—The Bystander Effect (1968)

In a famous 1964 case, a young woman named Kitty Genovese was stabbed to death on the sidewalk in Queens, a borough of New York, directly outside of a busy apartment building. She screamed for help, and nearly forty of the people living in the building looked out and saw her being stabbed, but according to contemporary reports, none of the people called the police for at least half an hour after the incident. In recent years, there has been some question as to when, exactly, people called the police and whether the observers recognized the seriousness of the incident, but the story of Kitty Genovese was enormously influential. It was seen as an indictment of Americans—especially those who lived in cities—who wouldn't do anything to help someone who was in trouble.

John Darley and Bibb Latané (1968) saw something different in the story. They argued that the case was similar to Asch's (1955) conformity experiments. In their study, seventy-two participants (undergraduates at New York University) were brought into a lab individually and seated in front of an intercom. They were asked to participate in a discussion about the difficulties of college life over the intercom, rather than face-to-face, to avoid any embarrassment and allow them to speak more freely. In addition, they were told that no one would be listening in on the conversation and that they would only be asked to answer questions about the content of the conversation afterward. The participants were asked to speak in turn, with each person speaking for about two minutes, and were told that the other microphones would be muted until the speaker was done. After the speaker was finished, one of the other microphones would be turned on so that another person could comment on what the first speaker had said. When any one microphone was on, all of the other ones were off.

The first individual to speak talked about how he was having a difficult time adjusting to New York City, and he even mentioned—though he was apparently embarrassed to do so—that he was prone to dangerous seizures when under stress. The others spoke in turn about their problems, including the participant, who spoke last. Then, the student prone to seizures spoke again. When his microphone came on, he began by speaking normally. He then grew increasingly loud and incoherent as he said that he was having a seizure and could die. It was clear that there was a problem seventy seconds after he started talking. About two minutes after he started talking, his microphone cut off because his allotted time was up.

What the participants didn't know was that all of the other voices over the intercom were actually prerecorded, and there wasn't a real emergency. The experimental manipulation was the number of other people that the participants thought were in on the conversation: just the participant and the individual having a seizure, a three-person group with one extra recorded voice, or a six-person group with four extra voices. The participants also didn't know that their microphones were recording the whole time so that the experimenters could see exactly how they responded to the apparent emergency (and carry out a manipulation check to make sure that the participants thought that the emergency was real).

The key measure in Darley and Latané's (1968) experiment was how long it took the participant to leave the room, ostensibly to get help. Once the participant left the room, the experiment was terminated, and an experimenter let the participant know that there wasn't really an emergency. The participant then filled out various surveys.

Eighty-five percent of participants who thought that they were the only ones hearing the seizure rushed out of the room before the end of the seizure, in an average of fifty-two seconds. This figure dropped to 62 percent of participants in the three-person group condition, and only 31 percent of the participants in the six-person group condition. If a participant didn't come out after six minutes, the experiment was terminated.

Darley and Latané (1968) also varied the composition of the groups. In some cases, the other bystanders were male, whereas in others they were female. In some conditions, one of the other bystanders mentioned that he or she was a pre-med student training at a local hospital, but none of these conditions had a significant impact on the likelihood of the participant responding or the speed with which he or she did. (These two additional conditions mean that the study was a $3 \times 2 \times 2$ factorial study, with 12 experimental cells.)

The participants who didn't report the emergency didn't seem apathetic or unconcerned. On the contrary, when the experimenter entered the room to end the experiment, the participants generally asked if the first speaker was okay and made sure that someone was taking care of him. The participants who didn't respond—most of the participants in the large-group condition—seemed torn between wanting to help the person having the seizure and looking foolish by overreacting because someone else may have already gotten help. They even took into account the problems arising from ruining the experiment if they left their room or met the others who were supposed to be anonymous voices. These countervailing concerns didn't matter much to the participants who thought they were the only ones who could help, but the participants in the larger groups thought that someone else was already doing something. Regarding the Kitty Genovese case, then, Darley and Latané (1968) did not think that people watched her being attacked and did nothing because they didn't care or because city life had turned them all into sociopaths. Rather, they argue, no one responded precisely because there were so many people watching, and they all figured that someone else would help.

Darley and Latané's (1968) study is an obvious case where both debriefing and manipulation checks would be very important. If the participants didn't think that there was a real emergency (as was the case with two of the participants), then the results for those cases would be meaningless. Debriefing would be necessary to ensure that participants didn't think that there was even a possibility that their inaction resulted in someone else's death.

The study is important because of what it says about the external validity of experiments. Lack of external validity—the applicability of the results of a study to an outside case—is one of the most common criticisms levied against experimental research. When researchers take surveys of public opinion or carry out participant observations, there's no question that their results apply to the real world, or at least to those participants. Experiments, though, put people into situations that would not otherwise exist, so there's always the question of whether participants' actions in these created scenarios are applicable to the outside world.

Some researchers try to increase the external validity of their studies by making the lab where the experiment is carried out feel less artificial. Researchers studying the effects of media exposure might let the participants eat snacks or flip channels on the television, rather than having them watch a video in a small, windowless room. Darley and Latané's (1968) research shows that these adjustments aren't always necessary. The key to the external validity of their study is not that it directly simulates the circumstances of the Kitty Genovese case, but rather that it simulates the relevant characteristics of that situation. In some respects, trying to make an experimental simulation equivalent to something going on in the real world is a fool's errand. There's no way that Darley and Latané could have set up a scenario in which participants looked out the window of an apartment building and watched someone get attacked, all the while knowing that a large number of others were watching as well. This scenario is complicated. How convincing is the actor playing the girl being attacked or the actor playing the murderer? What do the people in the other windows appear to be doing? The experimenter can't ensure that every facet of the experience is the same for every single participant. Any differences in how the study is carried out would potentially be confounds, and there's no reason to believe that the results of such a study would be more compelling.

Darley and Latané (1968) boiled down the Kitty Genovese scenario into its most basic components: someone is in trouble, and there are a number of other people who can help. Once these components were established, the only question was how well the experiment was carried out: Did the experimental manipulation work? Were there any confounds?

NATURAL EXPERIMENTS

Amalia Miller—Miscarriages and the Gender Wage Gap (2005)

There have been any number of attempts to explain why women in the United States earn less money than similarly situated men, but even when researchers account for obvious factors such as differences in education or jobs, a large part of the difference remains unexplained. In recent years, one of the most popular explanations for the remaining unexplained wage gap is how having a child affects men and women differently. Even in modern America, where mothers and fathers are likely to both work while raising a child, the burden of child care rests disproportionately on women. Indeed, wage analyses show that there's very little difference in the earnings of men and women working the same jobs among people who don't have children; however, people with children experience a big difference between the wages of men and women.

Still, this doesn't provide a full explanation for the wage gap because there are a couple of ways to interpret the result. It could be the case that employers discriminate against women with children, assume that they're not going to put in as much effort as men, and pay them less or provide fewer opportunities for advancement. It could be that employers favor men with children because they may be more stable. It could be that women with children end up working fewer hours to take care of the kids, while men with children don't. It could even be that women who choose to have children don't care as much about work as men with children and opt-out of higher levels of responsibility that could lead to more money. Or perhaps women who think that their careers aren't going so well decide to have a family instead, reversing the causal arrow.

These last explanations are the most troubling for feminist scholars. If the gender wage gap is the result of employers or society treating men and women differently, this problem can and should be rectified by new laws and policies, or enforcement of existing ones. However, if women who choose to have children are just less concerned with work, it's unclear what could be done, or even if something should be done. Ideally, this question could be resolved through an experiment: take women who don't want to have children and randomly impregnate some of them. There's no difference in the existing desires of the women for work or children, so if the women with children wind up making less money, it can be safely concluded that it isn't their fault; there's some form of discrimination going on. Of course, such an experiment would be completely unethical, but that doesn't mean that researchers can't simulate what would happen.

To do this, University of Virginia economist Amalia Miller (2005) looked at longitudinal survey data—information collected on the same participants on a regular basis—to trace the earnings of women based on their reproductive histories. However, she wasn't just looking at the effect of children on these women's earnings, but rather at the effect of miscarriages.

The comparison Miller (2005) was making was between women who had a baby and women who suffered a miscarriage in the same year. All else being equal, it would be fair to assume that the two women wanted a baby equally: they were both pregnant at the same time, but one was fortunate enough to have the baby. What Miller found was that the women who had a miscarriage instead of having a baby wound up making more money than women who actually had the baby, and the effects were pretty big. Each year delay in having a baby during a woman's twenties increased her lifetime earnings by about 10 percent, partially because women without children work longer hours and partially because these women earn 3 to 5 percent more pay for their work.

Of course, it's possible that there's something about women who have miscarriages that also leads them to get higher wages, even if it's difficult to think of what that might be. So, Miller (2005) also conducted additional analyses. In one, she looked at women who got pregnant while using birth control at age twenty-four, comparing them to women who had a baby when they were twenty-five. In this case, neither group wanted to have a baby when they were twenty-four, but some of them became pregnant despite their best efforts. Again, she found that the women who accidentally had babies at age twenty-four earned less than women who had waited another year. To further back up her claims, she did one more analysis, looking at women who reported that they had been trying to get pregnant. Some succeeded earlier than others, and those who did succeed wound up earning less money than women who had a baby later. The women all wanted babies at the same point in their lives, but factors that probably aren't related to their performance at work led some to have a baby later than others. Based on these studies, it seems that it really is having a child—and not the factors that lead women to have a child—that depresses women's wages.

Miller's (2005) study isn't an experiment, but it looks at factors that are assigned on a relatively random basis, or at least on a basis that isn't related to the dependent variable of interest. She was able to show that miscarriages aren't normally the result of risky behaviors, or any identifiable behaviors on the part of the women, but rather random chance. Miller treated women as if they were randomly assigned to one of these conditions—having a miscarriage or not—and saw how women who were put in the miscarriage condition differed from those who were put in the baby condition. In a sense, Miller took advantage of a random assignment that happened in the world and treated the results of that random assignment as if they were an experiment, a method referred to as a *quasi-experiment*, or a **natural experiment**.

The defining element of a natural experiment is that the researcher does not control placement of participants into groups. This is not to say that the placement isn't random. Suppose researchers wanted to study the effects of money on happiness and compared lottery players who won big jackpots with lottery players who didn't. The assignment of participants into groups would be random—based on the lottery drawing—but since the researcher didn't make the assignments, this would be a quasi-experiment rather than an experiment. In any quasi-experiment, the first job of the researcher is to show that the assignment of participants into groups—however it happened—was at least meaningfully random. Assignment doesn't have to be purely random, as it would be in a well-designed experiment. Rather, the factors that led to the assignment can't be related in any way to the outcome being studied. In Miller's (2005) case, this means establishing that women who suffer miscarriages aren't different from those who don't in ways that might affect their work habits or income. It's not necessary to establish that the assignment is purely random, which would probably be impossible. Rather, Miller needs to establish that factors that led to the miscarriage don't serve as confounds to the result.

In a quasi-experiment, there will almost always be concerns like this, which is part of the reason why Miller (2005) makes use of several quasi-experiments, all showing the same outcome, to bolster her results. Even if critics argue that one of the studies is confounded by factors that led to the miscarriage and to the lower income, they can't argue that all three of the studies have exactly the same confound leading to the same result.

This idea of meaningfully random assignment applies to laboratory experiments as well. Ideally, participants should be assigned to a condition as they enter the lab through a random process: a flip of the coin, a number generated by a computer, the roll of a die. However, if researchers in a lab study decide to place everyone who comes in during an even-numbered minute in the experimental group, the assignment wouldn't be purely random. It would, however, be meaningfully random because it's hard to imagine what experimental results would correlate with this assignment process. If the researchers instead decide to assign participants based on what day they come to the lab, the assignment likely wouldn't be random at all.

Quasi-experiments are only useful in situations that are truly determined by chance, such as winning the lottery or having a miscarriage. Miller (2005) couldn't have carried out the same study by comparing women who had abortions with women who had babies because there are certainly differences between the two groups that are not caused by chance and could work as confounds. Similarly, in the hypothetical study of lottery winners' happiness, researchers couldn't compare lottery winners with people who didn't play the lottery or lottery winners with people who were born into wealth, at least not if they wanted to call it a quasi-experiment.

The same logic can apply to studies of whole groups, rather than just individuals. Researchers in political science have treated judicial decisions in one state as a random event. For instance, a judge's decision to release inmates because of overcrowding in one state could be treated as a quasi-experiment in comparisons of that state with similar states nearby to test the impact of releasing prisoners on crime rates. A judicial decision could be used in this way, but it probably wouldn't be appropriate to use a law passed by a state as a quasi-experiment because there are almost certainly differences between states that lead to differences in the laws passed by their representatives.

Similarly, events can be used as experimental conditions to separate groups based on time. Political scientists at Stony Brook University on Long Island were carrying out a study of political attitudes in 2001 when the September 11th attacks occurred (Huddy et al., 2002). They continued the study after the terrorist attacks and treated the attacks as an experimental assignment; they compared people's attitudes before and after the event. Suppose that attitudes about patriotism or civil rights were different immediately after the terrorist attacks; it's difficult to imagine that the changes were caused by anything other than the attacks themselves.

THREATS TO INTERNAL VALIDITY: WHAT CAN GO WRONG?

In addition to the problems faced in the experiments that have been discussed so far, there are many other problems that can invalidate the results of an experiment. **History effects** occur when events in the outside world interfere with the results of the experiment. For instance, if a researcher was studying the relationship between anxiety and political attitudes and a terrorist attack occurred while the study was being carried out, the results would almost certainly be thrown off by the extraneous event. Such events essentially work as a natural experiment, separating out participants by when they participated in the study in addition to what condition they were placed in, and these factors have to be accounted for. Even in the absence of such dramatic events, smaller events such as the start of darker, colder winter months or the beginning of final exams can serve as potential confounds.

There is nothing, of course, that a researcher can do to prevent terrorism or the change of the seasons, but there are things that can be done to minimize their effects. First, researchers should make use of fully random assignments whenever possible. That way, participants affected by the event will at least be equally likely to be in each condition. Second, researchers should always try to run experiments in as short a time frame as possible: if there's a choice, testing all of the participants in a week is preferable to testing them over the course of a semester.

Maturation effects refer to emotional, physical, or psychological changes in the participants over the course of an experiment. For example, participants in a study on memory and learning might begin to forget words because they're tired or bored. The treatments in experiments often involve separating groups by the order in which they carry out tasks (both the experimental and control groups do the same things, but in a different order), which could be a confound. This is a bigger problem in experiments that are mentally or physically taxing or that use children as participants. To reduce the likelihood of maturation effects, researchers should be careful to limit the length of experiments, or at least provide regular breaks for participants.

Attrition or **mortality** is the problem that arises when participants selectively leave the study. In any experiment, participants have the right to leave without completing the study and not be penalized. As noted in Chapter 3, this doesn't happen terribly often, but it is a possibility. In experiments that take place over a long period of time, participants might move or, as the name "mortality" implies, even die. When a participant leaves without completing the study, there generally isn't any usable data for that participant, so he or she is removed from the record.

Mortality isn't a problem as long as participants from all of the groups in the experiment are equally likely to leave the study, but if participants from one of the groups are more likely to leave, this can be a confound. In Alexander and Fisher's (2003) fake lie detector study, one group of participants was asked to answer questions about sex while hooked up to the fake lie detector. Suppose that a large number of these participants just got up and left. It wouldn't be hard to imagine that the participants who had the most embarrassing sexual histories would be more likely to leave, and this could affect the results of the experiment.

Demoralization and **compensatory behaviors** refer to participants' responses to which group they're assigned. If participants know—or believe— that they're in a control group, they may be disappointed or discouraged, which may affect their behavior. If this reaction only happens in one of the groups, it's a potential confound. Similarly, participants who believe that they're in a control group may change their behaviors to make up for the placement. Suppose researchers were studying the effect of a weight-loss drug. Participants who receive—or think that they are receiving—the placebo could be disappointed that they're missing out on the real drug, and this disappointment could lead to further weight gain. This demoralization effect would work as a confound, making the drug seem more effective than it really was. On the other hand, participants who don't think that they are getting the drug could decide to diet more because they're not getting the pill to help out. In this case, the compensatory behavior would reduce the apparent effect of the drug. Ensuring that an experiment follows blinding (or even double-blinding) procedures can help to reduce the likelihood of these effects.

Regression to the mean refers to the tendency of outliers to become more similar to other members of a group over time. Sports fans are familiar with this concept as the *Sports Illustrated* Curse. When a team or an individual appears on the cover of *Sports Illustrated* (generally because of better-than-expected performance), the team or individual tends to stop performing as well shortly thereafter. This isn't because there's bad luck associated with being on the cover of the magazine, but rather because anyone who's performing far better than he or she should be is likely to go back to normal performance before long.

The same holds true in experimental studies. Participants who have very high scores tend to do worse in follow-up testing—even if nothing changed—just as participants with very low scores tend to do better. Suppose researchers were studying the effect of study techniques on math scores. Participants who scored very low on the pretest would probably do better on the posttest, regardless of whether the treatment actually did anything. Pre- and posttest scores are rarely identical, and those participants who scored poorly on the pretest can't do any worse. Similarly, participants who had very high scores on the pretest can't do any better and might even do worse on the posttest. To avoid this problem, researchers make sure that their pre- and posttest scales are properly pilot tested so that very few participants wind up on the top or bottom of the scale. They also ensure that experiments contain adequate control groups. Regression to the mean happens equally in experimental and control groups, so the comparison between the groups can help to control for these effects.

Testing effects are the responses of participants to the expectation that they will be evaluated. Suppose the girls in Stice, Spangler, and Agras' (2001) study of the effect of *Seventeen* magazine on body images knew that their dietary habits and body images were going to be evaluated. They may decide to go on a diet or attend a self-esteem workshop beforehand. Participants with poor body image are more likely to take these steps and could make it look as if the treatment had smaller effects than it really did. *Seventeen* might have a smaller impact on the body images of girls who preemptively went on diets, and the girls who already had good body images wouldn't have been as affected by exposure to the magazine in the first place. On the whole, it could easily have looked as if getting the magazine didn't have much of an effect at all. To reduce these problems, researchers try to keep the purpose of the study relatively vague before the debriefing (as Stice, Spangler and Agras did) so that there's no way that participants can prepare. In addition, researchers may make use of Solomon Three or Four Group Designs to eliminate the pretest entirely for some participants, thereby eliminating any effects it may have on the participants.

Pygmalion effects (also referred to as Rosenthal effects or observer expectancy effects) are participants' responses to the expectations of researchers. Robert Rosenthal and Lenore Jackson (1992) studied these effects in schools. They found that students perform better in class when teachers have higher expectations of them, with the teacher's expectations becoming a self-fulfilling prophecy. In experimental studies, this can be a confound when the researcher puts pressure on participants in one of the groups to do better. Suppose a researcher is testing participants' ability to remember words using one of two teaching techniques: a traditional one and an experimental one developed by the researcher. Because the researcher believes in the technique that he or she has developed, he or she might push participants assigned to the new technique to do better. As such, the participants in the experimental condition would do better, even if there isn't any real benefit to the new technique.

A common remedy is to conduct a double-blind study. Remember, in a blind study, the participants do not know which group they are in. Double-blind studies also ensure that the researcher does not know which group individual participants are in. A neutral third party has access to the group assignment information, but the researcher who interacts with the participants does not. This practice ensures that the researcher cannot provide preferential treatment to one group over the other.

To preserve the integrity of the study, members of the experimental and control groups must not interact. Interaction of the control and experimental groups is referred to as **contamination**. What are the potential problems of contamination? First, when two groups interact, they might compare notes and find out which group they belong to. Second, they might provide each other with the result of the pre- or posttest, resulting in a bias.

Placebo Effect

In a well-designed experiment, participants do not know which group they are assigned to. A blind study ensures that the participants are treated the same way, regardless of their group assignment. In a classical design study for a new cholesterol drug, the experimental group receives the new cholesterol-lowering pill and the control group does not. However, if the control group is given nothing, then the participants in the control group will easily figure out their group assignment, which could result in demoralization.

To remedy that, the control group is given an identical-looking pill, or **placebo**. It has the same shape, color, and appearance and is dispensed at the same times as the experimental group. The only difference is that it is a placebo, meaning that it is a sugar pill and not the actual cholesterol drug. However, many participants assigned to the control group actually believe they are taking the experimental drug. The idea of being chosen for the experimental group often results in positive effects. The morale boost of being chosen for the experimental group results in psychological benefits. However, the effects of the drug are not real—they are psychological artifacts.

Nocebo Effect

In placebo effects, participants in the control group who are given the placebo experience a positive effect (their cholesterol decreases, they lose weight, they feel better, and so on). Recent studies show that participants can also experience detrimental side effects, even if they are in the control group and are taking a placebo. Eleven percent of participants in a fibromyalgia drug trial who were taking the placebo dropped out of the study because they experienced the side effects of the experimental pill: dizziness and nausea (Häuser et al., 2012). Even though they were given the fake drug, these participants reported experiencing the potential side effects. This is important because these participants dropped out of the study, resulting in participant mortality. Even though these side effects are not considered real, they were experienced by the participants and caused physical harm. Researchers blame these **nocebo** effects on the increased awareness of side effects of drugs, resulting from long warnings at the end of pharmaceutical commercials, which have made participants more likely to know about the potential negative side effects of drugs.

ADVANTAGES AND DISADVANTAGES OF EXPERIMENTAL METHODS

Experiments have many advantages. While most methods can only make a claim to association, carefully designed experiments can claim causality, a huge advantage over other methods. Experimental design can also allow researchers to study phenomena they do not have the chance to observe in the real world. For instance, Asch (1955) might have wanted to observe how people would behave if they were in a smoke-filled room and others didn't react, but that's not a situation that's likely to present itself. In an experiment, Asch could create the desired scenario and observe the outcome. However, this artificiality is a potential problem. Such experiments have been criticized because it isn't clear how well the results translate to the real world.

In many cases, the participants in experiments are university students because they are easily available to academic researchers and relatively cheap to recruit. This, too, serves as a limitation on external validity. While college students may be similar to the general population in some ways, they're also different in some important characteristics (they're more educated, for one thing), and experimental stimuli that affect them may not work the same way on everyone.

Ethical Issues

Experimental designs have also been criticized because of the potential for ethical problems. Since many experimental settings involve creating a situation that does not naturally exist, it may be necessary to make use of deception. While deception isn't inherently unethical, it is problematic. The researcher must show that there's no way to carry out the experiment without the deception and that the deception doesn't cause any further harm to the participants. He or she must also ensure that all participants are fully debriefed.

This debriefing is important. In Asch's (1955) study of visual perception and peer pressure, many participants believed that they could not see and began to doubt their vision or even their neurological health. Similarly, in Milgram's (1974) study (discussed in Chapter 3), the subjects were led to believe that they were administering electric shock, causing serious injury and even death. Only by fully debriefing the participants and, in some cases, offering counseling can researchers fully remediate the harm caused by deception. It is up to the researcher—and the Institutional Review Board—to ensure that deception is justified.

FURTHER EXPERIMENTAL STUDIES

Jack Hollis and colleagues—The Effects of Weight Loss Diaries (1998)

Even if participants have been randomly assigned to a condition in an experiment and the materials for the experiment have been properly pretested, there is still the potential for things to go wrong. Confounds can arise from the structure of the experiment itself. Jack Hollis and his colleagues (1998) analyzed the effects of various manipulations on participants' weight loss. Some participants were asked to attend weekly meetings to discuss their weight loss with others in the study; others were not asked to attend. The goal of the meetings was twofold. First, the meetings were thought to put greater pressure on individuals to lose weight by introducing a social element. People may be more likely to try to lose weight if they know that their weight loss—or lack thereof—will be seen by others. Second, the meetings were supposed to help the people trying to lose weight by reviewing weight-loss techniques, such as monitoring portion size and estimating calorie counts. To see how well the manipulations worked, researchers asked participants to keep a food diary, in which they recorded everything that they ate.

In this study, the experimental manipulation was supposed to be attendance at the weight loss meetings. What Hollis and his colleagues (1998) found, though, was that the most important predictor of weight loss was actually how good the participants were at keeping their food diaries. Participants who recorded their meals in the diaries lost a great deal more weight than those who didn't, regardless of which experimental condition they were in.

SUMMARY

Unlike most research techniques, experimental studies allow researchers to isolate causality. If there are a sufficient number of participants, who are randomly assigned to conditions, and the only difference between the participants is the condition to which they are assigned, any difference between the participants at the end of the study must have been due to the experimental condition. While this seems straightforward in theory, the logistics of ensuring that these conditions are met can be daunting.

In the most basic experimental designs, participants are sorted into experimental and control groups, with the experimental group receiving the stimulus and the control group not. However, such simple designs can lead to potential confounds, encouraging many researchers to adopt more complex designs, with the Solomon Three and Four Group Designs considered the best. These designs, and others like them, try to ensure that aspects of the experiment themselves do not lead to extraneous differences between the experimental and control groups—factors that researchers refer to as confounds.

Of course, not all experiments are carried out in the controlled conditions of a laboratory. Laboratory studies have the benefit of giving researchers a great deal of control over the participants' experiences and therefore help to avoid confounds, but researchers face obstacles for establishing external validity. In an effort to increase the external validity of experiments, some researchers make use of field experiments (studies in the real world), in which participants may not even know that they are part of a study. Although these studies increase external validity, they may do so at the cost of internal validity because the researchers have much less control over the experiment and may be unable to control for all potential confounds. At the extreme, in what's called a quasi-experiment or natural experiment, researchers don't even carry out the random assignment themselves. They allow some other factor in the outside world to carry out the assignment, then look for differences between the randomly sorted individuals.

Study and Review

What characteristics of experiments allow researchers using them to make greater claims about causality than researchers using other techniques?

Explain why random assignment is so important to experimental research.

What problems with classic experimental design lead researchers to adopt Solomon Three and Four Group Designs?

Are field experiments really experiments? Why or why not? What about quasi-experiments?

Explain the trade-off between internal and external validity in experimental research.

CHAPTER 10

Designing Surveys: Writing Questionnaires

Learning Objectives

- Be able to explain the relationship between survey design and validity
- Be able to identify the importance of survey introductions
- Be able to assess the importance of including missing data categories
- Be able to explain the benefits and costs of using different types of survey questions
- Be able to identify the function of various scales

WHAT SURVEYS TELL US

In your experience, about how much does an eight ball (a certain amount of a type of illegal drug) cost around here?	
Don't know	80.6%
Less than $20	3.8%
Between $20 and $50	6.4%
Between $50 and $100	5.4%
More than $100	3.8%

Source: Fairleigh Dickinson PublicMind poll 2011, $N = 2{,}230$

Surveys have been used in America since the 1820s: one of the first asked respondents if they were going to vote for Andrew Jackson or John Quincy Adams in a presidential election. In terms of being a tool for scientific analysis of the opinions, beliefs, and actions of the population as a whole, however, surveys have only become so in the last eighty years. Many of the early polls failed for various reasons. The most famous of these polls is the *Literary Digest* poll of 1936, which polled 2.3 million voters—the biggest sample ever recorded by a survey and about one third of the entire electorate—and decided that Alf Landon, the Republican candidate, was going to beat Franklin Roosevelt by a landslide in that year's presidential election. As it turned out, Roosevelt won by a landslide. *The Literary Digest* had only polled people who owned telephones— fatally biasing its results toward wealthy respondents who preferred Landon—so the sample size did not matter; *The Literary Digest* went out of business soon afterwards. The lesson of this debacle is that if the sample isn't representative or if the questions are flawed, it doesn't matter how many people take a survey. In this chapter, we will explore the ways in which researchers design surveys and write questions.

The aim of **survey research** is to collect comparable and reliable information from a large number of respondents. Participants in a research survey are generally called *respondents* rather than *participants*. Surveys allow researchers to reach larger groups of respondents and collect information on attitudes, behaviors, values, and beliefs. Public opinion polls, political polls, and marketing surveys all use survey methodology, and many of us have taken surveys without even noticing.

In survey research, researchers distribute **questionnaires**, which are formal and structured. Because the aim of survey research is to provide comparable data on a large number of respondents instead of very detailed information about fewer cases, the researchers provide potential answers for the respondents to choose from, which are called **closed-ended** questions. In contrast, in-depth interviews are conversational in tone and use semi-structured, **open-ended** questions. Researchers simply pose the questions and do not provide options for the respondents. Since the tone of in-depth interviews is conversational, the researchers have time to explain, interpret, and clarify questions if needed. On the contrary, surveys are distributed to a very large body of respondents, and the researchers generally do not have the option to clarify or explain questions or add follow-ups to explore an especially interesting response. The majority of the questions in survey methodology are closed-ended questions because open-ended questions require a great deal of time and effort before analysis can be carried out.

The wording of the survey questions is extremely important and will determine the quality of the results. Poorly written questions will result in respondents not understanding what the question is about, refusing to answer, or even giving an incorrect answer. The most important step in designing a survey is writing questions. Researchers have one chance for the respondents to answer their questions, no matter how personal, embarrassing, or undesirable the answers could be. In that short time, the researchers want the respondents to answer as many questions as possible without becoming bored, distracted, or, most important, untruthful.

Respondents will often try to give what they think is the socially desirable and acceptable answer rather than the truth. This tendency is referred to as **social desirability bias**. The question above is part of a survey that was administered to middle and high school students between 2006 and 2013 and was part of an effort to determine the effectiveness of random drug testing programs in schools. To measure the effectiveness of the drug testing programs, students in schools that had the program were compared with students in schools that didn't have the program—but there was a problem. When it comes to potentially embarrassing, criminal, or controversial issues such as drug use, respondents often alter their responses in order to appear a certain way to whoever is going to review their answers. The goal of the above question is to sort out students who have been exposed to drugs from those who haven't been but want the researcher to think that they have.

An eight ball—two ounces, or one-eighth of a pound, of heroin or cocaine—typically costs several hundred dollars, so anyone who's bought one or been around someone who has bought one would find this to be an easy question: an eight ball costs well over $100. However, from the point of view of someone who doesn't know what an eight ball is, the question is difficult. If students don't know what an eight ball is or how much it costs, they should pick the first option, "don't know." But, if students want to make the researcher think that they know about drugs, despite the fact that they don't, they will guess, and when people guess, they very rarely choose the extreme options, like "less than $20" or "more than $100." Thanks to years of taking standardized tests, respondents know that the middle options are more likely. This means that the 16 percent of respondents who answered anything other than "don't know" and "more than $100" are just guessing. For whatever reason, they want the researcher to think that they know about drugs when they don't.

This question seems to work pretty well. Students who know that an eight ball costs more than $100 are more likely than others to know about the prices of other drugs and are more likely to admit to using drugs and alcohol, but this isn't the original form of the question. As originally written, the question asked students, "In your experience, about how much does an eight ball cost around here?" When the question was asked in this format—omitting the explanatory text about what an eight ball is—respondents were much more likely to say that it cost "less than $20."

This chapter explores the ways in which researchers word survey questions and design the actual questionnaire. How researchers word their questions, design their options, and even present the questions visually will help elicit the most honest answers without alienating respondents.

THE BASICS OF ITEM DESIGN

Introduction to the Questionnaire

Typically, the focus of designing a survey is question construction and wording. However, the instructions are just as valuable. In particular, the introduction of a survey is the key. No matter which mode is used to administer the surveys (in-person, over the telephone, online, or mail), the introduction is very important. The introduction is the respondent's first encounter with the study. A good introduction will help increase response rates; it will ensure that the respondents chosen for the study will choose to participate. It will also help build rapport with the respondents and ensure useful answers rather than refusals. A typical introduction informs the respondents what the study is about. However, it is very important that the hypothesis is not given to the respondents. Once the respondents know what the researchers are trying to prove, then there will be a reactivity bias. They will answer in the way they think the respondents want to hear. Therefore, "This is a study about the workplace" is a better option than "In this study, we are trying to measure the extent of gender bias in promotions."

The introduction also informs the respondents how long the survey takes. This should be an honest number. The researchers should not mislead respondents into thinking a survey will take only five minutes when in fact it takes half an hour. Being upfront about the length of the survey is an ethical practice: it informs potential respondents about the costs of being in the study. It is also important to be upfront about the length of the study because misleading a potential respondent will often result in respondents refusing to answer some questions and ending the survey before the completion. This will result in many missing values and incomplete questionnaires for the researchers. It is also important to design surveys that do not take too long. Many respondents get distracted, tired, and fatigued, which reduces the quality of the data if the survey design is too long.

Once the introduction has been settled, researchers move on to the hard part: designing the questions. (Researchers often use the more generic term *items*, since not everything asked on a survey is phrased as a question.) How a question is worded will determine the overall quality of the data collected by the researchers. Poorly worded questions will result in poor quality data: respondents being untruthful, getting confused about the questions, or even getting offended and refusing to answer. Below are some basic guidelines for writing questions.

No Jargon, Acronyms, Abbreviations, or Slang

Every social group has expressions and idioms of its own. There are many "inside" expressions that people take for granted. Psychiatrists talk about "SSRIs." People in warm states talk about "snowbirds." College students try to finish their "gen eds." Technical terms an individual knows because of his or her professional or educational experience are referred to as *jargon*, while terms that arise from a subculture or social group are called *slang*. American English is also filled with acronyms for professional terms, such as *SSRI* for *selective serotonin reuptake inhibitor*, and common terms, such as *AC, OJ,* or *ASAP*. If someone has "CIA" training, she could be a spy for the Central Intelligence Agency or a chef from the Culinary Institute of America. People often use slang, jargon, and acronyms without thinking, but these terms are difficult for outsiders to understand—enough so that there are dictionaries devoted to deciphering them.

In normal conversation, these terms aren't especially problematic. The people whom you're talking to are probably from the same subgroup that you're from, and if not, there's generally enough context to figure out what's being discussed. In surveys, though, this isn't always the case. Questions must be written in clear, concise language, without any unnecessary jargon, slang, or acronyms to make sure that the question means the same thing to all of the respondents.

For people who have been in or around drug culture, the meaning of "eight ball" is clear, but for the sample of students, there's no guarantee that it will be. "Eight ball" can mean a lot of things, from a quantity of drugs, to something on a pool table, to a child's toy that answers questions a user poses to it. The writers of the question have one meaning in mind, but the respondents may well have another, and this could have a significant impact on the answers given. The sort of eight ball used in pool costs just a few dollars; the Magic Eight Ball toy costs about the same. The researcher could easily decide that respondents giving the "less than $20" answer were trying to misrepresent their exposure to drug culture when they just had a different understanding of the meaning of the question.

Awareness of jargon, slang, and acronyms is part of the solution to this problem. When writing questions, researchers should be careful to avoid these terms whenever possible. However, the ubiquity of these terms means that researchers may not even notice that they're using them. As such, the first step in administering a survey is the use of pilot or cognitive testing in order to determine what the questions mean to respondents. In pilot testing, the questions are asked to a smaller number of respondents than will be used in the final survey, with researchers paying careful attention to the number of "don't know" responses or refusals to answer the question. High numbers of either of these can indicate a problem with the question. Researchers who are not carrying out the survey themselves (for instance, if workers in a call center are talking to respondents) may observe the administration of the survey by listening in on the calls or observing face-to-face interactions to see if respondents have problems with any questions or ask for clarification about the meaning of a question. If the researcher observes any problems, he or she can change the wording of the question to address the problem before the full survey starts.

Cognitive testing is a process in which the researchers don't administer the initial form of the survey but rather discuss each of the questions with people who are similar to the respondents the researcher would like to target. This technique is most often used when researchers are trying to survey subgroups that may have very different understandings of words or phrases than the researcher. For instance, researchers working for the census have to prepare questions in dozens of languages. To ensure that all of the groups understand the question in the same way, they bring in a few dozen people from each linguistic group to discuss what they understand the question to mean and if there are any hidden meanings to the words used that might not be evident to an outsider. These cognitive testing sessions can be in an individual or focus group format and typically involve going through each question, one by one, asking what the respondents think the questions and the responses mean.

Since the eight ball question was going to be asked of a sample of middle and high school students, cognitive testing was used to ensure that they understood all of the questions. A group of middle schoolers went through the questionnaire, and several told the researchers that they thought of the eight ball as the question-answering toy. The explanatory phrase "a certain amount of a type of illegal drug" was enough to resolve the ambiguity and ensure that the researchers and the respondents were all on the same page.

Item Specificity

Last week, were you working full time, part time, going to school, keeping house, or what?

Working full time	50.5%
Working part time	10.8%
In school	3.6%
Keeping house	16.8%
Retired	11.1%
Other	7.1%

Source: General Social Survey 1972–2006, $n = 51{,}012$

In addition to the questions that researchers are substantively interested in—measuring drug use, voting, racism, or criminality—nearly every survey also includes a section of **demographic questions**. These demographic questions, normally included at the very end of the survey, ask the respondents about their race, income, education, gender, and other characteristics that may help the researchers ensure that the sample is representative or to make sure that comparisons between groups are accurate. (Representative samples are discussed later in the chapter.)

The above question is used by the General Social Survey (generally abbreviated as the GSS) to find out about the respondent's employment status. People who don't have a job may have very different views on some issues, such as the state of the economy, than people who do have a job, so it's important for researchers to know whether someone is currently working or not. The results include all responses to the survey between 1972 and 2006, which accounts for the relatively high numbers of people describing themselves as keeping house. In recent years, the proportion has been much lower, and the proportion of individuals listing themselves as retired has been much higher.

These demographic questions may seem very straightforward, but the way in which they are asked can have important ramifications for the answers that are given. For instance, race is an important part of demographic information. Whites, African Americans, and Hispanics have very different views on any number of issues, and researchers need to account for this when tabulating and presenting survey results. Race may seem like an easy question, but there are a number of important decisions that need to be made. Should respondents be allowed to pick more than one racial category? Are all of the multiracial individuals—of which there are an increasing number in America—going to be lumped in a multiracial or "other" category? What about people who just refer to themselves as "American"? What about Hispanics who consider themselves to be white? Is an immigrant from Spain Hispanic? All of these issues are bound to come up in any large-scale survey, and the question and response choices must be carefully thought through before the survey is put in the field. As with other questions, pilot testing and cognitive testing are important tools for ensuring that the question works the way that the researchers would like.

As the above question demonstrates, even categories less controversial than race can become very complex. While some researchers might be tempted to simply ask respondents if they're employed, unemployed, or retired, having too few categories might lead to confusion among respondents. Is someone who's retired from his or her job but works a few hours a week retired or working part time? Is a full-time student employed or not? Is someone on maternity leave from work employed? Increased specificity in the wording of the questions can also help to reduce reactivity effects. If a respondent doesn't easily fit into any of the prescribed categories, or doesn't understand the question, he or she is more likely to pick the category that leads to a more desirable self-presentation. For instance, the retiree picking up a few hours here and there would be more likely to describe himself or herself as retired, not wanting the interviewer to think that he or she needs to work for the money. The woman on maternity leave could well describe herself as employed, even if she hasn't been at work in months. There's nothing necessarily wrong with these classifications—a researcher might properly consider women on maternity leave to be employed or retirees who work less than a certain number of hours to be retired—but the decision should be made by the researcher, not by individual respondents. After all, if the question isn't properly worded, respondents in the same circumstances might give very different responses.

The GSS employment question is also specific in another way: the time frame that it asks about. Rather than just asking respondents if they are employed or not, it asks what they were doing "last week." In some ways, this may seem as if it makes the question more difficult to interpret. After all, someone could have a full-time job but have been on vacation, out sick, or not working last week for any number of other reasons. Alternately, someone could be taking a month off between two full-time jobs or be a full-time student enjoying summer break. What was going on last week may or may not be an accurate indicator of what's going on the rest of the time.

However, there are good reasons to make the question that specific. As noted before, specificity in the wording of questions tends to reduce reactivity effects. A respondent who just lost his or her job or is just about to start one might consider himself or herself to be employed, even though he or she has more in common with unemployed people than with employed people. The phrase "last week" would push the person to categorize himself or herself as unemployed, rather than employed. Respondents generally don't want to lie in response to questions, but they do tend to pick the truthful response category that presents themselves in the best light. By increasing the specificity of the time frame that the question is referencing, the number of truthful categories a respondent might fit in decreases, making it more likely that people in similar situations will categorize themselves in similar manners. This sort of specificity also reduces reactivity by limiting the scope of the question: being unemployed in general is not the same thing as having been unemployed last week. Someone who was unemployed last week could be in a great new job this week, so respondents may be more willing to admit to being in a category that would otherwise be relatively unflattering since it's applied to a particular period in time, rather than being a general state of being.

Questions in the body of the survey should also be as specific as possible, both to reduce reactivity effects and to make it clear to the respondents how they should categorize themselves. This sort of specificity can sometimes mean that researchers have to include additional categories in the response options to ensure that some odd cases might be properly categorized. In the above question, for instance, 2.2 percent of respondents said that they had a job but weren't at it in the past week for whatever reason. If this category had not been included, some respondents wouldn't have been sure how to answer the question. For the other 97.8 percent of respondents, though, the increased specificity is expected to elicit far more accurate and truthful information.

Clear and Unemotional Language

> Some people say that gay marriage should be legal in New Jersey. Others oppose legalizing gay marriage. What is your position? Do you support gay marriage or oppose gay marriage?
>
> | | |
> |---|---|
> | Support gay marriage | 52% |
> | Oppose gay marriage | 36% |
> | Support civil unions but oppose gay marriage (volunteered) | 3% |
> | Don't know | 9% |
>
> Some people support marriage equality in New Jersey. Others oppose

marriage equality. What is your position? Do you support marriage equality or oppose marriage equality?

Support marriage equality	61%
Oppose marriage equality	25%
Support civil unions but oppose marriage equality (volunteered)	2%
Not familiar with term "marriage equality" (volunteered)	3%
Don't know	9%

Source: Rutgers-Eagleton poll October 2011, combined $N = 992$

Both of these questions are asking about the same thing—allowing members of the same sex to marry in New Jersey—but in the second question, support for same-sex marriage is nine points higher than in the first. This, by itself, may not be so strange, but both questions are actually from the same survey, taken at the same time. Half of the respondents in the survey were randomly assigned to receive the first wording of the same-sex marriage question, and the other half received the second wording, a technique referred to as a **survey experiment**.

Because respondents were randomly assigned to one question or the other, the difference between the groups isn't likely the result of random chance. Rather, people who hear the words "marriage equality" are more likely to approve of same-sex marriage than those who hear "gay marriage." In this case, and for many other emotional issues, the particular questions that are used have an enormous impact on the answers that respondents give. "Gay marriage" makes it sound as if same-sex couples are asking for a privilege that's traditionally not been accorded to them. "Marriage equality" makes it sound as if same-sex couples are asking for the same thing that everyone else has. As a result, a significant portion of the population would say that they oppose "gay marriage" but are in favor of "marriage equality," despite the fact that these terms mean the same thing.

In both questions, a small portion of the respondents—about 2 percent—said that they support civil unions between same-sex couples but oppose the use of the term "marriage" to describe them. In the results, these responses are noted as having been volunteered (often abbreviated as "vol"). This means that the option was not among the options that were read to the respondent in a telephone survey or were shown in an online or paper survey, but interviewers were told to accept it as a valid response anyway. In this case, this option represents a nice middle ground between supporting or opposing same-sex marriage, so many respondents would be likely to pick it if it were listed with the other options. By not listing it, the researchers are hoping to push people to categorize themselves as being on one side or the other of the issue.

The difference in support between the two questions is important. At the time, the New Jersey legislature was considering a bill that would legalize same-sex marriage, and legislators were eager to find out if it was popular among their constituents or not. Either way, a majority in the state supports same-sex marriage, but supporters would much rather hear that 60 percent of constituents support same-sex marriage and only 25 percent oppose it than to hear that 52 percent approve it and 36 percent oppose it. So, what's the real level of support? It's both. Support for same-sex marriage, like support for many policies, depends on how the issue is framed. People who think about the issue in terms of equality are more supportive than those who think about it in terms of granting rights to minority groups. Findings such as these have led many supporters of same-sex marriage to talk about the issue in terms of marriage equality in order to build support for their position.

The researchers at Rutgers University who designed this experiment, led by political scientist David Redlawsk, didn't have to decide which version of the question to include on the survey. They just went ahead and used both. However, this isn't always a good approach because it requires a larger sample size and may make it difficult to compare various groups within the study. If researchers can only use one wording of a question, it's important to phrase the question in terms that are emotionally neutral and are well understood by respondents. When asking about same-sex marriage, for instance, "homosexuals" or "same-sex couples" might be considered less emotional terms than "gays."

Similar issues arise on almost every policy question. For instance, responses to questions about abortion differ enormously depending on whether the question asks about "aborting a pregnancy" or "ending a pregnancy"; whether what is being aborted is referred to as an "embryo," an "unborn fetus," or an "unborn child"; or whether the person doing the aborting is referred to as a "woman" or a "mother." Respondents who support the right of a woman to end a pregnancy might not be as supportive of the right of a mother to abort her unborn child. Respondents are very sensitive to emotional terms such as "mother," "abortion," and "child," and their responses will reflect that.

Even in generally less fraught issues, such as tax policy, the inclusion of emotional words can make a difference. There has been a long-standing controversy over the policy of taxing income that comes from an inheritance among very wealthy Americans. Respondents are generally supportive of an "inheritance tax," but they don't like the "death tax" at all. Taxes are bad, but death is worse, and a combination of the two is terrible. In the above question, the term "gay marriage" may well elicit a stronger emotional response than "marriage equality," so in this way, the second question may be a better reflection of public opinion.

A second consideration is ensuring the terms used in the question are understood by the respondents and are as close as possible to the way that respondents actually think about the issue. In the above question, 3 percent of respondents admitted that they didn't know what "marriage equality" was, and it seems likely that there are many more who weren't willing to admit that they didn't. As a result, some respondents were supporting or opposing the issue without really knowing what they were saying, and given that this was the only question in the survey on the issue, there wasn't any context to help them out. It's better to use terms that will be widely understood by respondents, even if the question has to define the terms within the question itself. Such a question might ask if respondents "support marriage equality—giving the same legal recognition to same-sex couples that is given to opposite-sex couples—in New Jersey." The question is certainly less concise, but it makes sure that all of the respondents are on the same page. This is especially important because respondents are generally unwilling to admit that they don't understand a topic or don't know who someone is. Dozens of surveys have asked respondents for their views on made-up people or issues and found that people are more than willing to offer opinions about a person or controversy that doesn't really exist. Since respondents aren't going to tell the interviewer when they don't understand the question, it's vital to ensure that they do, even if it sometimes means overexplaining an issue.

Balanced Questions

Some people feel that women should have an equal role with men in running business, industry, and government. Others feel that women's place is in the home. Where would you place yourself on this scale, or haven't you thought much about this?

Equal role [1]:	64%
2	15%
3	5%
4	8%
5	3%
6	2%
Women's place is home [7]:	2%
Haven't thought about it	2%

Source: American National Election Study 2008, *n* = 1167

The above question has been asked for forty years as part of the American National Election Study (ANES), a large, federally funded national political poll run at least every two years since the 1950s, with the results available for free. Over that time, there has been a dramatic shift in responses. In 1972, only 31 percent of respondents agreed that women should have an equal role in society, and 19 percent said that a woman's place was in the home. From that point, the shift has been gradual, but by 2008, almost 80 percent place themselves in the first two categories. The ANES is most often run as a face-to-face survey, and for this question, the interviewer asks the question and then shows the respondent a card that lays out the responses: a scale ranging from 1 (representing full equality) to 7 (meaning that women should stay home). If the question were part of a telephone survey, it would have to be asked in a different way, probably laying out what the different responses from 2 to 6 actually meant.

One of the reasons that emotional words have such an impact on respondents is that respondents are constantly looking for cues as to how the interviewer wants them to answer the question. The use of certain emotional words can give respondents hints as to how they should answer, and in order to avoid this sort of reactivity, researchers need to ensure that questions are as neutral as possible. The above question, like the marriage equality questions discussed previously, has a construction that's commonly used in asking about controversial issues to avoid reactivity. Both of these items lay out both sides of the issue before actually asking the question; the formula used in this question ("some people feel this way, while other people feel the other") is one of the most common constructions. If respondents think that they have an opinion that's in the minority, they are less likely to offer it. By telling respondents that some people feel one way and some people feel the other, the researcher is sending the message that both views are acceptable.

Of course, respondents are always looking for cues as to what they should say in response to a question, and when presenting arguments in this way, researchers need to be very careful that they don't bias responses one way or the other. For instance, when using questions like this, researchers often vary the order in which the two options are presented. Half of the respondents might hear the question as given above, while the other half would hear, "Some people feel that women's place is in the home. Others feel that women should have an equal role with men in running business, industry, and government." It's possible that some respondents might simply agree with the first option given to them, so by altering the order in which options are presented, researchers can eliminate any bias resulting from this.

Statements about the options can also be used to give the respondent additional information about the question, to explain unfamiliar terms or reasons why people favor one side or the other. This is most useful when asking about issues that respondents don't fully understand. For instance, explanatory introductions to questions have been used widely in asking about ballot initiatives in California. Ballot initiatives require voters to wade through paragraphs of dense text that often include double-negatives and vote "yes" or "no." Researchers in California have found that their results are more reliable when they add a brief explanation of the ballot initiative in question. However, if statements about the options go beyond relatively simple phrases such as "some people think," it's important to make sure that both sides are represented equally so that respondents aren't pushed toward one option or the other. To ensure that the statements are perceived equally, researchers generally need to do some cognitive or pilot testing and refine the questions based on the results.

When researchers are concerned that respondents might avoid giving their real views on a controversial topic, they may also make use of verification questions. A verification question is simply a restatement of the original question, using slightly different wording or response options, asked much later in the survey or in a different context. The idea is that respondents who lie about their views on one question may have difficulty maintaining the lie on the second version of the question. If the two answers are very different, researchers will often use the less socially desirable response as being indicative of the respondent's true feelings. These secondary questions, used to verify the truthfulness of previous questions, are called **lie detectors**.

For example, many people lie about their age. Rather than asking respondents their age (which they can quickly lie about), researchers ask what year they were born. Typically, as a lie detector, researchers ask respondents what year they graduated from high school. The advantage of the question is that many people have trouble doing math in their heads that quickly. Second, unlike college, the majority of the population graduated from high school. This question functions as a lie detector. If researchers subtract sixteen, seventeen, or eighteen from the reported year graduated from high school, they should end up with the reported year of birth. If not, they know that the respondent was not truthful.

Double-Barreled Questions

Let me read you some statements about the Middle East. For each, tell me if you agree or disagree. Israel is a small, courageous, democratic nation, which is trying to preserve its independence.

Agree	79%
Disagree	12%
Not sure (vol)	9%

The Arabs are determined to destroy Israel, so Israel is justified in building itself up militarily to defend itself.

Agree	71%
Disagree	19%
Not sure (vol)	10%

Source: Harris poll February 1987, $N = 1,250$

These questions were used by the Harris poll repeatedly over the course of more than ten years, as part of a series of questions on attitudes toward Israel and the Middle East. In general, the questions show that Americans are largely supportive of Israel in its conflict with other countries in the Middle East—or do they? In the first item, respondents are asked to agree or disagree with a statement that asserts that Israel is small, democratic, courageous, and trying to preserve its independence. Some of those descriptors are factual: Israel is a small country and, by most measures, a democratic one. The other descriptors are opinion based: respondents could differ on whether they think Israel is courageous or if it is just trying to preserve its independence. So, if a respondent agrees with some of the statement, but not all of the statement, what is that respondent supposed to say? Does "agree" mean that the respondent agrees with all of the statements in the item? Most of them? Just one or two? The same issue makes the second item difficult to interpret as well. It contains two statements: Arabs want to destroy Israel, and an Israeli military build-up is justified. A respondent could easily agree with one statement, but not the other. What should that respondent say?

The above questions are classic examples of what researchers call **double-barreled questions**. Double-barreled questions ask the respondent for one answer to a question that has multiple parts. Respondents are asked to give an "agree" or "disagree" response to a question that could be answered in more ways than that: respondents could agree with some parts of the question but disagree with others. The researchers could have resolved this issue by increasing the number of response options. For instance, the second item could have asked respondents if they agreed that the Arabs are determined to destroy Israel and that the arms build-up is justified, agreed that the Arabs are determined to destroy Israel but that the arms build-up isn't justified, and so on. These response options would be unwieldy enough that the researchers at the Harris poll probably would have been better off simplifying the items. The first item could ask if Israel is just trying to defend itself; the second item could ask if Israel is justified in an arms build-up.

Double Negative Questions

Does it seem possible or does it seem impossible to you that the Nazi extermination of the Jews never happened?

Possible	22%
Impossible	66%
Don't know (vol)	12%

Source: Roper poll April 1993, *N* = 992

When the results of the Roper poll were released in 1992, they caused a media uproar (the final response option, "don't know," wasn't given to the respondents; as noted later in the chapter, it had to be volunteered). "What have we done?" asked Nobel Peace Prize winner Elie Wiesel, a Holocaust survivor who has written extensively about his experiences in Nazi concentration camps. "I am shocked that 22 percent—oh my God" (Kirchner 1994). Newspapers began pushing for more education about the Holocaust, more memorials, more steps to silence Holocaust deniers.

After the initial media uproar, though, researchers began asking about the validity of the results. In the question, respondents aren't asked if the Holocaust happened or not; they're asked if it's possible that it didn't happen. If respondents are sure that the Holocaust happened, they are supposed to say that it's impossible that it didn't happen. Remember, in most cases survey respondents aren't seeing the question—they're hearing it and may not even be paying full attention to what the interviewer on the phone is saying to them. Reading the question, it's not too hard to parse out what the response options mean; critics of the poll, though, argued that respondents just didn't know what they were saying. To their credit, the Roper poll conducted the survey again, adjusting the wording of the question so that it asked, "Does it seem possible to you that the Nazi extermination of the Jews never happened, or do you feel certain that it happened?" When the question was asked in this way, only 1 percent of respondents said that it was possible that it hadn't happened, with about 8 percent saying that they weren't sure.

The above question asks respondents to respond to a **double-negative**, in this case, to say whether or not it is impossible that something didn't happen. As a result, not all respondents gave answers that accurately reflected their views of the Holocaust; apparently, 21 percent of respondents said that it was "possible" that the Holocaust didn't happen, when they meant that it was "possible" that the Holocaust happened, or not "impossible" that it didn't happen. In telephone surveys, respondents can't see the question they're being asked. In online surveys, they may be able to see the questions, but they're not necessarily paying much attention. Often, respondents are just trying to finish the survey as quickly as possible. As a result, they are easily tripped up by items that have a complex structure. Researchers should make sure, therefore, that all questions are phrased in the simplest and most intuitive way possible. *Simple* means that questions should comprise short, declarative sentences. *Intuitive* means that the response options should resemble how people normally talk about the issue. If people normally talk about being for or against same-sex marriage, the "for" option in a question should indicate being for same-sex marriage, not being against it.

Also interesting in the responses to the two questions is the change in the number of respondents who said that they didn't know how to respond. In the initial double-negative form of the Holocaust question, 12 percent of respondents said that they didn't know; in the simplified form of the question, that figure dropped to 8 percent. This demonstrates one of the reasons why respondents sometimes say that they "don't know"—they just don't understand the question. There are, however, lots of other reasons why respondents give the "don't know" response. They may not want to offer an opinion on a controversial topic, may feel that the interviewer won't like the response they give, or may not be willing to offer an opinion on something that they don't know much about. It's important to allow respondents to skip to the next question by saying that they don't know—after all, researchers don't want to force respondents to give an answer that they may not agree with—but "don't know" is almost always a volunteered response, meaning that respondents aren't told that it's an available option. The idea is to allow respondents to opt-out of answering a question while not encouraging them to do so. After all, if respondents are overtly given the option to say that they "don't know," they'll take it far more than researchers would like.

In telephone surveys especially, it may be tempting for researchers to rely on the interviewer to help the respondent understand the question. Most telephone surveys use professional interviewers who are skilled at getting respondents to give answers that fit into the listed categories and complete the survey. However, it's problematic whenever an interviewer gives additional instructions, explanations, or prodding because it means that different respondents hear different things when answering the questions and therefore may understand the questions differently. One or two interviewers who explain a question in a certain way may introduce significant bias into survey results. Of course, there's no way to stop interviewers from going off the script, and in some cases, it may be desirable for them to do so if it means getting information that the researchers otherwise wouldn't be able to get. However, researchers can and should minimize the extent to which these sorts of ad hoc explanations are necessary, and they can do this by making sure that the questions and response options are clear and succinct.

Missing Data: "Don't Know" and Refusals

Which age group do you fall into? Are you...	
18–29	15%
30–44	28%
45–59	28%
60 and older	27%
Refused (vol)	2%

Source: Fairleigh Dickinson University PublicMind poll March 2012, *N* = 1185

Age is another of the demographic questions that nearly every survey includes, generally toward the end of the questionnaire. This seems to be a very straightforward question, but there are lots of ways to ask it. The information above actually combines results from two separate questions. In the first, respondents were asked what year they were born. Respondents who refused to answer that question—and there will always be some who do—were then asked to give their age as a general category, as in the above question. Some respondents still refused to answer, but fewer than if a specific age had been requested.

While previous examples have listed respondents who didn't know the answer to a question, asking about age almost always results in a large number of refusals. (There are respondents who don't actually know their age because they were born before birth certificates were standard, but such people are uncommon and are becoming more so.) For the above question, there's a different volunteered response: refusal to answer the question.

Responses of "don't know" should be differentiated from refusals to answer the question. Some respondents will simply refuse to answer questions on controversial topics. Just as with "don't know" responses, the interviewer should immediately move on to the next question and record the response as a refusal. The researcher should also be sure that the number of "don't know" and "refuse" responses are recorded separately because they provide different information about the respondents. A high number of "don't know" responses might mean that the question should be simplified or some explanatory text should be added. A high number of refusals might mean that the question should be phrased in a different way or taken out entirely to avoid unnecessarily antagonizing respondents. In the case of age questions, researchers have found any number of ways to minimize refusals. Generally, in nationwide polls, about 5 percent of respondents will refuse to answer when they're asked their age. If respondents are instead asked what year they were born—which is the same thing to anyone who knows how to subtract—the standard refusal rate drops to about 3 percent. Asking about age cohorts or asking age indirectly by asking about life events (what year the respondent finished high school) can drive down refusal rates even further.

Many of these strategies can also help researchers minimize the amount of lying on questions. When researchers ask about controversial or embarrassing topics, respondents may be likely to misremember or lie. For instance, the ANES generally asks respondents which candidate they voted for in the previous presidential election and has found that some people who voted for the losing candidate won't admit to doing so. Similarly, researchers asking about crime—whether it's arrests or victimization—find that respondents tend to underreport incidents. Sometimes, these concerns can be resolved by adding some explanatory text: noting how many people have been victims of crime or been arrested or emphasizing how close the presidential election was. In other cases, as with age questions, lying can be minimized by tricking the respondent. Respondents may want to lie about their age, but it's harder for them to figure out what year they're claiming to have been born in or what year they were supposed to have graduated high school.

Mutually Exclusive and Exhaustive Response Options

What is your religious preference? Is it Protestant, Catholic, Jewish, some other religion, or no religion?	
Protestant	50%
Catholic	27%
Jewish	2%
None	16%
Other (Specify)	1%
Don't know (vol)	4%
Source: GSS 2006, $N = 4{,}479$	

Questions about religion aren't used quite as commonly as some other demographic items, such as age, race, or employment status, mostly because they don't tell the researcher much and take a lot of time to answer. In the above question, for instance, if a respondent says that he or she is "Protestant," there is a follow-up question to determine which sect the respondent belongs to. Given the number of Protestant sects, coding the response can be a nightmare for interviewers, and that's assuming that the respondent even knows the particular sect that his or her church belongs to. For a large-scale social survey such as the GSS, though, religion is considered important enough that the researchers are willing to put in the additional questions.

The other thing that's interesting about this item is the response option of "other." Only about 50 respondents—from the overall sample of almost 4,500—

said that they were from some other category, but that category includes many groups, such as Hindus, Muslims, and Buddhists. Since listing all of the other categories that someone could fit in would make the question unreasonably long—and apply to only a few respondents anyway—researchers commonly add an "other" category. All of the Muslims, Hindus, members of Native American churches, and members of other religious groups would simply answer "other" and would then be asked to specify exactly what their religious preference is. This way, data is collected on everyone, but the length of the question is kept down for the vast majority of respondents.

The other major function of the "other" category is to ensure that the response options are exhaustive. In a well-designed survey question, every individual should fit into exactly one of the response options. To achieve this, the response options must be both **exhaustive** and **mutually exclusive**. *Exhaustive* means that every respondent fits into at least one of the response categories. *Mutually exclusive* means that no respondent fits into more than one of the response categories. For instance, if "other" was not one of the response categories, Buddhists, Muslims, Orthodox Christians, or even Jedi wouldn't fit into any of the response categories, so the response options wouldn't be exhaustive. Answers by these respondents might be recorded as "don't know" or "refused." A respondent might even try to fit into one of the named categories—none of which really capture information about that respondent appropriately. It is always a good idea, though, to ask respondents in "other" categories to specify their answer. In this question, that could be as easy as asking the respondent, "What would that be?" If enough respondents give the same response to the follow-up question, it can be included in later analysis of the results as if it were one of the named categories.

A lack of mutually exclusive response options could arise in the above question if "Christian" was included as a response category. There might be good reason to do so—perhaps in an attempt to capture Mormons or respondents who are part of nondenominational Christian sects—but if it were included, the categories would not be mutually exclusive because Catholics are both Catholic and Christian. As a result, some Catholics would choose "Catholic," and others would choose "Christian," making the results uninterpretable. Because of problems like this, researchers need to ensure that all respondents fit neatly into just one of the categories, and they need to adopt several strategies to make sure that this happens. The easiest way is to simply look at how other researchers have phrased the response options in the past and to use or adapt the options these researchers gave respondents. If past questions on the topic aren't available, researchers can make use of pilot or cognitive testing to make sure that the response options work as intended. If the problem is with the way in which some respondents are interpreting the question, researchers sometimes add explanatory text to the response options. So, instead of just "Christian," the response option could be, "Christian, but not a member of any major sect."

CLASSIC ITEM TYPES

Contingency Questions

Generally speaking, do you usually think of yourself as a Republican, a Democrat, an Independent, or what?

Republican	26%
Democrat	34%
Independent	40%

[If Republican]: Would you call yourself a strong Republican or a not very strong Republican?

Strong Republican	13%
Not very strong Republican	13%

[If Democrat]: Would you call yourself a strong Democrat or a not very strong Democrat?

Strong Democrat	19%
Not very strong Democrat	15%

[If Independent or Other]: Do you think of yourself as closer to the Republican or Democratic party?

Independent Democrat	17%
Independent Independent	11%
Independent Republican	12%

Source: ANES 2008, total $N = 2,293$

The above item is a more complex question than those that have been previously used as examples. All told, if has four parts, though every individual respondent is asked only two questions. Despite its complexity, it has become the standard measure for party identification in American political surveys, and the seven-point scale that results from the questions is used in almost every analysis of political views or voting behaviors. It also represents a conceptual leap in political science, as the earliest versions of the question from the ANES were among the first to operationalize partisanship as something other than voting behavior: someone can be a Democrat who votes for a Republican, or vice versa. This view just wasn't an option when researchers thought of attachment to parties solely in terms of who the respondent voted for.

The question begins by asking respondents to categorize themselves as a Republican, a Democrat, an Independent, or something else, though almost no one takes the last option. Just based on this question, there are more Democrats than Republicans, but there are more Independents than anything. However, that doesn't give the whole story. Many Americans say that they are Independents because it's the more socially desirable category; they want the interviewer to believe that they're free thinkers who don't blindly follow either party. To clarify, the ANES question has a follow-up for each category. Partisans—respondents who said that they were Republicans or Democrats—are asked if they are "strong" or "not very strong" partisans. Independents are asked which of the parties they feel closer to. As the responses show, most Independents admit that they prefer one party to the other, making them what political scientists call "leaners." When the responses to all of the follow-up questions are combined, they form a seven-point scale, ranging from strong Republicans to strong Democrats, with Independents in between. This scale tells a rather different story than the initial responses do. There are some true Independents (respondents who claim that they don't really identify with either party), but not many. There are more Democrats than Republicans—especially in 2008, with a presidential election that led many Americans to identify with the Democratic Party—but there are more Independents on the Democratic side, meaning that their supporters are generally less reliable in elections and are more likely to vote for the other party at the polls.

The party identification question is an example of what researchers call a **contingency question**. A contingency question is asked to a respondent only if that respondent has given a specific response, or set of responses, to previous questions. In this case, the question asked after the initial item depends on what the respondent said first. Respondents who said that they were Democrats got one question; respondents who said that they were Independents got another. As in the partisanship question, these contingency questions are generally used to get more information about certain subgroups—in this case, to find out how Independents lean or how strongly partisans feel about their side. In the religious affiliation question shown earlier, a contingency question might ask Protestant respondents what particular sect they identify with, a question that wouldn't be applicable to respondents who said that they were Catholic.

This may seem like an overly complicated way to get the information the researcher is looking for. After all, if the goal is to assemble a seven-point party identification scale, why not just ask respondents to place themselves on that scale? Instead of asking four different questions, the researcher could just ask if the respondent was a strong Democrat, a not so strong Democrat, an Independent who leans toward the Democrats, and so on. There are several reasons why a series of contingency questions is a better idea in this case. First, respondents have an easier time understanding a series of contingency questions, even though these questions are more difficult for researchers to program into a telephone poll script or analyze the results from. A respondent might not understand the difference between a weak Republican and an Independent that leans toward the Republicans. After all, many researchers don't fully understand it, either! A series of questions that simplifies the scale down to just two or three options at a time might be easier for respondents to understand. The same respondent that doesn't know the difference between a weak Republican and an Independent that leans toward the Republicans probably does know the difference between a weak and a strong Republican or an Independent that leans toward one side or the other.

Second, the contingency questions can be used to minimize social desirability effects. As noted previously, many Americans think that being an Independent is more desirable than being a partisan, so given the choice of calling themselves partisans or Independents who just happen to lean toward one party or the other, they'll choose the latter. By using a series of contingency questions, the researchers can ensure that most respondents don't have the option to give in to perceived social pressure in this way. If all of the options were given up front, the distorting effects of social desirability would be much worse.

Third, the careful use of contingency questions can actually save time on the survey. There aren't too many people who really enjoy taking social surveys, especially over the phone, so researchers are constantly trying to achieve a balance between collecting all of the information that's desired and keeping the survey short enough that respondents won't give up. As such, any technique that can keep surveys shorter is useful. Explaining the seven-point scale, and reading all of the possible responses to it, would take more time than the shorter, more intuitive contingency questions. Think about it this way: the way the contingency questions are set up, no one hears more than six possible response options. Combining all of the responses into the standard seven-point scale might take effort from the researcher, but if it gets more and better responses, it's well worth it.

Open-Ended Questions

The next questions are about freedom in America today. Freedom means different things to different people. When you think about freedom, what comes to mind? Can you tell me in a couple of sentences what freedom means to you?

Doing what I want	33%
Autonomy, self-realization	5%
Choices, making decisions	11%
Rights: religion and speech	19%
Movement and travel	8%
Negative: slave or subordinate	5%
Citizen, political participation	4%
Security, economic independence	4%
Other	10%
Don't know	2%

Source: GSS 2000, $N = 1,414$

The above question is different from the others that have been discussed so far. First, it deals with a more difficult subject matter. Instead of asking respondents how they feel about something, it asks them to describe what a fairly nebulous concept means to them. Second, the responses listed are never actually read to the respondents—if for no other reason than it would take forever! Instead, respondents are asked the question, and their responses are coded into the listed categories by researchers looking at their answers later on.

Of course, respondents didn't actually say that freedom means "autonomy or self-realization" or any of the other responses. These codes are used to approximate the actual responses given. For instance, if a respondent said that freedom means that "nobody can tell me what to do," the response would be coded in the autonomy category.

All of this coding means that the question is a lot more work for the interviewer, the respondent, and the researcher looking at the results, but sometimes it may be the only way to ask a question. For any given individual, freedom means many—or perhaps even all—of these things, so the researcher can't just ask respondents to choose one of the responses. This format also means that the researcher isn't imposing his or her ideas of what freedom means on the respondents. A researcher probably couldn't sit down and list all of the things that freedom might mean to Americans. By letting the respondents give whatever answer they like and building the response codes around their answers, the researcher is letting the people being interviewed define the answers.

Open-ended questions, like the above item, are those that don't have a defined response set. Rather than picking from a list of options, the respondent can say whatever he or she likes in response to a question. In some ways, these questions are much easier for respondents. After all, open-ended questions are more like actual conversations than normal survey questions. When was the last time someone asked you, "How was your day? Was it wonderful, good, so-so, kind of bad, really terrible, or don't you know?" The downside to these open-ended questions is that they are often difficult for researchers to work with. For example, the GSS has four questions asking respondents about their job and the industry they work in. There are so many possible industries (and possible jobs) that there really isn't any way to have a fixed set of response options, so the four questions are open ended. It's up to the interviewer to input the responses in a way that researchers can understand. To do this, interviewers have two full pages of instructions for the four questions. According to Tom Smith, the long-time director of the GSS, that's ten times as many instructions as there are for any other question in the study.

Open-ended questions are used for several reasons. First, as seen in the freedom question above, researchers don't want to impose an artificial structure on the respondents. If the freedom question were asked as a normal survey question, it would be like telling respondents, "These are various definitions of freedom. Which do you agree with most?" It's a perfectly valid question, but it eliminates the possibility of respondents surprising the researchers by coming up with their own definitions. This is also the justification for political surveys that ask respondents what they like best and least about candidates. What the respondents might like about a candidate might be something that the researchers never thought of—or something that's factually incorrect—but that doesn't mean that it's not important to know. Americans might tell an interviewer that they don't like Barack Obama because he was born in Kenya. This information isn't true, and researchers probably wouldn't include it in a defined response set, but that doesn't make the response any less valid.

Second, open-ended responses help to eliminate some forms of reactivity. Depending on the question, respondents may be more likely to pick the first response, the last response, the one that is most thoroughly described, or the one that seems least extreme. By removing the response sets, there's no way for respondents to try to figure out the "best" option based on the options given or what they think the interviewer wants them to say. Third, as seen with the GSS job and industry questions, a question may have so many possible responses that it's simply more efficient to code an open-ended response than it is to have respondents wade through all of the possible options.

Finally, researchers might choose to use an open-ended item to record additional responses to standard survey items. This might take the form of a contingency question. In the GSS religion question shown earlier, respondents who say that they belong to some religion other than those that have been listed are asked to specify that religion. This means that their response is open ended. In other cases, interviewers may be asked to record any additional comments that a respondent makes about a question. For instance, in the 2010 ANES, respondents were asked to choose between Barack Obama and Mitt Romney for President. One respondent told the interviewer, "Jesus, I'd have to shoot both of that pair of communists." The answer is not one of the response items, but it's illuminating nonetheless, and it was worth recording for the researchers to see later.

Once researchers have decided to use an open-ended question, they then have to decide how to deal with the resulting responses. Normally, the data turned in by interviewers takes the form of a series of numbers: the respondent chose Option 4 for Question 1, Option 5 for Question 2, and so on. For open-ended items, the responses can be sentences or even paragraphs, which makes the researcher's job difficult. The simplest way to deal with open-ended questions is by coding a response set without reading that response set aloud or showing it to the respondent. Essentially, every response is treated as a volunteered response. So, in the above GSS freedom question, the interviewer would see the categories listed above and decide which of those categories applies to the answer given by the respondent. This has the advantage of simplifying the data that's given to the researcher, but it puts a great deal of trust in the interviewer to be able to quickly and accurately categorize a potentially lengthy response. As such, this strategy is best used when researchers are looking for one particular answer. So, if the GSS researchers simply wanted to see how many Americans would say that freedom meant something about civil rights, such as speech and religion, the interviewer would simply have to decide if the answer had to do with civil rights or not—a much easier decision.

The second way to deal with these questions is by recording the entire response, then letting the researcher form the categories later. This is easiest in online or paper-and-pencil surveys, in which the respondent simply writes down an answer. In telephone or face-to-face surveys, the interviewer often has to write down the entire response very quickly. Many interviews, especially those carried out face to face, are recorded, allowing the researchers to go back and listen to the responses. They can then carry out what amounts to a content analysis on the responses to put them into appropriate categories.

Finally, most researchers adopt a hybrid technique in which responses that easily fit into one or more previously defined categories are recorded as such, but any other responses are saved to be coded by the researchers later. This does require some additional work on the part of the interviewers, but it helps to ensure that any difficult-to-code responses are left up to the researcher to categorize.

Matrix Questions

The above question asks respondents to assign blame for the economic crisis that began in 2008. They were given the same five response options for the six individuals or groups that could be to blame. This means that the responses to the six items are comparable in a way that they wouldn't be if there were different response options for each of them. In the above question, for instance, respondents are most likely to blame Wall Street bankers for the crisis, with consumers and President Bush just about tied as the second most blamed. President Obama received less blame from Americans than the others, with only 20 percent saying that he bore "a great deal" of the blame.

These sets of items, when used in surveys that present questions visually (as in online or paper-and-pencil surveys), are called **matrix questions**. The name refers to the presentation of the questions, in which respondents would generally just check the box corresponding to the level of blame that they want to assign to each individual or group. There are both benefits and problems with presenting items in this way. The biggest benefit is speed. Because respondents don't have to read through a different set of response options for each item, they can answer the questions quickly. They know what the question is; they just have to check the box for each item. A second benefit is that respondents tend to assign their responses in a relative fashion. In the above question, for instance, even though there's no instruction telling individuals that not all of the individuals or groups can be blamed "a great deal," nearly all of the respondents assign a low level of blame to some and a high level of blame to others. Respondents treat the question as if it's asking "Who is the most to blame?" That's often useful for

	A great deal	A lot	A moderate amount	A little	Not at all
How much is each of the following people or groups to blame for the poor economic conditions of the past few years?					
President Obama	20.0%	16.0%	24.1%	21.0%	18.8%
President Bush	28.3%	20.6%	26.1%	18.1%	6.9%
Democrats in the U.S. Congress	21.8%	24.3%	32.9%	15.4%	5.7%
Republicans in the U.S. Congress	24.3%	26.9%	30.2%	14.3%	4.3%
Wall Street bankers	45.4%	26.7%	18.3%	5.9%	3.7%
Consumers who borrowed too much money	30.0%	30.0%	25.2%	11.1%	3.7%

Source: ANES 2010, *N* = 1,263

researchers because it allows for easier comparison of the responses across the items. If a respondent said that all of the individuals or groups bore "a great deal" of the blame, there wouldn't really be anything to analyze. Because respondents treat the matrix items as if they're being compared, they give more variance in their responses. That comparability is the third benefit of matrix questions. Using the above set of items, researchers can look at which individuals and groups are most blamed for the economic crisis and which are least blamed. If there were different response options for each of the items, this would be much more difficult. In upcoming chapters, techniques for comparing responses across different items will be discussed, but setting the items up in a matrix makes the comparison a great deal easier.

There are also significant problems with using the matrix question format. The first is the speed that was discussed before. Because respondents tend to answer these questions quickly, they may not be thinking about their responses. It would be easy, for instance, for a respondent to quickly check or click the boxes for "a great deal" for all of the items without thinking much about it. To deal with this issue, researchers often include a **verification item** in the matrix questions. This verification item (or **quality–control check**) may be a simple instruction, such as "In this row, check the box labeled 'A little.'" If respondents aren't paying attention to the items, they may select the wrong box, and the researcher will know to ignore their responses. The verification item might be something more sophisticated, such as a fictional group or something irrelevant to the question. If a respondent says that Count Chocula shoulders "a lot" of blame for the financial crisis, researchers can be pretty sure that the respondent wasn't paying attention.

The second major problem with matrix questions is that researchers may use them when they don't really fit. The above ANES question is an example of when a matrix question is appropriate: the six items are asking the same thing about different individuals or groups. The problem would arise if the researchers tried to fit more questions into the matrix. For instance, researchers could ask respondents how much they approve of President Obama's handling of the economy using the same response options. Even if the response options fit—a respondent could like his handling of the economy "a lot" or "not at all"—the shift between the types of questions would tend to lead respondents to try to answer in a way that's relative to the other items in the matrix or consistent with what was said in other items. Perhaps more important, response options that don't quite fit the question actually cost time on the survey because respondents have to stop and figure out what they should say. As discussed previously, response options should be clear, succinct, and phrased in the way that respondents generally talk about the issue, and giving up on those guidelines to fit an item into a matrix is a bad deal.

Finally, because matrix presentation of questions lets researchers fit so many items into a limited amount of space, there is a tendency to increase the size of the matrix, but this should be avoided. The more items there are in a matrix, the more likely it is that respondents will get bored and just start checking boxes, necessitating more verification questions and possibly having to throw out responses.

While a matrix presentation can't be used in surveys in which the interviewer is reading items to a respondent, questions for a telephone survey can be structured in a similar way. In a telephone survey, an added instruction would tell the respondent, for example, "I'm now going to read the names of a number of individuals or groups who might be blamed for the poor economic conditions of the last few years. For each, tell me if they are a great deal to blame, a lot to blame. . ." and so on. This sort of item set retains some of the benefits of the matrix presentation (responses are fast, though they're not as relative) but also some of the problems. Respondents are just as likely to answer quickly and without thinking over the phone as they are when filling out an online survey.

Regardless of whether the items are presented verbally or visually, researchers should be careful about primacy and recency effects. Respondents tend to pay more attention to the items at the beginning and the end of a series. To make sure that this doesn't bias responses in the aggregate, researchers generally rotate the order in which the items are presented. So, some respondents might get "President Obama" first, while others get "Wall Street Bankers."

Sakamura Items

Respondents in the last pre-election poll carried out by PublicMind before the 2009 New Jersey gubernatorial elections were randomly assigned to one of the items above. The two items are the same in all respects except for the name of

If the election were held today, who would you vote for in a race between . . . and . . . and . . .? [ROTATE NAMES] [If "don't know," ASK: "At this moment, which way do you lean?" If "other," ASK: "Who would that be?"]	
Jon Corzine, the Democrat	39%
Chris Christie, the Republican	41%
Chris Daggett, the Independent	14%
None or Other	3%
Don't know [vol]	3%

If the election were held today, who would you vote for in a race between . . . and . . . and . . .? [ROTATE NAMES] [If "don't know," ASK: "At this moment, which way do you lean?" If "other," ASK: "Who would that be?"]	
Jon Corzine, the Democrat	38%
Chris Christie, the Republican	38%
Gary Steele, the Independent	12%
None or Other	3%
Don't know [vol]	8%

Source: Fairleigh Dickinson University PublicMind poll October 6, 2009, $N = 347$ for each item

the Independent candidate given. In some polls for that election, one of the Independent candidates, Chris Daggett, had received as much as 20 percent support. If that support translated into actual votes in the election, it would be unprecedented in New Jersey and could easily swing the election one way or the other. There were, however, reasons to not believe these results. First, Daggett's support was only present when his name was listed along with the two major party candidates. When his name wasn't read, only about 5 percent of respondents said that they were going to vote for an "other" candidate and named Daggett. Second, many respondents reported strong negative feelings toward both of the major party candidates, so it seemed likely that they were just saying that they would support anyone who wasn't one of those two. Third, the actual election ballots in New Jersey are set up so that the major party candidates are on the top, and all of the third-party candidates are presented at the bottom, in an order that varies by county. This survey experiment was used to see if Daggett's support was real or just a result of the way the question was being asked. So, half of the respondents were asked to choose between the Republican, the Democrat, and Daggett. The other half were asked to choose between the Republican, the Democrat, and Gary Steele, another third-party candidate who had not even received 1 percent support in the polls. When Steele's name was substituted for Daggett's, he received 12 percent support, compared to Daggett's 14 percent in the other form of the question.

This result led the researchers, headed up by political science professor Peter Woolley, to conclude that Daggett's support wasn't real. Respondents were simply saying that they would vote for anyone other than the major party candidates. Daggett had only been doing so well in the polls because he was the Independent candidate who was named in the question. Actual support for Daggett was the difference between the 14 percent he received in the first version of the question and the 12 percent that Steele (who didn't have any actual significant support) earned in the second version, or about 2 percent. As it turns out, that's pretty much exactly what he got in the actual election.

These types of questions, in which the name of an actual individual being evaluated is substituted for a lesser-known, or even fictional, name are variously called Prufrock items or **Sakamura items**, and they can be used in all sorts of studies. For instance, researchers who want to understand how much people support the police or the suspect in police brutality cases could easily use one or two real cases and one fake case. If a respondent supports the police (or the suspect) in the real cases and in the fake case, the researcher knows that his or her responses aren't based on the facts of that particular case. Instead, the respondent always supports one side or the other.

Feeling Thermometers

I'd like to get your feelings toward some person or group. I'll read the name of a person or group, and I'd like you to rate that person or group using something we call the *feeling thermometer*.

Ratings between 50 degrees and 100 degrees mean that you feel favorable and warm toward the person. Ratings between 0 degrees and 50 degrees mean that you don't feel favorable toward the person or group and that you don't care too much for that person or group. You would rate the person or group at the 50-degree mark if you don't feel particularly warm or cold toward the person or group.

If we come to a person or group whose name you don't recognize, you don't need to rate it. Just tell me, and we'll move on to the next one. How would you rate…Mormons?

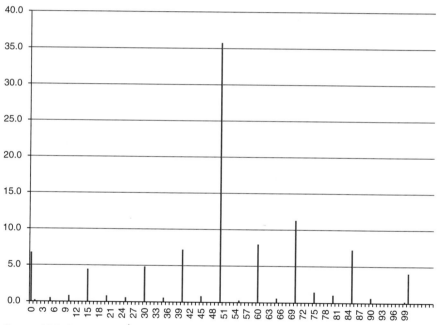

Source: ANES 2010, $N = 1,271$

In the run-up to the 2012 Presidential election, there was a great deal of interest in the public perception of Mormons and whether feelings toward Mormons would affect former Massachusetts Governor Mitt Romney's run for the Presidency. By themselves, these results don't mean very much, but the ANES, the GSS, and other prominent surveys have been using these sorts of feeling thermometer questions to measure feelings toward various groups for some time, allowing them to compare views of Mormons with views of other religious and ethnic groups. The average for Mormons was 51, comparable to other groups. This is largely driven by the number of respondents who rated Mormons right in the middle of the scale at 50; almost 36 percent did so. More revealing are the relative proportions who have very positive or very negative views of Mormons.

About 9 percent of respondents gave Mormons a 10 or less, while only 5 percent gave them a 90 or more.

The first thing to notice about these **feeling thermometer** items is how long the instructions are. Because of how long it takes to explain these scales to respondents, they're normally used in long lists of items; reading all of those instructions for just one or two items simply isn't worth it. The idea of these types of questions is to allow respondents to give a more nuanced evaluation of individuals and groups. Rather than have just four or five response options, respondents have 101. This is especially important for researchers who want to use the responses as dependent variables in regression analyses, which will be discussed in Chapter 13. The more categories the dependent variable has, the better regression analysis works, so a feeling thermometer works very well, at least in theory.

The reason feeling thermometers seem to work better in theory than in practice is that while respondents have 101 possible response options, they don't use them all. In the above item asking about Mormons, nine responses (0, 15, 30, 40, 50, 60, 70, 85, and 100) accounted for 90 percent of all of the answers. Only 1.3 percent of respondents gave an answer that ended in something other than a 0 or 5, and almost all of these were just above or just below one of the common answers (like 49, 1, or 99). So, while there are theoretically 101 responses respondents can give, in reality, there's more like 10. Still, that's far more than researchers would be able to get out of a standard set of response options.

The other potential problem with feeling thermometer questions is that, like matrix questions, respondents tend to treat them as if they're relative. So, if respondents have given a 50 to one group or individual, they tend to use that as a baseline for evaluating other groups. If they like another group a little less, they give it a 40 or even a 49. If they like it a little more, they give it a 51 or a 60. This isn't bad in and of itself, but it does mean that if the first group got a 60, the ratings for all of the other groups down the line will be driven up—what would have been a 49 is now a 59, and so on. Researchers have adopted a number of strategies to deal with these problems. One is to treat all of the feeling thermometer ratings as relative. Instead of worrying about what number, exactly, each group was given by a respondent, researchers look at the order of the items. The difference between a 49 and a 50 isn't as important as the fact that one group was rated higher than the other. In addition, researchers generally make sure to rotate the items in the feeling thermometer series, just as they do with matrix questions. While some respondents might see Mormons as the first group, other respondents would see it last or in the middle. By rotating the order in which the items are given, researchers can ensure that the effect of item order on the responses of individuals averages out when they look at the whole sample.

Despite these problems with feeling thermometers, they do allow for a much wider range of responses than most other types of questions. For that reason, researchers continue to use them and just deal with any problems as they arise.

CLASSIC ITEM SCALES

In addition to individual items, researchers often make use of groups of items that are designed to work together. These scales of items can be difficult to develop, but researchers typically don't have to do so. By adapting existing scales, researchers can ensure the validity of the items without having to reinvent the wheel.

In **Likert** items (named after organizational psychologist Rensis Likert, pronounced *LICK-ert*), participants are asked to rate their views using a range of responses, often from "strongly disagree" to "strongly agree." Likert items typically have five or seven points (as in the second set of examples), with the middle category representing a neutral response (such as "neither agree nor disagree"). Likert items without such a middle category (as in the first set of examples) are called *forced-response items* because they force participants to take a stand on the question, either for or against it. Many researchers prefer forced-response questions because participants may be reluctant to agree or disagree to any extent with controversial statements, such as those in the examples.

These Likert items are often referred to as Likert scales, but a Likert scale properly refers to a series of Likert items on the same topic. The first example is a Likert scale, in which the researcher could measure a participant's opinions on

Likert Scales

	Strongly agree	Agree	Disagree	Strongly disagree
Now, I'm going to read several more statements. As I read each one, please tell me whether you strongly agree, agree, disagree, or strongly disagree with it.				
A working mother can establish just as warm and secure a relationship with her children as a mother who does not work.	23%	42%	28%	8%
A preschool child is likely to suffer if his or her mother works.	9%	32%	49%	10%
It is much better for everyone involved if the man is the achiever outside the home and the woman takes care of the home and family.	9%	26%	47%	17%

	Strongly agree	Agree	Neither agree nor disagree	Disagree	Strongly disagree
Now, I'm going to read several more statements. As I read each one, please tell me whether you strongly agree, agree, neither agree nor disagree, disagree, or strongly disagree with it.					
Family life often suffers because men concentrate too much on their work.	10%	48%	15%	25%	2%
Because of past discrimination, employers should make special efforts to hire and promote qualified women.	17%	46%	14%	19%	4%

Source: General Social Survey 2006, weighted cumulative results

women's role in the household and workplace by combining the responses to the various items.

Because there are often a relatively large number of responses available to participants on a Likert item, it's tempting to treat responses as if they are interval-level, or even ratio-level, variables. In the second example, for instance, the responses could be numbered from 1 to 5, with "strongly agree" at 1, and "strongly disagree" at 5. However, any results stemming from this would be misleading. While it may seem that the difference between "strongly agree" and "agree" is about the same as the distance between "strongly disagree" and "disagree," researchers can't assume that this is the case. It's also been suggested that the middle category in a nonforced response Likert scale is somewhat sticky; all else being equal, participants like to pick the middle category. If this is the case, then the conceptual distance between the middle category and the categories next to it might well be greater than the distance between the middle categories and the more extreme categories. Adding to this is the common problem of *moderation bias*, in which participants tend to avoid picking extreme responses such as "strongly agree" and "strongly disagree."

Finally, Likert scales face the problem of *agreement bias*. On the whole, participants would rather agree with a statement than disagree with it. To combat this, researchers ensure that the various items in the Likert scale are coded in opposite directions. For instance, in the first example set of Likert items, participants who are more in favor of women working would tend to agree with the first statement and disagree with the second two statements. While it may be the case that the conceptual difference between one category and the next is constant throughout the scale (that is, the difference between "strongly agree" and "agree" is the same as the distance between "agree" and "neither agree nor disagree"), it's unlikely, and researchers can't establish it without sophisticated statistical analyses. As such, responses to individual Likert items are best treated as ordinal-level variables. Respondents who say that they agree with a statement are higher on the scale than those who say that they disagree, but researchers can't say exactly how big the difference is. As a result, it's not really appropriate to report the mean score of a Likert item (though researchers do it all of the time); rather, researchers should report the median or modal score or, even better, the distribution throughout the entire scale (what percent fell into each category).

This limitation on the interpretation of results from individual Likert items is what drives researchers to make use of the larger Likert scales. In the scales, researchers look at the responses to a large number of Likert items. (Rensis Likert argued that eight was about the right number.)

Developed by psychologist Louis Leon Thurstone in the 1920s, **Thurstone scales** are designed to measure attitudes toward a given construct. In a Thurstone scale, the respondents are asked a series of questions about the construct, and they may agree or disagree with each. Typically, the attitude of the participant is expressed as the proportion of the items that he or she agreed with. For example, a participant who said that a woman should be allowed to have an abortion if she is pregnant as a result of rape, serious defects, or health reasons (three of the seven conditions) would score a .43 on the GSS abortion scale shown above. Someone

Thurstone Scales

	Yes	No
Please tell me whether or not you think it should be possible for a woman to obtain a legal abortion if. . .		
There is a strong chance of serious defect in the baby?	80.2%	19.8%
She is married and does not want any more children?	43.3%	56.7%
The woman's own health is seriously endangered by the pregnancy?	89.8%	10.2%
The family has a very low income and cannot afford any more children?	47.0%	53.0%
She became pregnant as a result of rape?	81.9%	18.1%
She is not married and does not want to marry the man?	43.7%	56.3%
The woman wants it for any reason?	39.4%	60.6%

Source: GSS 1972–2006, weighted cumulative results

who said "yes" to all of the conditions would score a 1, and someone who said "no" to all of the conditions would score a 0.

To construct a Thurstone scale, researchers begin with a large number of statements about the construct they wish to measure attitudes on. Rather than seven statements, as in the GSS abortion scale, they might start with thirty or forty different circumstances under which a woman might want an abortion. They then narrow down these statements through pilot testing. In this pilot testing, researchers ask a group of participants to sort all of the statements and rate them on a scale (often an eleven-point scale, though it doesn't have to be) of how favorable they are to the concept being measured. For instance, the statement "It should be possible for a woman to obtain a legal abortion if the woman wants it for any reason" is very favorable to abortion, while "It should be possible for a woman to obtain a legal abortion if there is a strong chance of serious defect in the baby" is not nearly as favorable. That is, lots of people who aren't in favor of abortion would still agree with the serious defect statement. Once the pilot testing participants have sorted all of the statements individually, the researcher looks at where each of the statements was placed, on average, and how consistent that placement was (specifically, the mean and standard deviation of the placement). The researcher then picks out the statements that were placed most consistently (have the lowest standard deviation) and best represent the full range of attitudes. The researcher would pick out the statement that was placed, on average, lowest (in this case, the woman's health being endangered), the statement that was placed highest (the woman wants it for any reason), and statements that were placed along the spectrum: some at the low end, some in the middle, and some at the high end.

The idea of this placement is to make sure that there none of the items will always go together. There's no point in having two different items on the scale if all of the participants who agree with one also agree with the other. Research has shown that support for abortion in cases of rape is almost exactly the same as support for abortion in cases of incest. In a Thurstone scale, then, it doesn't make sense to ask the incest question if the rape question is already present. In addition, statements that almost no one agrees with, or almost no one disagrees with, are generally not included. If 99 percent of participants agree that a woman should be allowed to have a legal abortion if she would certainly die in childbirth, knowing someone's response to that item doesn't help the researcher distinguish between that respondent and anyone else. As such, there's no point in including it in the scale. Researchers call such items *nondiscriminatory* because they don't help identify the difference between groups; good items that do tend to divide up the respondents into groups are *discriminatory*.

When using Thurstone or similar sets of items, researchers generally make sure to include some items that are reverse-coded. In the above scale, all of the items are coded such that saying "yes" means greater support for abortion rights. This corresponds with the way respondents naturally talk about abortion rights—people are more likely to talk about being for or against abortion, rather than being for or against bans on abortion—but it also means that respondents may be just saying "yes" or "no" reflexively, without really thinking through the items. There's also the issue of agreement bias. All else being equal, respondents tend to agree more than they tend to disagree. This agreement bias could be leading researchers to overstate support for abortion rights. To correct for these problems, researchers could include one or two items in which "no" indicates support for abortion rights. For instance, asking if the respondent supports the requirement of spousal or parental notification before an abortion is allowed or supports restrictions on the use of government funds to provide abortions for poor women. Such items can be problematic, leading to double-negative questions or questions that aren't phrased naturally, but careful wording of the questions can minimize these issues. Also, these issues must be weighed against the problems arising from agreement bias and reflexive answering.

A **Guttman scale** is a broad term for any scale that can be rank-ordered such that agreement with one of the items higher up in the scale also means agreement with all of the lower items. In the above scale of religious beliefs, pretty much all participants who say that they believe in religious miracles also say that they believe in life after death and heaven. Similarly, almost all participants who say that they believe in hell also believe in religious miracles, life after death, heaven,

Guttman Scales

Do you believe in. . .	Yes, definitely	Yes, probably	No, probably not	No, definitely not
Heaven?	67.9%	18.2%	7.8%	6.2%
Life after death?	59.3%	21.4%	9.5%	9.8%
Religious miracles?	49.1%	27.1%	14.5%	9.3%
Hell?	56.9%	18.2%	13.1%	11.8%
The devil?	46.0%	19.5%	16.9%	17.7%

Source: GSS 1998

and so on. Conversely, almost no participants who say that they do not believe in heaven say that they believe in any of the other items, and participants who believe in life after death and heaven but not religious miracles are very unlikely to believe in hell or the devil.

Any scale that has these properties of rank ordering is a Guttman scale, even if there doesn't seem to be a logical relationship between the items. In the above scale, it seems silly that there is about 6 percent of the population that believes in heaven but doesn't believe in life after death, but as long as the rank-ordering relationship holds, it's a Guttman scale.

Guttman scales are useful because they are an easy way of making certain that a scale is unidimensional, meaning that all of the items are measuring the same underlying concept. In this case, the concept is religious belief; because the items have a rank-ordered relationship, researchers can be pretty certain that all items are measuring the same thing. Researchers can also look for unidimensionality with a set of sophisticated statistical techniques called *factor analysis*, but Guttman scales are still considered an acceptable way of measuring it.

This isn't to say that the relationship between the variables has to be perfect in the dataset. Even if the scale is a Guttman scale, some responses won't fit the pattern. For instance, there are a few participants in the GSS dataset who say that they believe in the devil but don't believe in hell. Leaving aside some troubling theological implications, in a Guttman scale, this is referred to as an *error* (which doesn't mean that the individual participant made a mistake in his or her response, just that the response doesn't fit the pattern established by the scale). As long as no more than about 5 percent of the sample makes the same error, the scale is still considered a valid Guttman scale.

To create a Guttman scale, researchers start out in much the same way as they do for a Thurstone scale. Based on pilot studies or previous research, researchers generate a large number of items that could measure the concept they're trying to examine. Then, the researchers carry out another pilot test in which they ask participants to agree or disagree with each of the statements. Once researchers have this data, they arrange the responses of each participant in what's called a *scalogram analysis*. In the scalogram analysis, the participants are sorted, top to bottom, according to how many of the items that they agreed with. (Participants who agreed with more items go to the top.) The items are sorted left to right, according to how many participants agreed to them. (Items that were agreed to more often go on the left.) In the resulting scalogram, the "yes" responses should be clustered at the top and left, with the "no" responses at the bottom and right. The researchers can then identify the errors (shaded in the scalogram below) and remove any items that don't fit the pattern more than about 5 percent of the time. The items that are left after the troublesome ones have been removed constitute the Guttman scale. Note that the items don't have to be presented in the same order that they're listed in the scalogram, and researchers often mix them up on the final survey.

In the past, the abortion scale discussed in the section on Thurstone scales (known as the Rossi Abortion Scale) was considered to be a Guttman scale, but it's easy to see why that view has fallen out of favor. If it were a Guttman scale, the

Example scalogram analysis, error responses bolded

	Heaven?	Life after death?	Religious miracles?	Hell?	The devil?
Respondent 1	Yes	Yes	Yes	Yes	Yes
Respondent 2	Yes	Yes	Yes	Yes	Yes
Respondent 3	Yes	Yes	**No**	Yes	No
Respondent 4	Yes	Yes	Yes	Yes	No
Respondent 5	Yes	Yes	Yes	No	No
Respondent 6	Yes	Yes	No	No	No
Respondent 7	Yes	No	No	**Yes**	No
Respondent 8	Yes	No	No	No	No
Respondent 9	No	No	No	No	No
Respondent 10	No	**Yes**	No	No	No

assumption would be that agreement with one item would imply agreement with some or all of the others. The "wants it for any reason" question is the hardest, and it might make sense to assume that someone who agrees with it would agree with all of the other questions, as in a Guttman scale. However, that logic doesn't hold for items in the middle of the scale. A participant could (and many do) easily say that a married couple shouldn't have an abortion just because of low income, but an unmarried woman who doesn't want to get married should be allowed to have one. If it were assumed that this was a Guttman scale, such a response would be classified as an error (the respondent should have given a different response), so the researcher would ignore the actual response. If it's instead treated as a Thurstone scale, the researcher assumes that participants know what they're saying and treats all of the responses as valid.

Bogardus Scales

Bogardus scales are based on the work of Emory Bogardus, one of the leading figures of early American sociology (among many other things, he founded AKD, the sociology honors society). In his initial research, he was trying to measure social distance by asking participants how close they would be willing to get to members of an immigrant group. His initial scale was seven points—ranging from willingness to marry a member of that group down to wanting to exclude members of that group from even visiting the country—with each level being assigned a numerical value. He asked participants to rate thirty different groups and found an overall mean of 2.14 across them, indicating that, on average, the participants were not willing to have a member of one of the groups marry into their family and probably would not be willing to have them as friends, but they would be willing to have them live on the same street. By 2001, when researchers in New Jersey carried out a replication among students at twenty-two colleges with a slightly different set of groups, the overall mean had fallen to 1.45. Even the means of the groups that were seen as the most distant, Muslims and Arabs (not surprising since the study was carried out in September and October 2001), were 1.88 and 1.94. There was less perceived distance to Arabs than there had been against the average immigrant when Bogardus first carried out his research.

In a Bogardus scale, there's a definite order to the responses. It doesn't make sense for participants to say that they would be okay with having someone as a co-worker but not be okay with that individual living in the same country. As such, the social distance between an individual and a given group is determined by looking at the left-most positive response. Someone who says that he or she would be okay with a member of a group being related to him or her by marriage is scored as a 1 on the scale, regardless of what else he or she says. Similarly, someone who says that he or she would be okay being close friends with a member of that group gets a 2, no matter what else he or she says, and so on. This means, of course, that a Bogardus scale is actually a special case of a Guttman scale.

Today, full versions of the Bogardus scale are most widely used in studies outside of the United States. Researchers looking at views of Roma (gypsies) in Eastern Europe have used them, along with scholars looking at ethnic integration in Balkan and Baltic countries. Within the United States, they have become less useful because Americans are often unwilling to admit that they would not want to work with, marry, or live near a member of another ethnic group (as mentioned in Chapter 2's discussion of the operationalization of racism). In their stead, researchers have developed alternative scales to measure social distance, such as the GSS scale showed above. In some cases, modifications to the scale are necessary depending on the nature of the group; for example, it doesn't always make sense to ask someone if they would be willing to marry a homosexual. In other cases, participants aren't willing (or maybe able) to give honest answers to the questions. Finally, scales such as these may be used to give a more general measure of tolerance, rather than Bogardus' concept of social distance. These scales are commonly used to measure tolerance of ideological or belief-based minorities, such as atheists or communists, especially since participants in surveys may be more willing to express discomfort with such groups than they would be for ethnic minorities. In the types of questions used on the GSS, though, there is no necessary ordering to the responses. (Participants could logically say "yes" to any one of the options but not the others.) Tolerance is normally determined by recording the proportion of the items the participant gave the more tolerant response.

Still, researchers continue to use Bogardus' original scale, mostly because of the scale's rich history and continuity. By asking the same questions about the same groups, researchers can track how some of these groups (such as African Americans or Jews) have become more integrated into American society over time.

OTHER CONSIDERATIONS

Visual Considerations

Wording of the questions is the central component of survey research, but simply having good questions is not enough to create a good survey. In a survey, the order of the questions is also very important. Typically, researchers start with easier, more general questions and build up to more personal, invasive, and potentially unpopular questions. There are two reasons for this order. First, ordering the questions from easier ones to more difficult ones builds rapport with the respondents. As respondents answer questions, they build rapport with the researcher, and they will be more likely to answer more personal, private, and difficult questions. Second, in the cases where the respondents refuse to answer a more difficult, personal, or invasive question, researchers do not risk having all the questions unanswered. If such a difficult, personal question is placed at the beginning of the survey, researchers risk alienating the respondent.

Demographic Questions

Typically, the last section of a survey is reserved for demographic questions. *Demographic questions* are survey questions about the background of the respondent and include age, gender, race, ethnicity, political affiliation, income, education, marital status, and union membership (as well as any number of other items, depending on the purpose of the survey). These demographic variables are not very interesting or exciting; therefore, starting with these questions does not attract the interest of the respondents. Early questions should be interesting enough to attract the interest of the respondents and draw them into the survey.

ADVANTAGES AND DISADVANTAGES OF SURVEY RESEARCH

Survey research has many advantages. It is one of the only research methods that allows researchers to gather information from a large body of respondents. Many large-scale surveys such as the GSS collect information on sample sizes over 2,000. Unlike in-depth interviews, survey methodology allows researchers to collect data on a very large group of respondents. Surveys are the best method for research topics that require large samples. They are great tools for describing populations, gathering public opinion, or determining political affiliation. They can describe very large populations and also allow for comparisons with different countries.

If the sample is selected appropriately, then survey research can use samples to come to conclusions about larger populations. Unlike other methods, if surveys are distributed to samples recruited through probability sampling, then researchers can use statistics to generalize from the results. In that case, this method has very high external validity. The results do not just apply to the sample, but researchers can use these results to come to conclusions about the wider population. For example, many political polls use samples to determine how the population will vote in a national election. The important point is that they do not have to talk to the entire population to know how the entire country will vote; they come to conclusions about the entire country based on a small sample.

Finally, because individual questionnaires are so standardized, they can be relatively easy to replicate. A researcher simply has to ask the same question again in order to see if the results hold. In that sense, surveys have high reliability.

However, it is important to note that the wording of the questions is essential for reliability. As too many researchers have found, even a small change in question wording can lead to a big difference in results.

Standardization allows survey methodology to collect comparable and reliable information on a large group of respondents. However, standardization can also be considered a weakness of surveys. Some argue that respondents are forced into rigid categories when in fact the choices do not necessarily represent them. That is why pilot testing, cognitive testing and open-ended items are crucial in the development of the survey questions to allow the researchers to offer appropriate categories. Researchers have a difficult time offering categories that apply to a wide range of people and still are applicable and relevant to individual respondents.

Survey methodology has also been criticized due to the potential artificiality of the process. Respondents can say they support a candidate, believe in an issue, or follow a television show; however, the information provided on a questionnaire might not translate into real life. This is less of a problem for in-depth, qualitative interviews because the respondents can explain themselves by walking the researchers through their thinking process and explaining how they came to the decisions they did. In surveys, respondents do not have that choice, and researchers do not know for sure if the opinions expressed on the survey do in fact translate into action. Another potential problem is operationalization. If researchers do not operationalize properly, they might not be measuring what they intended to measure in the first place. Therefore, they might end up with survey results that do not represent the initial concept being measured.

Ethical Considerations

Survey research has some ethical considerations, just like other research methods. Typically, surveys do not pose as big an ethical risk as some other research methods. However, this does not mean that they do not involve any risk or potential harm to the subjects. At the very least, survey questions could cause emotional distress among respondents. For example, asking about finding jobs when the respondent is unable to find a job might stress out the respondent. Using value-neutral wording and allowing respondents to easily refuse to answer questions can help mitigate this possibility.

Unlike a face-to-face, in-depth interview, where anonymity is not possible, surveys can be anonymous, depending on how they are administered. Even when a survey is not anonymous (that is, the researcher knows the address, phone number, or name of the respondent), it is important that individual answers cannot be traced back to the respondents. Many researchers assign numbers to the actual surveys and separate the name, phone number, and contact information from the data. This helps to ensure that all the information shared will be reported only in aggregates and no participant can be personally identified.

SUMMARY

It's important for researchers to take great care in how they structure the items they use on surveys. Because the same questions need to be administered many times to a large number of respondents, everyone who hears the question needs to be able to understand it easily and give a comparable response. Unlike in interview situations, survey researchers can't depend on prompts and follow-ups to clarify answers; everything has to be crystal clear from the start.

In addition to the words of the question itself, researchers also need to be careful about the response items that are given to respondents in closed-ended questions. If the response items are double-barreled or some respondents don't fit into any of the categories, the results of the question may be uninterpretable. To make sure that the target population will understand the items, researchers often make use of cognitive testing, a process that involves simply asking people who are like the respondents what they understand the item to mean.

Often, researchers make use of scales, series of items that are designed to work together to tell the researcher more than individual items could. These scales can be difficult to develop, but most researchers simply adapt scales that have already been used in other contexts, a strategy that helps to increase validity.

On top of the structure of the actual items and scales, researchers also need to pay attention to the order in which the items are asked. The introduction, at the top of the survey, sets the stage for the entire survey experience and can have a substantial impact on completion and acceptance rates. Items are typically ordered from least to most sensitive over the course of the questionnaire, with most surveys ending with a series of demographic items. While surveys often have fewer ethical concerns than other research techniques, researchers should still be careful about difficult or sensitive topics and ensure that a respondent's statements can never be traced back to the individual.

Study and Review

Under what circumstances, if any, would it be appropriate to make use of technical terms or similar jargon in a questionnaire?

Are more specific response sets necessarily more valid than less specific ones? Why or why not?

Suppose that you were asking a survey question on which there isn't any serious disagreement: whether or not the holocaust occurred or whether divorce should be allowed. Would it still be suitable to use balanced-item wording?

Why would you include separate (volunteered) responses for "don't know" and "refused"? Is there really a difference between the two?

Which are more valid: open-ended or close-ended questions? Why?

Under what circumstances is it ethical for researchers to include Sakamura items?

What's the difference between Guttman scales and Thurstone scales? Does it really matter?

CHAPTER 11
Administering Surveys

Learning Objectives

- Be able to assess the external validity of surveys
- Be able to explain the utility of face-to-face surveys
- Be able to explain why telephone surveys are so widely used
- Be able to explain the functions of mail surveys
- Be able to explain the circumstances under which internet surveys are most useful
- Be able to explain how sample results can be generalized to populations of interest
- Be able to identify non-SRS sampling techniques

GENERALIZING FROM SURVEYS

Laurence Steinberg and Alex R. Piquero—Jail for Juveniles? (2010)

Widespread fears that young men were becoming criminal "super predators" (violent criminal offenders without guilt or remorse) led public opinion to become increasingly in favor of harsh penalties for juvenile offenders the 1980s and 1990s. This wave of change in public opinion led lawmakers to adopt tough-on-crime policies that sent minors to adult courts and prisons. However, the extent to which the public supports such policies—and the circumstances under which they do so—has been a matter of some debate. Criminologists have generally concluded that the public wants juvenile offenders to be held accountable and that only older teenagers who have committed multiple violent offenses should be treated as adults. If that's the case, though, why do polls on the subject come to such varied conclusions?

Laurence Steinberg and Alex R. Piquero (2010) argue that the differences in the results of polls on juvenile offenders can be traced to variations in the ways in which the questions are asked and that even small differences in the question wordings can lead to significant differences in the results of the poll. To see exactly how the differences in wording affect the outcome of these studies, they carried out a survey experiment. In the experiment, respondents were given slightly different versions of the same question, "How much do you support trying [some or all] [first-time or repeat] [fourteen-year-old or seventeen-year-old] offenders arrested for [theft or rape] in adult court?" Each respondent was randomly assigned to one of the two options for each of the four variables, so one respondent might be asked about trying some repeat fourteen-year-old offenders in adult court, while another might be asked about first-time seventeen-year-old offenders. This led to a total of sixteen possible experimental conditions (a 2 × 2 × 2 × 2 factorial design), which meant that Steinberg and Piquero (2010) needed a relatively large **sample** for their **telephone survey**. These options weren't picked without good reason. The researchers did cognitive testing with college undergraduates to make sure that they understood what the offenses entailed; they initially wanted to use "assault," or "burglary," but found that many people didn't understand what exactly they were. They also chose fourteen and seventeen as the comparison ages because previous research showed that people tended to draw the age at which people should be held accountable at fifteen or sixteen, so fourteen and seventeen put them safely on either side.

In order to collect this sample, Steinberg and Piquero (2010) made use of a random-digit dialing process, in which a computer randomly creates and dials numbers. (This process and others are discussed in greater detail later in the chapter.) Of course, most of the numbers dialed aren't valid. The researchers dialed 29,352 numbers, and only 7,132 of those were actually eligible to participate in the survey. The rest were businesses, government offices, fax machines, disconnected numbers, or numbers that had never been used in the first place. However, that 7,132 *does* include calls that went to answering machines, to houses with owners who never picked up the phone, or to houses in which no one was eligible to participate in the survey (because there were no English speakers, no one was over eighteen, or similar reasons). Of those 7,132 calls that reached numbers for places where someone could conceivably have picked up, 2,282 people actually completed the survey, giving the researchers between 118 and 169 respondents in each experimental condition. (In survey experiments, the number of respondents in each cell is almost never even, and that's fine as long as the process that assigns respondents to a cell is truly random.) When researchers refer to the "response rate" of a study, they're generally referring to this figure: the number of completed surveys out of the total number of eligible numbers. The response rate for Steinberg and Piquero's survey was 2,282 out of 7,132, or about 32 percent.

Not surprising, Steinberg and Piquero (2010) found that respondents who were in the condition in which they were asked about older offenders charged with a more serious crime were more likely to support trying the offender as an adult. About 60 percent of respondents said that they had a "great deal" of support for trying a seventeen-year-old rapist (first-time or repeat offender) as an adult, compared with about 37 percent who said the same about a fourteen-year-old first-time rapist, and only 15 percent for a fourteen-year-old first-time thief. In sum, when the question was asked about older teens or teens who had committed a more serious crime, respondents were far more likely to support trying juveniles in adult court (though the "some or all" experiment had no effect) and sending them to adult prison, and the size of the differences was enormous. The results suggest that almost half of the public would switch opinions based on the age of the offender and the crime that was committed.

Steinberg and Piquero's (2010) study is a fairly simple survey experiment: researchers randomly assigned respondents to one of sixteen possible experimental conditions and compared the results for each. If we're just considering the respondents for this survey, the results are fairly unambiguous: respondents were more likely to support trying juveniles as adults when the juveniles were older and the crimes more serious. That said, this study is not important because of what it says about the respondents, but rather what it says about the public as a whole. With this or any other survey, the question is one of external validity, or generalizability. What do these results tell us about all the people who weren't respondents in the survey? The key point in survey methodology is to be able to generalize from our findings in the sample. We want to make statements and come to conclusions about the bigger **population**. In this chapter, we will discuss the many ways to administer surveys. With rapid changes in technology, the methods used to distribute and administer surveys have changed as well. Surveys can be administered face to face, in the mail, over the telephone, and online.

SURVEY MODES

Face-to-Face Polls

Despite some early failures, such as the *Literary Digest* poll discussed in Chapter 10, telephone surveys have been regarded in recent years as a good way to achieve a generalizable (or what survey researchers refer to as *representative*) sample of the population. The gold standard, or absolute best way, to measure a cross-section of the American public remains **face-to-face interviews**. Although some surveys (like the ANES) still use face-to-face interviews, they're very expensive and time consuming, so they have largely been replaced by telephone surveys. Face-to-face interviews are conducted by an *interviewer*, who reads the questions to a *respondent* and records the answers.

The main advantage of face-to-face surveys is that they increase response rates. Having an interviewer ask the questions directly also ensures that no questions are skipped. Especially with longer surveys, face-to-face administration is a preferable option. Respondents are less likely to stop the survey halfway if the person administering the survey is there.

However, training interviewers and arranging face-to-face interviews is often very time consuming and costly. Although they increase response rate, face-to-face surveys are not suitable for questions that are more personal or challenging. Surveys on sexual behavior and history or criminal and illegal activity may be more challenging to administer face to face than they would be over the telephone, or through other means.

Second, administering surveys face to face creates potential reactivity. The presence of the interviewer might affect the results of the survey and the answers respondents provide. Research shows that respondents answer differently based on the interviewer's race and gender. To control for this bias, many surveys collect information on the race and gender of interviewers to allow researchers to eliminate any such systematic bias.

Training interviewers is essential to reduce bias. One of the most important features of survey research is that all respondents are treated equally to allow for comparable data. Therefore, it is very important that the interviewers do not offer explanations, views, or definitions. To ensure comparability of results, interviewers are trained to only read the questions as they are written; they are not allowed to change wording, offer explanations, or give clarification when asked. This is, of course, a challenging task. Oftentimes, because an interviewer is administering the survey, respondents ask questions and request clarification. This is where writing good questions really pays off (as we saw in Chapter 10). Typically, researchers anticipate which concepts will need clarification and where they will need to offer more information. Pilot studies usually help with that. Many researchers will have prewritten scripts for the interviewer, offering clarification or definitions. For example, " In the past week, did you work full time? By *full time*, I mean 40 hours of paid work outside the home per week."

Researchers not only provide scripted definitions and clarifications, but they also create **prompts**. These instructions help interviewers better communicate with respondents. They are only given to the interviewers and help guide them through the survey.

Telephone Surveys

Telephone surveys are well-regarded for a number of reasons. First, nearly everyone in America has a telephone. That means that, theoretically at least, researchers could build a list of every person in the country along with one phone number for that individual. To create a true random sample of the entire country then (more on true random samples later in this chapter), they could simply randomly pick numbers from that list. That list, of course, is hypothetical. It doesn't exist, and even if it did, it would be hopelessly out of date before anyone got a chance to use it, but contrast this with the state of **Internet surveys**. Since not everyone in the country has access to the Internet, it would be impossible to make this sort of list for email addresses, and so it would be impossible to even theoretically get the true random sample that survey researchers would like.

Second, telephone surveys generally make use of trained interviewers. In an online or mail survey, there's no one for respondents to ask for clarification if they don't understand a question. Respondents to a telephone survey, however, can get help from the person at the other end of the line. Ideally, researchers should make use of cognitive testing and pilot studies to ensure that there is as little confusion about the questions as possible, but there's always going to be some confusion. It's better to offer a little clarification than to have respondents give up on the survey entirely. Unlike interviewers in a face-to-face survey, interviewers in a telephone survey can talk to people all over the country in one evening, meaning that researchers need fewer people to carry out a survey. These interviewers are also able to create a rapport with the respondents, putting them at ease and making them more likely to both answer questions honestly and complete the survey.

Third, there has been an enormous amount of technology developed to aid in telephone-based surveys. Most modern call centers make use of **computer-assisted telephone interviewing (CATI)** systems that show the interviewer the script of the interview as it happens, allow the interviewer to quickly input the responses given, and automatically tabulate basic results for the researchers. These systems have been around long enough that they've become fairly easy to program and use, while systems for online surveys are still young. These systems can even allow researchers to measure things such as how long a respondent took to answer a question (often referred to as *latency*) or even the relative loudness of the response.

Still, the reason most researchers make use of telephone surveys is that they allow for what is recognized as a good representation of the American public for less money and time than it would take to do a face-to-face survey. While telephone surveys remain the standard, there are problems with them, including some issues that are getting worse with time. The biggest problem facing telephone surveys is declining response rates. Steinberg and Piquero's (2010) survey had a response rate of about 32 percent, meaning that 68 percent of the time that they called a valid number, they weren't able to get a completed survey. This becomes a problem if the people who pick up the phone are systematically different from the people who don't pick up the phone. For instance, suppose that only people over sixty-five completed the survey, or only Democrats, or only women: the results of the survey wouldn't represent the views of the American public at all. We'll talk more about response rates, and how to deal with low response rates, later, but for now it's enough to know that the response rates for telephone surveys have been declining precipitously in recent years. Thanks to caller ID, among other things, fewer people are picking up their phones to answer questions, and this makes telephone surveys less efficient and potentially representative of the public. Proponents of telephone surveys argue that they're still pretty good—and still better than online polls—but the problem is getting worse.

A second emerging issue with telephone surveys is the rise of cell phones. Steinberg and Piquero (2010) didn't include any cell phones in their sample, but most telephone surveys carried out today do so. A lot of people don't have landlines at home, so the only way to reach them is via a cell phone, but this creates a lot of complications for researchers. First, calling cell phones can be dangerous. People sometimes pick up while they're driving, so researchers have to find out if the respondent is driving and call back later if he or she is. Second, most people with cell phones also have home phones, and this can make them twice as likely to be included in the survey, so their views might be overrepresented. Third, respondents sometimes have to pay for the minutes they use in answering a call on their cell phone, which can lead them to resent being asked to complete a survey. Finally, federal law prohibits the use of automatic dialing devices to call cell phones. This means that interviewers have to manually dial cell phone numbers. This isn't difficult: the number comes up on the CATI system, and the interviewer just punches it in. In a survey such as Steinberg and Piquero's, however, the researchers dialed almost 30,000 telephone numbers to get 2,282 responses. Dialing one number isn't a problem, but dialing ten or more numbers to get one response takes a lot of time and, therefore, costs more money.

Finally, telephone surveys are also relatively slow when compared to online or mail surveys. Telephone surveys require that the interviewer reads the question aloud to the respondent, and this generally takes more time than simply having the respondent read the question and response options himself or herself. In telephone surveys, time is money. Interviewers have to be paid by the hour, so the longer it takes to ask a question, the fewer surveys can be completed in a given amount of time. Surveys that take too long can also lead respondents to quit and hang up before the survey is completed, and a survey that's half completed is generally useless to researchers.

In recent years, some public opinion researchers have begun to use automated survey response tools, popularly referred to as *robocalls*. In these surveys, the interviewer is simply a recording, and respondents speak or press buttons on their phone to indicate their answer. Such polls have the advantage of being cheap—some firms will return a sample of 1,000 respondents for $500 or so—and fast. Since there are no live interviewers, the survey firms can carry out hundreds of calls simultaneously, returning results in hours for surveys that could take days for trained interviewers to get through. However, such methods should be used only with great caution. There's some evidence that potential respondents are more likely to hang up on robocalls, leading to a worse sample, and may be less likely to give thoughtful or truthful answers to a recording than they would to an interviewer with whom they have a rapport.

Telephone surveys remain the dominant mode, or technique for carrying out, survey research, but the increasing difficulties with response rates and the complication of cell phones has led many researchers to look into alternative modes of carrying out surveys. There is still general agreement that telephone surveys are the most cost-efficient way of reaching a cross-section of the American public, but there are certain circumstances under which mail or online surveys may be more appropriate.

Mail Surveys

Mail surveys have been around longer than telephone surveys; however, they tend to be used less frequently due to the availability of other media. Mail surveys typically have low response rates. Especially today, when many respondents are bombarded with junk mail on a daily basis, it is very difficult for researchers to distinguish their studies from marketing and advertising material. Sending a questionnaire for a respondent to complete on his or her schedule is also challenging. In face-to-face surveys, the interviewer creates potential peer pressure for the respondent to complete the survey. The respondents for mail surveys, however, might toss the survey somewhere and forget about it. Mail surveys can also be quite costly. Researchers pay for printing costs as well as postage costs. Typically, they also enclose a self-addressed stamped envelope for the return of the survey. Despite low response rates and high costs, mail surveys are still useful in certain circumstances. They enable researchers to collect information on more sensitive topics and conduct longer surveys.

Christopher Bader, F. Carson Mencken, and Paul Froese—The Baylor Religion Survey (2007)

As sociologists studying the role of religion in American life, Christopher Bader and his colleagues (2007) found that there simply wasn't much data on the topic available. Looking at the articles published in the leading journals on the topic, they found that most relied on samples of particular religious groups, and nearly all of those that used national samples relied on the GSS. However valuable the GSS is, though, it covers a range of topics of interest to sociologists, so any given subfield, like religious sociology, will only have a few questions included in the survey in any given year.

Many surveys measure the views of a subset of Americans. For instance, surveys that try to predict electoral outcomes are only interested in talking to people who are likely to vote. Other surveys might be targeted at American citizens, members of the military, students, or people who drive regularly. In their survey of religious views, though, Bader and his colleagues wanted to get a snapshot of the views of everyone in the country—a more difficult task. To do it, they hired the Gallup Company to dial random digits of telephone numbers. This isn't a process that's used very often. Generally, researchers pick telephone numbers randomly from a list that they've obtained. The random-digit dial technique, though, means that every phone number in the country has an equal chance of being called, whether it's a cell phone, an office line, or a fax number, listed or unlisted. This means that the researchers are including everyone—even people who have unlisted numbers—but it also means that they have to make a much larger number of calls (because many of the numbers won't work) and they have to correct for the fact that some people have more than one telephone number (for instance, a home line and a cell phone) and are therefore more likely to be called. Gallup called 7,041 numbers and asked the people on the other end of the line if they wanted to participate in the study: 3,002 (43 percent) agreed to do so.

The researchers made sure that there was no mention of religion in the description of the study, in order to avoid talking to people who were more involved or interested in religion than the average American. The people who agreed to participate were randomly assigned to take part in a mail version of the survey or a mixed mail and telephone version. Bader and his colleagues (2007) explain that they used mail surveys in order to ask more questions than they reasonably could over the telephone. In general, telephone surveys can't be much longer than twenty minutes, whereas mail surveys allow respondents to stop and come back to the survey later if they need to; respondents can also read questions faster than interviewers can read to them.

One thousand and two respondents were assigned to do the interview over the phone, and after the interview, 660 agreed to do a mail survey as well (though only 603 of them actually gave an address to which the researchers could mail a survey). The rest of the respondents just received the mail survey. Of the 2,603 surveys sent out, 1,721 (66 percent) were returned. In total then, the researchers received mail surveys back from 1,721 of the initial 7,041 numbers that were called, a response rate of 24 percent.

The mail survey was pretty long—sixteen pages, including the cover. It included a cover letter explaining the survey and giving a contact number in case the potential respondents had any questions about the study. The survey also included $5 cash as a thank-you for filling out and returning the survey. After the initial mailing, the potential respondents were sent a follow-up letter thanking them for agreeing to participate. Potential respondents who didn't send their surveys back were sent another packet, with a whole new questionnaire, another $5, and a postcard reminding them to send the survey back.

In a mail survey, a 24 percent response rate isn't bad, but Bader and his colleagues (2007) were worried that there might be some systematic biases in the data. For instance, the 2007 survey—there have been several since—included a set of questions on belief in the paranormal, asking about ghosts, reincarnation, and the like. People with very conservative religious beliefs might have been offended by these questions and therefore less likely to return the questionnaire. If there were any such systematic biases in the likelihood of responding, the views of the people returning the questionnaire wouldn't be a good representation of the views of Americans on the whole. To check for any such biases, the researchers compared the demographic characteristics of the people who responded to the survey with the known demographic characteristics of the population as a whole and the respondents to a similar survey, the GSS. For characteristics such as age, race, and gender, the researchers were able to compare the respondents to their mail survey with U.S. census data. For other characteristics, such as religious beliefs and specific denominations, they compared their sample with the GSS. If their sample had the same religious beliefs, age, education, income and other demographic characteristics as the entire population, then their beliefs on other topics should be representative of the overall population as well.

Although they've been largely supplanted by telephone and Internet-based surveys in recent years, mail surveys are still useful in many instances. Bader and his colleagues (2007) argue that a mail survey was especially useful for their research for a couple of reasons. First, their survey was especially long. There are prominent surveys—such as the ANES and the GSS—that are even longer, but those surveys are generally carried out by interviewers talking to people face to face. Face-to-face interviews may be the best way to carry out such lengthy surveys, but they're very expensive. Researchers have to carefully train interviewers all over the country and pay them an hourly rate. Face-to-face interviews also may be subject to high reactivity effects. If the questionnaire isn't carefully designed to avoid such effects, respondents talking about race to an African American interviewer or gender issues to a female interviewer might give very different responses than they would otherwise. Second, while some people have no telephone, or multiple telephones, pretty much everyone lives in one place or another. So, by selecting potential respondents on the basis of address rather than telephone number, mail surveys arguably can do a better job of representing the views of the whole country than other ways of collecting data.

The way Bader and his colleagues (2007) carried out their mail survey is fairly representative of how mail surveys are carried out in modern social science research. While other countries have a fairly high response rate for mail surveys—the United Kingdom is commonly used as an example—the overall response rate for unexpected mail surveys in the United States is remarkably low. It's low enough that it's hard to argue that the people who return the surveys aren't fundamentally different in some way from the people who don't return the surveys. Researchers can't just mail out the surveys to random addresses if they want to have any chance of a representative sample of the public. Instead, like Bader and his colleagues, they contact potential respondents beforehand and ask if they would be willing to fill out a mail survey. That way, the potential respondents know that the survey is coming, are less likely to throw it out as junk mail, and are more likely to actually return it.

Most mail surveys today also include a small amount of money as an incentive; the $5 that Bader and his colleagues (2007) used is pretty typical. The money isn't a payment for filling out the survey. Most people wouldn't fill out a lengthy survey for such a small amount of money, and response rates may actually go down if potential respondents view it as payment. It's important that the materials accompanying the survey and the money make it clear that the money is a gift in recognition of the help that the potential respondent is giving. The materials should also make it clear that it isn't a quid pro quo. After all, there's no way to get the money back if the respondent doesn't return the survey. The goal of the money is threefold. First, it is an acknowledgment that the potential respondent is putting effort into filling out the survey and that the researchers know that. Second, it creates some pressure on the respondent to return the study. While there's certainly no obligation to fill out the survey, money can often make the respondents feel as if they should do so. Just as participants in an experiment can leave whenever they want but usually continue to participate in order to fulfill their part of a social script, potential respondents to a mail survey who take money often feel as if they should do their part and return the survey. Third, if potential respondents know that a survey is coming and that there's cash in the envelope, they're more likely to open the envelope in the first place. Once they do that, the likelihood of returning the survey goes up significantly.

Ethically, the use of money in mail surveys is far less fraught than it is in other types of research. Because there's no way for the researcher to take the money back if the respondent doesn't return the survey, there's less of a chance that the respondent will feel that he or she needs to complete the survey because of the amount of money involved. Monetary coercion, as such, is less of a problem. The problem with money, as noted before, is that too much money will make respondents feel as if they're being paid to participate, and if they decide that the money isn't worth the time, they may become less likely to return the survey.

While mail surveys are cost efficient, can arguably achieve a better representation of the American public than some other methods, and can include a larger number of questions than telephone surveys, they're only useful for certain research questions. Bader and his colleagues (2007) were interested in the religious and spiritual beliefs of the American public, and those beliefs weren't likely to change much over the course of weeks or even months. It doesn't matter if one respondent fills out the survey a week or a month before another. If researchers are interested in attitudes or behaviors that are likely to change in a matter of weeks or months, they need to use another mode for collecting survey data. For related reasons, researchers nearly always ask respondents to mail surveys to give the date that the survey was completed. That way, if something happens during the administration of the survey that might affect responses, the researchers can look at any differences between those surveys carried out before and after the event.

INTERNET SURVEYS

Markus Prior—Soft News and Political Knowledge (2003)

Since Bill Clinton famously went on Arsenio Hall's late-night program to play the saxophone and sit down for an interview, American politicians have been increasingly prone to reach out to the public through entertainment programs and what scholars refer to as "soft news" shows. These soft news programs generally cover Hollywood gossip or lifestyle issues. Daytime and late-night talk shows are good examples, as are entertainment news programs such as *Extra* or *Access Hollywood*. While these programs aren't generally political, they do sometimes cover political issues: Barack Obama and his wife went on *The Oprah Winfrey Show*. Political candidates go on *The Tonight Show*. Jimmy Fallon and Jon Stewart make jokes about politics. As these programs and formats have become more popular, researchers in political science have seen a chance for the American public to become more informed about politics and current events. People who wouldn't watch news shows watch *Oprah* or *The Ellen Degeneres Show*, and they may learn something about politics by doing so.

However, it isn't clear that what people learn from these soft news sources will actually be useful in making informed decisions about politics. Marckus Prior's (2003) research looks at several different categories of political knowledge: political scandals, foreign policy, and basic facts about American government. To measure the effect of soft news on political knowledge in these various areas, Prior used an online survey sample, run by a company called Knowledge Networks, with a total sample size of 2,538. Like the Baylor Religion Study discussed above, Knowledge Networks starts with a telephone poll, and this poll is used to build a sample that's representative of all Americans. Of course, since it's an online poll, not everyone can participate: not everyone has Internet access at home. To resolve this problem, individuals selected for the Knowledge Networks sample who don't have Internet at home are given a device that allows them to access the Internet, provided that they agree to complete a certain number of surveys per month. If the potential respondent already has Internet access, Knowledge Networks pays for it, provided that the respondent completes the surveys. The total number of people in the Knowledge Networks sample is in the tens of thousands: for any individual survey, a few thousand respondents are randomly chosen.

Although previous research had found that people who watch soft news programs are more interested in news stories than people who don't watch any news at all, soft news didn't help the respondents in Prior's (2003) online sample learn much about politics and current events. Watching soft news did increase the likelihood that respondents would be able to correctly answer questions about personal scandals affecting politicians (at the time, these included a murdered Washington intern and the congressman she worked for, another Congressman's illegitimate child, and the arrest of then-President Bush's daughter for underage drinking), but it didn't help them answer substantive questions about foreign affairs or Washington (questions about the war in Afghanistan, foreign aid, or even which party had a majority in Congress).

Prior (2003) admits that it's possible that people are following the news, and maybe even making decisions based on it, without being able to recall the facts—a model political scientists refer to as *online processing*—but argues that soft news, in general, doesn't do much to inform the American public, at least in ways that such information is normally measured. He also argues that this isn't as big a problem as others might think, mostly because people who actually follow the news still tend to watch hard news programs such as evening news broadcasts. The people who want entertainment out of their programs by and large watch entertainment shows rather than soft news.

The vast majority of online surveys aren't terribly useful for social science researchers for two main reasons. The first is that while most Americans today have Internet access, not all of them do, and a survey that's based just on the Internet is going to miss large portions of the population. Members of minority groups, residents of inner cities, people living in rural areas, and the elderly are all less likely to have reliable Internet access than other Americans, so any survey that only gets respondents who have access to the Internet is going to miss or underrepresent these groups and fail to provide a cross-section of the American population. Second, even if people who have Internet access do represent a cross-section of the American population, there's no easy way to get a random sample of people who use the Internet to take a survey. Researchers running telephone surveys can randomly dial houses; researchers doing mail surveys can send questionnaires to random addresses, but there's no equivalent for online surveys. When they're online, potential respondents receive so many unsolicited emails and see so many ads that it's very hard to attract them to take a survey. Oftentimes, researchers offer cash incentives to fill out a survey, but that doesn't necessarily fix the problem because the people who are willing to take a survey online for money aren't a random subset of everyone online anyway. Because of this, most online surveys don't tell researchers much about the views of the American public, or even the views of Americans who go online regularly. To put it another way, the results of online surveys often cannot be generalized, so they have low external validity.

Knowledge Networks and similar services get around this issue by providing Internet access to any potential respondents who don't already have it, allowing these companies to include a random sample of all Americans as potential respondents. By requiring that participants then fill out a certain number of surveys in a given period, they also ensure that the people who actually take the surveys are a random subset of their total sample. This isn't a perfect approach by any means (ideally, their overall sample would be replenished after every survey, but that would be enormously expensive), but it comes much closer to a random sample of the American population than other online survey approaches.

The problems with online surveys are significant, but there are also some major benefits to administering surveys online. First, online surveys can be much cheaper to carry out than other modes. Unlike mail surveys, researchers using online modes don't have to worry about printing questionnaires or paying postage. Unlike telephone surveys or face-to-face surveys, researchers using online surveys don't have to pay trained interviewers to ask the questions. The survey only needs to be programmed once, and as many potential respondents as the researcher wants can be sent to the same website. In mail and telephone surveys, the amount of money available is the real limit on the size of the sample that the researcher can achieve. Internet surveys change the calculation dramatically. Internet samples can be very large, though, as will be discussed below, a larger sample doesn't mean much if it isn't representative. For online surveys, money still matters, as it can help the researchers achieve a better, more representative sample. A survey carried out by a group such as Knowledge Networks, for instance, will be much more expensive than one carried out by a group not worried about achieving a representative sample.

Second, online surveys can be carried out very rapidly. It may take weeks or months to gather all of the responses to a mail survey and somewhere between days and weeks to carry out a telephone survey. An online survey, in contrast, can be put into the field and completed in a matter of hours. It may not always be desirable to complete a survey that quickly—the people who are around to do a survey at 10 in the evening or 9 in the morning are probably not a random sample of the public—but if researchers want to quickly gage responses to a fast-moving event, online surveys can be very useful.

Third, online surveys allow researchers to include all sorts of media that would be impossible to include in telephone or mail studies. In Prior's (2003) study, respondents were asked to identify a participant in a scandal by looking at a picture of the young woman in question. Other political scientists have put campaign ads, audio clips of speeches, or news items into their surveys. Such items can be tremendously useful and are simply impossible to do in mail and telephone studies.

Finally, it has been argued that respondents may be more willing to answer embarrassing or controversial questions truthfully in an online survey. In telephone surveys, and especially in face-to-face interviews, the respondent is talking with another person, and this may lead to increased reactivity effects. While online surveys aren't really any more or less anonymous than any other kind of survey, respondents tend to feel that responses given online are less likely to be traced back to them. This is most likely a result of past experiences with anonymity on the web, and while it isn't necessarily accurate, it may be useful for researchers asking questions that respondents might not want to talk about with another person.

Because most online survey providers do not provide access to the Internet in the same way that Knowledge Networks does, their results are generally not based on a representative sample of the American public. However, this does not mean that the sample is necessarily bad or that the results are invalid. Proponents of online surveys argue that they can use weighing processes and other techniques to simulate a random sample. They also make the case that low response rates to telephone surveys mean that those samples aren't true random samples of the population, either, so the online sample isn't any worse than a telephone sample. There is some validity to these arguments, but the issue is far from settled. For now, most researchers remain very careful about generalizing from online samples to the population at large, relying on trusted providers with a proven track record.

SAMPLING

Robert S. Erikson, Costas Panagopoulos, and Christopher Wleizen—Likely Voters and the 2000 Presidential Debates (2004)

Before the first Presidential debate of the 2000 election, then-governor George W. Bush was widely perceived to be in trouble. In the most trusted pre-election poll, the Gallup poll, he trailed Vice President Al Gore by eleven points among likely voters, fifty-one to forty. After the first debate, in which Bush was widely thought to have done well, if not spectacularly, he made what seemed to be a miraculous leap in the polls. In the Gallup poll released just after the first debate, he went from being eleven points down to being eight points up, forty-nine to forty-one.

In American politics, this is an enormous change: it appears that 19 percent of the voting public changed their minds after seeing the debate, with 10 percent abandoning Gore and 8 percent going to Bush. Swings of that size, though, seem implausible, and Robert Erikson and his colleagues (2004) decided to look more closely at the Gallup poll to see what might have caused it. Erikson and his colleagues aren't arguing that voters weren't swayed by what they saw in the debate, but rather that the enormous swing in the pre-election polls was caused by a shift in who Gallup considered to be a "likely" voter.

To determine who is likely to vote in an upcoming election, Gallup asks respondents seven questions. For each question, respondents can get either zero or one point, depending on their answer. For instance, Gallup asks respondents how much thought they've given to the election. Respondents who say that they've given it some thought or quite a lot of thought get one point. Respondents who say that they know where their polling place is get a point, as do respondents who voted in the last midterm election, and so on. Gallup then adjusts the scores based on the age of the respondents (young voters might not have been able to vote in past elections) and on whether or not the respondent is registered to vote (if they're not, they're assigned a score of zero). Gallup then makes a best guess, based on the type of election and overall voter enthusiasm, as to what score will get people to vote. For an election that a lot of people might not be paying attention to, Gallup might consider only scores of six or seven to be likely voters. For a Presidential election that's expected to have high turnout, a score of five might make someone a likely voter.

Erikson and his colleagues (2004) argue that the big shift in support toward Bush after the first debate was most likely a result of greater enthusiasm among Bush's voters and less enthusiasm among Gore's supporters. Gallup's questions ask respondents if they plan to vote, how much thought they've given to the election, and how certain they are to vote, and all of these questions might change based on what's going on in the campaign. When Bush did well in the debate, his supporters started thinking about the election more and became more likely to say that they were going to vote, while Gore's voters became less certain that they were going to cast a ballot. As a result, the category of "likely voters" contained many more Bush supporters and fewer Gore supporters after the debate than it did beforehand. A lot of people did not change their minds because of the debate, but rather a lot of people started paying attention.

The main reason to use surveys rather than other techniques for social science research is the ability to generalize the answers given by respondents to some larger group. Researchers don't really care about what 1,200 people in a national Gallup poll have to say; they care about what the responses of those 1,200 people say about American voters as a whole. Once researchers have decided which survey modality to use, the next step is to determine which group they want the results to generalize to. Gallup wants its polls to generalize to Americans who are likely to vote in the upcoming election. Bader and his colleagues (2007) wanted the results of the Baylor Religion Study to generalize to the entire American public. Other surveys might be interested in one racial group, residents of one city, parents, or small business owners.

There are two ways to survey one particular group. The first is to identify everyone in that group, make a list, and randomly choose potential respondents from that list. This approach is most commonly used when membership in the group being surveyed is set. For instance, there have been a series of surveys of American business conditions that have talked just to graduates of the Harvard University MBA program. There are a limited number of Harvard MBA graduates. Their identities and contact information are known or can be obtained, so a researcher who wants to just look at Harvard MBA graduates could acquire such a list—and there are companies that specialize in putting together such contact lists—and randomly select potential respondents. The same approach could be used to survey residents of a particular city or a particular school district; interviewers could randomly choose addresses in the city or contact numbers from the school district list in order to get a random sample of all of the people in the group.

Such an approach doesn't work, however, if membership in the group is at all nebulous. For instance, researchers who wanted to survey Catholics wouldn't be able to just get the contact information from every church because that would exclude Catholics who don't go to church. Moreover, the cost and effort that would be necessary to create a list for such a large group would be enormous. Similarly, a Gallup poll of likely voters runs into the problem of defining who a likely voter is. Someone who is likely to vote today may not be likely to vote tomorrow. To put it another way, Harvard MBA graduates are defined by something that they have done in the past, making membership in the group easy to define. Likely voters are defined by an action that may or may not happen in the future, so there's no certain way to know who will and will not be a member of the group. There are also an enormous number of likely voters, perhaps 40 percent of the population, and not very many Harvard MBA graduates.

For these large or nebulous groups, it's generally easier for researchers to begin with a sample that includes all Americans, then use screening questions to determine if the respondent is part of the group that the researcher wants to survey. These screening questions are the first questions asked in any survey and can be simple or complex, depending on what group the researcher is trying to reach. A survey that wants to reach Catholics could simply ask the respondent if anyone in the household is Catholic; researchers would end the survey if the answer is "no." This approach wouldn't work with a smaller group like Harvard MBA graduates. About 1 in 4 Americans is Catholic, but fewer than 1 in 50,000 Americans has a Harvard MBA. So, a telephone survey that wants to reach a given number of Catholics would have to make about four times as many calls as they would need to get a random sample of the overall population. A telephone survey that called random numbers to get a sample of Harvard MBA graduates would have to make millions of calls in order to contact enough respondents to provide for reliable results.

The Gallup poll's battery of likely voter questions is an example of a much more complex screening process. The group of all likely voters—what survey researchers refer to as the *population*—is both very large and very nebulous, so screening questions are an appropriate way to determine if a potential respondent is part of the population that Gallup is trying to sample. However, the researchers at Gallup have reason to believe that potential respondents may lie about their likelihood of voting, so they make use of many of the techniques discussed in Chapter 10 to determine if someone really is part of the population. For instance, they use very specific questions. Rather than ask a potential respondent if he or she generally votes in elections, researchers ask if he or she voted in the last midterm election and if the respondent knows where his or her local polling place is. This takes a lot more effort than just asking if people are going to vote or not, but Gallup researchers argue that it gives them a better idea of who is and is not part of the population that they are trying to sample. The problems that Erikson and his colleagues (2004) identify are really problems with the nebulous nature of the population that Gallup researchers are trying to survey: people move in and out of the population, so estimates of the views of the population change accordingly.

These concepts are vital to the practice of survey research. At the highest level is what survey researchers call the *universe*: the set of everyone who could potentially be reached by the survey mode they are using. For instance, the universe of a telephone survey is everyone who has a home telephone; if cell phones were included in the survey, the universe would also include everyone with a cell phone number. The next task is to narrow the universe down into the population that the researchers are interested in. This could be something as large as all Americans or all likely voters or as specific as all Harvard MBA graduates. This narrowing can be done through contact lists or through screening questions. The goal of any survey is to talk to some portion of the population, normally chosen through a random process. The subgroup of the population that's included in the survey is referred to as the *sample*, and if the process of sampling is done correctly, the answers that the sample gives to the survey questions can be used to tell researchers about the views of the entire population.

In theory, a survey can simply be administered to everyone in a population. This is what the U.S. government tries to do every ten years with the census. If this tactic is successful (if the entire population of interest is sampled), researchers don't have to generalize from the sample to the population—the sample *is* the population. For almost everyone outside of the U.S. Census Bureau, though, reaching the entire population normally isn't an option, and some sampling process is necessary.

Robert G. Morris and John L. Worrall—Prison Architecture and Inmate Misconduct (2010)

A little less than 1 percent of all of the people in the United States are currently in prison or jail, the highest rate of incarceration in the world (about 30 percent higher than the number two country, Russia), so understanding prisons is important to American scholars and policy makers. There have been any number of factors that have been found to predict which prisoners will get into trouble while behind bars (length of sentences, previous violent behavior, gang membership, and so on) but Robert G. Morris and John L. Worrall (2010) decided to look at characteristics of prisons and how they affect inmate behavior.

Modern American prison designs generally fall into two categories. There is the traditional "telephone pole" prison, in which multistory cell blocks are placed parallel to each other with only one or two corridors connecting them, making them look, from above, like a telephone poll with rungs attached. Other prisons make use of a campus-style layout, in which the cell blocks are divided up around a central outdoor area. The telephone pole design was created, in part, to make it harder for inmates to escape—there's only one way in or out—but has been criticized for having very long corridors that may be difficult for guards to monitor. The campus-style buildings are easier for guards to monitor and are thought to be less degrading for prisoners.

To see if the design of the prison makes a difference, Morris and Worrall (2010) looked at the prison records of male inmates sentenced to between three years and life in Texas prisons, who had been assigned to either telephone pole or campus-style prisons (not including private prisons, local jails, and drug-punishment prisons). Overall, this resulted in a total population of 12,981 inmates. The researchers then randomly chose 2,500 records to analyze and tested if the architecture of the prison to which the inmates were assigned had any impact on the likelihood of committing further crimes while in prison. After controlling for other factors, such as the initial crime that the inmate committed, length of the sentence, age of the inmate, and so on, the researchers found that while the style of the prison didn't have an effect on violence, inmates in campus-style prisons were more likely to have been reprimanded for property offenses (such as stealing) and security-related offenses (such as making threats or violating safety rules). These findings are interesting because they seem to indicate that older-style, seemingly more dehumanizing prisons actually led to fewer reprimands for inmates than the newer-style prisons, though, as the authors point out, it could just be that inmates in the campus-style prisons are more likely to be caught.

The process of identifying respondents for research is called **sampling**. Since the researchers are interested in inmates generally, all inmates constitute the population in this research. Since it is not possible to administer surveys to all inmates in the United States, the idea is to select a smaller group (a sample) to represent the entire population. The sample selected needs to reflect the characteristics of the population; in other words, it needs to be **representative**. The best way make sure the sample is representative of the population studied is to select randomly to avoid systematic bias.

SIMPLE RANDOM SAMPLES (SRS)

Morris and Worrall's (2010) research isn't a traditional survey—after all, they didn't talk to the prisoners in question—but it is a perfect example of how **simple random samples** work. First, Morris and Worrall defined the population that they were interested in: male prisoners serving at least three years, but who were not on death row, and were housed in telephone pole or campus-style prisons. They had good reasons for all of these decisions. For instance, inmates are most likely to commit infractions during their first three years in jail, so inmates in prison for less than three years are much less likely to get into trouble, and including them could throw off the results. By doing so, the researchers turned the universe of all inmates in Texas prisons into a population that they could make generalizations about. Once they established the population, they proceeded to draw a sample of it—and a large sample at that. Of the 12,981 prisoners who met their criteria, they randomly selected 2,500 files for analysis. Their sample, therefore, was almost 20 percent of their population, a rate that's far higher than would be possible for most surveys. (A national public opinion survey, for instance, might survey 1 out of every 300,000 or so people in the country.)

Done correctly, this constitutes a perfect simple random sample (often abbreviated SRS). In an SRS, every case within the population has an equal chance of being selected to be in the sample. Just as the logic of experiments depends on random assignment of participants into experimental cells, the logic of the SRS depends on random assignment from the population into the sample. If there is, as in Morris and Worrall's (2010) research, a list of all of the people in the population, then creating an SRS is fairly straightforward: rolling a die (or having a computer generate a random number) for every name and picking that name when the dice come up with a certain value.

Starting with the list of the population, researchers can also randomly select by choosing the *n*th case, where *n* is the sampling interval. When there is no actual list of the population (as in Gallup polls of likely voters, for instance), researchers make use of techniques designed to get as close to picking every *n*th name as possible, such as the random-digit dialing procedures described earlier. In cases where there is an actual list (like the list of voters in a previous election, which is public record), researchers may choose the *n*th case, creating what's referred to as a **systematic sample**.

Morris and Worrall's (2010) sample is large relative to the size of their population, and this has implications for how well the results of their sample can be generalized to the population. Morris and Worrall were looking at the

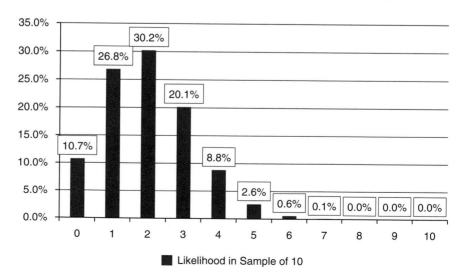

Likelihood in Sample of 10

rate of various kinds of infractions among prisoners in the two types of prisons. Suppose that they only had looked at a few records: only ten. In their survey, about 20 percent of prisoners had committed some kind of infraction. In a sample of ten, two of the prisoners should have been caught committing some kind of infraction. However, in a sample of ten, there's an 11 percent chance that none of the prisoners will have committed an infraction and only a 30 percent chance that two of the prisoners will have. If the researchers were to attempt to generalize from this very small sample, there's a 70 percent chance they'd get the figure wrong—and almost a 25 percent chance that they'd get it very, very wrong, getting a figure of zero or greater than three.

If the size of the sample increases, the likelihood of this sort of catastrophic failure decreases. Just using simple arithmetic—and assuming that any of the prisoner files chosen has a 20 percent chance of having an infraction—increasing the size of the sample to even fifty dramatically decreases the risk of getting the figure catastrophically wrong. In the sample of fifty, there's a 14 percent chance of exactly 20 percent of the sample have committed an infraction, and there's a 62 percent chance that the researchers will find that between eight and twelve inmates in the sample (16 to 24 percent) have committed an infraction.

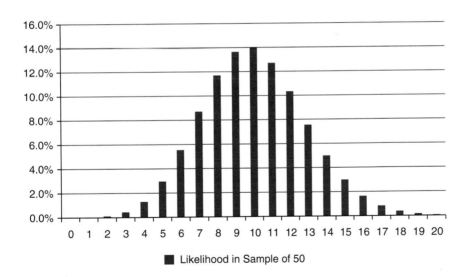

Likelihood in Sample of 50

As the sample size increases even more, the likelihood of a good result—one that's pretty close to the actual value in the population—increases. In a sample of 100, the odds of getting a sample value of between 16 and 24 percent goes up to 74 percent. In a sample of 200, the odds of being that close rise to 87 percent, and so on.

There are three things that should be evident from this example. The first is that in an SRS, a larger sample size means a result that comes closer to the actual population values. When researchers are trying to generalize from a sample to a population, they are more likely to be accurate when they have a large sample

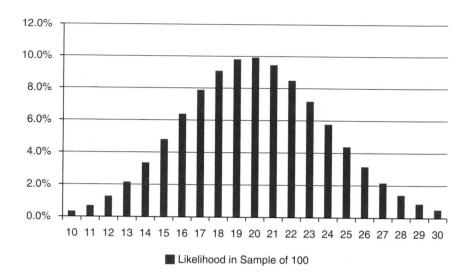

■ Likelihood in Sample of 100

than a small one because the odds of a few cases throwing off the accuracy of the sample decrease as the total size of the sample increases. If Morris and Worrall (2010) only sampled ten cases, the odds of getting a weird sample in which 10 percent or less of the sample had an infraction are more than one in three. With a sample size of one hundred, the odds of randomly picking a weird sample that just happens to consist of only 10 percent of the sample having infractions is less than 1 percent. If the researchers were to go to the extreme of sampling every case in the population, there's no chance that they would have a sample that deviated from the characteristics of the true population—but that's because they wouldn't have a sample at all!

The second is that while accuracy increases along with sample size, it only works to an extent. Going from a sample of ten to a sample of fifty increases accuracy dramatically. Adding another fifty to the sample on top of that helps, but not as much as the first forty did. Adding another one hundred on top of that still helps, but not as much as going from fifty to one hundred. The exact relationship will be discussed later, but it's enough to know that a bigger sample only helps to a point; after that, gains in accuracy from a larger sample size generally aren't worth the cost and effort of collecting additional responses.

Third, as sample size increases, the distribution of responses looks more and more like what statisticians refer to as a *normal curve*. The likelihood of the various responses (what's technically a *probability density function*, or PDF) for the sample of one hundred is a pretty good approximation of the normal curve: it's thick around the middle, with the likelihoods trailing off slowly as they get farther and farther away from the middle. The normal curve is also symmetrical, with the two sides of the distribution about the same. As sample size in an SRS increases, the distribution gets closer and closer to a normal curve, a characteristic that is enormously helpful to researchers. Researchers know a great deal about the normal curve and, therefore, about any sample that resembles it. These properties of the normal curve will be discussed in detail in Chapter 12.

These characteristics of an SRS make survey research so useful: as long as we have an SRS, we can very easily generalize to the population. But these characteristics only hold as long as we actually have an SRS, and that's not as easy as it may seem. In Morris and Worrall's (2010) research, getting an SRS was straightforward: they had 12,981 inmates who had the characteristics they were looking for, and they pulled the files of a randomly chosen 2,500. The key was that they actually had a list of the entire population they were interested in. Every case in the population had an equal likelihood of being chosen for the population, and no one in the population could avoid being part of the sample. In any survey in which researchers are collecting information by actually talking to respondents, this just isn't possible.

Darren E. Sherkat—Religion and Survey Response Rates (2007)

In 1998, researchers at the Pew Research Center—one of the leading survey houses in the United States—began a series of studies trying to find out why many polls, especially those in the American South, had done such a bad job of predicting election results. In one North Carolina U.S. Senate race, surveys had predicted a four-point victory for the Democratic candidate. On Election Day, the Republican won by six points. Similar errors occurred in governors' races in Virginia and mayors' races in Chicago and New York. Even as late as the 2004 Presidential election, most polls had the race as a dead heat between incumbent George W. Bush and challenger John Kerry, but Bush wound up winning the popular vote by four points. It was common among Republican groups to simply accuse the polls of having a liberal bias—of trying to make the Democrat look better—but Pew and other survey groups recognized that these results indicated that something was wrong with the way that they were carrying out their polls.

The Pew Researchers and Darren E. Sherkat (2007), a sociologist at Southern Illinois University, identified the same culprit for the problems in these surveys: response bias. In the Pew study, researchers examined the differences between respondents who initially agreed to be a part of the survey and those who initially refused and had to be convinced to take part. In their study, they found that the respondents who initially refused were more likely to express negative views of African Americans. If individuals who hold negative views of African Americans were less likely than other respondents to participate in the polls, but not less likely to vote, the polls would likely have too few of them in the sample, which could bias the results against the candidate those individuals voted for. Sherkat argues that racial views are just one characteristic that leads people to be less likely to participate in polls and that religious views underlie all of these characteristics. Individuals with fundamentalist religious views are more likely to hold negative views of African Americans, as well as negative views of women, of media outlets that might sponsor polls, and of science in general.

Any or all of these views could easily have an impact on how accurate a survey is. Most large polls, especially those that are conducted face to face, use many more female than male interviewers because female interviewers tend to be more able to get people to respond than male interviewers. Interviewers for the GSS, for instance, are more than 90 percent female. Interviewers also tend to have higher educational achievement than the average American, another factor that generally helps the response rate. However, suppose that one group or another feels threatened by women, especially educated women. That group would be less likely to agree to participate in the survey. If that group was also likely to vote for the Republican candidate in the election, the results of the survey would make the population seem less Republican than it really is.

To see if religious beliefs and related factors really are associated with response rates, and if this problem has been getting worse, Sherkat (2007) looked at interviewer judgments of respondent cooperativeness in the GSS. In the GSS and many other large surveys, the interviewer records a great deal of information about the respondent other than the answers to the questions. This information includes things such as the appearance of the house, if there were other people around, and so on, including how cooperative the respondent was. Sherkat examined GSS data between 1984 and 2004 and found that religious views had a significant effect on these measures of cooperativeness. While most respondents were rated as being friendly and interested—the highest level of cooperation— respondents who said that they believed that the Bible was the literal word of God were fifteen points more likely to be in one of the less cooperative categories. The relationship between religious views and cooperativeness also seemed to shift over the course of the data analyzed. During the Reagan and Bush years, fundamentalist respondents were more cooperative than they were during the Clinton years, when a Democratic President was in power.

Sherkat's (2007) research is just one example of how difficult it is to get an SRS in the real world and what the consequences of that failure can be. Error in a survey due to certain people being less likely to participate is generally referred to as *nonresponse bias*. In this case, Sherkat found that people who hold certain fundamentalist religious beliefs are less likely to participate in surveys, and this could be for any number of reasons, ranging from their views of women to their views of media groups to their views of social science in general. What really matters here, though, is that there is a systematic relationship between factors that are leading them to be less likely to participate in the survey and the outcomes that the survey is interested in (vote choice, in this case). Individuals holding these beliefs generally supported the Republican candidate, and since they were less likely to agree to take part in a survey, the sample underrepresented support for the Republican candidate.

Of course, in any survey, some people just aren't going to pick up their phone, answer the door, or check their email, and this doesn't generally lead to bad results. There are a lot of reasons why someone might not participate in the survey: maybe when the interviewer called they were on vacation, were out to lunch, or were trying to put a baby to sleep. There's no reason to believe that people who are on vacation are more likely to support a Republican or a Democratic candidate, so if researchers only care about vote choice, the fact that some people are on vacation really doesn't matter. It would be great to be able to talk to everyone, but if the traits that lead a potential respondent to not be in the actual sample aren't systematically related to the outcomes that the researcher is interested in, it really doesn't matter. Having to make more calls means that the survey might be more expensive, or take longer, but the results aren't going to be any better or any worse. However, suppose that the researchers were carrying out a study on where Americans like to go on vacation and called during the fourth of July holiday. A lot of potential respondents wouldn't pick up their phones because they were on a trip already, and the sample that was left might not be representative of the vacation plans of the population.

For social and political polls, the factors that generally lead potential respondents to not take part in the survey are pretty well known. Women are more likely to pick up the phone than men, and older people are more likely to pick up the phone than younger people. Democrats are more likely to be home on weeknights; Republicans are more likely to be home on weekends. Put together, this means that a telephone survey that calls households randomly is going to have a sample that is older and has fewer men than the overall population, and to the extent that older people and women have different views on the topics of interest, this is a real problem.

To some extent, these problems can be remedied with instructions at the start of the poll. Many surveys, for instance, ask to speak to the youngest male in the household or the person in the household with the closest upcoming birthday in an attempt to get a random person in the household, rather than the person who tends to pick up the phone. This doesn't solve all of these issues: if, as Skerkat (2007) argues, people with certain political and social views are less likely to participate, there's not much that can be done. To minimize these problems, survey researchers often make use of multiple call backs. If no one picks up a telephone number selected to be in the sample or the person who picks up doesn't want to be in the study or answer questions at that time, survey researchers will almost always try to convert the refusal into a completed survey. Part of this is to minimize costs. Many numbers just aren't valid, and the interviewer might have to call several other numbers before reaching another number that could potentially be part of the survey. The other part is to increase the quality of the sample. Researchers are afraid, with good reason, that the same factors that lead someone to not want to be in the study are also factors that might lead to different views on the topics of interest in the survey. As such, if the researchers only talk to the people who really want to talk to them and are available the first time they call, this will lead to a sample that's not a good representation of the population. Survey researchers will often call back the same number as many as seven times in order to get someone in the household to complete the survey, and surveys often include scripts telling interviewers what to say in order to convince reluctant respondents to complete the survey. For instance, interviewers might remind respondents that the interview will be short, that they're not selling anything, that the answers are confidential, and so on. The goal is to get as many people initially included in the sample to complete the survey as possible, in order to get the best possible representation of the population.

This is also why the issue of cell phones has become so important to survey researchers in recent years. While the number of households that only have cell phones varies widely from state to state, individuals who only have cell phones are much younger, more educated, and poorer than households that have both cell phones and landline phones. As such, it's been argued that surveys that exclude cell phones are missing a large part of the population that may well have different political and social views than those people who have landlines. So far, the evidence is mixed, and while most large surveys now include cell phones in one way or another, it doesn't seem to change the results of the surveys very much, mostly because young people are less likely to pick up the phone anyway.

STRATIFIED SAMPLING

David Kimball, Brady Baybeck, Cassie Gross, and Laura Wiedlocher—How Much Do Poll Workers Know? (2009)

Since the 2000 Presidential election, in which the outcome of the race was decided by a few hundred votes in Florida and there were widespread reports of voters not understanding the ballots there, there has been a concerted effort to modernize the American voting process. Despite some concerns about secrecy and the potential for result tampering, most municipalities have adopted electronic voting machines to replace the punch-card devices that many areas were using, even in the last ten years. These computerized devices make it easier to vote and make the tabulation of results much faster, but there's one element in the voting process that hasn't been updated: the workers. As the voting equipment has become more complex and legislatures have passed laws requiring voters to show identification before casting a ballot, the training and knowledge of these workers has become increasingly important. Kimball and his colleagues (2009), a research team at the University of Missouri at St. Louis, decided to look into this issue by carrying out a survey of election officials across the country.

Carrying out such a survey, though, is harder than just taking a random sample of all election officials. There are a bit more than 10,000 governmental jurisdictions in the United States that carry out election: towns, counties, school districts, and so on. Most of these jurisdictions are pretty small, with half serving less than 1,000 voters. However, a few jurisdictions in large —418, or about 4 percent—serve more than 50,000 voters each and are responsible for 64 percent of all of the voters in the country.

Since the people responsible for elections are public officials, getting their contact information and building a list of the entire population wasn't a problem. The real problem came from the odd distribution of jurisdictions. The fact that so many of the country's voters and election workers are concentrated in just a few jurisdictions meant that Kimball and his colleagues (2009) couldn't just take a random sample of all of the election officials in the country. Had they done that, the vast majority of their sample would be from the smallest jurisdictions, and their results wouldn't have told them much about the very large jurisdictions in which most Americans actually cast their ballots.

So, instead of an SRS, Kimball and his colleagues (2009) divided up the population into three groups based on the size of the jurisdiction. They then treated each of these groups as being a separate population and took a random sample from each of them. For instance, there were 5,021 jurisdictions serving less than 1,000 voters, and they took a random sample of 500. There were 4,931 jurisdictions with between 1,000 and 50,000 voters, and from that group, they took a separate random sample of 2,000. Because of the small number of very large jurisdictions, they sampled the entire population.

The 2,919 surveys were sent to the election administrators for each of the sampled jurisdictions, via email (with links to a web survey) if the researchers could find email contact information for the official, or via standard mail if they couldn't. Both the standard mail and the email surveys were the same. About 30 percent of the surveys were completed, with officials from the larger jurisdictions being the most likely to do so.

The results of the survey showed how different the large and small jurisdictions are. In small jurisdictions, the poll workers are mostly people with other government jobs who run the polls on Election Day, have been doing so for a long time, don't get paid much to do it, and don't have much training. In large jurisdictions, officials reported a constant struggle to get enough workers to man the polls on Election Day, but the officials were much more likely to require training, testing, and interviews before letting people work at the polls. For example, only 36 percent of small jurisdictions require training for potential poll workers before an election, compared with 80 percent of large jurisdictions. Despite the low pay and lack of training, the officials in the small jurisdictions are generally happier with the poll workers than those in the large jurisdictions.

Kimball and his colleagues (2009) made use of a common alternative to an SRS: a **stratified sample**. In a stratified sample, the overall population is divided into subpopulations, and an SRS is taken from each of the subpopulations, called **strata**. As a result, the samples of each of the subpopulations can be considered as representative of the population that it's drawn from. There are several reasons to use a stratified sample. The first is when researchers are interested in groups that don't make up much of the overall population. Kimball and his colleagues were carrying out a survey of election officials, and while election officials overseeing very large numbers of voters only make up a small portion of the total population of election officials in the country, they run elections for most voters in the country. If the survey had used an SRS, only about 4 percent of the election officials surveyed would have been from very large jurisdictions: in a sample of 3,000 that's only about one hundred officials. That sample of one hundred represents the relative number of election officials from very large jurisdictions, but it's too small a number to allow Kimball and his colleagues to draw any meaningful conclusions about the group. Just as the similarity of the sample and the population increase as the size of the sample increases, the accuracy of conclusions about subgroups increases as the size of that subgroup in the sample increases. A sample of one hundred is too small to tell us much about a population, so it's also too small to tell us much about any particular subpopulation, such as election officials in large jurisdictions.

Suppose that Kimball and his colleagues (2009) had wanted to use an SRS and still be able to draw conclusions about election officials from very large jurisdictions. If they decided that they needed a sample of 250 administrators from large jurisdictions to be able to draw conclusions about them, their SRS would have to have a sample of almost 7,000, doubling the cost and effort needed to carry out their study. Such a large sample size would also mean that they would have a huge sample of election officials from small jurisdictions, probably way more than they would need to draw conclusions about that group.

The same logic applies to any subpopulation. If a researcher is interested in how the views of Asian Americans differ from the rest of the population, he or she would almost certainly have to survey more Asian Americans than would be present in an SRS. When used in conjunction with an SRS, a stratified sample is often referred to as an *oversample*. In the study of Asian Americans, for instance, a survey of the entire population would be combined with an oversample of Asian Americans. The same questions would be asked of an SRS of the overall population and a stratified sample of Asian Americans, and the results could be compared.

The second reason to use a stratified sample is to ensure that all desired groups are included in a sample. A survey of religious views, for instance, might want to ensure that Jews, Muslims, and Mormons are all included in the survey, but there's a good chance that an SRS with a reasonable sample size would miss one or more of these groups. A stratified sample that included a certain number of representatives from each religious group would ensure that all of the groups are included.

The third reason to use a stratified sample is to try to overcome nonresponse bias. If researchers know that a certain group, for whatever reason, is less likely to be a part of an SRS, they can establish a stratified sample for that group. For instance, researchers know that young men are the least likely demographic group to participate in landline phone surveys, so an SRS would have fewer young men than it should if it represents the overall population. To correct for this, researchers might make a concerted effort to get a certain number of young men as an oversample, ensuring that at least some of them will be in the sample.

NONPROBABILITY SAMPLING

The above three methods of sampling—simple random sampling, stratified sampling, and systematic sampling—all are types of probability sampling. **Probability sampling** gives all members of the population equal chance to be selected into the study. By providing every person an equal chance to participate, probability sampling techniques randomize the selection process. That means that there will be no systematic bias in the selection process, and the samples selected through probability sampling will be representative of the entire population. Researchers typically use probability sampling in cases where they want to generalize the findings to a much larger population.

However, sometimes researchers cannot easily define their population. In those cases, they do not give everyone in their defined populations equal chance to participate in the study. This type of sampling is called **nonprobability sampling**. Nonprobability sampling is typically used when researchers do not want to generalize and use statistics to come to conclusions about the lager population.

Convenience Sampling

One type of nonprobability sampling is **convenience sampling**. Convenience sampling administers the surveys to any respondent who is available. Instead of thinking about the population, the researchers administer the survey only to respondents who are convenient. Typically, convenience sampling is not rigorous or systematic enough for an actual research project. However, typically convenience sampling is used at the early stages of a survey to work out the problems of a survey. It is a very good way to try out new questions and formats. The main advantage of convenience sampling is the ease and convenience. Unlike some other methods of sampling, it is very easy and cost effective. Convenience sampling is a helpful technique at very early stages of a survey to pretest wording, order, or structure of a survey before researchers invest too much time and money. However, it is not typically used for the actual study.

SNOWBALL SAMPLING

A nonprobability sampling that is often used in research is **snowball sampling**. Snowball sampling is still a nonprobability method: it does not give everyone an equal chance to participate in the study. Researchers cannot use statistical techniques on data collected through this method. They also cannot generalize findings to the entire population easily. However, the main reason why researchers use snowball sampling is that they are studying populations for which they do not have a list. In fact, in some situations, the group or phenomenon they are interested in is so specific and small that it is difficult to find a population list. In fact, the population of interest might be so small that it is difficult to locate individual respondents. In those cases, researchers typically locate one key respondent and find other potential respondents through that initial respondent. Like a snowball, the sample grows from the connections and recommendations of each respondent. Typically, snowball sampling is used in qualitative methodology, but snowball sampling is used for surveys of difficult-to-reach populations as well.

Pamela J. Smock, Wendy D. Manning, and Meredith Porter— Cohabitation, Money, and Marriage (2004)

In recent years, the number of couples cohabiting before marriage has risen dramatically. In past decades, living with a significant other before marriage was socially unacceptable in America, but this seems to have changed, as more and more couples live together before marriage: estimates are that almost half of Americans born in the 1990s will live with their spouse before marriage. Pamela J. Smock, Wendy D. Manning, and Meredith Porter (2004)—sociologists at Bowling Green State University—look at the transition between cohabitation and marriage: what factors lead some cohabiting couples to tie the knot, while others don't. Most of the research done on cohabitation, based on large-scale survey data, has identified money as the main difference between cohabitating couples who get married and those who do not. Richer cohabitating couples get married, while poorer ones do not. What Smock, Manning, and Porter want to know is *why* that is. After all, marriage has financial as well as social benefits—married couples pay less in taxes than unmarried couples, for instance—so it would make sense for poorer couples to feel more pressure to get married.

To look into what leads cohabitating couples to get married, Smock, Manning, and Porter (2004) carried out in-depth interviews with 115 individuals age twenty-one to thirty-five years, who were in a cohabiting relationship or had recently been in one. They were also interested in looking at differences between racial groups, so they made sure to have at least fifteen African American and fifteen Hispanic respondents. While cohabitation is increasingly common, it still doesn't account for a very large proportion of all of the households in any given area, so the use of a telephone or mail survey to find cohabiting couples—especially from specific ethnic groups—would have been wasteful. Instead, Smock, Manning, and Porter began by seeking out individuals in the community (at Laundromats, restaurants, and the like) and making arrangements for further interviews. Still, they weren't getting enough respondents from minority ethnic groups, so they asked the respondents that they already had from those ethnic groups to refer other cohabiting couples from that ethnic group, essentially asking respondents if they knew anyone else from their ethnic group that the researchers could talk to. The individuals referred in this way were then added to the study, if they were willing to participate, and made up about 30 percent of all of the respondents.

The researchers used semi-structured interviews that lasted, on average, about an hour and a half and talked to the respondents about their relationship, from the beginning to the present: how they met their partner, how they decided to move in together, how they decided to get married, their perceptions of marriage, and so on. While a number of researchers were used to recruit the respondents, Smock, Manning, and Porter (2004) used just one trained interviewer to carry out all of the interviews, in order to minimize the reactivity effects. All told, about half of the sample was currently cohabiting, a quarter was married after cohabiting, and a quarter was single after cohabiting. All of the respondents were from the Toledo, Ohio, metro area, which, the researchers argue, is demographically similar to the nation as a whole.

To analyze the responses, Smock, Manning, and Porter (2004) used computer-assisted content analysis, in which a computer program pulled out all of the references to money in the interviews, and coders then looked at those statements to determine the meaning. These statements were especially prevalent in the question that asked respondents "What would need to be in place for marriage?" Overall, 23 percent of respondents mentioned only economic factors in response; another 50 percent named economic factors and something else. One respondent told them:

I: Ok. How then, like what would have had to been in place for you to have gotten married?
R: Money.

I: Ok. Tell me a little bit about what that means.

R: Money means um … stability. I don't want to struggle, if I'm in a partnership, then there's no more struggling, and income-wise we were still both struggling.

Many others talked about needing to pay off debt before marrying. Others wanted to have a "real" wedding: until they had enough money to throw the big ceremony that they wanted, they saw no point in getting married. Having a justice of the peace officiate at town hall just wasn't the same thing. Even the poor people in the sample talk about how going "downtown" to get married is shameful, the sort of thing poor people do. The final source of resistance to marriage came from gender expectations: both men and women feel that the man should be able to take care of the family financially before marriage.

The researchers conclude that money is important because cohabiting is considered to be cheaper than marriage and that marriage is an end goal, something that happens after a series of other (mostly financial) goals are met. In contrast with other researchers, who argue that cohabitators feel that marriage will change their lives, Smock, Manning, and Porter (2004) find that cohabitators see marriage as something that happens *after* their lives change.

The sample Smock, Manning, and Porter (2004) collected is obviously nothing like an SRS, but that doesn't mean that it isn't a survey or that it can't tell us anything about a population. The technique the researchers in this study used to collect their sample (snowball sampling) is most commonly used to recruit participants for qualitative research or for surveys within very small populations. In a snowball sample, the researchers ask respondents to help them find more respondents, either by asking the existing respondent for someone else's contact information or by asking the respondent to give the researcher's contact information to someone else. As each respondent refers more potential respondents, the sample gets bigger and bigger, like a snowball rolling downhill.

Most of the time, snowball sampling is used when it may be difficult or impossible to independently contact enough individuals in the target population. Most research on sex workers, for instance, relies on snowball samples because respondents tend to know other sex workers, and sex workers aren't likely to talk to interviewers who just call them on the phone. Similarly, it would have been difficult for Smock, Manning, and Porter (2004) to find enough cohabiting couples through a random-digit dialing survey. Even if they did, it seems unlikely that the couples that could be found through such a survey would be a good representation of the entire population of cohabiting couples: most likely, they'd be more stable and richer than most cohabiting couples.

The use of a different sampling technique would be further complicated by the researchers' desire to have representatives from racial minority groups in the sample. They could have tried a stratified sample, but if the rates of cohabiting couples are low, the rates of cohabiting couples who happen to be Hispanic or African American are absurdly low. The number of calls the researchers would have to make to get a good sample would be enormously expensive and inefficient.

Qualitative researchers carrying out in-depth interviews are also more likely to use snowball sampling because of the extra effort required by the respondents.

People may be willing to talk with an interviewer for ten or fifteen minutes without knowing too much about what's going on, but expecting someone to sit for an hour and a half in-person interview is a bit different. Respondents may be more likely to cooperate if they know that their acquaintances have done the same, giving them confidence that the research isn't a scam and creating some social pressure for them to participate.

In surveys, though, researchers are generally interested in what a sample tells about the population of interest. No one outside of their family cares why certain cohabiting couples in Toledo get married or don't, but outsiders care about cohabitation in general and what these couples in Toledo can tell them about it. The external validity of a snowball sample is dependent on how carefully the sampling is done. The best snowball samples recruit their initial contacts from very different places within the population, making it more likely that the resulting sample will be similar to the overall population. For instance, Smock, Manning, and Porter (2004) found respondents not just in Laundromats, but also at parties, bars, restaurants, and other places around the community that were frequented by young couples. The cohabiting couples found in a Laundromat are likely very different from those found in a trendy bar, who are very different from those found in a late-night diner. By starting with couples recruited from all of these places, then talking to *their* acquaintances, the researchers were able to get a better sample than if they had just talked to couples at one of the places and built the snowball sample from there. The more diverse the core of the snowball is, the better the sample will be.

In SRS and related sampling techniques, researchers can evaluate how good a sample is by looking at the sample size, the response rate, and similar factors, but things aren't as clear-cut in a snowball sample. In many cases, researchers can get some idea of the quality of a sample by comparing the demographic characteristics of the sample to that of the overall population, if it's known. For instance, researchers have a pretty good idea of the average income, age, and education levels of cohabiting couples, and if the sample Smock, Manning, and Porter (2004) gathered is very different from these known characteristics, it probably doesn't tell us much about the overall population.

The best snowball samples also have a relatively low number of referrals for any given respondent. Imagine two snowball samples: in one, a single respondent refers twenty-nine of her friends to take part in the study. In the second, fifteen respondents each refer one other person to take part. All else equal, the second sample would be more representative of the population because the people one respondent knows are likely to be similar to each other in various ways that may not be evident to outsiders. (They may all shop at the same stores, work in the same office, belong to the same book clubs, and so on.)

Finally, researchers using snowball samples can also increase the external validity of their study by incorporating some random processes into the respondent selection process. Suppose that each respondent is asked for the names of five people who might be interested in taking part in the survey. Rather than just starting from the top of each respondent's list, the researchers would be better off putting all of the names into a unified list and then randomly choosing which participants to approach from the full list. That way, the sample won't disproportionately favor respondents' close friends or people who are close to one of the previous respondents.

In the past, snowball samples were generally limited geographically, just as Smock, Manning, and Porter (2004) only talked to individuals living in Toledo. Most of the people that respondents knew well enough to refer for the study tended to live near the respondent. This has the potential to create problems for external validity. The best that researchers can hope for is that respondents happen to live in an area that is fairly similar to the country as a whole: Toledo may be fairly similar to much of the country, but Brooklyn probably isn't. For researchers doing anything other than face-to-face interviews, this is less of a problem now because respondents may be able to refer contacts from social networking websites, who don't live anywhere near them. Even researchers doing face-to-face interviews may be able to do them via Skype or other video-conferencing services, making geography less of a limiting factor.

While it's possible for snowball samples, if carried out the right way, to be representative of a population, researchers don't generally use them for that purpose, mostly because it's difficult to tell exactly how representative they are without the use of advanced statistical techniques. Smock, Manning, and Porter (2004), for instance, wouldn't use a snowball sample to determine how long cohabitating couples stay together before marriage. Rather, snowball sampling is best used to answer the same questions that qualitative researchers generally look at: *how* something happens or *how* it is perceived, rather than *what* happens or *why* it happens. Smock, Manning, and Porter were looking at how cohabitating couples view marriage and how money plays into that: for this kind of question, a well-constructed snowball sample is perfectly appropriate.

The most important consideration for researchers using a snowball sample is ensuring that their snowball sample is not really a convenience sample. Convenience samples, sometimes called *availability samples*, are built based on whatever group is easiest for the researcher to get to, with no regard for how well the sample represents the population of interest. Students carrying out surveys for a class typically talk to their friends or other people in the class. Psychology departments at large universities typically require students to enroll in departmental participant pools, in which they agree to participate in a certain number of studies. Economics researchers pay students to come to the lab to take part in simulations. If a snowball sample starts with the researcher's friends or co-workers and doesn't go far beyond that, it's actually a convenience sample and has very little external validity.

There are certain circumstances under which this sort of sample is useful. For instance, researchers carrying out experimental research have been using student samples for decades, and while there is some skepticism about such studies, they remain generally accepted. The key to convenience samples, though, is that they cannot be used to tell us anything about the population of interest. Even if the population of interest is psychology majors at one university, the psychology majors taking a particular course aren't a random sample of all of the psychology majors, so they can't reliably tell us anything about the population. These convenience samples are useful only for pilot testing surveys (to identify problems with the questions or format of the survey) or for studying processes. Researchers using experiments, for instance, have made use of student samples on the assumption that, while students may be very different from the overall population, their brains work in about the same way as everyone else's, so the difference between experimental cells in a student sample is about the same as it would be in the general population. Even this might not always be the case. For instance, while a convenience sample is probably fine for a study of visual perception—everyone's vision is about the same—it might not be fine for a study of factors that lead individuals to associate with one political party or another, as students often have less stable political views than the general population. In sum, while snowball samples are often useful, convenience samples are only good for telling researchers about processes, and even then, only useful for studying processes that are the same in the convenience sample and in the general population.

SUMMARY

There's no single right way to carry out survey research: the best technique for one research question may not work well for researchers trying to reach a different population or find out about a different topic. The first major consideration researchers have to contend with is the mode of the survey. While telephone surveys have been the dominant mode for the past fifty years, the advent of cellular phones and caller ID has made them more difficult and expensive. On the other hand, Internet surveys can be very fast and very cheap—but face serious problems of validity. After all, there are many populations of interest in which not everyone has access to the Internet, and creating a representative sample from a purely Internet-based sample may be difficult or impossible. Other studies are best carried out via expensive face-to-face interviews or even mail surveys. No matter what survey mode is used, researchers are trying to achieve the greatest validity for their sample; they want to be able to leverage what they know about the fairly small group of people contacted by the survey to find out about the larger population of interest.

In addition to determining the proper mode for a survey, researchers also have to determine what the best sampling technique is. The gold standard in survey research is the SRS, in which every individual in the target population is equally likely to be picked to be some random process to take part in the survey. If an SRS is carried out correctly, it has the admirable quality of increasing the validity of conclusions about the population as the size of the sample increases. However, this only happens if there's no bias in the sampling process: if members of one group are systematically less likely to take part in the survey than another group, a greater sample size will do nothing to reduce the resulting bias. In some circumstances, researchers may be able to reach valid conclusions about a population from a non-SRS sample through the use of stratified or systematic sampling.

Sometimes, though, the population of interest is too rare for these sorts of probability-based sampling techniques, and researchers turn instead to nonprobability sampling, such as snowball samples. These techniques can be valuable, but they don't allow researchers to draw valid conclusions about the overall population, and researchers need to be careful that the sample does not devolve into a mere convenience sample.

Study and Review

Explain the relationship between sample size and survey validity.

Could the Baylor Religion Survey have been carried out through another survey mode? Why or why not?

Explain the special challenges facing researchers who want to survey nebulous populations, such as likely voters or fans of a certain television show.

Under what circumstances would a non-SRS probability sample be most appropriate?

CHAPTER 12

Quantitative Methods I: Descriptive Statistics

Learning Objectives

- Be able to navigate the data and variable views in SPSS
- Be able to carry out basic data visualization functions in SPSS
- Be able to explain the uses of the different measures of central tendency
- Be able to explain the functions of various measures of dispersion
- Be able to explain the function of z-scores
- Be able to explain the function of a margin of error

FROM SURVEY TO DATASET

Until this chapter, we've been focusing on the ways in which researchers can collect data, but we haven't spent much time on what they do with this data once it's collected. In quantitative analyses, especially, it's the job of the researcher to turn lists of numbers into information and conclusions that can be understood by other researchers and members of the public. This process also allows researchers to uncover patterns in the data that aren't obvious at first glance and get closer to understanding what factors lead to the outcomes that they are interested in.

These data analysis techniques most commonly are used to understand survey data, but there's no reason that the same techniques can't be used to look at other types of data, such as crime rates in various cities, number of wars over time, or the economic performance of different countries. In general, researchers need to collect a certain critical mass of data before quantitative analysis is really useful, and the more sophisticated the analysis, the more data is needed to make it worthwhile. This is why survey data is so often used, as it allows researchers to collect comparable data from a large number of individuals, giving them a large enough sample size to make the analysis worthwhile.

In this chapter and Chapter 13, we'll focus on showing how the analysis can be done with computers, rather than by hand. There are several reasons for using computers. The first is that nearly all modern data analysis is done using specialized software, such as SPSS, Stata, or R. The second is that doing these analyses by hand, or even with the help of a calculator, gets more difficult as the amount of data increases. As computer techniques become more useful, analyses by hand are less feasible. Third, many of the techniques we'll discuss require the use of integral calculus, which many students in the social sciences haven't mastered. Because these students can use computers, this isn't an obstacle: the computers, or even the printed tables, do the work for them. Without computers, students would have to carry out lengthy and complicated equations to do even the most basic analysis.

As we introduce data analysis techniques, we'll discuss the logic underlying them, as well as how to carry them out in SPSS. For the purpose of these chapters, we're assuming that the data to be analyzed has been downloaded from an archive or the website for this text. However, the same principles and techniques apply to data that researchers have collected and analyzed themselves, as this is sometimes the only way to find answers to specific research questions.

The Basics of SPSS

In this chapter and the next, we'll be using examples from a particular statistics program, SPSS. This doesn't mean that social scientists don't use other programs, such as SAS, Stata, and R, but SPSS is the program most commonly used by students and allows users to do much of the work through pull-down menus, rather than by typing in commands. As researchers do more and more work with SPSS, they often find it easier to type in commands rather than use the pull-down menus and dialog boxes.

SPSS (the acronym previously stood for Statistical Package for the Social Sciences, but no longer does) is a statistical program that researchers use to analyze data. In some ways, SPSS resembles simple spreadsheet programs, like Excel, and new users who have experience with spreadsheets may find some functions that they recognize. However, SPSS has many more functions than a spreadsheet program, and it helps social science researchers carry out the functions they commonly need. Also, most large datasets that researchers want to access are available in SPSS format, including the datasets used as examples in these chapters. Finally, the techniques discussed here for SPSS are easily transferable to other programs: running a regression analysis in Stata isn't much different from running one in SPSS, so once researchers learn SPSS, they can move to other programs without too much difficulty.

When the SPSS program is open, researchers need to pay attention to three different screens. The first of these is the Data View screen, which can be accessed by pushing the button for Data View in the bottom left corner of the main screen. In the Data View screen, columns (running up and down, like columns holding up a building) represent variables, and rows (running side to side, like people rowing a boat) represent individual cases. So, if a researcher has collected information on the age of each respondent in a survey, there would be one column for age, and each row would represent the age of a different respondent. The next column would represent a different variable, but the same respondents.

With some variables, it's easy to figure out what the numbers in the Data View screen signify. If the variable is age, for instance, the numbers in the column could easily represent the age of the respondent in years or the year in which the respondent was born. If a respondent is twenty years old, the value in the age column for the row representing that respondent could be 20. While this works fine for interval- or ratio-level variables (the different levels of measurement were discussed in Chapter 1), it doesn't work for ordinal- or nominal-level variables. For instance, in the 2010 American National Election Survey (ANES) respondents were asked how much the government should increase or decrease spending on crime prevention. There were ten possible responses, ranging from "increase a great deal," to "cut out completely." In the data, "increase a great deal" was coded as 1, "increase a moderate amount" was coded as 2, all the way down to "cut out completely," which was coded as 8. (The other two categories represent respondents who didn't answer the question, either because they said that they didn't know or refused to answer.) There's an order to the responses (which is why it's an *ordinal* variable), with higher values signifying less desired spending on crime prevention, but it's not obvious what that order is just from looking at the numbers in the Data View screen. Similarly, nominal-level variables, such as race or gender, don't have a meaningful order at all, so it's not immediately clear what the different numbers mean.

If the researcher is looking at a dataset that's been set up beforehand, he or she can determine what a 1 in the gender variable or a 5 in the race variable means by looking at the Variable View screen. The Variable View screen can be accessed in SPSS by clicking on the Variable View button in the bottom left corner of the

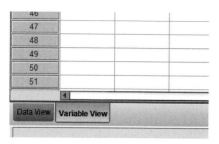

main screen, just to the right of the Data View button. Users can also get to the Variable View screen by double-clicking the name of the variable on the top of the screen in the Data View screen. In the Variable View screen, information is flipped from the Data View screen. Each row represents a variable, and each column represents a characteristic of that variable. Some of these columns tell how the data is presented—how wide the columns are or whether the columns are aligned to the right or left—but others have a direct impact on the data analysis.

The first of the important columns is the name of the variable. In general, large datasets use codes for the names of the variables rather than descriptive names, so the spending on crime prevention variable mentioned above isn't called "crime prevention spending," but rather "v083144x". These codes make certain things easier, but also mean that researchers have to take note of exactly which variables they're working with. Users can also rename variables to make them easier to find or remember, as long as the new names are fairly short and don't contain any illegal characters, such as *$*, *%*, *&*, or spaces, which cause conflicts when the program tries to process them. The next column to the right is called Type. Users have a number of options for this column, but two are most frequently used: numeric and string. *Numeric* means that the value is in normal numbers, like 0, 8, or −3. *String* means that the values for that variable are made up of words, which can be useful sometimes (as with volunteered responses), but also means that SPSS won't do any analysis of that variable.

The next important column in the Data View screen is the Label column. This gives a description of what the variable is. Since it isn't clear what variable v083144x is just from the name, users can get a better idea by looking at the label for the variable. In this case, it reads, "SUMMARY: increase or decrease spending on crime." This may or may not be enough for users to figure out what the variable is, and users may need to consult with a separate codebook, which can be downloaded from the same place the data was obtained. This codebook will give details on the exact question wording, the order in which the question was asked, and anything else that researchers might want to know. When researchers create a variable, they generally create their own labels in SPSS to remind themselves what the variable means. If these new variables are going to be shared with other people, the researchers may even build their own codebook.

Just to the right of the Label column is the Values column. This column gives information about what the numbers seen in the Data View screen actually signify and is where researchers would go to find out what an 8 on the crime prevention spending variable means. Just as in the Label column, researchers need to add the appropriate information to the Values column when creating a new variable to ensure that they remember what the value means and so others who might use the data can also figure it out. This column is also important for determining which values of the variable don't correspond to responses to the questions—for example, respondents who said "don't know" or refused to answer the question. To look at all of the values for a given variable, or change the values if necessary, users can click on the Values column in that variable's row, then click on the blue box that shows up on the right side of the cell.

P1d1x. SUMMARY: increase/decrease spend on science and tech...	{-9, -9. Refu...	None
P1e. Federal Budget Spending: dealing with crime	{-9, -9. Refu...	None
P1e1. How much increase or decrease spending on crime	{-9, -9. Refu...	None
P1e1x. SUMMARY: increase or decrease spending on crime	Refused}... [...]	None
P1f. Federal Budget Spending: welfare programs	{-9, -9. Refu...	None
P1f1. How much increase or decrease spending on welfare	{-9, -9. Refu...	None
P1f1x. SUMMARY: increase or decrease spending on welfare	{-9, -9. Refu...	None
P1g. Federal Budget Spending: child care	{-9, -9. Refu...	None
P1g1. How much increase or decrease spending on child care	{-9, -9. Refu...	None
P1g1x. SUMMARY: increase or decrease spending on child care	{-9, -9. Refu...	None
P1h. Federal Budget Spending: foreign aid	{-9, -9. Refu...	None

This will bring up the Value Labels dialog box; users can scroll up or down to see all of the values, or add values and labels by typing them into the blanks at the top of the dialog box. Note, however, that changing the names or listed values doesn't actually change the data; it just changes how the values are labeled. In general, when dealing with datasets that have been set up by others, users should be very careful about adding or removing values. However, when users add their own variables, by manually entering them or by calculating them based on other variables, they should ensure that the value labels are correct.

Finally, the Missing column tells SPSS to ignore certain values of a variable. In the crime prevention spending variable, values of 1 through 8 signify the opinions that respondents have on increasing or decreasing spending on crime prevention, but there are other values: −8 and −9. (Note that 9s and 99s are commonly used for these values, dating back to the use of punch cards that could only contain one or two digits for a response.) A value of −8 means that the respondent said that he or she didn't know whether spending should go up or down, and a value of −9 means that the respondent refused to answer the question. It's vital that researchers tell SPSS that these values don't represent meaningful answers to the question. Remember that lower values on the variable mean that respondents want more spending on crime prevention, and higher values mean that they want less spending. If a user forgot to tell SPSS that −8 and −9 weren't meaningful values, SPSS would treat a response of −9 as being on the same scale as the 1 through 8 responses. Respondents who answered "don't know" would be treated as if they wanted greater increases in spending than respondents who gave an answer coded as a 1 or a 2.

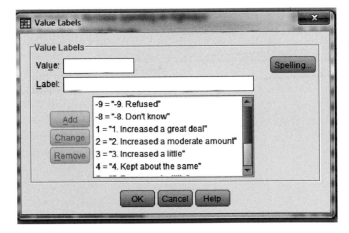

Even if there aren't many respondents who give the "don't know" response, they could throw off the analysis. To make sure that this doesn't happen, researchers using this data need to specify −8 and −9 as missing, meaning that these values shouldn't be included in any analysis of the data. It might be tempting to delete these responses to make sure that they won't cause problems, but this would eliminate any opportunity to look for patterns in them. For instance, it could be that individuals with high levels of racism are more likely to refuse to answer questions about race. If a researcher were to just delete the data, there would be no way of looking for such a pattern.

To set a value to missing, click on the cell in the Missing column in the row for the variable of interest. Just as with the Values column, a dialog box to show the current missing values can be opened by clicking on the blue button on the right side of the cell. In this case, the values of −8 and −9 should be set to missing; there are several ways users can do this. If there are just a few missing values—as is the case for this variable—users can enter discrete missing values. They simply click on Discrete Missing Values and enter −9 and −8 in the boxes below.

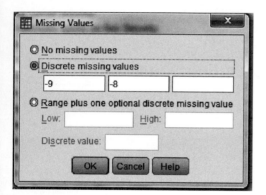

Alternately, users could enter a range of values. In this case, the range could go from −9 to −8, or −9 to 0. When entering a range, users also have the option of one additional discrete value. This option would be useful if there were more than three discrete missing values, a situation that doesn't often arise.

The third screen in SPSS is Output. This screen is used to record any analyses done on the first two screens or any changes that are made to the dataset. This separate document is automatically created when a user does anything in the other two screens, and it must be saved independently of the dataset. Once the user does anything in SPSS—even open a dataset— it's recorded in the Output document. When the user is done working, he or she generally saves the Output document; he or she can even use a Save As command to turn the document into another type of file (such as a Microsoft Word or PDF file) that can be more easily manipulated. By keeping track of the Output document, the researcher can see exactly what he or she did and what the outcome of those changes were. If the researcher does any analyses or makes any graphs, they're automatically saved to the Output document.

DESCRIBING DATA

Frequencies

The first step in analyzing a variable is to examine the **frequency table**. The frequency table tells the researcher the number of data points in the sample that have each value of the variable. Knowing this information is important for a couple of reasons. First, researchers can make sure that any missing values in the variable have been removed and that the order of the remaining values actually makes sense. Second, the table gives a basic idea of how the variable is distributed. There are a number of other ways to measure the distribution of a variable, but looking at the frequency table is always a good first step. It can tell the researcher if the data are concentrated in one category, spread across the entire range of the variable, or have another distribution.

In general, a frequency table gives information on the number of cases that are in each category of the variable and what percent of all cases that category represents. So, if a researcher is interested in using the number of days per week that people watch TV news in an analysis, he or she would start by examining the frequency table. In SPSS, the table would look like this:

A12b. [NEW] Days in typical week watch news on TV

		Frequency	Percent	Valid Percent	Cumulative Percent
Valid	0. None	98	4.2	8.4	8.4
	1. One day	51	2.2	4.4	12.8
	2. Two days	85	3.7	7.3	20.1
	3. Three days	67	2.9	5.7	25.8
	4. Four days	79	3.4	6.8	32.6
	5. Five days	139	6.0	11.9	44.5
	6. Six days	64	2.8	5.5	50.0
	7. Seven days	584	25.2	50.0	100.0
	Total	1167	50.3	100.0	
Missing	-1. INAP, R selected for version OLD	1155	49.7		
Total		2322	100.0		

The categories of the variable are listed on the left side of the table, with the characteristics of that value listed across to top. In this example, ninety-eight of the respondents said that they watched the news on TV zero days in a typical week, fifty-one said one day, and so on. The next column is where things get interesting. In this survey, half of the respondents were asked the question one way, and the other half were asked the question in a different way (denoted in the dataset as the "old" way). Because there were a total of 2,322 respondents in the survey, the ninety-eight who said that they watch TV news zero nights a week represent 4.2 percent of the total sample—but 8.4 percent of those people who were actually asked the question. The Percent column gives the percent in that category out of the entire dataset, while the Valid Percent column gives the percent as a function of only the cases that are not set to missing, for whatever reason (in this case, because the respondents were not asked the question). Generally, the valid percent is the more useful figure. Finally, the Cumulative Percent column gives the sum of all of the valid responses at or below that row. So, 12.8 percent of respondents watch news on TV for zero or one day in a typical week, 20.1 percent watch it for zero, one, or two days, and so on. This last column is only useful in ordinal-, interval-, and ratio-level variables; for nominal-level variables, which don't have a meaningful order, the cumulative percent doesn't really mean anything.

Looking at the frequencies, there are some immediate patterns evident. The first is that nearly everyone in the survey said that they watch the news some of the time; only about 4 percent admit to not watching any TV news. The second is that the largest group is people who say that they watch news on TV every day. The third is that a lot of respondents seem to watch it five days a week, perhaps because they skip TV news on weekends. These basic findings might lead a researcher to analyze the data differently than he or she otherwise would. Rather than look at the difference between people watching 0 and 1, or 1 and 2, days a week, the researcher might be better served by dividing people up into groups based on whether they watch TV news 7 days a week or less than that.

Creating a frequency table in SPSS is easy. Using the pull-down menus, users can select Analyze → Descriptive Statistics → Frequencies, select the variable of interest, then click on the arrow button in the middle of the dialog box to move that variable to the box on the right. Users then click OK, and the frequency table will appear in the Output screen.

Graphs

While frequency tables are useful, they are not always the best way to represent what's going on with a variable. Patterns may be more evident—especially in variables with large numbers of categories—if the variable is graphed. However, the kind of graph that is best used to represent a variable depends on the type of variable: what works for a nominal variable will probably not work for an interval variable, and vice versa.

Pie Chart

If the variable is measured on the nominal or ordinal level, a **pie chart** may be the best way to graph the findings.

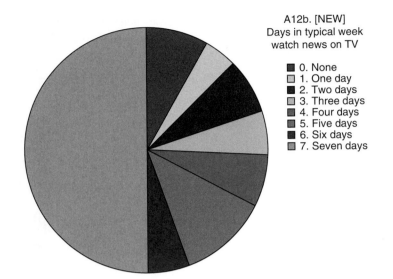

A12b. [NEW]
Days in typical week
watch news on TV

- ■ 0. None
- □ 1. One day
- ■ 2. Two days
- ▨ 3. Three days
- ▨ 4. Four days
- ▨ 5. Five days
- ■ 6. Six days
- ▨ 7. Seven days

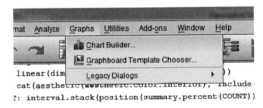

A pie chart represents all valid categories of the variable as parts of a circle, with the percent of the circle occupied by a category based on the valid frequency of that value. Pie charts are most useful when the goal is to compare the relative frequencies of the categories. The **legend** beside the pie chart provides information on which category is represented by which color.

In SPSS, there are several ways to create a pie chart. The easiest is through the chart builder, accessible by going to Graphs → Chart Builder.

This brings up the Chart Builder dialog boxes. To make a pie chart, users pick Pie/Polar from the menu at the bottom left of the dialog box. Then, they choose the variable of interest from the list on the top left side of the dialog box.

For a basic pie chart, users can just click OK to generate the pie chart.

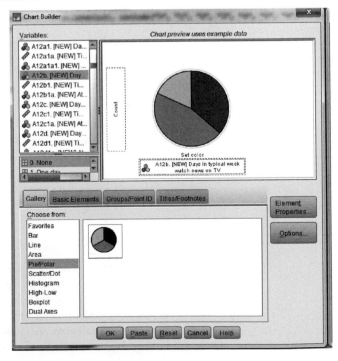

Bar Chart

Another option for nominal and ordinal levels of measurement is a **bar chart**. Bar charts are graphs where the *x*-axis represents the categories of the variable and the *y*-axis shows the frequency of each category. The bars do not touch each other because they represent different categories. Bar charts are visually effective choices for variables to highlight the difference between two categories. For example, the bar chart below clearly shows that there are far more people watching TV seven days a week than any of the other categories.

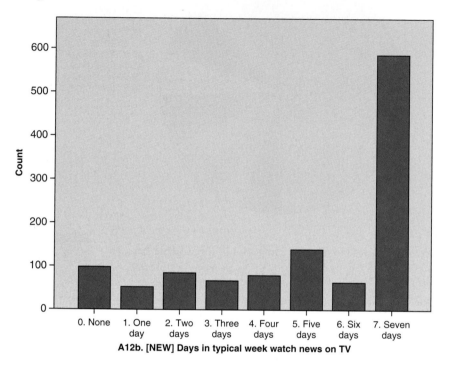

A12b. [NEW] Days in typical week watch news on TV

To create a bar chart, users go through the same process as for the pie chart; they simply pick Bar from the menu on the bottom left.

Histogram

For interval- or ratio-level variables, in which there is continuity across the categories, a **histogram** is used instead of a bar chart. Visually, a histogram looks like a bar chart in which the bars representing the frequencies of the categories touch.

In SPSS, making a histogram is no different from making any other kind of chart in the graph builder.

MEASURES OF CENTRAL TENDENCY

The most basic question researchers ask about data distribution—the list of values across all respondents for a single variable—is the **central tendency**. Commonly, people refer to this as the "average," but this term can mean several things depending on the type of variable being analyzed. Researchers typically use a more specific term: mean, median, or mode. These measures are different ways of talking about the middle of a distribution.

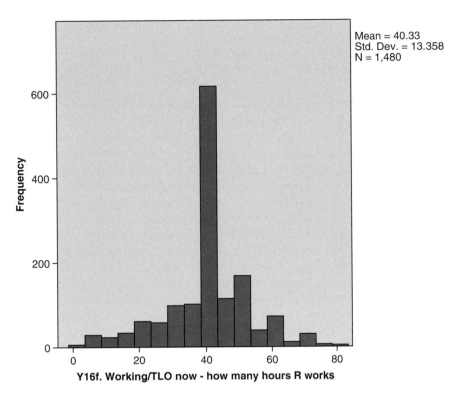

Mean = 40.33
Std. Dev. = 13.358
N = 1,480

Y16f. Working/TLO now - how many hours R works

The Mean

The most familiar measure of central tendency is the **mean** (also called the arithmetic mean to distinguish it from other calculations, like geometric means and harmonic means), which is what most people are referring to when they talk about an average. To obtain the mean, researchers simply add all of the scores in the distribution and divide the sum by the number of scores added (as discussed in a previous chapter, this is generally denoted by N). The mean is a basic-enough function that most students can do it without thinking, but the equation, when written out, looks a bit daunting.

$$\overline{X} = \frac{\sum_{i=1}^{N} X_i}{N}$$

Researchers denote the mean of a sample with the $\overline{X}$ symbol; rarely, texts may refer to the mean value of an entire population, in which case the Greek letter μ (mu) would be used instead. The uppercase X in the equation refers to the value of the variable that the researcher is trying to take the mean of. The subscript i below the X is the value for one individual case. The Greek letter Σ (sigma) means to sum all of the numbers that come afterward, starting at the value listed on the bottom ($i = 1$, meaning the first case) and repeating until the number at the top is reached (N, meaning the total number of cases in the data distribution). The sum of all of the cases is then divided by the number of cases, N.

This equation looks like a terribly complicated way of representing something that most people already know how to do, but it is important. First, it shows that even the most daunting equation—and research papers in social science can use some daunting equations—can be broken down and made simple. Second, this equation will come up later as part of other equations that make use of mean values.

While the mean has the advantage of being intuitive, it also has some drawbacks. First, it is not a resistant measure—a few scores on the edge of a distribution can have a large impact on the mean. Scores that are much higher or lower than the other recorded scores and don't reflect the overall distribution are often called **outliers**.

To understand why these outliers matter, suppose that your professor tells you the mean score on a test is 75 percent. In most classes, that would mean a C grade, so the class didn't do so well. However, that mean of 75 could correspond to a data distribution across ten students that looks like this:

36 72 75 76 80 81 81 82 83 84

The mean may be 75, but only two students did worse than that; most of the students in the class got scores in the 80s. The mean is made artificially low by the outlier—the one student who failed the test miserably, scoring a 36. Alternately, the data distribution could look like this:

66 68 71 72 73 74 74 75 77 100

The mean of the distribution is still 75, but now, nearly everyone scored lower than that. The mean is pulled upward by one student who did very well on the test, getting a perfect score. This illustrates the problem with the mean: a single outlier can have a disproportionate impact on the value. For instance, the mean salary for students graduating from the University of North Carolina with a degree in cultural geography in 1986 was over a quarter of a million dollars. This might make it sound as if cultural geography is a good degree to have. Maybe it is, but the high mean salary is more likely the result of Michael Jordan's earnings playing for the Chicago Bulls and the relatively small number of graduates in the major. The presence of even one big outlier can dramatically alter the mean of a data distribution.

This may make it seem as if researchers should ignore outliers, perhaps removing them from the data distribution, but this is generally a bad idea. First, outliers represent information, and researchers generally want to avoid deleting information from their data if at all possible. Second, removing outliers generally is not necessary because researchers can simply use techniques to minimize the impact of outliers.

The other problem with the mean is that it simply isn't useful for all types of variables. It makes sense to use a mean to talk about the central tendency of ratio- and interval-level variables, such as income, age, or feeling thermometer measures. It doesn't make sense to use the mean to talk about nominal- or ordinal-level variables. For instance, in the 2010 ANES, race is given as:

1. White
2. Black/African American
3. White and Black
4. Other Race
5. White and Another Race
6. Black and Another Race
7. White, Black and Another Race

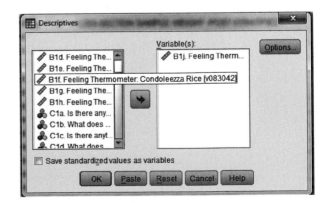

Ethnic group membership, such as being Latino, is treated separately. The mean score on this variable is 1.64, but what does that indicate? That the average person in the distribution is white, but kind of black? It doesn't actually indicate anything; for a categorical variable such as race or gender, the mean just isn't an appropriate measure. For variables like these, researchers need to use a different measure of central tendency.

SPSS makes it easy to calculate the mean of a variable. Using the pull-down menus, users can select Analyze → Descriptive Statistics → Descriptives.

From there, users can simply highlight the desired variables, then click on the arrow button in the middle of the dialog box to move the variable to the right. Clicking OK creates a short description of the variable, including the mean, in the Output document.

The Median

To overcome the problem of outliers, or when dealing with ordinal (though not categorical) variables, researchers use the **median**. When using the median, researchers look for the middle value of the distribution, regardless of how high the top values are or how low the bottom values are. This means that the median is much more resistant to outliers than the mean is. It takes account of the outliers, but they don't have an undue impact on the value of the median.

Generally, researchers don't even use a mathematical formula to express the median. The symbol for the median is simply Md. To find the median, researchers sort the data distribution from smallest to largest, count the total number of valid data points (so, missing values like refused or "don't know" responses wouldn't be counted), then go to the exact middle of the distribution. If there are an odd number of valid data points, the median would be the point with an equal number of data points above and below it. If there are an odd number of data points, it would be halfway between the two points at the middle. So, if there are 101 valid data points in a distribution, the median is the fifty-first value when the data are sorted. If there are 100 valid data points, the median is halfway between the fiftieth and fifty-first values.

Going back to the test scores from the previous section, the benefits of the median for datasets with outliers are immediately obvious. Remember that both distributions of test scores had a mean of 75:

$$36\ \ 72\ \ 75\ \ 76\ \ 80\ \ 81\ \ 81\ \ 82\ \ 83\ \ 84$$
$$66\ \ 68\ \ 71\ \ 72\ \ 73\ \ 74\ \ 74\ \ 75\ \ 77\ \ 100$$

Since there are ten (an even number) data points in each distribution, the median is halfway between the fifth and sixth values: 80.5 for the first one, and 73.5 for the second one. In both cases, the median is much more representative of what the actual scores on the test look like: mostly in the 80s for the first one and mostly in the 70s for the second.

There are any number of real-world examples in which the median is much more useful than the mean. For instance, the median household annual income for Americans in 2011 was $49,842: half of American households made less than this, and half made more. However, 5 percent of American households made more than $186,000, and about 1 percent made more than $400,000. The very high earnings at the top of the scale pull up the mean household income substantially. While the median is less than $50,000, mean household income is $69,677. In cases like this, the median is generally a better way of describing the central tendency than the mean because it does a better job of reflecting what the middle of the distribution is really like.

This example also shows one of the benefits of having multiple ways of describing central tendency: researchers can better understand the data distribution by comparing the median and the mean. Statisticians sometimes calculate a characteristic of a data distribution called *skewness*, or the extent to which there are more data on one side of the distribution or the other. If a variable has negative skewness, it has low outliers; if it has positive skewness, it has high outliers (as in the household income distribution). In general, a mean that is higher than the median indicates positive skewness, and a mean that is lower than the median indicates negative skewness. If the mean and the median are

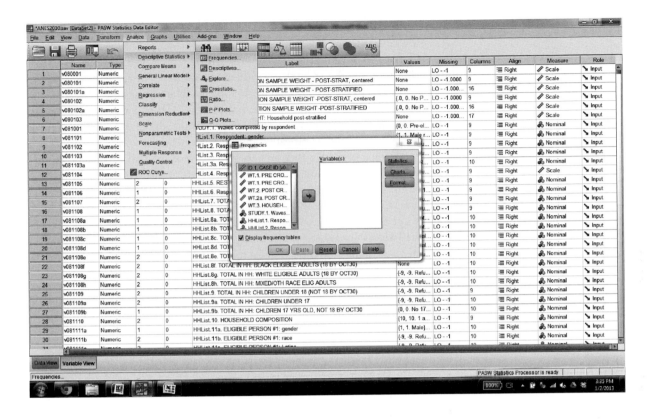

about the same, the data is probably distributed fairly evenly. So, researchers could simply note that the mean income is much higher than the median income and figure that there are some high-income households pulling the mean up. This simple test doesn't work in all circumstances—if there are lumps in the data distribution (what researchers call *multimodality*) or if the variable doesn't have a useful mean (if it isn't interval or ratio level)—but it works most of the time.

In SPSS, finding the median is fairly easy. From any of the screens, users can go to Analyze → Descriptive Statistics → Frequencies and select one or more variables.

Clicking on Statistics in the top right corner of the dialog box will bring up a new dialog box, in which users can choose which measures of central tendency they want reported, including the mean and the median. SPSS will put the median into the Output document if the user selects Median, clicks Continue, and then clicks OK in the two dialog boxes.

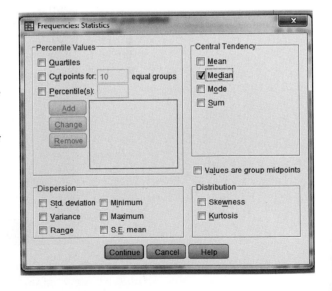

The Mode

The final measure of central tendency is the **mode**. The modal score in a distribution is simply the score that comes up most often. For interval- or ratio-level variables, there are a lot of potential problems when using the mode. First, there might not be a mode: in a distribution such as income, it's unlikely that two people in a sample will have the exact same annual income down to the penny. As such, no values would be repeated, and there wouldn't be a mode. Second, there might be many modes. Researchers generally assume that data distributions are smooth, with one big lump toward the middle. If this isn't the case, though, and there are a number of lumps in the data distribution (what researchers call a *multimodal distribution*), the mode is less meaningful. Third, modes that do exist might not be representative of the data distribution as a whole. For instance, in the General Social Survey, respondents are asked a series of seven questions to assess when a woman should be allowed to obtain an abortion (a scale discussed previously in Chapter 10). These questions can be combined on a scale, running from 0 to 7, in which a score of 0 indicates that the respondent thinks abortion should never be allowed, and 7 indicates that abortion should always be allowed.

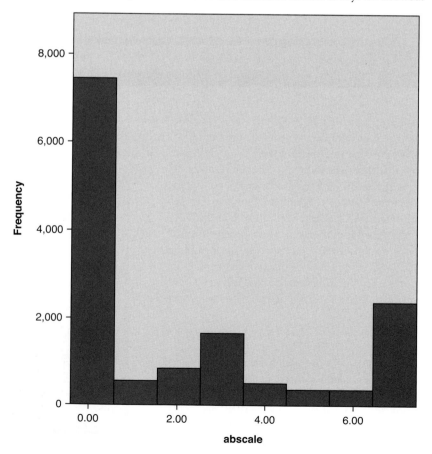

Looking at the distribution, the mode is clearly at 0. Fifty-two percent of respondents say that abortion should never be allowed. But the second biggest peak is at 7. Seventeen percent think abortion should be allowed for any reason. So, there is a very strong mode, but in a data distribution like this, the mode doesn't necessarily tell us about the central tendency of the distribution. Instead, the mean (2.1 on the seven-point scale) may be more informative because the median in this case would also be 0.

However problematic the mode may be as a measure, it is sometimes the only appropriate measure for a variable. As noted before, the mean and median simply aren't appropriate when dealing with a nominal-level variable, such as race or gender, or an ordinal-level variable, such as party identification. In these cases, where there is no meaningful order to the variable or the space between the defined values isn't meaningful, the mode is the only appropriate measure of central tendency. Even in these cases, though, researchers may be better served by simply presenting the information visually, to show readers what the distribution looks like.

To obtain the mode of a variable in SPSS, follow the same steps used for the median, then simply click on the Mode option in the Frequencies: Statistics dialog box.

MEASURES OF DISPERSION

So far, we have differentiated between data distributions based solely on the central tendency—but even data distributions with the same mean or median can be very different. These two data distributions show the scores of a scale ranging from 1 to 10, with the height of the bars corresponding to how often that score came up in the distribution. In both distributions, there is an N of 30, and both the mean and median are 5.5. Still, even a cursory examination shows how different the distributions are. What makes them different, despite their similarities, is the degree of **dispersion** in each data distribution.

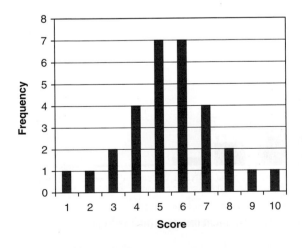
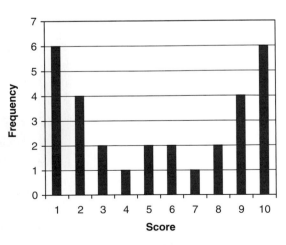

In the data distribution on the left, the values are all clustered more tightly around the middle of the distribution; in the data distribution on the right, the values tend to be farther away from the middle of the distribution. This difference is the essence of dispersion.

Range and Interquartile Range

The most basic measure of dispersion is the **range** of the data distribution. The range is simply the difference between the highest and the lowest valid scores present in the data. (Missing values aren't considered valid and wouldn't be included—another reason to be sure that they're set properly.) The 2010 ANES includes questions on the number of children under eighteen currently living in the respondent's household. The minimum number of children is 0, and the highest value in the dataset is 7. The range of the variable, therefore, is 8.

The main advantage of the range is the ease of calculation—it only requires subtraction. However, there are some big disadvantages. The first is that the range is often driven by outliers—the extreme scores on the edge of a distribution. In the 2010 ANES, exactly 1 respondent has seven minor children in her household, and only 11 out of 2,314 (that's about half a percent) have more than 4. It seems silly to let this very small group drive characteristics about the data distribution as a whole.

Finding the range of a variable in SPSS is straightforward. It may seem like users could simply look at the Values column in the Variable View screen, but

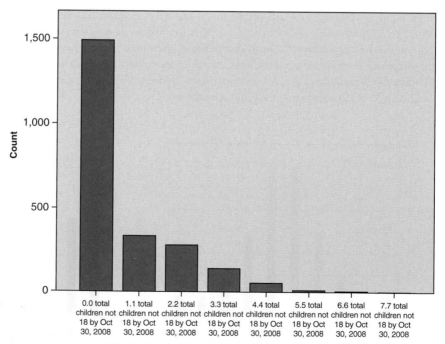

HHList.9. TOTAL IN HH: CHILDREN UNDER 18 (NOT 18 BY OCT 30)

Descriptive Statistics

	N	Minimum	Maxmum	Mean	St. Deviation
HHList.9. TOTAL IN HH: CHILDREN UNDER 18 (NOT 18 BY OCT30)	2314	0	7	.69	1.109
Valit N (listwise)	2314				

datasets don't always list all of the possible values for a variable in the Values column, especially if there are a large number of them, as in age or feeling thermometer variables. It's safer to use the Analyze → Descriptive Statistics → Descriptives command, as discussed in the section on finding the mean. This will put the minimum and maximum value, along with the mean, in the Output screen, making the calculation of the range simple.

Because the range can be so easily driven by outliers, researchers will sometimes use the **interquartile range** instead. The median of the data is also called the *fiftieth percentile*—the data point at which 50 percent of the distribution is above and 50 percent is below. Similarly, it's often useful to find other percentiles within the data, such as the twenty-fifth percentile (the point at which 25 percent of the data is below and 75 percent is above) and the seventy-fifth percentile. By finding the difference between the twenty-fifth percentile (also called the *first quartile*) and the seventy-fifth percentile (also called the *third quartile*), researchers can find the range that encompasses the middle half of the data. This measure gives a range that ignores outliers on the top and the bottom, leading to a more resistant measure.

In the number of children measure in the 2010 ANES, 64 percent of the respondents had no minor children living at home, so the twenty-fifth (and fiftieth) percentile is 0. Less than 25 percent of respondents had more than one child at home, so the seventy-fifth percentile is 1. Subtracting 0 from 1 gives an interquartile range of 1. This tells us that while there are people who have seven children at home, for the most part, the number of children only varies between zero and one.

SPSS makes finding the interquartile range fairly easy. Users can go to Analyze → Descriptive Statistics → Frequencies, select the variables they're interested in, then click on the Statistics button in the top right corner of the dialog box (just as in the description of how to obtain the median). From there, users can select Quartiles in the top left corner, click Continue, and then click OK in the dialog boxes.

SPSS puts the quartiles on the Output document: the interquartile range is just the difference between the seventy-fifth and twenty-fifth percentiles.

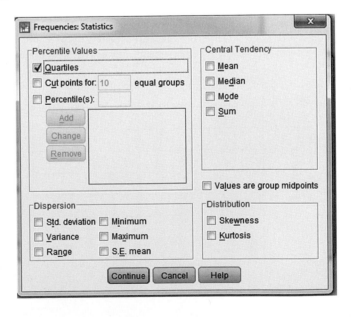

Statistics

HHList.9. TOTAL IN HH:
CHILDREN UNDER 18 (NOT 18 BY
OCT30)

N	Valid	2314
	Missing	8
Percentiles	25	.00
	50	.00
	75	1.00

The interquartile range is more resistant to outliers than the simple range, but it still relies on just two values to determine the spread of the data. It also doesn't reveal much about how concentrated the data are. If researchers want more detail about how dispersed a distribution is, more sophisticated methods are needed.

Variance and Standard Deviation

Because the various calculations of range depend on only two values— the top and bottom, or the twenty-fifth and seventy-fifth percentiles— researchers looking for more sophisticated analyses generally use measures of dispersion that take all of the data in the distribution into account. The basic idea underlying such measures is finding how far the data are, on average, from the mean. Going back to the two data distributions presented earlier, the benefits of such an approach are clear.

While both of the distributions have the same mean and range (the distribution on the right has a slightly larger interquartile range), the data in the distribution on the right are much more widely dispersed than the data in the distribution on the left. Another way to express this is to say that the data in the distribution on the left are, on average, much closer to the mean of 5.5 than the data in the distribution on the right.

Remember that the mean of a distribution is denoted as $\bar{X}$, with the value of any particular data point in the distribution denoted as X_i. Finding the mean is just a matter of summing up all of the values, from the first through the Nth (where N is the number of data points in the distribution), and dividing by the total number of data points.

$$\bar{X} = \frac{\sum_{i=1}^{N} X_i}{N}$$

If, instead, a researcher wants to find the mean distance to the mean, he or she should replace the Xi with an equation for the distance to the mean: $X_i - \bar{X}$.

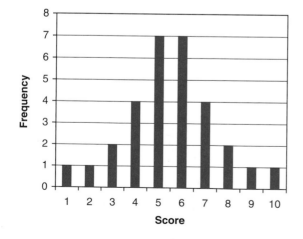

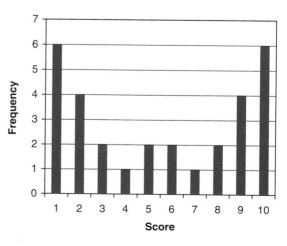

$$= \frac{\sum_{i=1}^{N}\left(X_i - \bar{X}\right)}{N}$$

Although this approach is pretty simple, it has a problem. If a data point is above the mean, then $X_i - \bar{X}$ will be positive; if the data point is below the mean, $X_i - \bar{X}$ will be negative. The problem is that there will always be exactly as much density of the data above the mean as below. No matter what the distribution looks like, the areas above and below the mean will just cancel each other out—that's the definition of the mean! As a result, it's necessary to carry out a mathematical operation that will turn the negative values into positive ones. Once all of the distances are positive, then the equation will be closer to giving the mean distance to the mean.

There are two obvious contenders for mathematical operations that can do this: squaring (a squared negative value turns positive) and taking the absolute value. There's no immediate reason why taking the absolute value won't work, and it even has some advantages in terms of leading to a more resistant measure of variance, but researchers nearly always square the $(X_i - \bar{X})$ term instead because it makes later calculations easier. Simply squaring $(X_i - \bar{X})$ leads to a measure called the **variance** of the distribution, represented mathematically as S^2.

$$S^2 = \frac{\sum_{i=1}^{N}\left(X_i = \bar{X}\right)^2}{(N-1)}$$

This resolves the most basic problem—all of the values of $(X_i - \bar{X})^2$ are positive—but instead of giving the mean distance to the mean, the equation gives the mean squared distance to the mean. Researchers can get a more easily interpretable figure by taking the square root of both sides. It also may seem strange that the denominator of the equation is $(N-1)$, rather than just N. The reasons for this have to do with what researchers call *degrees of freedom* in a sample. A full explanation is beyond the scope of this section, but it's similar to a Sudoku puzzle: once someone knows all of the numbers in a row except one, he or she automatically knows the last one. The same applies in statistics. If a researcher knows the mean and all of the values except one, he or she can work backward to figure out the last value. (Alternately, if the researcher knows all of the values, he or she can quickly calculate the mean.) As a result, having the mean and all of the values of Xi in the equation is kind of like counting one data point twice, so one is subtracted out. If a data distribution included the entire population, rather than just a sample, the denominator would just be N, though this almost never happens. (In such a case, researchers use the Greek letter σ [sigma] instead of S in the equation.) In practice, though, the difference isn't really important. If a researcher has a dataset so small that the difference between N and $(N-1)$ is an issue, the dataset has much more serious problems. Taking the square root of both sides of the equation results in the expression for s, or the **standard deviation** of the distribution.

$$S = \sqrt{\frac{\sum_{i=1}^{N}\left(X_i = \bar{X}\right)^2}{(N-1)}}$$

Descriptive Statistics

	N	Minimum	Maxmum	Mean	St. Deviation
HHList.9. TOTAL IN HH: CHILDREN UNDER 18 (NOT 18 BY OCT30)	2314	0	7	.69	1.109
Valit N (listwise)	2314				

The standard deviation isn't the same thing as the mean distance to the mean, but it's pretty close. A larger standard deviation means that the data in the distribution are more spread out, and a smaller standard deviation means that the data are more concentrated around the mean. It's not a perfect measure—outliers can drive the standard deviation up because the distances from the mean are squared before they're averaged—but it's generally good enough.

While the logic behind the equation is pretty straightforward—find the mean distance to the mean, square it to get rid of negative values, then take the square root to cancel out the squaring—plugging data into the equation is a laborious process. Thankfully, SPSS can do it very easily. To find the standard deviation of a variable in SPSS, users can simply use the Analyze → Descriptive Statistics → Descriptives command, as discussed in the section on finding the mean. Doing so creates a table on the Output screen that includes the standard deviation. For the number of children variable discussed previously, the standard deviation is 1.1—about the same as the interquartile range. While some people in the dataset have up to seven minor children at home, the mean is a bit less than 1 and generally doesn't go much past 2. (One standard deviation above the mean would be about 1.8.)

Z-SCORES

Once a researcher knows the mean and standard deviation of a dataset, he or she can use this information to compare individual data points in one distribution with individual data points in another distribution. To do this, researchers first standardize the value of individual data points by expressing that value in terms of how many standard deviations away from the mean it is. This standardized value is called a **z-score**.

$$z_i = \frac{\left(X_i - \overline{X}\right)}{S}$$

The z-score (z_i for any particular data point in a distribution (X_i) is simply the distance from the mean, divided by the standard deviation of the distribution. Because the distances from the mean haven't been squared, z-scores can be positive or negative—and in any distribution, the sum of all of the positive scores will be equal to the sum of all of the negative scores—but since there's no need to sum all of the z-scores, this isn't really a problem. Values bigger than the mean will have positive z-scores, values below the mean will have negative z-scores, and a value that's equal to the mean will have a z-score of 0. (It's zero standard deviations away from the mean.) It's pretty easy to carry out this equation manually for individual values of a variable, but SPSS can be helpful for transforming all of the values of a variable into the equivalent z-scores. To do this, users can again use the Analyze → Descriptive Statistics→ Descriptives command and simply check the box on the bottom of the dialog box for Save Standardized Values as Variables.

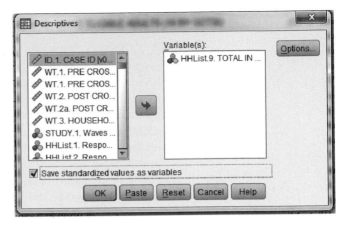

Doing so creates the normal descriptive table in the Output screen and also creates a new variable in the Data View and Variable View screens that is the z-score equivalent of each value of the variable specified. The new variable is listed as the last variable in the dataset, and SPSS automatically names it Z, plus whatever the old variable was called, and creates an appropriate label for it. Be careful to exclude any missing values from the variable before running this command, or the values will be wrong.

1952	v085409f	Numeric	2	0	ZZ09f. POST IWR OBS: Mention 6 - R reactions to IW	{-4, -4. NA (
1953	v085409g	Numeric	2	0	ZZ09g. POST IWR OBS: Mention 7 - R reactions to IW	{-4, -4. NA (
1954	v085409h	Numeric	2	0	ZZ09h. POST IWR OBS: Mention 8 - R reactions to IW	{-4, -4. NA (
1955	Zv081109	Numeric	11	5	Zscore: HHList.9. TOTAL IN HH. CHILDREN UNDER 18 (NOT 18 BY OCT30)	None

By itself, this is interesting, but not terribly useful. The real power of z-scores comes in comparing values from two different distributions and finding the relative likelihood of different values of a distribution. Doing so requires some assumptions. The most important of these is that both data distributions roughly follow a z-distribution—what's commonly referred to as a *normal curve*. A normal curve is unimodal, with one big lump in the middle, and gets smaller and smaller as it stretches out on either side. It's also symmetrical, with the areas above and below the mean mirror images of each other. As with all probability distributions, the total area under the curve is equal to 1. Thankfully, there are lots of real-world variables that fit these requirements, and as long as a data distribution has a very large N (at a minimum, bigger than about 100) and doesn't have any obvious dissimilarities to a z-distribution (for instance, if the distribution were very multimodal or very skewed), researchers can generally treat a variable as if it were normally distributed.

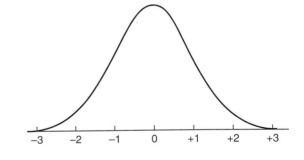

As long as a variable follows the normal distribution, the z-score tells a researcher about the position of an individual data point on the distribution. A z-score of 0 is right in the middle. A 2 is pretty far to the right, and a −3 is very far to the left. It's important to note that while it looks as though the normal curve goes to zero around three standard deviations from the mean, it never quite touches zero. In a normally distributed variable, the frequency of a score three standard deviations from the mean is very, very small, but it's not zero, and in a large enough sample, there will be some cases in which there are z-scores bigger than 3 or smaller than −3.

Using z-scores as relative positions, it's possible to compare very different distributions, as long as they both follow the normal distribution. To show how this works, we can compare impressive records from across sports. Suppose two sports fans were arguing about which is more impressive: Michael Jordan's National Basketball Association (NBA) record of 30.12 points per game across his career or Kareem Abdul-Jabbar's NBA record of 38,387 career points. It might seem as if there's no way to resolve the question, but if these records are distributed according to a normal distribution, it's easy. For each record, we can use the list of the top 100 scores for that record as a data distribution and calculate the z-score for the record at the top of the list. For instance, Michael Jordan has an NBA record career 30.12 points per game. If we look at the top 100 scores for that record (Jordan's record, the second highest career points per game, all the way down to the 100th highest career points per game: Calvin Murphy's 17.91 mean points per game), the mean of the top 100 is a record of 21.30 points per game, with a standard deviation of 2.77. With this information, Jordan's record can be converted to a z-score:

$$z_{Jordan} = \frac{(30.12 - 21.30)}{2.77} = \frac{8.82}{2.77} = 3.18$$

The same can be done for Kareem Abdul-Jabbar's record. Looking at the list of the top 100 NBA total points scored, the mean is 20,885.35, with a standard deviation of 4,725.97, giving Abdul-Jabbar a z-score of:

$$z_{Abdul-Jabbar} = \frac{(38,387 - 20,885.35)}{4,725.97} = \frac{17,501.65}{4,725.97} = 3.70$$

Assuming that the record scores follow a normal distribution, both records are very impressive, with z-scores above 3, but Abdul-Jabbar's record is much farther out on the right of the z-distribution and could therefore be considered more impressive. Note that it doesn't matter that one of the records is expressed in thousands of points while the other is mean points per game because the comparison is just based on the number of standard deviations away from the mean. These same records could be compared with something from another sport entirely, like Cy Young's Major League Baseball (MLB) record of 511 career wins. The list of the top 100 career wins in MLB has a mean of 261.06 wins and a standard deviation of 55.16, giving Young's record a z-score of 4.53—more impressive than either basketball record. No wonder it's a record that's lasted more than a century!

There's no reason why a z-score can't be converted back into a nonstandardized score. Suppose that the arguing sports fans wanted to see how many points per game Jordan would have to have scored in order for his record to be as impressive as Young's amazing record of 511 career wins. Solving the z-score equation for X_i results in:

$$Z_i = \frac{(X_i - \bar{X})}{s}$$

$$S \star Z_i = (X_i - \bar{X})$$
$$(S \star Z_i) + \bar{X} = X_i$$

Put another way, the nonstandardized value corresponding to a given z-score is just the z-score times the standard deviation of the distribution, plus the mean. So, in order for Jordan's record of career mean points per game to be as impressive as Young's record, it would have to be 4.53 standard deviations away from the career points per game mean of 21.30:

$$X_i = (2.77 \star 4.53) + 21.30 = 12.55 + 21.30 = 33.85$$

To be the Cy Young of basketball, Michael Jordan would have to have a mean of 33.85 points per game over his career.

By itself, comparing z-scores from various distributions might be useful for resolving arguments about sports, but z-scores become much more useful when they are turned into likelihoods. The normal curve is important precisely because it's been well studied, and researchers know how to translate any spot in the normal curve into a likelihood. Normally, if a researcher wanted to find the area under a curve above and below a particular point, he or she would need to use integral calculus. For a normal curve, though, the calculus has already been done, and researchers can just consult a table that gives the results.

People's heights, for instance, follow a normal distribution. The mean height of an American male is 1.78 meters, or 5 feet 10 inches (for American women, the average height is 1.63 meters, or 5 feet 4 inches), with a standard deviation of 2.8 inches for both men and women. So, a man who is one standard deviation above the mean—or about 6 feet 1 inch—is the equivalent of a woman who is also one standard deviation above the mean, or about 5 feet 7 inches. We could use this information in any number of ways. For instance, it's thought that men tend to exaggerate their height in online dating profiles. They may believe that women are looking for men who are at least 6 feet tall, and so they list their height as at least 6 feet. A survey of American online dating profiles found that 44 percent of men's profiles on one popular dating site listed their height as 6 feet or greater. Assuming that men on dating sites aren't generally taller or shorter than American men on the whole, it's possible to determine if men on the dating sites are lying about their heights.

The first step is to convert the value of interest into a z-score. In this case, the goal is to determine what percentage of American men are 6 feet or taller. For simplicity, all of the heights are converted to inches (so 6 feet is 72 inches, and the mean of all American men is 70 inches).

$$Z_{6 ft} = \frac{(72 - 70)}{2.8} = \frac{2}{2.8} = .71$$

Because 72 inches is taller than the mean of 70 inches, the z-score is positive; .71 means that a man who is 6 feet tall is .71 standard deviations taller than the mean American man. Then, the z-score table is used to determine the corresponding proportion of the population.

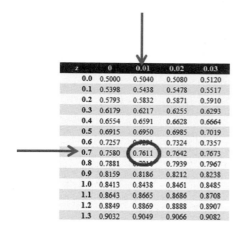

z	0	0.01	0.02	0.03
0.0	0.5000	0.5040	0.5080	0.5120
0.1	0.5398	0.5438	0.5478	0.5517
0.2	0.5793	0.5832	0.5871	0.5910
0.3	0.6179	0.6217	0.6255	0.6293
0.4	0.6554	0.6591	0.6628	0.6664
0.5	0.6915	0.6950	0.6985	0.7019
0.6	0.7257	0.7291	0.7324	0.7357
0.7	0.7580	0.7611	0.7642	0.7673
0.8	0.7881	0.7910	0.7939	0.7967
0.9	0.8159	0.8186	0.8212	0.8238
1.0	0.8413	0.8438	0.8461	0.8485
1.1	0.8643	0.8665	0.8686	0.8708
1.2	0.8849	0.8869	0.8888	0.8907
1.3	0.9032	0.9049	0.9066	0.9082

To use the z–score table, go down the columns to the correct tenths place. In this case, that would be 0.7. Then, go across to the proper hundredths place of the z–score. In this case, the z–score is 0.71, so the hundredths place is 0.01.

At the intersection of the two values is a number that corresponds to the percentage of the population that's expected to have a score less than that z–score. For a z–score of 0.71, the number is 0.761, which tells us that we would expect 76.1 percent of a normally distributed population would have a z–score of less than 0.71. In this case, it means that 76.1 percent of American men are expected to have a height of less than 6 feet. Because the total area under the normal curve is equal to 1, it's also possible to calculate what percent of men have a height greater than 6 feet: $1 - .761 = .239$, or 23.9 percent.

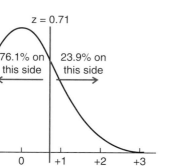

With this result, we can draw some conclusions about men on the dating site. Since 44 percent of men on the dating site listed their height as 6 feet or greater, and only 23.9 percent of men in the overall population are expected to have that height, one of two things is happening. Either men on the dating site aren't a random sample of the overall population—for some reason, tall men use Internet dating more, or short men use it less—or about half of the men who claim to be 6 feet tall on the site are lying about it.

Using the z–score table is a little more complicated for a negative z–score, but not much. Remember that the normal distribution is symmetrical, so the negative values are just mirror images of the positive ones. The procedure for finding the percentage is the same; the only thing different is the interpretation. For negative z–scores, the number in the table represents the percentage of scores in the population that are *greater* than the negative score (rather than less, for positive z–scores). To find out what proportion of men are shorter than 5 feet 6 inches, we'd go through the same process as before, converting the height to a z–score:

$$Z_{5'6"} = \frac{(66 - 70)}{2.8} = \frac{-6}{2.8} = 2.14$$

Then, find the corresponding z–score in the table, this time ignoring the negative sign. The number at the intersection of 2.1 and .04 is .9838. If this were a positive z–score, this would mean that 98.38 percent of the population would be expected to have a score less than this. Since it's a negative z–score, it means that 98.38 percent of the population is expected to have a z–score *greater* than -2.14, or that 98.38 percent of American men are expected to be taller than 5 feet 6 inches. With this number, it's then easy to figure out that $1 - .9838 = .0162$, or 1.62 percent of American men are 5 feet 6 inches or shorter.

These z-scores have lots of other applications, as discussed below and in the next chapter, when they are used to create margins of error and standard errors of estimates and form the basis for hypothesis testing.

MARGIN OF ERROR

In Chapter 11, there is a discussion of how larger sample sizes in a survey tend to reduce the likelihood of getting a result that's far away from the actual value in a population. If this sounds like a standard deviation, there's a reason. In fact, the range attached to a survey estimate is calculated in much the same way as a standard deviation. Anyone who's read about public opinion surveys is familiar with the concept of a margin of error: press reports of surveys generally say something along the lines of "25 percent of Americans, plus or minus 3.5 points, believe that President Bush knew about the 9/11 attacks before they happened." The 3.5 points, in this case, is the margin of error attached to the estimate. Calculating this margin of error is just

z	0	0.01	0.02	0.03	0.04	0.05
0.0	0.5000	0.5040	0.5080	0.5120	0.5160	0.5199
0.1	0.5398	0.5438	0.5478	0.5517	0.5557	0.5596
0.2	0.5793	0.5832	0.5871	0.5910	0.5948	0.5987
0.3	0.6179	0.6217	0.6255	0.6293	0.6331	0.6368
0.4	0.6554	0.6591	0.6628	0.6664	0.6700	0.6736
0.5	0.6915	0.6950	0.6985	0.7019	0.7054	0.7088
0.6	0.7257	0.7291	0.7324	0.7357	0.7389	0.7422
0.7	0.7580	0.7611	0.7642	0.7673	0.7704	0.7734
0.8	0.7881	0.7910	0.7939	0.7967	0.7995	0.8023
0.9	0.8159	0.8186	0.8212	0.8238	0.8264	0.8289
1.0	0.8413	0.8438	0.8461	0.8485	0.8508	0.8531
1.1	0.8643	0.8665	0.8686	0.8708	0.8729	0.8749
1.2	0.8849	0.8869	0.8888	0.8907	0.8925	0.8944
1.3	0.9032	0.9049	0.9066	0.9082	0.9099	0.9115
1.4	0.9192	0.9207	0.9222	0.9236	0.9251	0.9265
1.5	0.9332	0.9345	0.9357	0.9370	0.9382	0.9394
1.6	0.9452	0.9463	0.9474	0.9484	0.9495	0.9505
1.7	0.9554	0.9564	0.9573	0.9582	0.9591	0.9599
1.8	0.9641	0.9649	0.9656	0.9664	0.9671	0.9678
1.9	0.9713	0.9719	0.9726	0.9732	0.9738	0.9744
2.0	0.9772	0.9778	0.9783	0.9788	0.9793	0.9798
2.1	0.9821	0.9826	0.9830	0.9834	0.9838	0.9842
2.2	0.9861	0.9864	0.9868	0.9871	0.9875	0.9878
2.3	0.9893	0.9896	0.9898	0.9901	0.9904	0.9906

a matter of knowing something about the question being asked and using the z-score table appropriately.

Whenever researchers try to draw conclusions about an entire population based on a randomly selected sample of that population, there's bound to be some error. No matter what precautions the researcher takes, there's always the chance that the randomly selected portion of the population was just weird in some way—too many men, too few minorities—and not representative of the population as a whole. The beauty of random sampling in surveys isn't that it minimizes that risk (though it helps) but that it allows researchers to precisely calculate how wrong they're likely to be.

There are three moving parts to this calculation. The first is the size of the sample. The most commonly used example of this is flipping a coin. If a coin is flipped just ten times, there's a pretty good chance that heads (or tails) will come up 70 percent of the time. If the coin is flipped 100 times, the probably of heads coming up 70 percent of the time is tiny. If the coin is flipped 1,000 times and comes out on one side 70 percent of the time, the coin is weighted. The same logic applies to survey samples: a very small sample might wind up not being very representative due to random chance, but as the sample size increases, that likelihood decreases. As described in Chapter 11, however, the relationship isn't that easy. There are decreasing marginal returns to increases in sample size. A sample of 1,000 is much more likely to be representative than a sample of 500, but a sample of 1,500 isn't much better than a sample of 1,000.

The second part of the margin of error calculation is the standard error of the estimate. "Standard error" sounds a lot like "standard deviation," and it is. How researchers determine the standard error depends on the kind of variable being analyzed. If the variable is a dichotomous variable—such as a question in which respondents can say "yes" or "no" to something, with no categories in between—then the standard error is:

$$SE = \frac{p(1 - p)}{\sqrt{N}}$$

In this equation, p is the proportion of respondents who say "yes" (or "no") to the question, while N is the size of the sample. Because N is in the denominator, the larger the sample size is, the smaller the standard error will be. In the numerator, the expression gives bigger standard errors when the proportion of yes or no responses is closer to .5, and smaller when it's closer to 0 or 1. In the 2010 ANES, for instance, 4.1 percent of respondents (p = .041) say that they are homosexual or bisexual. The N of the survey is 2,274, so the standard error of the estimate is:

$$SE = \frac{.041(1 - .041)}{\sqrt{2,274}} = \frac{.041(.959)}{47.69} = \frac{0.039}{47.69} = .00083$$

If the proportion of respondents were closer to .5, the standard error would be larger. For instance, 57.7 percent of respondents in the same survey, with the same sample size, identified themselves as belonging to a Protestant religious denomination. The only difference is the proportion in the category, but the standard error is six times as big:

$$SE = \frac{.577(1 - .577)}{\sqrt{2,274}} = \frac{.577(.423)}{47.69} = \frac{0.244}{47.69} = .00512$$

For variables that have more categories—and can be treated as interval- or ratio-level variables—researchers can use the standard deviation rather than the proportion in the category. As such, the equation for interval- or ratio-level variables is:

$$SE = \frac{S}{\sqrt{N}}$$

Once the standard deviation is calculated, this equation is straightforward: the larger the standard deviation of the variable, the larger the standard error will be. In the same dataset, 1,969 respondents gave their views of atheists on a feeling thermometer scale, ranging from 0 to 100, with higher values representing warmer feelings. The mean score given by respondents on the survey is 39.95, with a standard deviation of 26.27, so the standard error of the estimate is:

$$SE = \frac{26.27}{\sqrt{1,969}} = \frac{26.27}{44.37} = .592$$

The final element needed to find the margin of error of an estimate is the desired level of confidence in the estimate. When the margin of error is presented as "25 percent of Americans, plus or minus 3.5 points," there's an important element being left out. Generally, the margin of error presented in media reports is a 95 percent confidence interval, meaning that the researchers can be 95 percent certain that if they did the survey again, the result would be within 3.5 points of 25 percent, or between 21.5 percent and 28.5 percent. This can also be understood as meaning that the researchers are 95 percent certain that the true value in the population is somewhere within that same range. If the researchers wanted to be 99 percent confident that the true value in the population was within the range, the range would have to be bigger: maybe 4.5 points instead of 3.5. The question is, *how* much bigger does it have to be?

In order to make this calculation, researchers go back to the z-score table. Think of the mean of the estimate as being at z = 0. If the researcher wants 95 percent confidence in the estimate (also called a 95 percent confidence interval), that means just a 2.5 percent chance that the estimate is too low and a 2.5 percent chance that the estimate is too high. To calculate the z-score that corresponds to a 2.5 percent chance on either side, researchers use the z-score table in reverse. Since the z-score table gives the proportion that's less than that z-score, researchers just look for the value that corresponds to 97.5 percent.

z	0	0.01	0.02	0.03	0.04	0.05	0.06	0.07
0.0	0.5000	0.5040	0.5080	0.5120	0.5160	0.5199	0.5239	0.5279
0.1	0.5398	0.5438	0.5478	0.5517	0.5557	0.5596	0.5636	0.5675
0.2	0.5793	0.5832	0.5871	0.5910	0.5948	0.5987	0.6026	0.6064
0.3	0.6179	0.6217	0.6255	0.6293	0.6331	0.6368	0.6406	0.6443
0.4	0.6554	0.6591	0.6628	0.6664	0.6700	0.6736	0.6772	0.6808
0.5	0.6915	0.6950	0.6985	0.7019	0.7054	0.7088	0.7123	0.7157
0.6	0.7257	0.7291	0.7324	0.7357	0.7389	0.7422	0.7454	0.7486
0.7	0.7580	0.7611	0.7642	0.7673	0.7704	0.7734	0.7764	0.7794
0.8	0.7881	0.7910	0.7939	0.7967	0.7995	0.8023	0.8051	0.8078
0.9	0.8159	0.8186	0.8212	0.8238	0.8264	0.8289	0.8315	0.8340
1.0	0.8413	0.8438	0.8461	0.8485	0.8508	0.8531	0.8554	0.8577
1.1	0.8643	0.8665	0.8686	0.8708	0.8729	0.8749	0.8770	0.8790
1.2	0.8849	0.8869	0.8888	0.8907	0.8925	0.8944	0.8962	0.8980
1.3	0.9032	0.9049	0.9066	0.9082	0.9099	0.9115	0.9131	0.9147
1.4	0.9192	0.9207	0.9222	0.9236	0.9251	0.9265	0.9279	0.9292
1.5	0.9332	0.9345	0.9357	0.9370	0.9382	0.9394	0.9406	0.9418
1.6	0.9452	0.9463	0.9474	0.9484	0.9495	0.9505	0.9515	0.9525
1.7	0.9554	0.9564	0.9573	0.9582	0.9591	0.9599	0.9608	0.9616
1.8	0.9641	0.9649	0.9656	0.9664	0.9671	0.9678	0.9686	0.9693
1.9	0.9713	0.9719	0.9726	0.9732	0.9738	0.9744	0.9750	0.9756
2.0	0.9772	0.9778	0.9783	0.9788	0.9793	0.9798	0.9803	0.9808
2.1	0.9821	0.9826	0.9830	0.9834	0.9838	0.9842	0.9846	0.9850

A z-score of 1.96 corresponds to 97.5 percent of values that are smaller, and, therefore, 2.5 percent that are bigger.

Going back to the normal distribution, this means that the researcher can be 95 percent confident that the true value is within 1.96 standard errors (rather than standard deviations) of the estimated mean. The equation for this margin of error, then, is just

$$\text{MOE}: \overline{X} \mp SE \star Z^*$$

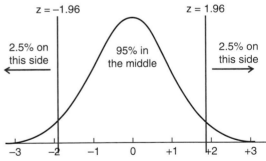

In this equation, the margin of error is the mean of the estimate, plus or minus the standard error multiplied by the appropriate z-score. For 95 percent confidence, the appropriate z-score is 1.96 because that score corresponds to a 2.5 percent likelihood of being too high and a 2.5 percent chance of being too low, for a total of a 5 percent chance of being within the range. If the researchers instead wanted a 99 percent confidence interval, they could find the appropriate z-score by looking in the z-score table for a value corresponding to a 0.5 percent chance of being too high or too low (for a total of a 1 percent chance of being out of the range). This means a z-score of 2.57.

z	0	0.01	0.02	0.03	0.04	0.05	0.06	0.07	0.08
0.0	0.5000	0.5040	0.5080	0.5120	0.5160	0.5199	0.5239	0.5279	0.5319
0.1	0.5398	0.5438	0.5478	0.5517	0.5557	0.5596	0.5636	0.5675	0.5714
0.2	0.5793	0.5832	0.5871	0.5910	0.5948	0.5987	0.6026	0.6064	0.6103
0.3	0.6179	0.6217	0.6255	0.6293	0.6331	0.6368	0.6406	0.6443	0.6480
0.4	0.6554	0.6591	0.6628	0.6664	0.6700	0.6736	0.6772	0.6808	0.6844
0.5	0.6915	0.6950	0.6985	0.7019	0.7054	0.7088	0.7123	0.7157	0.7190
0.6	0.7257	0.7291	0.7324	0.7357	0.7389	0.7422	0.7454	0.7486	0.7517
0.7	0.7580	0.7611	0.7642	0.7673	0.7704	0.7734	0.7764	0.7794	0.7823
0.8	0.7881	0.7910	0.7939	0.7967	0.7995	0.8023	0.8051	0.8078	0.8106
0.9	0.8159	0.8186	0.8212	0.8238	0.8264	0.8289	0.8315	0.8340	0.8365
1.0	0.8413	0.8438	0.8461	0.8485	0.8508	0.8531	0.8554	0.8577	0.8599
1.1	0.8643	0.8665	0.8686	0.8708	0.8729	0.8749	0.8770	0.8790	0.8810
1.2	0.8849	0.8869	0.8888	0.8907	0.8925	0.8944	0.8962	0.8980	0.8997
1.3	0.9032	0.9049	0.9066	0.9082	0.9099	0.9115	0.9131	0.9147	0.9162
1.4	0.9192	0.9207	0.9222	0.9236	0.9251	0.9265	0.9279	0.9292	0.9306
1.5	0.9332	0.9345	0.9357	0.9370	0.9382	0.9394	0.9406	0.9418	0.9429
1.6	0.9452	0.9463	0.9474	0.9484	0.9495	0.9505	0.9515	0.9525	0.9535
1.7	0.9554	0.9564	0.9573	0.9582	0.9591	0.9599	0.9608	0.9616	0.9625
1.8	0.9641	0.9649	0.9656	0.9664	0.9671	0.9678	0.9686	0.9693	0.9699
1.9	0.9713	0.9719	0.9726	0.9732	0.9738	0.9744	0.9750	0.9756	0.9761
2.0	0.9772	0.9778	0.9783	0.9788	0.9793	0.9798	0.9803	0.9808	0.9812
2.1	0.9821	0.9826	0.9830	0.9834	0.9838	0.9842	0.9846	0.9850	0.9854
2.2	0.9861	0.9864	0.9868	0.9871	0.9875	0.9878	0.9881	0.9884	0.9887
2.3	0.9893	0.9896	0.9898	0.9901	0.9904	0.9906	0.9909	0.9911	0.9913
2.4	0.9918	0.9920	0.9922	0.9925	0.9927	0.9929	0.9931	0.9932	0.9934
2.5	0.9938	0.9940	0.9941	0.9943	0.9945	0.9946	0.9948	0.9949	0.9951
2.6	0.9953	0.9955	0.9956	0.9957	0.9959	0.9960	0.9961	0.9962	0.9963

In the 2010 ANES, the mean score of respondents on the feeling thermometer for atheists was 39.95, with a standard error of .592, so the margin of error would be:

$$\text{MOE: } 39.95 \mp 0.592 \star 1.96$$
$$\text{MOE: } 39.95 \mp 1.16$$

The small standard error—a function of the small standard deviation and the large sample size—means that the researchers can be 95 percent confident that the true value for views of atheists in the population is between $(39.95 - 1.16 = 38.79)$ 38.8 and $(39.95 + 1.16 = 41.11)$ 41.1. If the researchers instead wanted a 99 percent confidence interval, the only difference in the equation would be replacing the z-score of 1.96 with one of 2.57, giving:

$$\text{MOE: } 39.95 \mp 0.592 \star 2.57$$
$$\text{MOE: } 39.95 \mp 1.52$$

Or a true value between 38.4 and 41.5. These results indicate that the survey estimates are very accurate—probably within a point or two of the true values in the population—but a lot of this is driven by the large sample size. If the sample size were smaller—say, 500 instead of 1,969—the standard error of the estimate would be larger

$$\text{SE} = \frac{26.27}{\sqrt{500}} = \frac{26.27}{22.36} = 1.17$$

And the 95 percent confidence interval would be much larger as well, giving a range that's between 37.6 and 42.3

$$\text{MOE: } 39.95 \mp 1.17 \star 1.96$$
$$\text{MOE: } 39.95 \mp 2.30$$

Researchers will often refer to "statistically significant differences," or even just "significant differences," and this is what they are referring to. If the 95 percent confidence interval around the estimate of 39.95 was 37.6 to 42.3, a researcher could say that the estimate was significantly different from any number less than 37.6 or more than 42.3. If the researcher wanted to compare it to a figure that was between 37.6 and 42.3, the researcher could say that the difference was not statistically significant. Also note that such statements always imply a confidence

z	0	0.01	0.02	0.03	0.04	0.05	0.06	0.07	0.08	0.09
0.0	0.5000	0.5040	0.5080	0.5120	0.5160	0.5199	0.5239	0.5279	0.5319	0.5359
0.1	0.5398	0.5438	0.5478	0.5517	0.5557	0.5596	0.5636	0.5675	0.5714	0.5753
0.2	0.5793	0.5832	0.5871	0.5910	0.5948	0.5987	0.6026	0.6064	0.6103	0.6141
0.3	0.6179	0.6217	0.6255	0.6293	0.6331	0.6368	0.6406	0.6443	0.6480	0.6517
0.4	0.6554	0.6591	0.6628	0.6664	0.6700	0.6736	0.6772	0.6808	0.6844	0.6879
0.5	0.6915	0.6950	0.6985	0.7019	0.7054	0.7088	0.7123	0.7157	0.7190	0.7224
0.6	0.7257	0.7291	0.7324	0.7357	0.7389	0.7422	0.7454	0.7486	0.7517	0.7549
0.7	0.7580	0.7611	0.7642	0.7673	0.7704	0.7734	0.7764	0.7794	0.7823	0.7852
0.8	0.7881	0.7910	0.7939	0.7967	0.7995	0.8023	0.8051	0.8078	0.8106	0.8133
0.9	0.8159	0.8186	0.8212	0.8238	0.8264	0.8289	0.8315	0.8340	0.8365	0.8389
1.0	0.8413	0.8438	0.8461	0.8485	0.8508	0.8531	0.8554	0.8577	0.8599	0.8621
1.1	0.8643	0.8665	0.8686	0.8708	0.8729	0.8749	0.8770	0.8790	0.8810	0.8830
1.2	0.8849	0.8869	0.8888	0.8907	0.8925	0.8944	0.8962	0.8980	0.8997	0.9015
1.3	0.9032	0.9049	0.9066	0.9082	0.9099	0.9115	0.9131	0.9147	0.9162	0.9177
1.4	0.9192	0.9207	0.9222	0.9236	0.9251	0.9265	0.9279	0.9292	0.9306	0.9319
1.5	0.9332	0.9345	0.9357	0.9370	0.9382	0.9394	0.9406	0.9418	0.9429	0.9441
1.6	0.9452	0.9463	0.9474	0.9484	0.9495	0.9505	0.9515	0.9525	0.9535	0.9545
1.7	0.9554	0.9564	0.9573	0.9582	0.9591	0.9599	0.9608	0.9616	0.9625	0.9633
1.8	0.9641	0.9649	0.9656	0.9664	0.9671	0.9678	0.9686	0.9693	0.9699	0.9706
1.9	0.9713	0.9719	0.9726	0.9732	0.9738	0.9744	0.9750	0.9756	0.9761	0.9767
2.0	0.9772	0.9778	0.9783	0.9788	0.9793	0.9798	0.9803	0.9808	0.9812	0.9817
2.1	0.9821	0.9826	0.9830	0.9834	0.9838	0.9842	0.9846	0.9850	0.9854	0.9857
2.2	0.9861	0.9864	0.9868	0.9871	0.9875	0.9878	0.9881	0.9884	0.9887	0.9890
2.3	0.9893	0.9896	0.9898	0.9901	0.9904	0.9906	0.9909	0.9911	0.9913	0.9916
2.4	0.9918	0.9920	0.9922	0.9925	0.9927	0.9929	0.9931	0.9932	0.9934	0.9936
2.5	0.9938	0.9940	0.9941	0.9943	0.9945	0.9946	0.9948	0.9949	0.9951	0.9952
2.6	0.9953	0.9955	0.9956	0.9957	0.9959	0.9960	0.9961	0.9962	0.9963	0.9964
2.7	0.9965	0.9966	0.9967	0.9968	0.9969	0.9970	0.9971	0.9972	0.9973	0.9974
2.8	0.9974	0.9975	0.9976	0.9977	0.9977	0.9978	0.9979	0.9979	0.9980	0.9981
2.9	0.9981	0.9982	0.9982	0.9983	0.9984	0.9984	0.9985	0.9985	0.9986	0.9986
3.0	0.9987	0.9987	0.9987	0.9988	0.9988	0.9989	0.9989	0.9989	0.9990	0.9990
3.1	0.9990	0.9991	0.9991	0.9991	0.9992	0.9992	0.9992	0.9992	0.9993	0.9993
3.2	0.9993	0.9993	0.9994	0.9994	0.9994	0.9994	0.9994	0.9995	0.9995	0.9995
3.3	0.9995	0.9995	0.9995	0.9996	0.9996	0.9996	0.9996	0.9996	0.9996	0.9997
3.4	0.9997	0.9997	0.9997	0.9997	0.9997	0.9997	0.9997	0.9997	0.9997	0.9998

Z-Score Table: Area under the Normal Curve below the Given Z-Score

interval. Generally, when researchers talk about a difference being statistically significant, they are talking about a 95 percent confidence interval because this is considered the default value for social sciences. Under some circumstances (if a 5 percent chance of error is too great for some reason or if there are limitations on the data that make a 95 percent confidence interval inappropriate) researchers may use a 99 percent, or even a 90 percent, confidence interval. When they do so, however, they will almost certainly state that they're doing so and explain why.

SUMMARY

Once the data from a survey—or any other quantitative research technique—have been collected, it's time to carry out analyses. The most basic analyses are descriptive, looking at the measures of central tendency and dispersion, and often involve making graphs of the variable. In the past, this could be a time-consuming process—university researchers even had art departments to help make graphs—but today, it's easy for anyone with the right software to carry out descriptive analyses or make graphs.

There are any number of programs that can carry out these sorts of analyses, but SPSS is the most widely used basic software for social science students. In SPSS, the user can choose from three different screens, each with a different function: the Data View screen, the Variable View screen, and the Output document. Using these screens, users can set up the data in order to facilitate analysis, then see the results of their work.

Although SPSS makes it easy to carry out analyses, users must be careful to pick the descriptives that are most useful for the variable in question. While mean and standard deviation are the most frequently used basic descriptives, they aren't useful for every variable. Under certain circumstances, the mean and standard deviation can be combined to create the standardized form of a variable, or the z-score. These z-scores can be compared across variables following a normal distribution and can be converted to percentages, telling researchers what percent of cases in a distribution are expected to be above or below that score. This same principle allows survey researchers using SRS to determine the margin of error around their sample statistics.

Study and Review

1. In the past 20 years, there has been increasing concern about an obesity epidemic in the United States. Since 1990, the mean weight of American men ages twenty to seventy-four has increased from 180 pounds to 196 pounds, while the mean weight of American women in the same age range has increased from 142 pounds to 160 pounds. However, over the same period, the median weight of Americans has only increased by six pounds for men and eight pounds for women. What does this imply about the distribution of this variable? About the obesity epidemic generally? If you were to graph the variable, what do you suppose it would look like?

2. Comparing the weight distribution of Americans in 1990 and now, would you guess that the standard deviation has gone up or down? Why?

3. Perhaps the most impressive record in NBA basketball is John Stockton's record of 15,806 career assists. In the list of the top 100 career assists, the mean is 5,765.84, with a standard deviation of 1,886.54. Stockton's record is often overlooked, as assists aren't as flashy as points or blocks, but how many points would Michael Jordan have had to have scored per game over his career in order to match Stockton's z-score? (Jordan's record is 30.12 career points per game; the list of the top 100 has a mean of 21.30 with a standard deviation of 2.77.)

4. The College Board, which administers the SATs and other standardized tests, ensures that every year the mean score on each of the subjects in the SAT is about 500, on an 800-point scale (the actual mean scores in 2012 were 496 for critical reading, 514 for math, and 488 for reading), so the mean total score is almost exactly 1500. The College Board also strives to ensure that the standard deviation of each section is 100, giving a total standard deviation across the three sections of 300. Approximately 1.6 million students take the test each year. Assuming that scores on the SAT follow a normal distribution, about how many get more than 2000 for a combined score? How many get less than 1500? How many get between 1800 and 2200?

CHAPTER 13

Quantitative Methods II: Multivariate Relationships

Learning Objectives

- Be able to explain the utility of crosstabs for social science researchers
- Be able to identify the parts of a scatterplot
- Be able to use correlations to summarize the relationships between two variables
- Be able to identify the functions of OLS regression for social science researchers
- Be able to generate and test hypotheses regarding regression coefficients
- Be able to make use of dummy and control variables when appropriate
- Be able to interpret the results of multivariate regression models

The techniques in the previous chapter only looked at the characteristics of a single variable, but researchers in the social sciences are often much more interested in the relationships between variables. While describing individual variables can help to familiarize researchers with social phenomena, the main job of a social science researcher is to think through cause and effect (independent and dependent variables) and test theories about the relationships.

This chapter is made up of ways to analyze the relationships between variables, but many of the decisions about what kind of analysis to use are driven by the types of variables being analyzed. Many of the more sophisticated techniques require that one or more of the variables are at the interval or ratio levels; when dealing with nominal- or ordinal-level variables, simpler techniques often must suffice.

CROSSTABS

The most basic way to look at the relationship between two variables is through a **crosstab** (also called a *contingency table* or a *two-way table*): essentially a frequency table for two variables at the same time. These tables simultaneously display the frequencies of the two variables of interest and give a basic idea of the relationship between them. Unlike many of the other techniques, which work best for interval- and ratio-level variables, crosstabs are generally most useful when both variables are on the nominal or ordinal level.

For instance, it's believed that one of the reasons that Americans have become more supportive of legal protections for homosexuals in recent years is that more homosexuals have come out of the closet, and people with a homosexual friend or relative are more accepting of homosexuality. To test the relationship between having a homosexual friend or relative and support for a particular issue (say, marriage equality), a researcher could run a crosstab.

In this crosstab, the columns denote whether a respondent has any family or friends who are homosexuals—1,121 out of the 2,195 valid cases on this variable said "yes"—and the rows denote the respondents' opinions on marriage equality. (The descriptions of the values have been changed slightly from the original dataset to make them clearer.) The values in the rows show that 841 respondents out of the 2,195 total valid cases support marriage equality, 805 oppose it, and 549 oppose marriage equality but support civil unions for homosexual couples. These total figures, found along the bottom of the chart for the columns and the

Count

		X12a. Sexual orientation of family and friends		Total
		1. Yes	5. No	
X16. R position on gay marriage	Marriage should be allowed	558	283	841
	Marriage should not be allowed	295	510	805
	Oppose Marriage, Support Civil Unions	268	281	549
Total		1121	1074	2195

side of the chart for the rows, are called the **marginals**, or marginal values. The figure at the bottom right shows the total number of respondents for which there are valid cases for both of the variables in the crosstab.

In addition to the marginals, the crosstab also has cells that represent the intersection of the two variables. The cells show, for instance, that there are 558 respondents who both have a homosexual friend or family member and support marriage equality, while there are 283 respondents who support marriage equality but don't have any homosexual friends or relatives.

Making this sort of crosstab in the software program SPSS is simply a matter of going to Analyze → Descriptive Statistics → Crosstabs and choosing the variables for the rows and columns in the crosstab. Users can select as many variables as they like, and SPSS will generate a crosstab in the Output screen for each combination of rows and columns listed.

The problem with this simple crosstab table, though, is that it requires the user to do quite a bit of math to draw conclusions about the relationships between the variables. For instance, the crosstab shows that there are more supporters of marriage equality who have homosexual friends and relatives (558) than there are supporters of marriage equality who don't (283), but there are also more respondents with homosexual friends and relatives (1,121) than there are respondents who don't (1,074). The real question isn't whether the number of respondents in one cell is bigger than the other, but rather whether respondents with homosexual family and friends are more likely to support marriage equality. To answer this question, it's necessary to look at percentages, rather than just frequencies. A researcher could do this by hand: divide the value in each cell by the appropriate marginal value and compare the results, but it's easier to have the computer do it.

To have the crosstab display the percentages, rather than just the frequencies, users can open the dialog box for Crosstabs, then click the Cells button on the top right side of the box. This opens up a new dialog box. To show the percentages for either the rows or columns, check the boxes next to Row or Column, as appropriate, then click OK. In addition, users can choose to look at just the percentages, and not the frequencies, by unchecking the box for Observed (under Counts) at the top left side of the dialog box.

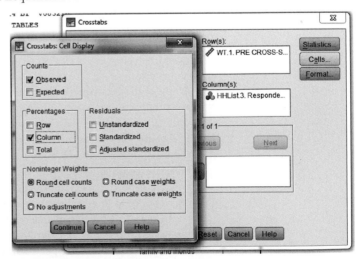

X16. R position on gay marriage *X12a. Sexual orientation of family and friends Crosstabulation

			X12a. Sexual orientation of family and friends		
			1. Yes	5. No	Total
X16. R position on gay marriage	Marriage should be allowed	Count	558	283	841
		% within X12a. Sexual orientation of family and friends	49.8%	26.4%	38.3%
	Marriage should not be allowed	Count	295	510	805
		% within X12a. Sexual orientation of family and friends	26.3%	47.5%	36.7%
	Oppose Marriage, Support Civil Unions	Count	268	281	549
		% within X12a. Sexual orientation of family and friends	23.9%	26.2%	25.0%
Total		Count	1121	1074	2195
		% within X12a. Sexual orientation of family and friends	100.0%	100.0%	100.0%

The resulting crosstab gives the total number of respondents in each cell, as well as the percentage of each row that the number of respondents represents. This shows that the 558 respondents who both have homosexual friends or family and are in support of marriage equality are 49.8 percent of all respondents who have homosexual friends or family. Only 26.4 percent of respondents without any homosexual friends of family members support marriage equality. Based on this, it seems likely that having homosexual friends or family members increases the likelihood that a respondent will support marriage equality. The table would look cleaner if the frequencies were removed, but researchers are generally cautious about doing this. If there are no frequencies on a crosstab, it's impossible to know if the percentages are based on a large sample or a small one, and researchers might wind up drawing conclusions when there isn't sufficient data to support them.

SCATTERPLOTS AND CORRELATIONS

Many of the basic questions about the relationships between variables can be answered with crosstabs, but crosstabs don't always work, especially if one or both of the variables have a large number of categories. When one or both of the variables are at the interval or ratio level, the easiest way to look at the relationship between them is through a **scatterplot**. The scatterplot is a bivariate graph, in which one variable is on the x-axis (horizontal) and the other variable is on the y-axis (vertical), and each respondent is represented by a point corresponding to its values on the two variables.

In the 2012 Presidential election, pundits and pollsters argued that the incumbent President, Barack Obama, would have a difficult time winning reelection because of the persistently high unemployment rate. As they pointed out, no President in the previous 100 years had ever won reelection when the unemployment rate was above 7.2 percent, and everyone agreed that it would be well above that on Election Day. (The unemployment rate on Election Day wound up being 7.8 percent.) Nate Silver (2011), a statistical analyst working for *The New York Times* (now working with ESPN), tackled this issue by looking at the relationship between the incumbent party's margin of victory in the Presidential election and the unemployment rate for all Presidential elections between 1948 and 2008. Both of the variables in the analysis are ratio level: a party's margin of victory could be positive or negative and could range from −100 percent to 100 percent, and the unemployment rate could be anywhere between 0 and 100 percent. As such, a crosstab wouldn't tell Silver much, but on a scatterplot, the relationship looks like this:

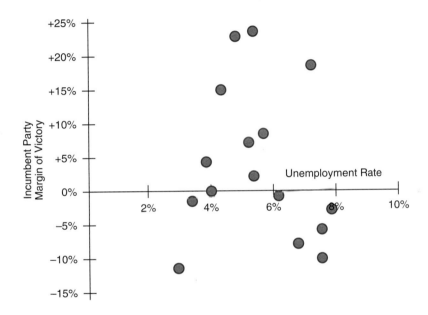

Based on this relationship and other ways of splitting up the data, he concluded that there was no significant relationship between the unemployment rate on Election Day and how many votes the incumbent party won in the Presidential election. While there are plenty of cases at the bottom right hand side of the scatterplot (representing cases in which there was a high unemployment rate and the incumbent party lost the election), there are also plenty of cases toward the top right (in which the incumbent party won despite high unemployment), and even some on the bottom left (in which the incumbent party lost despite low unemployment). He was sure to point out that this doesn't mean that the unemployment rate doesn't matter—just that the relationship between unemployment and a President's chances of reelection isn't that simple.

Silver's (2011) analysis, as he also notes, was hampered by the small number of data points. There simply haven't been that many Presidential elections similar to the one that he was trying to predict, and this makes it harder to find patterns in the data. Such patterns are more likely to emerge when researchers look at a large dataset, such as the 2010 American National Election Study discussed in the previous chapter. Suppose a researcher wanted to look at the relationship between a respondent's age and his or her view of homosexuals. In the 2010 ANES, age goes from 17 to 90, while the feeling thermometer measure for homosexuals runs from 0 to 100. That means that a crosstab would have (73 × 101 =) 7,373 cells—far more than any researcher can easily look through. Researchers could turn these ratio-level variables into ordinal categories—dividing age up into ten-year ranges, for instance—but this should generally be avoided, as it means throwing away some of the variance in the data unnecessarily. More important, while crosstabs don't work with interval- or ratio-level variables, there are many techniques that *only* work with them, and dividing up the variables into ranges wouldn't allow use of these techniques.

Where there's a very large sample size, however, the scatterplot can be too crowded to be easily interpreted. As a result, it's often easier to graph the median of one variable (in this example, feeling thermometer toward homosexuals) for each value of the other variable (age).

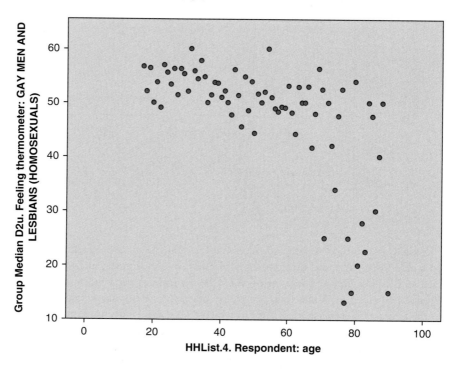

In this scatterplot, the relationship between age and the respondent's views of homosexuals seems clear. As respondents get older, they tend to have more negative views of homosexuals: as age goes up (moving to the right), the view of homosexuals goes down.

Making a scatterplot like this in SPSS is much like making other kinds of graphs. Open the Chart Builder with Graphs → Chart Builder. Choose

Scatter/Dot from the list on the bottom left of the dialog box, and drag the variables from the list on the top left to the *x*- and *y*-axis.

Clicking OK at this point will create a simple scatterplot—but because of the large sample size, it may be too crowded, with many of the points on top of each other, making it difficult to interpret. In this case, the problem is exacerbated by the fact that feeling thermometers aren't entirely continuous. Respondents can't choose values in between categories, and most respondents tend to pick values divisible by five. So, the simple scatterplot looks like this:

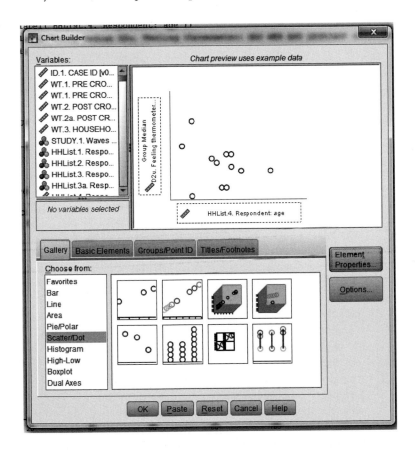

To get a cleaner, more easily interpretable scatterplot, users need to specify that the *y*-axis (which now shows a value of the homosexual feeling thermometer for each respondent) should instead show a median value for each value of age. Doing this is a matter of clicking on Element Properties on the right side of the Graph Builder dialog box, about halfway down. This brings up a separate dialog box: under Statistics, chose Group Median (or mean or any of the other available values), then click OK to create the scatterplot in the Output screen.

When researchers look at scatterplots, they're typically looking for linear relationships: ones that can be summed up by saying that when one variable goes

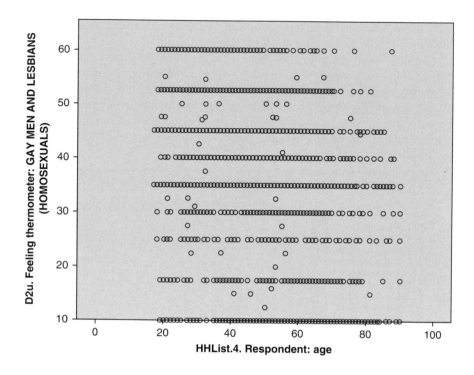

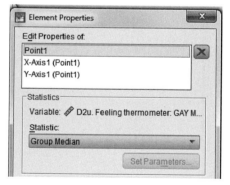

up, the other variable goes up (or down). If both variables tend to go up together, they have a positive relationship; if one goes down as the other goes up, they have a negative relationship. Of course, the direction of the relationship is dependent on how the variables are coded, so researchers need to be careful about keeping track of the coding of the variables when dealing with these relationships.

While researchers can get a sense of what the relationship between the two variables looks like by examining the crosstab, they can get a better idea by looking at the correlation between the two variables. The **correlation** is a summary of the linear relationship between the two variables. It's bounded by negative one and positive one, with negative values representing negative relationships, positive values representing positive relationships, and figures close to zero representing no relationship at all. In the examples below, the scatterplot on the top left represents a negative relationship, the scatterplot on the top right represents a positive relationship, and the scatterplot on the bottom is a correlation near zero.

The correlation between two variables—denoted in equations as r and often referred to as Pearson's r (after Karl Pearson, a German/British statistician who founded the world's first university statistics department and is otherwise best known for his work on eugenics) or the coefficient of correlation—isn't hard to calculate by hand, but for large datasets it takes a great deal of time, so it's better to let the computer do it. In essence, what Pearson's r does is create a line that summarizes the relationship between the variables. There's no real dataset in

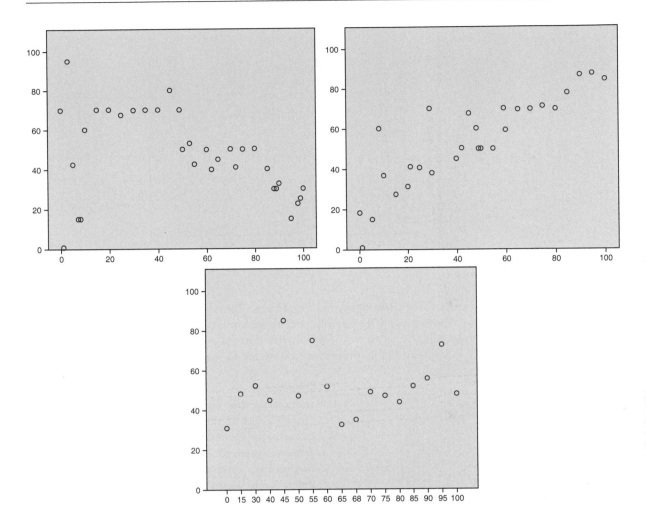

which all of the data fall perfectly along this line. If nothing else, there will be error in the reporting or recording of the data, so some of the data won't be on the line, even in a very strong relationship. The distance between any individual point and the line of best fit is what researchers refer to as *error*. This error could be the result of things such as respondents not understanding a question or lying or the data being recorded incorrectly. It could also be the result of another variable having an impact on the relationship. Often, there are outliers in the relationship—values that seem to be well above or below the line without any good reason. It's important to note this because correlation is responsive to outliers, and they tend to have a disproportionate effect on the correlation.

At first glance, it may seem as if correlation is the perfect way to describe the relationship between two variables, but there are some problems with it. The first is that it only describes linear relationships, and many of the most

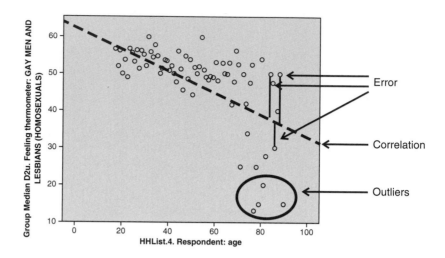

interesting relationships just aren't linear. The relationship between age and views of homosexuals, for instance, doesn't appear to be linear. From the scatterplot, it looks like the best way to summarize the relationship would be to say that it goes down very slightly from about age twenty to age sixty, then declines precipitously thereafter.

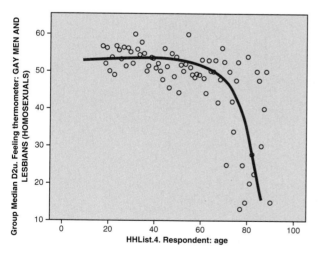

If researchers try to represent it as a purely linear relationship, they may miss out on some important characteristics. In this case, it seems likely that the relationship is being driven by a generational difference—people over a certain age don't like homosexuals as much—rather than a life-cycle difference, in which people like homosexuals less as they get older. The second problem with correlations is that they only analyze one relationship at a time, while social scientists generally want to look at multiple causes. Still, they're commonly used as a preliminary step in data analysis and as a way of describing a variable: in addition to talking about the mean and standard deviation of a variable, it's common for researchers to mention some significant correlations in the Data section of a research paper.

There are three important features to a correlation. The first is the magnitude of the correlation; this is similar to the slope of the line of best fit. The steeper the slope, the closer the correlation is to 1 or −1, and the stronger the correlation is. In this case, the correlation is −0.191, which implies that there is a moderately strong linear relationship between the two variables. Researchers throw around guidelines for what makes a "good" correlation, but there are no hard-and-fast rules. In physical science experiments in which physical laws are being tested with highly accurate equipment, a correlation of 0.95 might be quite low. In social sciences, where there are lots of measurement and reporting errors and other factors that might play a role, a correlation of 0.2 is perfectly reasonable.

Second is the direction of the correlation. This is simply whether the r is positive or negative, with a positive r meaning that as one variable increases, the other does as well. A negative r means the opposite. In this case, the correlation is negative, meaning that as age goes up, people tend to like homosexuals less. The correlation doesn't say anything about the causality of the relationship—whether age is driving views of homosexuality or views of homosexuality are driving age—the numbers just say that there's a negative relationship. As always, it's up to theory (and, in this case, common sense) to tell researchers which factor is the cause and which is the effect. Since a person's age keeps going up no matter what the person thinks of homosexuals, age is almost certainly the cause here, and views of homosexuality are the effect.

Finally, researchers have to pay close attention to the significance of the correlation. In the previous chapter, individual variables were described as having a mean and a standard deviation, and correlations can be thought of in the same way. In this case, though, the mean isn't a point, but rather a line—the line of best fit. Just as a standard deviation is similar to the mean distance from individual points to the mean, the equivalent of a standard deviation for the correlation is the *mean error* (technically, the square root of the mean squared error), or the distance between the individual data points and the line of best fit. A correlation in which all of the data are close to the line has a smaller degree of error than one in which the data tend to be farther from the line or one in which there are a lot of outliers.

Using this information, researchers can create a confidence interval around the line of best fit, in much the same way that they create a confidence interval around a mean estimate. In this case, though, the confidence interval tells the researcher what the slope of the line could be: the smaller the confidence interval, the more likely it is that the true relationship is similar to that described by the line. In the relationship between age and views of homosexuals, there are a lot

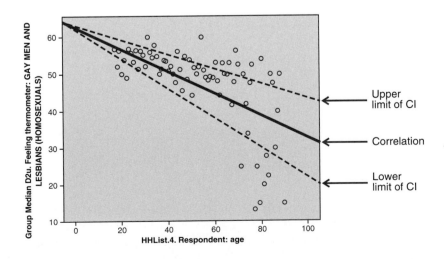

of outliers, so the error around the line of best fit is relatively large, and so is the confidence interval.

Just as the confidence interval around a point can be used to determine whether a difference between this 95 percent (or 90 percent or 99 percent) confidence interval can be used, the confidence interval around a line of best fit can be used to determine whether a correlation is significant or not. Remember that a correlation of zero means that there's no relationship between the variables at all: an increase or decrease in one has no relationship to an increase or decrease in the other.

Going back to Silver's (2011) analysis of the relationship between Presidential Election vote share and the unemployment rate, there was a small negative correlation between the two variables. But because of the small sample size, and the relatively high degree of error—lots of the data points are far from the line representing the correlation—the confidence intervals around that line are rather large.

They're large enough, in fact, that the upper limit of the negative correlation is horizontal. That's important because it means that the 95 percent confidence interval around the slope of the line representing the correlation includes 0. The estimate of the slope may be negative, but Silver (2011) can't say, with 95 percent confidence, that the slope isn't 0, which would mean that there's actually no relationship between the unemployment rate and the incumbent party's margin of victory in the election. There might be a relationship between the two variables, but there isn't a significant one.

On the other hand, the relationship between age and views of homosexuals is significant, because the calculated margin of error around the estimated correlation of −0.191 doesn't include 0. That means that researchers can be

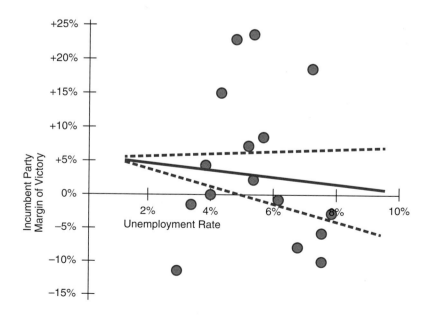

95 percent confident that there is a negative relationship. As such, SPSS reports that the correlation is significant and even gives a likelihood of the relationship happening by chance (in this case, it's less than 0.01 percent). If the error rate around the line was larger, or the relationship itself was weaker, this might not be the case. It's also important not to overinterpret the correlation. It can be helpful to think about the correlation coefficient as being a line that represents the relationship between the two variables, but actually generating that line involves a more complicated process called linear **regression**. All the correlation tells researchers is whether there is a linear relationship between the two variables, whether it's positive or negative, and whether it's significant. Correlation can't be used to predict values of one variable based on the other or for any discussion of causality: it simply says whether the values tend to go up together, or not, and nothing else.

In SPSS, calculating the correlation is easy. Users can go to Analyze → Correlate → Bivariate, and enter the variables. Users can enter as many variables as they like: SPSS will generate pair-wise correlations for each set of variables. Pearson's r is the default measure of correlation used (Spearman's r is sometimes used as well, though only with ordinal variables). A description of what the Two-Tailed and One-Tailed boxes mean will come later in the chapter, but for now, the Two-Tailed box is the best option.

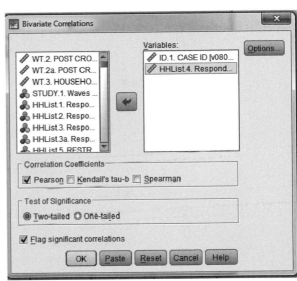

Once users click OK, SPSS generates the correlation matrix in the Output screen. In the correlation matrix, each variable is represented on both the columns and the rows, and in the same order. This means that the diagonal of the correlation matrix—going from the top left to the bottom right—is the correlation of each variable with itself, which is always 1. Off of the diagonals is the correlation of the variable in that row with the variable in that column. The top number is r (in this case, −0.191), and the number below it indicates whether or not the correlation is significant. For a 95 percent confidence interval, a value for this number of *less* than 0.05 indicates a significant correlation. Also note that each correlation shows up in the correlation matrix twice—once above the diagonal and once below it—and there's no difference between the two.

While correlation is a valuable tool for describing the relationship between certain kinds of variables, it does have some significant limitations. First, it doesn't allow researchers to predict values of one variable based on values of the other. In Silver's (2011) analysis, researchers would want to be able to say that a given level of unemployment should lead to a certain margin of victory for the President's party in the election, but correlation just doesn't allow for that. Second, in the social sciences, there's very rarely mono causation. Things aren't generally caused by one thing, but rather by a whole series of factors, each exerting its own influence. While it is possible to calculate partial correlations—correlations that

Correlations

		D2u. Feeling thermometer: GAY MEN AND LESBIANS (HOMO-SEXUALS)	HHList.4. Respondent: age
D2u. Feeling thermometer: GAY MEN AND LESBIANS (HOMOSEXUALS)	Pearson Correlation	1	−.191**
	Sig. (2-tailed)		.000
	N	2041	2023
HHList.4. Respondent: age	Pearson Correlation	−.191**	1
	Sig. (2-tailed)	.000	
	N	2023	2300

** Corelation is significant at the 0.01 level (2-tailed).

account for multiple variables at the same time—it quickly becomes unwieldy. As a result, when researchers want to isolate the effects of a number of variables at once, and make predictions about the likely result of changes in one variable on another, they turn to regression analysis.

UNIVARIATE REGRESSION ANALYSIS

A 2012 article in *The New York Times* profiled Andrew Pole, a statistician who was hired by the retail giant Target to answer a simple question: How can we identify people who are going to have a baby? For retailers, this is terribly important. Generally, consumers stick with the brands that they already know and use. People who use a certain brand of toothpaste, pasta sauce, paper towels, or whatever tend to keep on using it, and they tend to keep on buying it from the same place. However, when something major changes in a consumer's life—getting married, moving, having a baby, and the like—these set patterns are interrupted, and consumers may wind up buying different products or buying them at a different place. So, once companies find out that people are doing any of these things—because they start a wedding or baby registry, file a change of address with the post office, or apply for a mortgage—they flood consumers with advertisements, hoping to profit from their change in habits. What Target wanted from Pole was a way to identify women who were pregnant before they subscribed to parenting magazines, registered a stroller, or opened a baby registry somewhere. Executives at Target thought that if they could get to the pregnant women first, before the other retailers, they'd have a better chance of getting the women to change their habits and shop at Target.

In dealing with this question, Pole was aided by massive datasets that retailers and companies have built over the years. Whenever a consumer uses a loyalty card at a supermarket or drug store, the store tracks what the consumer buys; links it with facts about the consumer such as age, race, and address; and sells that data to a clearinghouse, who in turn sells it to other interested companies. Using this sort of data, Pole was able to isolate women who started baby registries and see what they had bought in the weeks before they started the registry. He found that in the early stages of pregnancy, women tended to buy unscented lotions, calcium and zinc supplements, cotton balls, and hand sanitizers. An uptick in the consumption of any one of these items could be coincidence, but if a woman of reproductive age starts buying lots of them, there's a very good chance that she's pregnant.

Target immediately began using this sort of analysis to send out coupons for baby-related items to pregnant women—but had to scale back the program when they received complaints that their coupons for diapers and strollers were sometimes arriving before the women had told their families that they were pregnant, or even after an early miscarriage. Instead, they started embedding the baby-related coupons in books of coupons for neutral items, like lawn furniture or paper towels, so that women wouldn't realize that Target was guessing that they were pregnant.

The sort of analysis that Pole was doing obviously goes well beyond the bivariate correlations and crosstabs discussed so far in this chapter. While the details of his analyses are secret, he was certainly making use of a more advanced relative of correlation, which researchers call *regression analysis*. Regression analysis allows researchers to model one variable (the dependent variable) as a function of one or more other variables (the predictor or independent variables) and predict values of the dependent variable conditional on values of the independent variable. For Pole, the dependent variable was starting a baby registry, and the independent variables were the changes in buying patterns leading up to the woman starting that registry. Once he knew how a woman's buying patterns had changed, he was able to predict, with very high accuracy, whether or not the woman was pregnant.

The basis of any regression analysis is what researchers call the "line of best fit." If two variables are arranged on a scatterplot, the line of best fit is the line that minimizes the mean squared distance from the data points to the line— what was previously referred to as *error*, or, in this case, *mean squared error* (MSE). In regression analysis, by convention, the dependent variable—the one that the researcher is trying to predict—is arrayed on the vertical, or y-axis, while independent variables are arranged on the horizontal, or x-axis. Sticking with this convention is important for a couple of reasons. First, since everyone does it the same way, putting the dependent variable on the x-axis would cause unnecessary confusion to readers. Second, putting the dependent variable on the y-axis allows researchers to talk about how changes in the independent variable make the dependent variable go "up" or "down." If the dependent variable were on the x-axis, researchers would have to talk about the dependent variable going "left" or "right," which isn't as intuitive.

This means that researchers can't use regression analysis without deciding which variables are causes (independent variable) and which variables are effects (dependent variables). Like correlation, regression analysis itself doesn't tell the researcher which is which: that decision can only come from theory or from empirical characteristics of the variable. An earlier example looked at the relationship between age and views of homosexuals. In a case like that, it's easy to figure out that age must be the cause (the independent variable) and views of homosexuals the effect (the dependent variable). Nothing, except the passage of time, can change someone's age, so if there is a causal relationship between views of homosexuals and age, age has to be the cause and views of homosexuals the effect. The causal relationship could also be clear if the variables are time dependent. In Pole's analysis, for example, buying the cotton balls and unscented lotions came before the women started a baby registry, so there's no way that starting a baby registry could be causing women to do something weeks in the past. Causal relationships may also be clear in a well-designed experimental study: if the only difference between groups is an experimental manipulation, any difference between the groups after the manipulation must be the result of the experiment. In other cases, it isn't nearly as straightforward. For instance, Republicans are much less likely to support abortion rights than Democrats are. It could be that people who join the Republican Party adopt the views of the party and prominent Republicans with regard to abortion, so being a Republican makes people less supportive of abortion rights. It also could be the case that people who oppose abortion rights tend to gravitate toward the Republican Party, so views on abortion are causing party identification. From the data itself, there's no way to tell which is the cause and which the effect. Researchers have to rely on theory and past research to decide how best to model the relationship.

While calculating a regression analysis can be very time consuming, especially as the number of independent variables increases, interpreting the results of a simple regression analysis—what researchers refer to as OLS, or ordinary least squares, regression—is not. The outcome of a regression analysis may look daunting, but it's actually based on what most students learned in junior high math class.

The starting point for understanding the results of a regression analysis is the equation for a line. In regression analysis, every line in a two-dimensional space can be represented by knowing the value on the x-axis (x), the slope of the line (denoted as m), and the point at which the line intercepts the y-axis (b). Put them together, and the result is simply:

$$Y = mx + b$$

When the value on the x-axis is equal to 0, the value on the y-axis is b. From there, when x increases by 1, y goes up by m (in this case, m is negative). It's all very simple, but it looks more complicated when the terminology for regression analysis is used instead of the equation for a line.

$$\hat{Y} = \beta_1 x_1 + C$$

In this version of the equation, Y has been replaced by $\hat{Y}$ (said "y-hat"), or the expected value on the y-axis for a given set of x-values. x_1 is simply the value

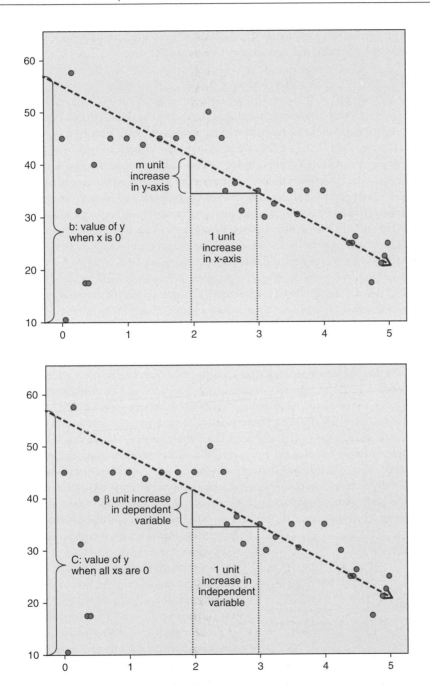

of the independent variable, and the subscript 1 is used with it to allow for multiple independent variables in the equation. β_1 is the slope of the line of best fit that summarizes the relationship between the independent variable x_1 and the dependent variable. C is exactly the same thing as b in the equation of a line: the value of $\hat{Y}$ when all of the xs are 0. Of course, since regression allows for multiple independent variables, this equation can be expanded to:

$$\hat{Y} = \beta_1 x_1 + \beta_2 x_2 + \beta_3 x_3 \ldots + \beta_k x_k + C$$

where k is the total number of independent variables in the equation. No matter how many independent variables there are, though, the interpretation of them remains exactly the same: x is the value of that independent variable, and β is the slope of the line that best represents the relationship between that independent variable and the dependent variable, *controlling for all of the other independent variables in the equation.* This last point is very important. The biggest advantage of regression analysis, even one as simple as OLS regression, is that it allows researchers to find the marginal effects of one independent variable, holding constant the effects of all of the other independent variables in the model. To understand what this means, suppose a researcher used OLS regression analysis to try and model the effect of age on people's feeling thermometer rankings of homosexuals. It's already been established that there's a significant correlation between the two, and because age can't be affected by anything other than the passage of time, it's clear which is the independent variable (age) and which the dependent (views of homosexuals). There are also several requirements that have to be met before OLS analysis is feasible, but the most important ones are ensuring that the dependent variable is measured on an interval or ratio scale (the independent variables may be ordinal, interval, or ratio) and ensuring that the relationship between the variables is actually linear. In this case, the dependent variable has a meaningful zero point, making it a ratio-level variable, and the correlation analysis (as well as just a glance at the crosstabs) shows that there is a significant linear relationship between the two. Before attempting to run any regression, it's also important that researchers check the variables they wish to use to make certain that all missing values have been set properly and all of the variables have a meaningful order. If they don't, the results of the regression analysis will be nonsensical. In SPSS, users run the OLS regression analysis by going through the menus to Analyze → Regression → Linear.

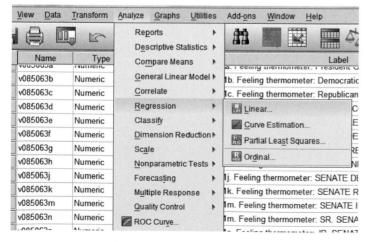

From there, users can select the dependent variable for the box in the top center and all desired independent variables for the box in the center of the dialog box.

There are many other options that users can specify from the Linear Regression dialog box. In the Statistics menu, users can specify the desired confidence intervals (the default is, of course, 95 percent). In Plots, the user can ask SPSS to output a scatterplot showing the relationship between one or more of the independent variables and the dependent variable. Once any desired options have been specified, the user can click OK to send the results of the regression to the Output screen.

This output is a little more complicated than it needs to be because it includes a great deal of information that generally isn't very useful. Rather than just giving the results of the regression, SPSS gives four different boxes. The first tells the user if any of the desired variables have been removed from the equation before the analysis was carried out. The most common reason this would happen is if two of the variables are actually the same thing. For instance, if a researcher put Age and Year of Birth into the same model as independent variables, the system would recognize that they're perfectly correlated ($r = 1.0$), and kick one of them out.

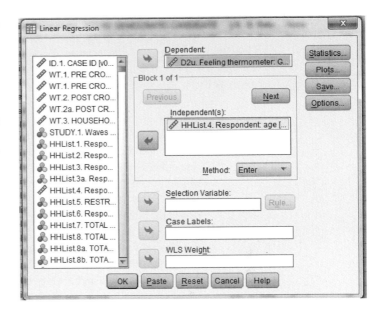

The next box is the Model Summary, and this actually has some important information in it. Most important is the R Square (r^2), also referred to as the *coefficient of determination*. Based just on the name, it's clear that it's the correlation, squared. In this case, there's only one independent variable (called **bivariate regression**), and it's already been established that the correlation between the dependent variable and the one independent variable is 0.191; 0.191 squared is 0.036. The r^2 is important because it's used as a measure of model fit: it tells researchers what percent of the total variance in the

Variables Entered/Removed[b]

Model	Variables Entered	Variables Removed	Method
1	HHList.4. Respondent: age[a]		Enter

a. All requested variables entered

b. Dependent Variable: D2u. Feeling thermometer: GAY MEN AND LESBIANS (HOMOSEXUALS)

dependent variable is explained by all of the independent variables included in the model. Since correlation is bounded by −1 and 1, the squared correlation can be as low as 0 or as high as 1, and generally a high r^2 is preferable to a low one. As with correlation, there's no magic number that makes for a good r^2. Measurement error can make r^2 lower, low sample sizes may contribute, as well as the general complexity of the variable being modeled. In social science, an r^2 of around 0.20 is considered pretty good, and one that's too high—more than about 0.90—is probably a sign that the researcher has done something wrong. In this case, the r^2 is fairly low: age, by itself, only explains about 4 percent of the total variance in feeling thermometer ratings of homosexuals. The rest of the variance in the dependent variable (96.4 percent) is made up of other factors that lead people to rate homosexuals higher or lower on the scale, as well as any error in the measurement (which can't be accounted for by any independent variable).

In addition to the r^2, this box also includes the adjusted r^2.

Model Summary

Model	R	R Square	Adjusted R Square	Std. Error of the Estimate
1	.191[a]	.036	.036	27.462

a. Predictors: (Constant), HHList.4. Respondent: age

In this case, the adjusted r^2 is equal to the actual r^2—but that's only because there's just one independent variable in this model. The major problem with using the r^2 as a measure of model fit is that adding any variable to the regression as an independent variable—including ones that don't predict the dependent variable at all—will increase the r^2 by a little bit, just through random chance. So, if researchers wanted to artificially increase a model's r^2, they could do so by simply adding random variables. This is one reason that researchers shouldn't use the r^2 as the only measure of how good a regression model is, and the adjusted r^2 is an attempt to correct for it. Essentially, the adjusted r^2 is the normal r^2 minus a small penalty for each independent variable added in. If the new independent variables are useful in explaining the dependent variable, the difference between the adjusted r^2 and the r^2 will be small. If they're not, the adjusted r^2 will be rather lower than the r^2.

The third box describes the analysis of variance for the model, abbreviated as ANOVA. Some researchers, especially in psychology, use these figures, but most social scientists just ignore them. The last of the four boxes, though, is the one that's of real interest to social science researchers. It gives the β coefficients and standard errors for each of the independent variables, allowing researchers to estimate the marginal effects of each of them on the dependent variable. In this case, there's only one independent variable, so there are only two sets of figures: one for the independent variable (the age of the respondent) and one for the constant.

Coefficients[a]

Model		Unstandardized Coefficients		Standardized Coefficients	t	Sig.
		B	Std. Error	Beta		
1	(Constant)	64.411	1.790		35.992	.000
	HHList.4. Respondent: age	−.314	.036	−.191	−8.729	.000

a. Dependent Variable: D2u. Feeling thermometer: GAY MEN AND LESBIANS (HOMOSEXUALS)

These figures allow researchers to estimate the value of the dependent variable—feeling thermometer ratings of homosexuals—as a function of all of the listed independent variables. To do this, researchers simply plug in the listed values of β and C into the equation for $\hat{Y}$.

$$\hat{Y} = \beta_1 x_1 + C$$
$$\hat{Y} = -0.314 x_{Age} + 64.411$$

So, for any value of age, which ranges in the dataset between seventeen and ninety, the expected value feeling thermometer rating is equal to the respondent's age times −0.314, plus 64.411. In a scatterplot, this would look like:

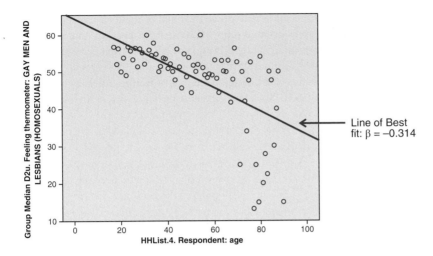

So, if a researcher wanted to calculate the expected feeling thermometer rating for a forty-year-old, for instance, he or she would simply put 40 into the equation as the value of xage, giving:

$$\hat{Y} = -0.314(40) + 64.411$$
$$\hat{Y} = -12.56 + 64.411$$
$$\hat{Y} = 51.851$$

Based solely on the participant's age, the researcher would expect that a forty-year-old would give homosexuals as score of 51.9 on the feeling thermometer. A thirty-year-old would be expected to have a higher rating by about 3.1 points, and a fifty-year-old would be expected to have a lower one by about 3.1 points (since the value of $\hat{Y}$ goes down by .314 for each one-unit increase in age, it goes down by 10 × .314, or 3.14, for every ten-year increase in age). The expected values of $\hat{Y}$ also function as a final check that the variables in the regression are coded properly: if the expected values of the dependent variable didn't make sense (if the regression were predicting a feeling thermometer score of −20 or 350), the researcher would know that something had gone wrong.

SIGNIFICANCE AND HYPOTHESIS TESTING

There's more to the regression results than just the β coefficient, however. In the column next to the β is the standard error of the estimate. This standard error is very similar to a standard deviation in that it indicates how far off the estimate is on the mean. A low standard error, relative to the size of the β, means that the researcher can be confident that the effect of the independent variable is significant. If the standard error is large, relative to the β, there is a greater chance that the effect of the independent variable isn't significant. Thankfully, determining whether the β is significant or not is just like finding a margin of error. Just like the confidence interval around a mean is equal to the standard error multiplied by the appropriate z-score (1.96 for a 95 percent confidence interval), the margin of error around a β is equal to the standard error multiplied by the appropriate z-score, found in exactly the same way.

In this case, the β for the effect of age on views of homosexuals is −0.314, with a standard error of 0.036. So, a 95 percent confidence interval around the estimate would be:

$$\text{MOE: } \beta \mp \text{SE} \star z^\star$$
$$\text{MOE: } -0.314 \mp 0.036 \star 1.96$$
$$\text{MOE: } -0.314 \mp 0.07$$

giving a confidence interval of between −0.38 and −0.24. Once the confidence interval is known, the question is, what is it being compared with, and for β coefficients, this is simple. With correlations, a significant correlation was one in which the confidence interval did not include 0: a value that indicates no relationship between the variables. The same is true for β coefficients. If the confidence interval around a β coefficient does not include 0, researchers can say that there is a significant effect of the independent variable on the dependent variable.

As with all confidence intervals, the confidence interval around a β coefficient is made more complex by the two factors that go into a confidence interval. The first of these was discussed when confidence intervals were introduced: 95 percent confidence intervals are the norm in social science research, but 99 percent and 90 percent confidence intervals are not unheard of. A low accepted rate of error—as in a 99 percent confidence interval—corresponds to a larger confidence interval, while a higher accepted rate of error corresponds to a smaller one. Researchers most commonly use a larger confidence interval when they're making a large number of simultaneous tests. If researchers use a 95 percent confidence interval, there's a 5 percent chance of finding a significant effect by chance: so, if the researchers carry out ten or fifteen analyses, there's a good chance that one analysis will look significant just by chance. In such a case, a 99 percent confidence interval might be more appropriate.

The other factor that affects confidence intervals, and determinations of significance, is whether the researcher is looking for a one-tailed or a two-tailed effect. In a one-tailed effect, the researcher has specified that the coefficient should be on one side of zero: either positive or negative. In a two-tailed effect, the researcher has not specified a direction, only that the effect of the independent variable is expected to be nonzero.

It's vital that these expectations about the likely values of coefficients (or of any relationship between two variables) be set before the analysis is actually carried out. In a research paper, they're included in the hypothesis section, and social scientists have formal ways of stating these hypotheses. In this case, if the researchers, before doing the analysis, believed that age would have a negative effect on views of homosexuals (as age increases, scores on the feeling thermometer for homosexuals go down), they would put a statement in the hypothesis section that:

$$H1: \beta_{Age} < 0$$

The hypothesis is labeled H1 because it's the first **alternative hypothesis**. If the researcher wanted more alternative hypotheses, perhaps relating to other independent variables in the model, they would typically be labeled H2, H3, and so on. It's also important to note that the hypothesis is stated mathematically, rather than in a sentence. In a research paper, it's important to state the hypotheses both ways: first in a plain language description, then mathematically. The plain language statement of the hypotheses (in this case, "The β for the effect of age on views of homosexuals will be negative") ensures that the reader understands what the hypothesis means. The mathematical statement of the hypotheses makes sure that the hypothesis is stated specifically enough that it can be tested rigorously. There's often some wiggle room in a plain language statement of a hypothesis, but there's none in the mathematical statement.

Like all alternative hypotheses, this one is stated as an inequality, using greater than or less than signs. This is what separates the alternative from the other type of hypotheses, **null hypotheses**, which make use of equal signs in addition to, or instead of, the inequality signs. In this case, for instance, the null hypothesis would be that the β for age would be 0 (no effect at all) or positive:

$$H\text{ø}: \beta_{Age} \geq 0$$

Together, the null (denoted with the empty set symbol "ø") and alternative hypotheses constitute all of the possible outcomes of the analysis. Once the researcher runs the regression and looks at the β, it must either be greater than, less than, or equal to 0. The null hypothesis simply consists of all of the outcomes that are not in the alternative hypothesis (or hypotheses): since the alternative hypothesis is that the β is negative, the null is what's left over. This is similar to making sure that survey responses are exhaustive; every possible outcome must be part of one of the hypotheses. To understand why the null hypothesis includes the equal sign but the alternative does not, it's helpful to look at what the outcome of this test would be. The 95 percent confidence interval for the β runs from −0.38 to −0.24. This means that the researchers can be 95 percent certain that the actual level of β is between −0.38 and −0.24 and can say, with 95 percent confidence, that the β is negative because all of the values within the confidence interval are below 0. In social science terminology, the researchers could say that they reject the null hypothesis that β is equal to or greater than 0. This isn't quite the same thing as accepting the alternative—and researchers are careful never to say that they've accepted an alternative hypothesis—but it's as close as they get.

Suppose that the alternative hypothesis had, instead, been that the β would be equal to 0: using an equal sign in the alternative hypothesis, rather than an inequality. Had the researchers done so, they could have rejected the null hypothesis because the β was greater or lesser than 0—or because the confidence

Null Hypothesis

interval was big. In essence, the researchers would be more likely to reject the null hypothesis just because there was a big standard error in the β, which could result from a small sample size, lots of outliers, measurement error, a nonlinear relationship, or other factors. Any of these factors make it more likely that the confidence interval will include 0—and none of them are good reasons to reject a null hypothesis. The equal sign, therefore, should always be in the null hypothesis, never in the alternative.

All of these are what researchers refer to as *one-tailed hypotheses*. They're one-tailed because the alternative hypothesis posits that the β is *less* than 0. If it were a two-tailed hypothesis, the alternative would posit that the β is greater *or* lesser than 0, leaving only the equal sign to the null hypothesis. The two-tailed hypotheses would be

$$H_1: \beta_{Age} \neq 0$$
$$H_0: \beta_{Age} = 0$$

In this case, the researchers would reject the null hypothesis if the β were low enough that the upper limit of the confidence interval were below 0, or if it were high enough that the lower end of the confidence interval was above 0. The decision to reject, or fail to reject, the null hypothesis is the essence of **hypothesis testing**. At first glance, this may make it seem as if researchers should always use a two-tailed hypothesis—they're twice as likely to reject the null hypothesis—but it's actually generally the opposite. The reason has to do with the z-score table. Suppose that the researcher assumed that there was no relationship between the independent and dependent variable, that the true value of β was actually 0. How far away from 0 would the β have to be before the researcher would be convinced that it wasn't actually 0? Well, that depends on the size of the standard error. If the standard error is small relative to the β, the researcher would be willing to believe that a small β was a real difference from 0. If the standard errors were large, even a big β might not be credible as a real difference. In essence, the researcher is seeing how many standard errors away from 0 a β coefficient is. In a 95 percent confidence interval, the researcher is looking for a number of standard errors away from 0 that corresponds to only a 5 percent chance of happening by random chance. If it's a two-tailed hypothesis, this 5 percent chance of happening by random chance is evenly split between the top and the bottom of the distribution.

This means that the researchers would be able to reject the null hypothesis that $\beta = 0$ if the β coefficient was 1.96 standard errors away from 0, which is the same thing as saying that the 95 percent confidence interval around the β coefficient does not include 0. For a 99 percent confidence interval, the z-scores would correspond to 0.05 percent on either side of the distribution, and the researchers would need to see a β that was 2.57 times as big as the standard error in order to reject the null hypothesis. The scores discussed here aren't actually z-scores. Z-scores refer to how many standard deviations away from the mean a value is. Since these scores are in terms of standard errors, instead of standard deviations, they're referred to as *t-scores* rather than z-scores. In very small sample sizes (less than about 120), t-scores can be different than z-scores, but researchers probably shouldn't be using regression with such small sample sizes anyway. For

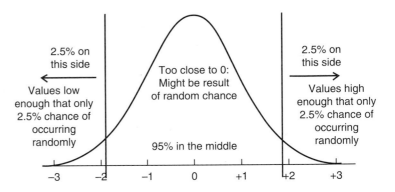

these purposes, at least, the t-scores and z-scores are functionally equivalent, and z-score tables work just fine for translating scores into probabilities.

If the researcher specifies a one-tailed hypothesis, though, things are a bit different. Rather than looking for 2.5 percent on either side of the distribution, the researchers are looking for values on just one side of the distribution—positive or negative. This means that they could reject the null with a smaller value, but only if it was in the hypothesized direction.

For a one-tailed hypothesis, the researchers would be able to reject the null hypothesis if the β was only 1.65 times as big as the standard error. The catch, though, is that the value has

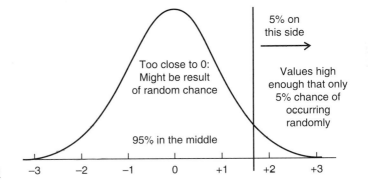

to be either positive or negative. Going back to the relationship between age and feeling thermometer ratings of homosexuals, the β is negative, and more than eight times as big as the standard error (β = −0.314, SE = 0.036, −0.314/0.036 = −8.7). As such, researchers would be able to reject the null hypothesis in a one-tailed negative test (H1: $\beta_{Age} < 0$). However, if the researchers had instead hypothesized a one-tailed positive test (H1: $\beta_{Age} > 0$), they would be unable to reject the null hypothesis, no matter how big the β was.

This brings up the next important aspect of hypotheses: they must be set before the analysis is carried out. If the researcher sets the hypothesis after doing the analysis, or changes the hypothesis after seeing the results, the results will be wrong. This seems strange at first glance—the results are just numbers, and they can't know when the hypotheses were set—but the math really doesn't work if the hypotheses are set after the fact. It's already been established that the β on the relationship between age and feeling thermometer ratings of homosexuals is negative and that the confidence intervals around it don't include 0. So, if researchers had set a two-tailed hypothesis (looking for a β that's at least 1.96 times as big as the standard error, positive or negative) or a one-tailed negative hypothesis (looking for a β with a negative value that's at least 1.65 times the standard error), they would reject the null. If, however, they had set a one-tailed

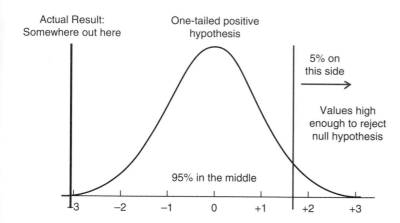

positive hypothesis, they would fail to reject the null hypothesis.

So, suppose that the researchers see the results and decide to just change the hypothesis from a one-tailed positive to a two-tailed hypothesis.

If they did so, they would be accepting a 2.5 percent chance that the finding occurred by random chance on the negative side, but that doesn't change the fact that they were already accepting a 5 percent chance of random error on the positive side. (If the β had been 1.65 times the size of the standard error, they would have rejected the null.) So, instead of having a 95 percent confidence interval, they actually have a 92.5 percent confidence interval. The situation is even worse if they changed the hypothesis from a one-tailed positive to a one-tailed negative. If they did that, what looks like a 95 percent confidence interval is actually a 90 percent confidence interval. Any change that's made to the hypothesis after the fact makes the confidence intervals wrong.

When researchers are able to reject the null hypothesis, they can say that the independent variable has a significant effect on the dependent variable. It's important to note, though, that *significant* is a dichotomous category: an effect cannot be very significant, or weakly significant, or almost significant. The β of age is almost 9 times as big as the standard error—but it's no more significant than a β that was just 1.96 times as big as the standard error, and a β in a two-tailed hypothesis that's 1.95 times as big as the standard error isn't any more significant than one that is 0.

DUMMY AND CONTROL VARIABLES

This all seems very clear-cut: age has a significant negative effect on feeling thermometer ratings of homosexuals, but there's one big problem. The problem is that there are lots of other factors that drive people to like homosexuals more or less. Political views, race, gender, education—all could be expected to have an impact on how people view homosexuals. This is problematic because some of these things are correlated with age. Older people tend to hold more conservative political views, for instance. Therefore, it's possible that what looks like an effect of age on how people view homosexuals is *actually* an effect of something else that's correlated with age.

The only way for a researcher to isolate the actual effect of age is to control for all of the other factors that could reasonably be driving people's views of homosexuals. If all of these additional variables are not included in the regression analysis, the estimates of the effects of the included variables simply aren't reliable. These additional variables—which typically include demographic characteristics such as race, gender, education, income, and, for political dependent variables,

WE FOUND NO LINK BETWEEN GREY JELLY BEANS AND ACNE (P > 0.05).

WE FOUND NO LINK BETWEEN TAN JELLY BEANS AND ACNE (P > 0.05).

WE FOUND NO LINK BETWEEN CYAN JELLY BEANS AND ACNE (P > 0.05).

WE FOUND A LINK BETWEEN GREEN JELLY BEANS AND ACNE (P > 0.05). WHOA!

WE FOUND NO LINK BETWEEN MAUVE JELLY BEANS AND ACNE (P > 0.05).

WE FOUND NO LINK BETWEEN BEIGE JELLY BEANS AND ACNE (P > 0.05).

WE FOUND NO LINK BETWEEN LILAC JELLY BEANS AND ACNE (P > 0.05).

WE FOUND NO LINK BETWEEN BLACK JELLY BEANS AND ACNE (P > 0.05).

WE FOUND NO LINK BETWEEN PEACH JELLY BEANS AND ACNE (P > 0.05).

WE FOUND NO LINK BETWEEN ORANGE JELLY BEANS AND ACNE (P > 0.05).

NEWS

GREEN JELLY BEANS LINKED TO ACNE!

95% CONFIDENCE

ONLY 5% CHANCE OF COINCIDENCE! SCIENTISTS...

party identification—are collectively referred to as *control variables*. A **control variable** is simply an independent variable included in the analysis in order to better isolate the effects of the variables that the researcher is actually interested in. This works because regression analysis calculates the marginal effects of each independent variable on the dependent variable; that is, the effect of that independent variable, controlling for the effects of all of the other included independent variables. So, if both age and party identification are included as independent variables, the regression will correct for the fact that older people tend to be more Republican and may hold more negative views of homosexuals because of that.

In this case, if the researchers are most interested in the effect of age on people's views of homosexuals, any other independent variable would be a control variable. (The other variables, like age in this case, are often referred to as *variables of interest*.) There is no hard-and-fast rule for which control variables need to be included in the model. It really is up to the researcher to decide what factors, aside from the variables of interest, can be expected to have an effect on the dependent variable. In general, indicators of race and gender are essential, but many other factors can be included.

In this case, it makes sense to include a number of control variables: race, education, income, party identification, church attendance, and having a homosexual friend or relative. A researcher wanting to use these control variables would first make sure that they were coded properly and that all of the missing values were properly accounted for. It should also be noted that many of these variables aren't interval or ratio level. Gender is typically a nominal-level variable, for instance. The type of regression discussed here, though, only requires that the dependent variable be on the interval or ratio level; the independent variables can be ordinal level. As long as there's a reasonable order to the variable, it can be used as a predictor.

By itself, though, this doesn't solve the problem. Party identification and education are ordinal variables, but some of the desired controls, like gender and race, are nominal-level variables. In order to use these in the regression model, it's necessary to turn them into ordinal-level variables. Researchers do this by creating what are called **dummy variables**. Dummy variables are dichotomous, ordinal representations of nominal variables. *Dichotomous* means that the variable only has two values—typically 0 and 1, though any two values can be used. *Ordinal* means that the values of a dummy variable are based on the values of a related nominal-level variable, coded to give some order to the nominal values. For instance, gender is the classic example of a nominal-level variable. There's simply no order to it. However, it wouldn't be difficult to recode a gender variable to make it ordinal. Rather than gender, a researcher could create a new variable, Female, that's coded as 1 if the respondent is a woman and 0 otherwise. There is an order to this variable—higher values indicate that the respondent is more female, lower values mean that the respondent is more male—so it can fairly be treated as an ordinal variable and included as a predictor in the model. For such a variable, the β in the regression results would be the average change in the dependent variable when the value of the dummy variable goes from 0 to 1. Alternately, it could be described as the difference between men and women.

Things are a little more complicated when the nominal category has a large number of values. In general, any nominal variable can be represented by a number of dummy variables equal to the total number of categories, minus one. In the case of gender, there are only two categories, so gender can be represented as just one dummy variable. If the researcher were to create a second dummy variable out of the gender variable—coded as 1 if the respondent is a man, and 0 otherwise—it wouldn't contain any additional information: if you know who the women are, you already know who the men are (everyone else). It works the same way with a nominal variable like race. Suppose the race variable had five categories. To fully represent it, the researcher would need to create four dummy variables.

		Dummy Variables			
		White	AA/Black	A/PI	Hispanic
	White	1	0	0	0
	African American/Black	0	1	0	0
Category	Asian/Pacific Islander	0	0	1	0
	Hispanic/Latino/a	0	0	0	1
	Other	0	0	0	0

This table shows how a five-category, nominal race variable could be turned into four different dummy variables. A white respondent would score a 1 in the White dummy variable and a 0 in all of the other dummy variables. An African American respondent would score 1 in the AA/Black dummy variable and 0 in all of the other dummy variables, and so on. There are only four dummy variables, but jointly they include all of the information found in the nominal variable. Although there's no dummy variable for Other, respondents who fall into that category can still be identified because they have a score of 0 on all of the dummy variables. Adding an additional dummy variable to represent the respondents in the "Other" race category wouldn't actually add any information, and if the researcher tried to use it in a regression, SPSS would kick it out beforehand.

When there are multiple dummy variables coming from the same nominal variable, interpretation of the β coefficients is a little more complicated. In all cases, the β coefficient attached to a dummy variable tells the researcher how respondents in that category differ from people who are in the excluded category, the one that didn't get a dummy variable. So, in the case of gender (where they are only two categories), the β of Female tells the researcher how women differ from men. But if there are dummy variables for White, African American, Hispanic, and Asian, the β coefficients attached to each of these tell the researcher how respondents in that particular category differ from respondents in the category that was excluded (in this case, Other). So, a positive β for White means that whites have a higher score on the dependent variable than people in the Other category—not necessarily higher scores than people in the African American or Asian categories (though that may also be the case).

Before creating these dummy variables in SPSS, users first have to ensure that they know how the existing nominal variable is coded and what dummy variables they want. Although a nominal variable can be represented by a number of dummy variables equal to the number of categories minus one, there's no requirement that researchers actually create that many dummy variables. For this analysis, two dummy variables—one for African American and one for Hispanic—should suffice. Using the Values column in the Variable View screen, users can see that a value of 2 on the existing race variable corresponds to African American.

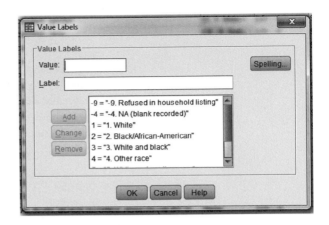

Once that's established, the user can go to Transform → Recode into Different Variables. From there, the user can specify the old nominal variable, as well as the name and label for the new dummy variable. Once they have typed in the Name and Label for the new dummy, users click Change to link it to the old variable.

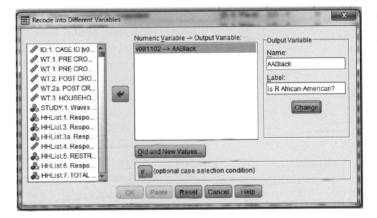

Next, the user clicks on Old and New Values. The old values, on the left side of the dialog box, are the values of the original nominal variable. The new values are those of the dummy variable being created. In this case, a value of 2 in the existing variable

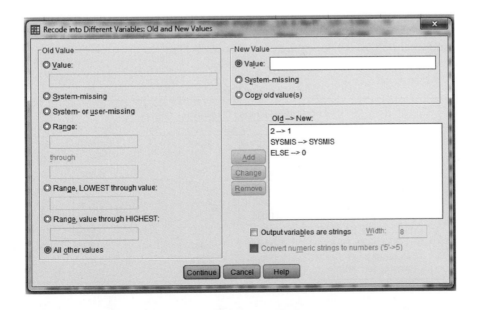

corresponds to a value of 1 in the new dummy variable, so the user can type "2" into Value on the left, and "1" into Value on the right before clicking Add on the bottom right.

Next, the user can set the missing values to be missing in the new variable as well. The user clicks System-Missing on the left and links it to System-Missing on the right. Finally, all of the remaining values—everything that isn't African American or missing—can be set to 0 in the new dummy variable. Once this is done, clicking Continue on the bottom left, then OK, creates the new dummy variable.

MULTIVARIATE REGRESSION ANALYSIS

Once the researchers have generated all of the necessary dummy variables and ensured that all of the variables have had their missing values accounted for and are otherwise ready to use, they can run the full regression. In this case, it is a **multivariate regression** model because it has many predictors, rather than just one, as in previous examples. With all of the control variables included, the r^2 of the model increases substantially, to 0.139 (with an adjusted r^2 of 0.130), but the important part is the β estimates.

The age of the respondents still has a significant negative effect on the respondent's views of homosexuals, but the effect is smaller than it was when age was the only independent variable included (−0.224, rather than −0.314). This indicates that some of the effect that was being attributed to age was actually an effect of one or more of the other independent variables now included in the model. This β would be interpreted as meaning that controlling for all of the other variables in the model, a one-year increase in age decreases the expected value of the feeling thermometer rating of homosexuals by 0.224.

There are a couple of ways to tell whether the effect is significant. The first is to look at the ratio of the β to the standard error. For a two-tailed hypothesis, with 95 percent confidence intervals, the β should be 1.96 times as big as the standard error. This is close enough to 2 that researchers can just look to see if

Coefficients[a]

Model		Unstandardized Coefficients		Standardized Coefficients	t	Sig.
		B	Std. Error	Beta		
1	(Constant)	39.568	6.042		6.549	.000
	Age of Respondent	−.224	.060	−.191	−3.717	.000
	R educational attainment	3.211	.662	.184	4.853	.000
	Household income	.036	.182	.008	.197	.844
	Is R African American?	−4.307	2.506	−.069	−1.719	.086
	Is R Female?	11.066	1.810	.201	6.113	.000
	Is R Latino/a	.871	2.363	.014	.369	.712
	R Party Identification	−2.241	.482	−.176	−4652	.000
	Attend religious services how often	2.666	.773	118	3.447	.001

a. Dependent Variable: D2u. Feeling thermometer: GAY MEN AND LESBIANS (HOMOSEXUALS)

β is twice as big as the standard error. (For two-tailed tests, it doesn't matter if it's positive or negative.) The second way to tell if the effect is significant is to look at the column labeled "t." This is the t-value, which is simply the β for that variable divided by the standard error—the exact ratio being used in the previous technique. If the t-value is greater than 1.96 (positive or negative) for a two-tailed, 95 percent confidence test, the effect of the β is significant, and the researcher can reject the null. The actual test values used will, of course, change based on whether the hypothesis is one- or two-tailed and what level of confidence is desired.

The final column in the regression results box is labeled Sig, short for "significance." This is essentially what would be found by looking up the percentage that corresponds to the listed t-score. For a 95 percent confidence interval on a two-tailed hypothesis, for instance, a value of less than 0.05 in this column would indicate a significant effect. However, researchers should be careful about relying on these results too much: the value needed for a significant effect depends on whether the hypothesis is one- or two-tailed and what the desired confidence interval is. As such, the t-value is generally more useful.

Based on this, it's clear that age has a significant negative effect on respondents' views of homosexuals, with a t-value of −3.7, the absolute value of which (3.7) exceeds the critical value (1.96) for a two-tailed 95 percent hypothesis test, and several other independent variables have significant effects as well. Education, for instance, has a significant positive effect, as does the frequency with which respondents attend religious services. These two variables, though, demonstrate the importance of keeping the coding of independent variables in mind. The Education variable is coded from 1 to 7, where 1 indicates a respondent who didn't attend high school, and values increasing until 7, which indicates respondents with a graduate degree. Regression results are always in terms of one unit increases in the independent variable, and in this case, a one-unit increase in education corresponds to a higher level of education; so, for each one-unit increase in a respondent's level of education, his or her feeling thermometer rating of homosexuals is expected to increase by 3.2.

The frequency with which respondents attend religious services also has a significant positive effect on views of homosexuals, but this only makes sense in the context of how the variable is coded.

In this variable, higher values indicate that the respondent goes to church less often. So, even though the β coefficient is positive, it means that the less frequently a respondent goes to church (and so the values of the independent variable increase), the higher the feeling thermometer ratings of homosexuals are expected to be.

Of course, not all of the independent variables have a significant effect on the dependent variable. Each one-point increase in household income, for instance, increases the respondent's expected feeling thermometer rating by just 0.036 points, with a standard error of 0.182. In this case, the standard error is five times as big as the β, so the confidence interval around the β certainly includes 0. A researcher could fairly conclude that, after controlling for the other variables in the model, there is no significant effect of household income on the feeling thermometer ratings.

Interpretation of the dummy variables is similar to that of the other independent variables. The β of the gender dummy variable indicates that women are expected to rate homosexuals 11.1 points higher on the feeling thermometer than the excluded category (men). Similarly, the β of −4.3 on the race dummy for African American indicates that African Americans are expected to have a rating 4.3 points less than the excluded category. Since the nominal race variable was split up into just two dummies (African American and Latino/a), the excluded category includes all respondents who are neither African American nor Latino/a: so, Whites, Asian Americans, and those who fall into the Other category. The β coefficients mean that African Americans are expected to give lower score on the feeling thermometer than this mixed White/Asian/Other group, while Latinos/as are expected to have slightly higher scores, though that difference is not significant.

It's tempting to compare the β coefficients of the various independent variables to try to see which has the largest effect on the dependent variable, but the comparison isn't quite that straightforward. In this case, the dummy variable for African Americans has a larger β (−4.3) than the party identification variable (β = −2.2). However, the African American variable only goes from 0 to 1, while the Party Identification variable goes from 0 to 6. So the biggest possible effect of being an African American on views of homosexuals is (1 × 4.3=) 4.3, while party identification can have an impact as big as (6 × 2.2=) 13.2. Since the relative impact of the independent variables on the dependent variable depends on the coding of the variable, the comparisons only make sense if the variables have the same range. To make these comparisons easier, SPSS calculates the standardized coefficients, which is the relative size of the effects if the independent variables all had the same coding. In this model, the standardized coefficients indicate that gender has the largest single effect on the feeling thermometer ratings, with education having the second biggest. While these figures are useful for comparing relative effect sizes, researchers need to be careful not to use them for anything else. If they were used to calculate predicted values of the dependent variable, for instance, the results would be incorrect.

Once the regression results are generated, though, calculating expected values of the dependent variable is just a matter or substitution and multiplication. Remember that the expected value of Y $(\hat{Y})$ is equal to:

$$\hat{Y} = \beta_1 x_1 + \beta_2 x_2 + \beta_3 x_3 \ldots + \beta_k x_k + C$$

In this equation, k is the number of independent variables in the model. For this model, then, the expected value of a respondent's feeling thermometer rating of homosexuals is:

$$\hat{Y} = \beta_{Age}x_{Age} + \beta_{Education}x_{Education} + \beta_{Income}x_{Income} + \beta_{AA}x_{AA} + \beta_{Female}x_{Female}$$
$$+ \beta_{Latino}x_{Latino} + \beta_{PartyID}x_{PartyID} + \beta_{Services}x_{Services} + C$$

$$\hat{Y} = -0.224x_{Age} + 3.211x_{Education} + 0.036x_{Income} + -4.307x_{AA} + 11.066x_{Female}$$
$$+ 0.871x_{Latino} + -2.241x_{PartyID} + 2.666x_{Services} + 39.568$$

It's clear from these equations that any calculation of the expected value of Y requires a value for each of the independent variables, even those that aren't significant. So, if researchers wanted to use these regression results to calculate an expected feeling thermometer rating of homosexuals, they would have to specify values for all of the variables in the model. For instance, the expected value for a forty-year-old (Age = 40) white (African American = 0, Latina = 0) Republican (Party Identification = 6) woman (Female = 1) with a bachelor of arts (BA) degree (Education = 6) and a household income at the mean of the scale (Income = 11) who goes to church every week (Services = 1) would be:

$$\hat{Y} = -0.224(40) + 3.211(6) + 0.036(11) + -4.307(0) + 11.066(1)$$
$$+ 0.871(0) + -2.241(6) + 2.666(1) + 39.568$$

$$\hat{Y} = -8.96 + 19.266 + 0.396 + 0 + 11.066 + 0 + -13.446 + 2.666 + 39.568$$
$$\hat{Y} = 36.824$$

This equals an overall expected value of 36.8. This calculation also shows why researchers prefer to create dummy variables with values of 0 and 1. While there's no reason that the gender dummy variable couldn't be coded 1 (male) and 2 (female), or even 53 (male) and 217 (female), coding it as 0 and 1 makes the calculation of the expected values much easier. The coefficient is multiplied either by 1 or by 0 (and is canceled out completely).

These OLS regression models are the simplest forms of regression, but they're still very powerful. Combined with theory, and for the right dependent variables, they can tell researchers about the factors that contribute to the dependent variable and allow them to predict values of the dependent variable. The key here, though, is that the regression analysis must always be guided by theory. Without theory to inform the hypotheses and tell the researcher which independent variables to include, the regression analysis is useless. Properly used, though, regression analysis is an invaluable tool for telling social scientists why things happen, even when the causes are very complex.

SUMMARY

As useful as descriptive statistics are, most researchers are interested in testing hypotheses about the relationships between different variables. The most basic ways of doing so are through crosstabs and graphs, with some of these graphs—especially scatterplots—capable of representing very complex relationships between two variables. Scatterplots are also useful for visualizing the simplest summary of the relationship between two variables: the correlation. A correlation, as discussed in earlier chapters, simply tells researchers if two variables tend to go together, without any necessary causal relationship between them. Correlations range from −1 to 1, with negative values meaning the two variables tend to move in opposite directions, positive values meaning that they move together, and correlations near 0 meaning that there's no relationship at all.

It's possible to summarize a correlation as a line on a scatterplot, and this is especially important because it allows researchers to establish a confidence interval around the correlation. This isn't always useful for correlations, but the same logic applies to regression analyses and allows researchers to test hypotheses about the value of the line that best summarizes the relationship between two variables. A regression involving just two variables isn't really any different from a correlation analysis—but the true value of regression becomes evident when researchers use control and dummy variables to isolate the effect of one variable on another, controlling for other factors that may play a part. Using multivariate regressions such as these, researchers can test hypotheses about the effect of one variable on another, holding other factors constant.

The process by which researchers assess the significance of relationships between variables is based on the hypotheses that they lay out beforehand, so if the hypotheses aren't chosen carefully or are changed after the analyses are carried out, tests of significance simply aren't applicable. However, if the analyses are done correctly, researchers can use regressions to determine the strength and direction of relationships between variables and even predict values of a dependent variable for given values of the predictors.

Study and Review

Based on the results of the final regression model of people's feeling thermometer ratings of homosexuals, would you suppose that education is correlated with the feeling thermometer rating? Would you suppose that this correlation would be significant or not?

Coefficients[a]

Model		Unstandardized Coefficients		Standardized Coefficients	t	Sig.
		B	Std. Error	Beta		
1	(Constant)	49.985	5.742		8.705	.000
	Age of Respondent	−.254	.061	−.144	−4.178	.000
	Household income	.407	.166	.086	2.455	.014
	Is R African American?	−5.651	2.527	−.090	−2.236	.026
	Is R Female?	10.838	1.835	.197	5.907	.000
	Is R Latino/a	−1.185	2.349	−.019	−.504	.614
	R Party Identification	−2.325	.489	−.182	−4.757	.000
	Attend religious services how often	2.360	.782	.104	3.019	.003

a. Dependent Variable: Feeling thermometer: Homosexuals

Coefficients[a]

Model		Unstandardized Coefficients		Standardized Coefficients	t	Sig.
		B	Std. Error	Beta		
1	(Constant)	41.415	6.549		6.324	.000
	Age of Respondent	−.220	.061	−.125	−3.635	.000
	Is R African American?	−6.302	3.702	−.100	−1.702	.089
	Is R Latino/a?	.178	2.546	.003	.070	.944
	Is R White?	−2.205	3.011	−.039	−.732	.464
	R Educational attainment	3.196	.662	.184	4.827	.000
	R Party Identification	−2.211	.484	−.174	−4.572	.000
	Attend religious services how often	2.669	.774	.118	3.450	.001
	Is R Female?	11.053	1.811	.201	6.104	.000
	Household income	.035	.182	.007	.194	.846

a. Dependent Variable: Feeling thermometer: Homosexuals

If education were not included in the final regression model, the results are as follows. In this version, household income has a significant positive effect on views of homosexuals. Why would this be the case? In addition, the coefficient for African American is now larger. Why would that be the case? What would you suppose happened to the r^2 of the model? Would it be higher or lower? Much higher or much lower? Why? What about the adjusted r^2?

Suppose that, in addition to the dummy variables for African American and Latino/a, researchers included a dummy variable for whites in the model. The results of such a model are as follows. How would this change the interpretation of the race dummy variables?

The text calculates the expected feeling thermometer for a forty-year-old white Republican woman with a BA and a mean household income who goes to church every week as 36.8. How would this estimate change if the researchers used the model that includes white as a dummy variable?

CHAPTER 14

Frontiers in Social Research

Learning Objectives

- Be able to explain how current technology is changing the way social scientists carry out research
- Be able to identify the advantages and disadvantages of using aggregated online search data in social science research
- Be able to explain why social networks have become an important site for social science research
- Be able to assess the validity of research making use of communications gathered from Twitter and similar services
- Be able to explain why newly digitized documents are useful for social science researchers
- Be able to explain the potential benefits and problems arising from online convenience samples
- Be able to explain why recent advances in medical information are different from information previously available to researchers

This book has explored the major methods used by today's social science researcher. Research methods and techniques are not static, though: they are constantly evolving along with technology. There's nothing new about these changes: advances in communication technology made telephone and Internet surveys possible; advances in computers made large-scale regression analysis possible. Today, however, is a particularly exciting time for social science and research methods. Emerging technology has made data more available to researchers than ever before, and online communication technology has allowed researchers to look at social networks in ways never before possible, and even recruit participants for studies in new ways. However, as these methods allow us to see deeper into people's lives than ever before, they also bring the potential for new ethical dilemmas.

Perhaps more important for students in social science, though, is the democratization of research that these new techniques have created. Doing research on census records used to mean going to archival libraries and spending days or weeks poring through microfilm. Now, individual-level census data from the past is available online. Carrying out an experiment used to require a laboratory. Now, online services make it possible for anyone to carry out experiments fairly cheaply. Researchers can—for free—use Google Analytics or Twitter to find out what people around the world are searching for and talking about. These techniques haven't replaced traditional data collection methods, and probably won't, but they have opened up new ways for young researchers to do cutting-edge work.

Throughout this book, we've tried to show not just how research can be done, but also how researchers—successful and not—have actually done it. Part of this is to show what's come before, part of this is to show the flexibility of these methods, and a big part of it is to show what's possible. Almost any of the research questions that the studies in this book have dealt with can now be examined cheaply and easily by anyone with a personal computer and Internet connection. That's why we can see no better way to conclude this book than with a showcase of some of the cutting-edge research that's being done in the social sciences, much of it by students. These cases are designed to bring together all the topics covered up until this point, but they can also serve as inspirations for students who want to start on their own research.

ANALYSIS OF SEARCH DATA

Seth Stephens-Davidowitz—Googling Racism (2012)

While there is broad consensus that racism still exists in American society, it has become increasingly difficult to measure. Some methods, such as the IAT discussed in Chapter 2, have shown an ability to detect at least some forms of racism in a lab setting, but such techniques don't necessarily tell us about the overall prevalence of racism in the general population, or about its effect on important social and political outcomes. Surveys are better at measuring these sorts of large-scale effects, but Americans are generally unwilling to admit to racist attitudes in surveys, even if they're aware of them.

These questions about the impact of racism on social and political outcomes received increasing attention during the 2008 Presidential election, in which the Democratic nominee, Barack Obama, was the first African American to be nominated by a major political party. Arguments arose about whether still-existing racist attitudes would make it more difficult for him to win, but in the absence of survey data, it was exceedingly difficult to test for the effects of racism on the likelihood of voting for Obama.

Seth Stephens-Davidowitz (2012), an economics graduate student at Harvard, decided to tackle this question not by asking people about racist attitudes, but rather by looking at the prevalence of searches on Google that included the *n*-word (though not a common variant of that word that frequently shows up in rap lyrics). Google provides information about the relative frequency of searches for terms by geographic area, though not by individuals, and this data seems to correlate well with people's interests in those areas: people in Southern California are more likely to search for "Lakers," people in Florida are more likely to search for "shuffleboard." It stands to reason, then, that people in areas with high levels of racism are more likely to search for the *n*-word.

This method of measuring racism has a few advantages over other techniques. First, people who are using Google to search for the *n*-word—most of whom are apparently searching for racist jokes—aren't taking part in a study of any kind and aren't trying to make themselves look good to anyone, making it a **nonreactive** measure of racism. Second, as a measure of racism, searches for racist material have a high degree of face validity. Researchers may argue about the validity of the Modern Racism Scale or the IAT as a measure of racism, but it's difficult to imagine why someone would search for racist material online—especially racist jokes—if they don't harbor racist attitudes.

In order to determine the impact of racist attitudes, as measured through the prevalence of these Google searches, on the likelihood of voting for Obama, Stephens-Davidowitz (2012) compared the frequency of the searches with Obama's vote share in that area. To do this, he determined how many votes Obama probably should have won in that area by looking at how many votes 2004 Democratic nominee John Kerry won in that area, plus the average gain of Democratic congressional candidates in that area. Essentially, Obama should have done as well as John Kerry did in 2004, adjusting for how well other Democrats in the area did in 2008. In the areas with a high prevalence of searches for the *n*-word, Obama did worse than he should have. For instance, Stephens-Davidowitz compares results from Denver, Colorado, and Wheeling, West Virginia. In both areas, John Kerry won 50 percent of the vote, and Democrats in general did about seven points better in 2008 than in 2004, so Obama should have won about 57 percent of the vote. In Denver, with a very low frequency of racist searches, Obama won 57 percent. In Wheeling, with one of the highest rates of racist searches in the country, Obama won 48 percent. All told, Obama's underperformance in areas with high prevalence of racist searches amounted to almost 5 percent of the national popular vote.

This research offers a new way to approach what's been one of the thorniest problems facing the social sciences. In this case, the prevalence of new information technology makes it possible to operationalize a familiar topic in a new way. This sort of research is only possible because such a large proportion of the population has access to the Internet and uses it for everyday activities. However, one of the reasons that using Google is so popular is that people think it's anonymous—they don't think that anyone is watching what they're searching for. If they knew that someone was going to know that they were searching for a racist joke, they may not have done it. In this case, the ethical concerns are somewhat moderated by the fact that the unit of analysis isn't the individual Google user, but rather entire regions, and regions don't have privacy that needs to be protected.

Still, the main source of ethical protection here isn't the researcher, but rather the company that collected the data in the first place. Although Google doesn't release information about individual users, it certainly has that information, and corporations aren't subject to the same ethical restrictions that individual researchers are. A similar situation arises from the sort of databases that corporations such as Target use to discover the buying habits of individual consumers (as discussed in Chapter 13). Can a researcher ethically gain access to information that corporations have collected? What if the data is on the individual level? Existing ethical rules are based on older technologies, but new technologies may require ethical regulations that reflect today's data collection techniques.

ONLINE FIELD EXPERIMENTS

Robert M. Bond et al.—Facebook Field Experiment on Voting (2012)

New technologies offer more than just new ways to operationalize existing concepts; they offer entirely new sites for researchers to work. Robert Bond, who has a joint appointment in Political Science and Communication at Ohio State University, and his colleagues were able to use Facebook in a study of the effects of peer pressure on voting. People who logged onto Facebook on November 2, 2010 (Election Day) were part of an enormous field experiment designed by Bond and his colleagues (2012). Ninety-eight percent of the people who logged in (a bit over 60 million users) received a special section in their news feed. The section included a "Vote" logo, a link to information about local polling places, a counter displaying the total tally of Facebook users who indicated they had voted, images of "friends" who had indicated they had voted, and a button that users could push to say that they had voted.

One percent of people who logged in—about 600,000 people—were shown everything except for the faces of friends who had already voted. The last group (another 600,000 people) didn't get any voting information in their feeds. Previous in-person field studies had shown that social pressure was one of the most effective ways to get people to the polling place, and the three-group design allowed the researchers to look at two different kinds of peer pressure. The main experimental condition looks at the effect of seeing the pictures of friends who had voted; the second experimental condition looks at the more diffuse social pressure of knowing how many people had voted overall. The effects of both of these conditions can then be compared with those of the control condition, where people didn't see any additional messages.

It seems that the researchers would be able to assess the effects of the experimental conditions by looking at how many people clicked the I Voted button in each condition, but it wasn't that simple. First, participants in the control group didn't have an I Voted button to push. Second, results based on which people pushed the button could just be telling the researchers that people felt pressure to tell their friends that they had voted, not that they actually did. To figure out which people actually had voted, the researchers compared actual voter rolls with Facebook profiles.

The researchers were able to show that the main experimental condition had a significant effect on actual voting behavior. While only about 7 percent of all Facebook "friends" are close friends in real life, seeing that real friends had voted made people in the main experimental condition about two points more likely to vote. This might not sound like a big effect, but it means that the researchers were able to prove, through examination of voter rolls, that about 280,000 people in thirteen states cast a ballot who otherwise would not have. Seeing close friends of close friends who had voted led to an increased likelihood of voting as well.

In addition to being, by far, the largest field experiment every conducted, there are some important implications to these findings. The first is that social pressure over social network sites is not as powerful as social pressure in the real world; the biggest effect on people was seeing real-world friends who had voted. The second is that the boundaries between the physical world and the virtual world are not as set as researchers might previously have thought. Social pressure in the virtual world does bleed over into real-world actions—in this case, leading to hundreds of thousands of people voting who otherwise would not have. The virtual world seems to matter most when it's giving people information about close friends, but it matters nonetheless. While the total number of additional votes generated by the experiment is small compared to the total turnout in the 2010 midterm elections, it is possible that the experiment changed the result of some individual races.

These findings go beyond the effect of voter turnout. In this case, the researchers used online social networks to encourage people to engage in a socially desirable behavior, and there's no reason that they couldn't be used to encourage other desirable behaviors. For instance, social scientists and health researchers are exploring the impact of social networks on weight loss and money management. This sort of research, however, is much more ethically fraught than the previous study of Google search patterns because it deals with individual-level data. Everyone who logged into Facebook in the United States on Election Day was part of an experiment without any informed consent, or even a way to opt-out of the study. This study is potentially ethical regardless because the people in the study (not participants, as they had never opted-in to the study and were not equal partners in the research process) didn't suffer any potential harm and weren't asked to volunteer any information that they wouldn't have willingly given out on Facebook anyway. Generally, research is exempt from Institutional

Review Board approval if it only involves information that people would be willing to give out under normal circumstances without informed consent; this is how university researchers are able to run public opinion polling centers, for instance. Today, however, people are willing to give out enormous amounts of potentially embarrassing information to websites—but does that mean that researchers can have free access to it?

While Bond's study was generally applauded by the public and the scientific communities, a later field experiment carried out via Facebook (Kramer, Guillory and Hancock, 2014) led to widespread condemnation of the ethics of the study. In the more recent study, the Facebook feeds of some users were experimentally changed to show either more positively valenced (like "happy" or "fun") or more negatively valenced words (like "bummer" or "cry") from the enormous list of potential messages that could be displayed. The researchers found that the individuals who had been exposed to more negative words tended to post more negatively valenced words themselves, in what they contend is an example of emotional contagion. The sizes of the effects were relatively small, but many in the media and academia were worried about the lack of informed consent from those individuals whose emotions may have been manipulated. Facebook argued that all users agree to be part of studies when they sign up for the service, and that they carry out research like this all of the time for research and marketing purposes. However, the fact that a company can legally carry out such studies doesn't necessarily mean that they're ethical, nor does it mean that university researchers – who have to answer to IRBs and all of the ethical standards discussed in Chapter 3 – can be a part of such research if the company doesn't conform to them. The Facebook mood experiment – as well as other studies like it – raises real questions about how research ethics applies in a world where large companies like Facebook and Google are increasingly taking the place of universities in all sorts of research.

Another important aspect of this type of research is that it shows how the online world functions as an entirely new site for research. Other examples (like the ethnography based in *World of Warcraft* discussed in Chapter 6) have used the online world as a site for research, but in this case, it's a research site that has strong connections and a strong effect on things that are of interest in the physical world. While students probably won't be able to get the owners of Facebook to agree to carry out a large-scale field experiment (though there's no reason not to ask), there are plenty of

FACEBOOK SHOULDN'T CHOOSE WHAT STUFF THEY SHOW US TO CONDUCT UNETHICAL PSYCHOLOGICAL RESEARCH.

THEY SHOULD ONLY MAKE THOSE DECISIONS BASED ON, OH...

HOWEVER THEY WERE DOING IT BEFORE.

WHICH WAS PROBABLY ETHICAL, RIGHT?

Research Ethics

other questions that can be addressed through these virtual environments: How does flirting work in a virtual world where people can look however they like? How do virtual discussions of a topic differ from those in the real world? Why are conspiracy theories so prevalent on the Internet? As people increasingly move life functions—such as communication, information gathering, and interaction with friends—into virtual worlds, the importance of studying these virtual worlds only increases.

CONTENT ANALYSIS OF ONLINE COMMUNICATIONS

Johan Bollen, Huina Mao, and Xiao-Jun Zeng—Tracking Market Fluctuations via Twitter (2011)

In the past twenty years—driven by research on limited rationality and prospect theory (as discussed in Chapter 4)—behavioral economists have found that people are affected by their emotions when they're making economic decisions. The earlier assumptions of rational individuals making calculated, rational decisions just don't seem to explain people's behavior. This has some very interesting ramifications for researchers studying financial markets. If all people buying and selling stocks were acting rationally, basing their decisions solely on facts about the stocks that they were buying and selling, there would be no way to predict which stocks will go up and which will go down. However, if people are making decisions about buying and selling stocks on the basis of emotions, it may be possible to predict the market—but only if researchers can measure aggregate emotions in the public on a real-time basis. **Collective mood** is a difficult concept to operationalize, but it's no more abstract than other concepts that researchers work with, like Robert Levine's (1999) pace of a city research discussed in Chapter 2.

Twitter provides a new way to operationalize collective moods. Millions of users in the United States post short, frequent messages on Twitter. Bollen, Mao, and Zeng (2011) decided to test if it is possible to use content analysis to extract the emotional content of these messages and then use the aggregate results to predict fluctuations in the stock market. They analyzed 9,853,498 public tweets posted by approximately 2.7 users from September 28, 2008, to December 19, 2008, and used several techniques to automatically extract mood information from the tweets (similar to the KWIK methods discussed in Chapter 8). These included OpinionFinder, which looks at individual word choice to discern the mood of the tweet, and the Google Profile of Mood States, which measures six "dimensions" of mood: alert, sure, vital, kind, happy, and calm. No matter what they call it, both techniques use about the same methodology as any content analysis: look at the frequency of certain words and phrases (or other characteristics of the message) and compare them with an established dictionary that has a score for each. In their analysis, Bollen, Mao, and Zeng found that the collective mood, as measured through the coding of these tweets, has a strong correlation (0.88) with movement in the Dow Jones Industrial Average.

One of the main reasons that researchers carry out public opinion polls is to gage the mood of the public on various topics, and that's exactly what these sorts of studies of Twitter are doing. The difference is that studies of public mood on Twitter are unobtrusive—people aren't intentionally talking to an interviewer—so the results may be more honest, with people being more willing to express socially undesirable beliefs.

The other benefit of analyzing messages on Twitter is the volume of communications that are publicly available to researchers: 500 million a day or so. With that amount of data to work with, researchers may be able to find signs of even small patterns in the messages. Unfortunately, these messages are about all sorts of things and probably aren't a replacement for standard public opinion surveys because they don't answer any particular question. Twitter probably isn't a good way to find out how people feel about a political candidate or a policy proposal, for instance.

The other problem with Twitter is the same problem that faces any online-based public opinion measure: it's not representative of the public at large. Bollen, Mao, and Zeng (2011) may have been able to predict fluctuations in the stock market using Twitter data because the population of people who buy and sell stocks has a substantial overlap with the population of people who use Twitter. This relationship may not hold for all populations, though. In the 2012 Republican Presidential primary election, for instance, Twitter traffic seemed to predict that Representative Ron Paul, a favorite among young people and on college campuses, would do very well in the primaries—but this turned out not to be the case. The population of people who use Twitter and the population of people who vote in Republican primaries, it seems, are very different, so generalizing from one to the other just doesn't work (for instance, African Americans are dramatically overrepresented on Twitter relative to the general population). That said, the online world presents enormous opportunities for anyone trying to carry out a content analysis. To do her research on gangsta rap lyrics (discussed in Chapter 8), Charis Kubrin (2005) first had to listen to hundreds of hours of CDs, transcribe the lyrics, and then code them. Now, researchers can easily find online the lyrics to just about any song ever recorded, already in a format that simple KWIC programs can read without a problem. The problem for researchers who want to carry out content analysis of online text is now when to stop collecting data. The enormous amount of information that's available for content analysis on the Internet may be of great use to researchers—but they still need to be very careful about the conclusions they draw from it.

ANALYSIS OF HISTORICAL DATA

Gregory Clark—Class Mobility in Europe and the United States (2012)

Throughout history, social scientists have explored social mobility in different settings. Can individuals succeed socially and economically on their own merits, or is their success limited by their parents' social status? This problem becomes even more interesting on the macro scale. It's thought that social mobility is a desirable trait in a society, and if it can be measured on a macro scale, country by country, researchers may be able to identify characteristics of societies that have higher levels of social mobility. This, in turn, may guide countries in shaping policies to create more of it. Typically, studies of social mobility have focused on one or two generations, operationalizing social class through income, education, and occupation. Such studies of upward mobility are particularly challenging because in order to trace upward mobility, researchers need to follow the same family for generations. Gathering such data, though, is exceedingly difficult and time-consuming. Small-scale studies have been done on isolated communities without much inward or outward migration, but these obviously have limited generalizability.

Gregory Clark (2012), an economic historian at the University of California, Davis, didn't set out to study social mobility. Instead, he was looking at the British elite before the Industrial Revolution to see how their families fared after that economic upheaval. Although he couldn't easily track individual fortunes, he was able to use newly computerized records to trace families with rare last names who attended Oxford or Cambridge University since the thirteenth century and see where members of those families were now. Attending one of these universities is a good sign of upper-class status, and his results indicate that once families have achieved this status, they're likely to retain it. He found, for instance, that if a British man today shares a rare last name with someone who attended Oxford or Cambridge University 200 years ago, he is nine times as likely to attend those same universities as someone from the general population. Similarly, he's much more likely to have a prestigious occupation, such as doctor or lawyer, and even live a few years longer than the average person. Historians have been carrying out this sort of **archival research** for decades, but it's only recently that they've been able to do so without having to seek out local records, potentially at hundreds of sites.

Clark (2012) used the same techniques to track social mobility in several other countries (Sweden, the United States, India, China, Chile, and others) and found that the degree of social mobility in each of them was almost exactly the same. Moreover, there wasn't any significant change in this rate of social mobility over time, even when Clark went as far back as the records could take him—almost 1,000 years, in the case of England. So, the United States might seem to be a society where parentage doesn't matter as much as it does in the United Kingdom or China, but that is an illusion. Similarly, none of the enormous social upheavals during the period Clark studied—the Industrial Revolution, Globalization, World Wars—seemed to change the rate of social mobility. The low rates of social mobility also explain some questions that researchers have about those societies: Why are members of low castes in India still disadvantaged after the caste system was formally disbanded years ago? Are the descendants of slaves in the United States still suffering the consequences of their ancestors' enslavement?

There are, of course, some limitations to this method. Looking at the names only lets the researchers capture the relative place in society: not income, overall wealth, or standard of living. It's also difficult to trace the ancestors of individuals with common last names. However, what's really interesting about this research is what it says about the democratization of data in the modern era. While getting historical data used to be a matter of going into dusty archives, the information in these archives is now increasingly available online for anyone to find, and it doesn't require researchers to travel or stock up on sinus medication. Researchers can download all of the data from past U.S. Censuses and the records of every entrant to Ellis Island. Data that wasn't available to anyone ten years ago—from the Dead Sea Scrolls to Shakespeare's First Folio—are now available to anyone who wants to look at them. The Internet hasn't just created new sites for data collection or text available for content analysis. It's made existing research techniques, like this sort of archival work, much simpler for researchers. This is valuable for researchers in all fields of the social sciences, as any researcher who wants to look at economic data from the nineteenth century or prison records from twenty years ago can attest.

BETTER CONVENIENCE SAMPLES ONLINE?

Adam J. Berinsky, Gregory A. Huber, and Gabriel S. Lenz— Using Mechanical Turk to Recruit Participants (2012)

Often, researchers at universities rely heavily on the use of student subject pools. Whether they're paid or given course credit, students are the most common convenience samples for researchers at a university. Provided that proper controls are in place to ensure a lack of coercion, there's nothing necessarily wrong with using student samples, but there is a problem with the representativeness of these samples. As discussed in Chapter 9, this isn't necessarily a problem as long as the goal of the study is to understand cognitive processes: students at universities may be different from the general public in a lot of ways, but their brains probably work the same way. However, in recent years, even this assumption has come under attack from scholars who argue that the reliance on undergraduate student samples biases research results. This leaves researchers who want to do experimental research in a quandary: either use student convenience samples that are easy to obtain and inexpensive (but may not be representative) or recruit nonstudent samples that are representative (but are much more expensive and difficult to obtain).

One solution to this problem comes from Internet sampling, specifically Amazon's Mechanical Turk (MTurk) service—named after a famous early automaton that seemed to be playing chess but was really controlled by people. MTurk is a web-based service that allows researchers to recruit participants to fill out surveys (or complete other simple tasks, such as proofreading) for pay. Although the participants aren't a representative sample of the public, they are cheap. Researchers can easily embed an experiment on a survey and have participants fill it out for far less money than it would take to have the same experimental survey done over the telephone. Researchers using the service for a short survey have reported paying as little as 10 to 15 cents per participant—far less than any other participant recruitment technique. Also, results are available very quickly, within hours or days, rather than weeks. Not surprising, researchers have been interested in using MTurk as a supplement to, or a replacement of, student samples—but does it work?

MIT political scientist Adam Berinsky and his colleagues (2012) examined the results of studies carried out with MTurk to determine if the service was worthwhile and if the results were reliable. The most important of their findings is that while the population of people who answer surveys on MTurk isn't representative of the overall population, it's more representative than a student sample. Compared with random sampling techniques, participant samples acquired through MTurk are younger, poorer, and more liberal than average Americans—but still better than a student convenience sample.

Second, the researchers find that **longitudinal research** is much easier to carry out over MTurk. In most survey modalities, finding the same participants repeatedly is enormously challenging and expensive, but in MTurk, it's fairly easy. Longitudinal studies are rare because of the cost and difficulty involved, but MTurk may make them much more common.

Berinsky and his colleagues' (2012) study also dismisses two prevalent myths about participants recruited through the Internet. The first assumption is that these participants will be less engaged in the study. The findings show that the MTurk participants actually pay closer attention to the study than a student convenience sample. (After all, they are being paid.) While this is an advantage for some researchers, it could also lead to complications. Participants paying close attention to the study may be able to detect the experimental conditions, discern the research question, and guess the researchers' expectations. This could potentially lead to changing or altering answers to please the researcher. Even without the researchers present, it might result in the Hawthorne effect (as discussed in Chapter 6). The second myth is that participants recruited online would be repeat customers; in other words, the same participants would be in the samples over and over. However, the Berinsky study does not find many repeat subjects in the subject pool.

Just as the Internet has allowed consumers to buy products much more cheaply than they were able to in the past, it's allowed researchers to get participant samples much more easily. Participants recruiting via MTurk are similar to companies building new factories overseas because the wages are lower. As long as the results are about as good, information technology makes the move worthwhile.

In some sense, this is just another way that the democratization of data has affected social science research. Just as documents that were only available to certain well-placed researchers are now available to everyone, the sort of large participant pools that were only available to researchers with lots of grant money are now available to everyone. The democratization of data also affects the types of studies that researchers run, allowing researchers to use more participants than they would otherwise and to conduct more longitudinal studies.

The use of online samples also raises some ethical questions: participants aren't supposed to be taking part in a study just for the money, but it's hard to argue that MTurk participants are doing it for the advancement of science. Still, the amount of money is small enough that it seems unlikely that there's too much monetary coercion.

MEDICAL TESTS AND IMAGING

Helen Fisher, Arthur Aron, and Lucy Brown –An fMRI Study of a Romantic Love (2005)

What is it like to feel romantic love? Romantic love is cross-cultural phenomenon. It feels like such a personal and individual thing, but romantic love is found in almost every time, place, and culture. Researchers have individual reports on how people feel when they are in love. People in love have a higher heart rate and body temperature, butterflies in their stomach, and sweaty palms, but these are only the reported symptoms. None of this tells researchers what's going on in the brains of people experiencing romantic love. To make matters more complicated, people experience similar symptoms with sexual attraction as they do with love.

To capture the difference, Helen Fisher and her colleagues (2005) put participants in an **fMRI** machine to see what happens to the brain when someone is in love. fMRI, which stands for functional magnetic resonance image, is a technique that allows researchers to watch the flow of blood in the brain in real time. This allows them to see exactly which parts of the brain are activated (or at least have more blood flow to them—there's been some question about how well that reflects activation) in response to certain stimuli. It's a fairly new technology and one that nonmedical researchers have only recently been able to make use of, though the cost is still high enough that sample sizes in fMRI studies are very small.

For this purpose, Fisher and her colleagues (2005) recruited ten women and seven men who reported that they were intensely in love. They varied in age from eighteen to twenty-six and had been in love for one to seventeen months. The study first started with semi-structured interviews to determine the intensity, duration, and the experience of the love. The researchers showed the participants pictures of their beloved for twenty seconds, then asked them to count backward from a large number. The researchers also showed the participants photos of a neutral acquaintance, followed by time to count backward from a large number. Counting backward from large numbers was expected to reduce the carryover effect of any feelings and responses.

The fMRI findings show that romantic love and sexual attraction are not the same thing from the perspective of brain activation. Even though the symptoms, and many times the experiences, of romantic love and sexual attraction are similar, the researchers show that they really are different. What people have thought for centuries—that romantic love is something very different from mere sexual attraction—is now supported by medical evidence.

Findings like these are only possible with the help of fMRI technology, and brain scans are just one of the medical technologies now being adapted to social science use. fMRIs allow researchers to look inside the brains of participants, possibly revealing what they are thinking and feeling, even if they have no desire to disclose such information to the researchers. Confidentiality protects participants from unwanted information about themselves being leaked, but researchers also need to be sure to keep information gained through these techniques from the participants themselves. Suppose Fisher and her colleagues (2005) were able to differentiate between participants who really were and were not in love. That's not the sort of information that would ever be ethical to disclose to participants.

Similar ethical concerns arise from the increase in genetic testing. When the genome was first cracked in the 1990s, genetic sequencing cost millions; now, individuals can get their own genes sequenced and analyzed for less than $1,000. This new data leads to new ethical concerns. As Francis Collins (2012), the director of National Institutes of Health was quoted in *The New York Times* as saying, "We are living in an awkward interval, where our ability to capture the information often exceeds our ability to know what to do with it." An example of this discrepancy came up with a woman whose family had a history of ovarian and breast cancer. Because of her strong family history, she planned to have her breasts removed in order to prevent an occurrence of cancer. She enrolled in a study to identify genes related to cancer and signed consent forms indicating that she did not want to be contacted by the researchers. Knowing her family history and intentions, the researchers were shocked to find out that she had none of the genetic markers for breast cancer—the genes that had led to cancer in her family weren't present in her genome. What should the researchers do? On one hand, the participant has signed a consent form saying that she does not want to be contacted. On the other, she's going to be going through major surgery for no reason.

In this particular case, after lengthy discussions with the legal team and the ethics committee at the National Human Genome Project, the researchers decided to breach the consent form and contact the participant. They offered their findings about the cancer gene to the participant and any other members of her family who wished to find out. This was an exceptional case: in most, the consent forms would not have been breached. As with all of these advances in research techniques, as horizons expand, the law and ethical considerations need to catch up.

SUMMARY

Technological advances, especially the widespread availability of the Internet, have transformed the way social scientists carry out research. Communications are increasingly carried out online—often in a way that makes them available to researchers, who can track the prevalence of online searches for various terms on Google and the emotional state expressed by tweets. While the individuals making searches for offensive terms online or tweeting about their day may understand that someone is watching, they're generally not censoring themselves, making this online activity an excellent site for nonreactive research designs. Perhaps more important, this sort of information is often available to researchers for free, allowing anyone so inclined to do large-scale studies that would have been impossible only a few years ago.

This democratization of research extends to the recruitment of participants. Services such as Mturk and many others allow researchers to recruit participants who may be more representative of the overall population than student samples at a much lower cost than before. These samples are still not perfect, and there's an enormous debate about their relative value, but the fact that researchers can run an experiment online for as little as a few dollars per participant is enormously democratizing. In at least one case, researchers were able to convince a major online service—Facebook—to volunteer its users for an experiment, leading to what's probably the largest field experiment in history.

However, these new techniques for collecting data still face the same sort of ethical problems as older techniques. If researchers can look inside the processes of someone's brain, what does that mean for privacy? What are the ethical responsibilities of researchers who can calculate the expected probability of an individual developing a disease? Does the fact that individuals have given private information to Facebook or Twitter mean that researchers don't have to worry about getting their consent to use that information? The fact that data is easier to get may lead some researchers to gloss over old questions about validity and ethics, but that doesn't mean that old questions no longer apply.

Study and Review

Compare the validity and ethics of Bond's (2012) Facebook field experiment and Stephens-Davidowitz's (2012) analysis of Google search terms. In both cases, they looked at online activity without collecting consent from individuals. Is this acceptable? Why or why not?

Can researchers generalize research results from an online sample to the population as a whole? Why or why not?

While the Facebook field experiment on voting was generally applauded, the later study on mood contagion was widely condemned as unethical. What makes these studies different, from an ethical perspective?

It seems pretty obvious that research participants gathered through Mturk are doing it for the relatively small sums of money involved. Does this amount to monetary coercion? Why or why not? If so, what would have to be done to ensure that coercion is not present?

What steps would researchers using fMRI data need to take in order to ensure that their research conforms to ethical standards?

Does the very small sample size of fMRI studies hurt their validity? Why or why not?

Bibliography

Adler, Patricia and Pete Adler. 2003. "The Promise and Pitfalls of Going Into the Field." *Contexts*. 3(2): 41–47.

Adorno, Theodore W., Else Frenkel-Brunswik, Daniel J. Levinson and Nevitt R. Sanford. 1950. *The Authoritarian Personality*. New York: Norton.

Alexander, Michele B. and Terri D. Fisher. 2003. "Truth and Consequences: Using the Bogus Pipeline to Examine Sex Differences in Self-Reported Sexuality." *The Journal of Sex Research*. 40(1): 27–35.

Almond, Gabriel and Bingham Powell. 1966. *Comparative Politics: A Developmental Approach*. Boston, MA: Little, Brown.

Asch, Solomon Elliot. 1951. "Effects of Group Pressure upon the Modification and Distortion of Judgment." In H. Guertzkow (Ed.) *Groups, Leadership and Men*. Pittsburg, PA: Carnegie Press.

Asch, Solomon Elliot. 1955. "Opinions and Social Pressure." *Scientific American*. 139: 31–35.

Bader, Christopher D., Carson F. Mencken and Paul Froese. 2007. "American Piety 2005: Content and Methods of the Baylor Religion Survey." *Journal for the Scientific Study of Religion*. 46(4): 447–463.

Beaman, AL, Klentz B, Diener E. and Syanum S. 1979. "Self-Awareness and Transgression in Children: Two Field Studies." *Journal of Perspective Social Psychology*. 37(10): 1835–1846.

Bearman, Peter S. and Hannah Brückner. 2001. "Promising the Future: Virginity Pledges and First Intercourse." *American Journal of Sociology*. 106(4): 859–912.

Belkin, Lisa "The Opt-Out Revolution." *New York Times*. Published: October 26, 2003.

Berger, Jonah, Marc Meredith, and S. Christian Wheeler. "Contextual priming: Where people vote affects how they vote." *Proceedings of the National Academy of Sciences* 105.26 (2008): 8846-8849.

Bergman, Brian. 2005. "Unlovely, Unloved? There's no Underestimating the Power of a Pretty Face – or of a Homely One." *Macleans*, March 30, 2005.

Berinsky, Adam J. Gregory A. Huber, and Gabriel S. Lenz. 2012. "Evaluating Online Labor Markets for Experimental Research: Amazon.com's Mechanical Turk." *Political Analysis*, 20.3 (2012): 351-368.

Bernhardt, P.C, Dabbs, J.M. Jr. Fielden, J.A and Lutter, C.D. 1998. "Testosterone Changes during Vicarious Experiences of Winning and Losing Among Fans at Sporting Events." *Physiological Behavior*. 65(1): 59–62.

Besen-Cassino, Yasemin. 2008. "The Cost of Being a Girl: Gender Earning Differentials in the Early Labor Markets." *NWSAJ Journal*. 20(1): 146–160.

Besen, Yasemin. 2005. "Consumption of Production: A Study of Part-time Youth Labor in Suburban America." *Berkeley Journal of Sociology*. 49(1): 58–75.

Besen, Yasemin. 2006. "Exploitation or Fun? The Lived Experience of Teenage Employment in Suburban America." *Journal of Contemporary Ethnography*. 35(3): 319–340.

Bittman, Michael, Paula England, Nancy Folbre, Liana Sayer and George Matheson. 2003. "When Does Gender Trump Money? Bargaining and Time in Household Work." *American Journal of Sociology*. 109(1): 186–214.

Blum, Linda M. and Nena F. Stracuzzi. 2004. "Gender in the Prozac Nation: Popular discourse and Productive Femininity." *Gender and Society*. 18(3): 269–286.

Blumer, Herbert. 1962. "Society as Symbolic Interaction". In Arnold M. Rose. *Human Behavior and Social Process: An Interactionist Approach*. Houghton-Mifflin. Reprinted in Blumer (1969).

Blumer, Herbert. 1969. *Symbolic Interactionism; Perspective and Method*. Englewood Cliffs, NJ: Prentice-Hall.

Blumer, Herbert. 1971. "Social Problems as Collective Behavior." *Journal of Economics and Sociology*. 18(3): 298–306.

Boelen, W.A. Marianne. 1992. "Street Corner Society: Cornerville Revisited." *Journal of Contemporary Ethnography*. 21(1): 11–51.

Bollen, Jonah, Huina Mao and Xiaojun Zeng. 2011. "Twitter Mood Predicts Stock Market." *Journal of Computational Science*. 2:1–8.

Bond, R. M. *et al.* "A 61-million-person experiment in social influence and political mobilization" *Nature*. 489, 295–298 (2012).

Brines, Julie. 1993. "The exchange value of housework." *Rationality and society*. 5.3: 302–340.

Campbell, Tom. 1981. *Seven Theories of Human Society*. Oxford: Clarendon Press.

Cancian, Francesca M. and Steven L. Gordon. 1988. "Changing Emotion Norms in Marriage: Love and Anger in U.S. Women's Magazines since 1900." *Gender and Society*. 2(3): 308–342.

Carnegie, Dale. 1964. How to Win Friends and Influence People. New York: Simon and Schuster.

Chen, M. Keith, Venkat Lakshminarayanan, and Laurie R. Santos. "How basic are behavioral biases? Evidence from capuchin monkey trading behavior." *Journal of Political Economy* 114.3 (2006): 517–537.

Childs, Erica Chito. 2005. "Looking Behind the Stereotypes of the 'Angry Black Woman:' An Exploration of Black Women's Responses to Interracial Relationships." *Gender and Society*. (19) 4:544–561.

Clark, Gregory and Neill Cummins. 2012. "What is the True Rate of Social Mobility? Surnames and Social Mobility, England, 1800–2012." Unpublished manuscript.

Connell, R.W. 2005. *Masculinities*. Berkeley, CA: University of California Press.

Cooley, Charles H. 1902. *Human Nature and the Social Order*. New York: Scribner.

Darley, John and Bibb Latané. 1968. "Bystander Intervention in Emergencies: Diffusion of Responsibility." *Journal of Personality and Social Psychology*. 8(2): 377–383.

David Kimball, Brady Baybeck, Cassie Gross and Laura Wiedlocher. 2009. "Poll Workers and Election Administration: The View from Local Election Officials." Paper presented at the annual meeting of the Midwest Political Science Association. Chicago, IL. April.

Davis, Kingsley and Wilbert E. Moore. 1945. "Some Principles of Stratification." *American Sociological Review*. 10 (2): 242–249.

De Castro, John M. "Social facilitation of duration and size but not rate of the spontaneous meal intake of humans." *Physiology & Behavior*. 47.6 (1990): 1129-1135.

DeVault, Marjorie L. 1999. *Liberating Method: Feminism and Social Research*. Philadelphia, PA: Temple University Press.

Dubner, Stephen J. and Steven D. Levitt "Monkey Business: Keith Chen's Monkey Research." New York Times June 5, 2005.

Durkheim, Emile. 1960 [1893]. *The Division of Labor in Society*. Translated by George Simpson. New York: The Free Press.

Durkheim, Emile. 1997. *Suicide: A study in sociology*. New York: The Free Press.

Dutton, Don G. and Aron, Arthur P. 1974. "Some Evidence for Heightened Sexual Attraction under conditions of high anxiety." *Journal of Personality and Social Psychology*. 30:510–517.

Ehrenreich, Barbara. 2001. *Nickeled and Dimed: On (Not) Getting By in America*. New York: Metropolitan Books.

Ellis, Carolyn. 1995. *Final Negotiations: A Story of Love, and Chronic Illness*. Philadelphia, PA: Temple University Press.

Émile Durkheim. 1982. *The Rules of Sociological Method*. New York: Simon and Schuster.

England, Paula, Emily Fitzgibbons Shafer and Alison C.K. Fogarty. 2007. "Hooking-up and forming Romantic Relationships in Today's College Campuses." *The Gendered Society Reader*, edited by Michael Kimmel. New York: Oxford University Press.

Entwisle, Doris R, Karl L. Alexander and Linda Steffel Olson. 2000. "Early Work Histories of Urban Youth." American Sociological Review 65(2): 279–297.

Erisen, Cengiz. 2007. "Priming Opinion Change". Unpublished manuscript.

Federico, Christopher M., and Jim Sidanius. "Racism, ideology, and affirmative action revisited: The antecedents and consequences of "principled objections" to affirmative action." *Journal of personality and social psychology*. 82.4 (2002): 488–502.

Festinger, Leon. 1956. *When Prophecy Fails: A Social and Psychological Study of a Modern Group that Predicted the Destination of the World*. New York: Harper.

Fink, Janet S. and Linda Jean Kensicki. 2002. "An Imperceptible Difference: Visual and Textual Constructions of Femininity in Sports Illustrated and Sports Illustrated for Women." *Mass Communication & Society* 5(3): 317–339.

Finkel, Steven E., and John G. Geer. 1998. "A spot check: Casting doubt on the demobilizing effect of attack advertising." *American journal of political science*: 573-595.

Fisher, Helen, Arthur Aron and Lucy L. Brow. 2005. "Romantic Love: An fMRI Study of Neural Mechanism for Mate Choice." *The Journal of Contemporary Neurology*. 493:58–62.

Fitzsimons, Gráinne M., Tanya L. Chartrand, and Gavan J. Fitzsimons. 2008. "Automatic effects of brand exposure on motivated behavior: how apple makes you "think different"." *Journal of consumer research*. 35.1: 21-35.

Freeman, Derek. 1983. *Margaret Mead and Samoa: The Making and Unmaking of an Anthropological Myth*. Cambridge, London: Harvard University Press.

Freeman, Derek. 1999. *The Fateful Hoaxing of Margaret Mead: A Historical Analysis of Her Samoan Research*. Boulder, CO: Westview Press.

Gans, Herbert. 1995. *The War Against the Poor: The Underclass and Anti-Poverty Policy*. New York: Basic Books.

Gard, Greta. (Ed.)1993. *Ecofeminism: Women, Animals and Nature*. Philadelphia, PA: Temple University Press.

Garfinkel, Harold.1967. *Studies in Ethnomethodology*. Englewood Cliffs, NJ: Prentice-Hall.

Gettler, Lee T., Thomas W. McDade, Alan B. Feranil and Christopher W. Kuzawa. 2011. "Longitudinal Evidence that Fatherhood Decreases Testosterone in Human Males." *Proceedings of the National Academic of Sciences of the United States of America*. 108(39): 16194–16199.

Giedd, Jay N., *et al*. "Brain development during childhood and adolescence: a longitudinal MRI study." *Nature neuroscience*. 2.10 (1999): 861–863.

Goode, Erich. 1996. "The Ethics of Deception in Social Research: A Case Study." *Qualitative Sociology*. 19(1):11–33.

Gray, P.B., Campbell, B.C., Marlowe, F.W., Lipson, S.F. and Ellison, P.T. 2004. "Social Variables Predict between- but not within-Subject Testosterone Variation in a Sample of U.S. men." *Psychoneuroendocrinology*. 29:1153–1162.

Greenwald, Anthony G., McGhee, Debbie E. and Schwartz, Jordan K. L. 1998. "Measuring Individual Differences in Implicit Cognition: The Implicit Association Test." *Journal of Personality and Social Psychology*. 74:1464–1480.

Harris, Scott. 2006. *The Meaning of Marital Inequality*. Albany, NY: SUNY Press.

Häuser, Winfried, Ernil Hansen, and Paul Enck. 2012. "Nocebo phenomena in medicine." *Dtsch Arztebl Int* 109.26: 459–465.

Henson, Kevin and Jackie Krasas Rogers. 2001. "Why Marcia You've Change: Male Clerical Temp Workers Doing Masculinity in a Feminized Job." *Gender and Society*. 15(2): 218–238.

Herman, Alexis. 2000. "Report on the Youth Lab Force." United States Department of Labor.

Hobolt, Sara B. and Robert Klemmensen. 2005. "Responsive Government? Public Opinion and Policy Preferences in Britain and Denmark." *Political Studies*. 53: 379–402.

Hobolt, Sara Binzer and Robert Klemmemsen. 2005. "Responsive Government? Public Opinion and Government Policy Preferences in Britain and Denmark." *Political Studies*. 53(2): 379–402.

Hobsbawm, Eric. 1969. *Bandits*. London: Weidenfeld & Nicolson.

Hochschild, Arlie Russell (with Anne Machung) 1989. *The Second Shift*. New York: Viking Press.

Holstein, James A. and Jaber F. Gubrium. 1995. *The Active Interview*. Thousand Oaks, CA: Sage.

Hu, Bill, Thomas McInish and Li Zeng. 2010. "Gambling in Penny Stocks: The Case of Stock Spam Emails." *International Journal of Cyber Criminology*. 4(1&2): 610–629.

Huddy, Leonie, Stanley Feldman, Charles Taber and Gallya Lahav. 2002. "Threat, Anxiety, and Support of Anti-Terrorism Policies." *American Journal of Political Science*. 49(3): 593–608.

Hughes, Mikayla, Kelly Morrison and Kelli Jean K. Asada. 2005. "What's Love Got To Do with It? Exploring the Impact of Maintenance Rules, Love Attitudes, and Network Support on Friends with Benefits Relationships." *Western Journal of Communication*. 69(1): 49–66.

Humphreys, Laud. 1970. *Tearoom Trade: Impersonal Sex in Public Places*. London: Duckworth.

Ingraham, Chrys. 1999. *White Weddings: Romancing Heterosexuality in Popular Culture*. London: Psychology Press.

Jary, D. and J. Jary (editors). 1991. "Social structure." In *The Harper Collins Dictionary of Sociology*, New York: Harper Collins.

Jones, Edward E. "Flattery Will Get You Somewhere." *Trans-action*. 2.4 (1965): 20–23.

Kanter, Rosabeth Moss. 1993. *Men and Women of the Corporation*. New York: Basic Books.

Kast, Eric, M.D. 1966. "LSD and the Dying Patient." *Chicago Medical School Quarterly*. 26: 80–87.

Katz, Lawrence, Jeffrey Kling and Jeffrey Liebman. 2001. "Moving to Opportunity in Boston: Early Results of a Randomized Mobility Experiment." *Quarterly Journal of Economics*. 116(2): 607–654.

Kimmel, Michael. 2009. *Guyland: The Perilous World Where Boys Become Men*. New York: Harper Perennial.

Kolata, Gina. 2012. "Genes Now Tell Doctors secrets They Can't Utter." *The New York Times*. August 25, 2012.

Korzeniewicz, Patricio Roberto and Timothy P. Moran. 1997. "World Economic Trends in the Distribution of Income 1965–1992." *American Journal of Sociology*. 102:1000–1039.

Kubrin, Charis. 2005. "Gangstas, Thugs and Hustlas: Identity and the Code of the Street in Rap Music." *Social Problems* 52(3): 360–378.

Kubrin, Charis. 2006. "'I See Death Around the Corner': Nihilism in Rap Music." *Sociological Perspectives.* 48(4): 433–459.

Landsbeger, Henry A. 1958. *Hawthorne Revisited.* Ithaca, NY: Cornell University Press.

Laner, Mary and Nicole Ventrone. 2000 "Dating Scripts Revisited." *Journal of Family Issues.* 21(4):488–500.

Laurence Steinberg and Alex R. Piquero. 2010. "Manipulating Public Opinion about Trying Juveniles as Adults." *Crime & Delinquency.* 56:487–506.

Le, Xuan, Ian Lancashire, Graeme Hirst and Regina Jokel. 2011. Longitudinal Detection of Dementia through Lexical and Syntactic Changes in Writing: A Case Study of Three British Novelists. *Literary and Linguistic Computing* 26(4): 435–461.

Lever, Janet. 1986. "Sex Differences in the Differences in the Complexity of Children's Play and Games," pp 74–89 in *Structure and Process*, edited by Richard J Peterson and Charlotte A Vaughan. Belmont, CA: Wadsworth.

Levine, Robert 1999. "The Pace of Life in 31 Countries." *Journal of Cross-Cultural Psychology.* 30(2): 178–205.

Libet, Benjamin. 2004. *Mindtime: The Temporal Factor in Consciousness.* Cambridge, MA: Harvard University Press.

Loftis, Jack Ross. 1974. "Effects of Misattribution of Arousal upon the Acquisition and Extinction of a Conditioned Emotional Response." *Journal of Personality and Social Psychology.* 30(5): 673–682.

Lukacs, Andre, David Embrick and Talmadge Wright. 2009. "The Managed Hearthstone: Labor and Emotion Work in the Online Community of World of Warcraft." *Facets of Virtual Environments Lecture Notes of the Institute for Computer Sciences, Social Informatics and Telecommunications Engineering*, Volume 33. Heidelberg: Springer Berlin. Pages 165–77.

Marlowe, Frank W. 2004. "What explains Hadza food sharing?" *Research in Economic Anthropology* 23:69–88.

Marlowe, Frank W. 2004. "Marital Residence among Foragers." *Current Anthropology.* 45:277–284.

Marx, Karl. 1867. *Capital.* New York: International Publishers.

McConahay, John B. 1983. "The Effects of Race, Racial Attitudes and Context on Simulated Hiring Decisions." *Personality and Social Psychology Bulletin.* 9 (4): 551–558.

Mead, George Herbert. 1962. *Mind, Self and Society from a Standpoint of a Behaviorist.* Chicago, IL: University of Chicago Press.

Mead, George Herbert. 1964. *Selected Writings.* Indianapolis, IN: Bobbs-Merrill.

Merton, Robert K. 1957. *Social Theory and Social Structure.* New York: Free Press.

Messner, Michael A. and Jefferey Montez de Oca. 2005. "The Male Consumer as Loser: Beer and Liquor Ads in Mega Sports Media Events." *Signs: Journal of Women in Culture and Society.* 30(3): 1879–1909.

Milgram, Stanley. 1963. "Behavioral Study of Obedience." *Journal of Abnormal and Social Psychology.* 67: 371–378.

Milgram, Stanley. 1974. *Obedience to Authority: An Experimental View.* Harper, New York.

Miller, Amalia. 2005. "The Effects of Motherhood Timing on Career Path." *Journal of Population Economics.* 24(3): 1071–1100.

Minnich, Elizabeth. 1977. Discussion in the The Scholar and the Feminist: Connecting Theory, Practice and Values. Conference Sponsored by the Barnard College Women's Center

Mitchell, Richard G. 2004. *Dancing at Armageddon: Survivalism and Chaos in Modern Times.* Chicago, IL: University of Chicago Press.

Moerman, Michael. 1988. *Talking Culture: Ethnography and Conversation Analysis.* University City, PA.: University of Pennsylvania Press.

Moffatt, Michael. 1989. *Coming of Age in New Jersey*. New Brunswick, ME: Rutgers University Press.

Moss, Phillip and Chris Tilly. 2003. *Stories Employers Tell Race, Skill, and Hiring in America*. New York: Russell Sage Foundation.

Mosteller, Frederick and David Wallace. 1964. *Inferred and Disputed Authorship: The Federalist*. Reading: Addison-Wesley.

Ochs, Elinor. 2009. "Opportunity for Interaction? A Naturalistic Observation Study of Dual-Earner Families After Work and School." *Journal of Family Psychology*. 23(6):798–807.

Otnes, Cele and Elizabeth Pleck. 2003. *Cinderella Dreams: The Allure of the Lavish Wedding*. Berkeley, CA: University of California Press.

Parillo, Vincent N. and Christopher Donoghue. 2005. "Updating the Bogardus Social Distance Studies: A New National Survey." *The Social Science Journal*. 42: 257–271.

Parsons, Talcott. 1951. *The Social System*. Free Press of Glencoe.

Parsons, Talcott. 1967. *Toward a General Theory of Action*. Cambridge, MA: Harvard University Press.

Parsons, Talcott. 1968. *The Structure of Social Action*. New York: Free Press.

Parsons, Talcott. 1977. *Social Systems and the Evolution of Action Theory*. New York: Free Press.

Peshkin, Alan. 1988. *God's Choice: The Total World of a Fundamentalist Christian School*. Chicago, IL: University of Chicago Press.

Prior, Markus. 2003. "Any Good News in Soft News? The Impact of Soft News Preference on Political Knowledge." *Political Communication*. 20 (2): 149–171.

Quinn, Beth. 2002. "Sexual Harassment and Masculinity: The Power and Meaning of Girl Watching." *Gender and Society*. 16(3): 386–402.

Reaney, Patricia. (2012, March 23). Average cost of U.S. wedding hits $27,021. Reuters. Retrieved from http://www.reuters.com/article/2012/03/23/us-wedding-costsid USBRE82M11O20120323

Redlawsk, David P. "Hot cognition or cool consideration? Testing the effects of motivated reasoning on political decision making." *Journal of Politics*. 64.4 (2002): 1021–1044.

Reinharz, Shulamit. 1992. *Feminist Methods in Social Research*. New York: Oxford University Press.

Riker, William H. and Peter C. Ordeshook. "A Theory of the Calculus of Voting." *American political science review*. 62.01 (1968): 25–42.

Robert G. Morris, and John L. Worrall. 2010 "Prison Architecture and Institutional Misconduct." *Crime and Delinquency*. November 2010.

Robert S. Erikson, Costas Panagopoulos and Christopher Wleizen. 2004. "Likely Voters and the 2000 Presidential Debates." *Public Opinion Quarterly*. 68:588–601.

Rosenthal, Robert and Lenore Jackson. 1992. *Pygmalion in the Classroom*. New York: Irvington.

Sapolsky, Robert M. 1998. *The Trouble With Testosterone: And Other Essays On The Biology Of The Human Predicament*. New York: Scribner Press.

Saxbe, Darby E., Rena L. Repetti, and Adrienne Nishina. 2008. "Marital satisfaction, recovery from work, and diurnal cortisol among men and women." *Health Psychology*. 27.1: 15.

Sentyrz, Stacey M. and Brad J. Bushman. 1998. "Mirror Mirror on the Wall: Who is the Thinnest One of All? Effects of Self Awareness on Consumption of Full-Fat, Reduced-Fat, and No-Fat Products." *Journal of Applied Psychology*. 83(6): 944–949.

Sherif, Muzafer, O. J. Harvey, B. Jack White, William R. Hood and Carolyn Wood Sherif. 1954. *The Robbers Cave Experiment: Intergroup Conflict and Cooperation*. Fishers, IN: Wesleyan.

Sherkat, Darren E. 2007. "Religion and Survey Non-Response Bias: Toward Explaining the Moral Voter Gap between Surveys and Voting." *Sociology of Religion*. 68(1):83–96.

Shor, Eran and Dalit Simchai. 2009. "Incest Avoidance, the Incest Taboo and Social Cohesion: Revisiting Westermarck and the Case of the Israeli Kibbutzim." *American Journal of Sociology* 114(6): 1803–1842.

Simmel, Georg. 1922 [1955]. *Conflict and the Web of Group Affiliations*, translated and edited by Kurt Wolff. Glencoe, IL: Free Press.

Smelser, Neil. 1964. *Toward a Theory of Social Change.* New York: Basic Books.

Smock, Pamela J., Wendy D. Manning and Meredith Porter. 2004. "*Everything's There Except Money: How Money Shapes Decisions to Marry among Cohabitors.* Ann Arbor, MI: Population Studies Center University of Michigan.

Snowdon, David, Susan Kemper, James Mortimer, Lydia Greiner, David Wekstein and William Markesbery. 1996. "Linguistic Ability in Early life and Cognitive Function and Alzheimer's Disease in Late Life: Findings from the Nun Study." *Journal of the American Medical Association.* 275(7): 528–532.

Sommers, Samuel R. and Michael I. Norton. 2007. "Race-Based Judgments, Race-Neutral Justifications: Experimental Examination of Peremptory Use and the *Batson* Procedure." *Law and Human Behavior.* 31(2): 261–273.

Spender, Dale. 1985. *For the Record: The Making and Meaning of Feminist Knowledge.* The Women's Press.

Steele, Claude M., and Joshua Aronson. 1995. "Stereotype threat and the intellectual test performance of African Americans." *Journal of personality and social psychology.* 69.5: 797.

Stephens-Davidowitz, S. 2012. The Effects of Racial Animus on a Black Presidential Candidate: Using Google Search Data to Uncover What Traditional Surveys Miss. Unpublished manuscript.

Stice, Eric, Diane Spangler and W. Stewart Agras. 2001. "Exposure to Media-Portrayed Thin-Ideal Images Adversely Affects Vulnerable Girls: A Longitudinal Experiment." *Journal of Social and Clinical Psychology.* 20(3): 270–288.

Stone, Pamela. 2007. *Opting Out: Why Women Really Quit Careers and Head Home.* California: University of California Press.

Suedfeld, Philip, P.E. Tetlock and S. Streufert, 1992. "Conceptual/integrative Complexity." In C. Smith (editor) *Handbook of Thematic Content Analysis* (pp. 393–401). New York: Cambridge University Press.

Van Honk, Jack and Dennis J.L.G. Schutter. 2007. "Testosterone Reduced Conscious Detection of Signals Serving Social Correction: Implications for Anti-Social Behavior." *Psychological Science.* 18(1): 663–667.

Walker, Karen 2010. "I am not Friends the Way She is Friends." In *Men's Lives*, edited by Michael Kimmel and Michael Messner. New York: Pearson Press (8th edition).

Wansink, Brian. 2006. *Mindless Eating: Why We Eat More than We Think.* New York: Bantam.

Weeber, Stan C. and Daniel G. Rodeheaver. 2003. "Militias at the Millennium: A Test of Smelser's Theory of Collective Behavior." *Sociological Quarterly.* 44(2): 182–184.

White, Jenny B. 2004. *Money Makes us Relatives: Women's Labor in Urban Turkey.* London, New York: Routledge.

Whyte, William Foote. 1993/1943. *Street Corner Society: The Social Structure of an Italian Slum.* Chicago, IL: University of Chicago Press.

Williams, Christine. 1992. "The Glass Escalator: Hidden Advantages for Men in the "Female" Professions." 39(3): 253–267.

Zimbardo, Philip. 1971. The Stanford Prison Experiment http://www.prisonexp.org/psychology/41.

Glossary/Index

Page numbers in bold refer to tables. Page numbers in italics refer to figures.